Paulus Venetus
Logica Parva

Analytica

Investigations
in Logic, Ontology and the Philosophy of Language

Editors:
Ignacio Angelelli · Austin (Texas/USA)
Joseph M. Bocheński · Fribourg (CH)
Christian Thiel · Erlangen

Editor-in-chief:
Hans Burkhardt · Erlangen

Philosophia Verlag München Wien

Paulus Venetus

Logica Parva

Translation of the 1472 Edition
with Introduction and Notes
by Alan R. Perreiah

The Catholic University of America Press
Washington, D.C.

Philosophia Verlag München Wien

CIP-Kurztitelaufnahme der Deutschen Bibliothek

Paulus ‹Venetus›:
Logica parva / Paulus Venetus. Transl. with an introd. and notes
by Alan R. Perreiah. –
München · Wien : Philosophia Verlag, 1984.
(Analytica)
Einheitssacht.: Logica ‹engl.›
NE: Perreiah, Alan R. [Übers.]
ISBN 3-88405-031-1 (Philosophia Verlag)
ISBN 0-8132-0587-5 (Cath. Univ. of America Press)

Published with subsidies from the Förderungs- und Beihilfefonds
Wissenschaft der VG WORT.

Library of Congress Cataloging in Publication Data
Paolo, Veneto, ca. 1370–1429.
    Logica parva.
    Includes bibliographical references.
    1. Logic-Early works to 1800. I. Perreiah, Alan R.
II. Title.
BC60.P3413   1983   160   83-2023
ISBN 0-8132-0587-5

Available in North and South America from The Catholic University
of America Press, Washington, D.C.

ISBN 0-8132-0587-5
ISBN 3-88405-031-1

Typesetting: SatzStudio Pfeifer, Germering
Manufactured by WB Druck GmbH, Füssen
Printed in Germany 1984

Table of Contents

Preface

Paul of Venice is a Janus figure who looks both backward into the Middle Ages and forward into the Renaissance. An Augustinian Friar educated at the Oxford Convent in the 1390's Paul returned to Italy and taught at Padua for more than 25 years.[1] In addition he was Provincial of his order and an ambassador of the Venetian Republic to Austria, Hungary and Poland. He has been called, "one of the most prolific writers of the century", and the *Logica Parva* is one of four works attributed to him in logic.[2] In Italy it enjoyed a circulation second only to Peter of Spain's *Summulae Logicales*.[3] Because of its wide readership the *Logica Parva* earned for Paul of Venice the reputation of having imported the "Oxonian dialect" to Italy.[4] Paul's many works in Logic, Science,[5] Philosophy[6] and Theology[7] not only record main currents in 13th and 14th century thought: they also anticipate major trends of the 15th and 16th centuries.

Several scholars have drawn attention to the increasing use of logic textbooks in the universities of the 13th century, and the *Logica Parva* is a manual in this same tradition.[8] The principal authors and works of the 13th century were: William of Sherwood, *Introduction to Logic*; Roger Bacon, *Summulae Dialectics*; Lambert of Auxerre, *Logica*; and Peter of Spain, *Summulae Logicales*.[9] The 14th century saw an even greater proliferation of logic texts, including William of Ockham's *Summa Logicae*, Walter Burleigh's *De Puritate Artis Logicae* as well as works by John Buridan, Albert of Saxony, Peter of Ailly and others.[10] Though Paul cites most of these authors elsewhere, he does not do so in the *Logica Parva*. The *Logica Parva* shows no trace of the works of the Dominican Thomists Harvey of Nedellec and St. Vincent Ferrer or the Augustinians Giles of Rome and Gregory of Rimini.[11] Moreover, it exhibits no evidence of influence by the documented sources of the *Logica Magna* including John Venator, Richard Brinkley, Richard Ferrybridge, Thomas Bradwardine and Peter of Mantua.[12] Finally, the author of the *Logica Parva* shows some familiarity with the views of Roger Swyneshed, William of Heytesbury and Ralph Strode.[13]

Paul was entering his prime at the start of the *Quattrocento* and his influence remained prominent in Italy for two centuries. His work in Logic is notable *directly* for those who continued it and *indirectly* for those who reacted to it. This can be shown by a brief consideration of his relationships to others — Scholastics as well as Humanists. Paul of Pergula, perhaps

Paul's most successful student, wrote an elementary text similar to the *Logica Parva* and held for many years the first chair of Logic in the Republic of Venice.[14] Cajetan of Thiene, another student, became a leading logician in the Paduan tradition.[15] One measure of Paul's esteem among later Scholastics is the fact that his works were published many times and by the end of the 15th century were required reading at Padua. At least half a dozen detailed commentaries on his logic were produced during this same period.[16] Paul was known to the Humanists in several ways. Lorenzo Valla recognized the *Logica Parva*.[17] Erasmus who knew of Paul's dominance at Padua may have him in mind in the *Praise of Folly*.[18] In several of his diatribes against the "Little Logicals" Thomas More cites examples which occur in the *Logica Parva*.[19] Finally, Juan Luis Vives explicitly names Paul of Venice and the *Logica Parva* in his polemical work *Against the Pseudodialecticians*.[20]

Many problems in the interpretation of medieval logic remain unresolved. Several of these center on three issues which have not been dealt with adequately in the literature. The first concerns the relationship between logic as a theoretical pursuit and logic as a practical discipline in later medieval education. A better understanding of how these two distinct functions intertwine would help to explain many of the idiosyncracies of late Scholastic logic. A second issue arises from the fact that the logic of the earlier Middle Ages was expressed primarily in an oral and not in a written or "literary" medium. This point is crucial not only for an accurate understanding of the language of medieval logic but also for a fair assessment of its achievements. A third issue turns around the question whether medieval logic is a formal logic in the strict sense or whether it is a theory of logical form. The present study offers some new hypotheses on each of these issues.

Considerable attention has been paid over the past three decades to the formal aspects of medieval logic.[21] A great deal of effort has been devoted to showing that the medievals anticipated, or failed to anticipate, this or that development in modern formal logic. As scholarship advances, however, it becomes increasingly clear that the logicians of the later Middle Ages were less interested in constructing systems of formal logic than they were in understanding the logical forms inherent in natural languages. Thus, there is need for an acceptable framework within which the research of the recent past might be better related to the task which the medievals set for themselves: namely, describing and explaining the structures of natural language. In an effort to bridge this gap many authors have alluded to the notion of "logical form" but with one or two exceptions no one has considered precisely what the medievals would have meant by a theory of logical form or what they would have included in it. In answering these questions the present study refers to work on the theory of logical form by Donald Davidson and Gilbert Harman.[22] Not only do they give a clear account of what many 20th century thinkers have meant by "logical form" but some of their observations accord well with what several later medieval thinkers meant on the subject. The introductory essays demonstrate that there is a close correspondence between the components of a theory of logical form and the contents of Paul of Venice's *Logica Parva*. Moreover, the essays show that comparisons between the medieval and modern theories are much more plausible when the former are regarded as theories of logical form rather than as works in formal logic.

To see medieval logic as a theory of logical form is to clarify at the same time medieval logic's relationship to medieval grammar in general and to speculative grammar *(grammatica speculativa)* in particular.[23] For a major theme of speculative grammar is that of the modes of signification *(modi significandi)*, and the concept of signifying or meaning *(significatio)* holds a prominent place in medieval logical theory. The traditional distinction between "realists" and "nominalists" in the Middle Ages (originally associated with the separate but related "problem of universals") calls to mind the fact that the medievals held widely differing views on the status of signification in a semantical theory. While the present study does not probe in detail Paul of Venice's views on this important topic it does open naturally onto such investigations.[24] In the longer run the issue will become even more important, for medieval theories of logical form no less than their modern counterparts must settle on the place of meaning within them. Clearly, the question of whether a theory of meaning is reducible to a theory of truth is central to the evaluation of such theories.[25]

What does the *Logica Parva* contribute to the theory of language? Modern linguistic theory has made such great strides that the medieval explanations of linguistic phenomena may not satisfy us. Nonetheless, the medievals wanted to know how the larger wholes of a language are systematically compounded from its smallest parts, and they were dedicated to describing the forms of natural language in ways which were as meticulous as they were precise. Thus their methods and techniques of description still hold considerable interest in the history of linguistics.[26]

The present translation of the *Logica Parva* is based on the 1472 Venice Edition published in 1970 by Georg Olms Verlag.[27] Although I consulted later editions especially the 1492 Venice Edition (Petrus de Quarengiis Bergamensis) and the 1565 Venice Edition (Johannes Bonadeus) in my initial work, the 1472 Edition remained the basis of the translation. Wherever I found reason to question it, I compared the 1472 text with the earliest known manuscript (MS 60) dated 1401 in the Collegio di Spagna in

Bologna, Italy. The correspondence between the 1401 manuscript and the 1472 edition is in fact so close that the latter appears to have been copied from the former. The translation departs rarely from the 1472 text. It does so only where a word or sentence has been omitted by the copyist or where at the end of an argument a conclusion is signaled by the elliptical "Therefore, etc." *(quare etc.* or *ergo etc.)* In the former instance I have supplied from the manuscript a translation of the missing phrase or clause; in the latter I have expressed the implied conclusion. In both cases I have marked the additions in the customary way with editorial brackets. In the large number of passages which I have checked the manuscript proved an invaluable aid to reading what was already present, though obscurely, in the edition.

During 1980–1981 I had an opportunity to conduct a census of manuscripts of the *Logica Parva* in Italy. My list now contains 80 manuscripts of the *Logica Parva* including fragments. Of those I inspected personally more than 50, and I carefully checked catalog descriptions of the remaining ones. On the basis of my examination of these manuscripts I have confirmed not only that the manuscripts are in substantial agreement with one another but also that the 1472 edition faithfully represents the manuscript tradition. I also examined several commentaries on the *Logica Parva*. The most famous of these is by Mengus Bianchellus.[28] But there are others, e.g. Jacob Ritius, Manfredus de Medicis, Bartholomeus Manzolus, Pamphilus of Bologna, Antonio Cittadini of Faenza and Juan Hidalgo as well as a number of anonymous commentaries.[29] Although this amounts to fifteen commentaries on the *Logica Parva* which I have studied, I suspect that there are still others which I have not seen.[30]

Acknowledgements

Work on this project has continued for several years. Research for the essays was begun in the Summer of 1971 when I participated in the Institute in the Philosophy of Language sponsored by the Council for Philosophical Studies at the University of California, Irvine. Initial work on the text was begun in 1974 when I was a member of the School of Historical Studies of the Institute for Advanced Study, Princeton. I also had the opportunity to participate in two medieval seminars: Carol D. Lanham's "Medieval Epistleography", at U.C.L.A. (Summer, 1978) and John Murdoch's "Unity of Learning in the Later Middle Ages", at Harvard University (Summer, 1979). By their matter and their spirit these seminars not only furthered my work: they afforded opportunities to study in major research libraries. To the foundations which made them possible, The National

Endowment for the Humanities (for grants in 1974, 1979 and 1980–81), the American Council of Learned Societies and the University of Kentucky Research Foundation I am most grateful. To the following libraries, the Collegio di Spagna in Bologna, Italy, the Lily Library at Indiana University, the U.C.L.A. Research Library, the Henry E. Huntington Library, the Folger Shakespeare Library and the Houghton Library, Harvard University, I am thankful. I also thank Mrs. Vivian Macquown of the University of Kentucky Interlibrary Loan Department as well as Mrs. Patricia Harris and Miss Fran McFall of the Department of Philosophy for typing the difficult text.

Several colleagues have read sections of the translation in its early stages: Professor Thomas Maloney, the University of Louisville (Chapters I and II), Ivan Boh, Ohio State University (Chapters III and IV), Paul V. Spade, Indiana University (Chapters V and VI) and Henry Schankula, the University of Kentucky (Introductory Essays). This acknowledgement in no way implies that these colleagues agree with the final form of the work. I am sincerely grateful for their generous help; but I alone am responsible for the translation and the introductory essays. Finally, I want to dedicate this work to the memory of Professor Julius R. Weinberg who first encouraged me to explore the relationships between modern theories of logical form and later medieval logic.

Note

All page references to the *Logica Parva* are to the 1472 Venice Edition published in reprint by Georg Olms Verlag, Hildesheim/New York, 1970. These are indicated by a number in square brackets e.g., '[7]'. Citations in the notes are keyed to the reference list by author, item number and page, e.g., 'Bocheński, 2, pp. 1–30'.

Notes

[1] For a fuller account of Paul's life see Perreiah, 1. For bibliographies on Medieval Logic see Ashworth, 8, and Spade, 5.
[2] See Roth, Volume I, p. 68. For a bibliography of Paul's writings see Perini, Lohr, 2. The present author has prepared a census of manuscripts which is being published separately. For early printed editions of the *Logica Parva* see Risse. The other works in logic which have been attributed to Paul are: the *Logica Magna* (an anthology of Fourteenth century logic), the *Sophismata Aurea* (a collection of 50 sophisms) and the *Quadratura* (a series of exercises in dialectical argumentation). For comparisons and contrasts between the *Logica Parva* and

13

the *Logica Magna* see the Appendix to this volume. Though greatly dependent on Heytesbury's *Sophismata* there is sufficient manuscript evidence to claim that the *Sophismata Aurea* is a genuine work by Paul of Venice. The *Quadratura* is a record of Paul of Venice's *annus oppositionis*, a year long series of disputations which were required in the Augustinian order for admission to bachelor status. See Perreiah, 9.

[3] On Peter of Spain's work see Mullally, 1, 2 and on the publication of the *Summulae Logicales* see 1, 1xxviii f. For a partial inventory of *Logica Parva* manuscripts and texts see Lohr, 1 *(nota bene:* only one of the manuscripts listed under *Logica Magna* is actually a manuscript of that work (viz., Vat. Lat. 2132 (XV); the remaining ones are manuscripts of the *Logica Parva*. See also the *Logica Parva* entries in Mohan 1, 2, Kristeller 2. Regarding the early 16th century Professor Ashworth writes: "Paul of Venice apparently met with the steadiest demand, for in Venice alone sixteen editions of his *Logica Parva* were produced, six of them between 1525 and 1580." Ashworth, 6, p. 3.

[4] Roth, Volume I, p. 68. For Paul's work in logic see Maierú and Vasoli.

[5] For Paul's work in science see Randall, Clagett and Wallace.

[6] For Paul's contributions to certain philosophical issues, e.g., the theory of mind, see Nardi.

[7] For Paul's work in theology see Perini. It is noteworthy that the commentary on the *Sentences* attributed to Paul by Perini and earlier bibliographers is in fact based on that of John of Ripa who taught at Paris in the mid-14th century. See Stegmüller and Ruello.

[8] On the 13th century see: De Rijk, 1, Volume 2, Part 1, pp. 126–176; Kneale, pp. 224–246; Ong, pp. 131–167.

[9] On Sherwood see Kretzmann, 1, 2. On Roger Bacon see Steele. On Lambert of Auxerre see Alessio. And on Peter of Spain see Mullally and De Rijk, 6.

[10] On Ockham see Gál and Brown; On Walter Burleigh see Boehner, 4. The contributions of the other authors are introduced in Moody, 2, 4; Boehner, 3; Bocheński, 2 and Kneale.

[11] On St. Vincent Ferrer see Trentmann, 1, 4 and Perreiah, 3, p. 5 ff.

[12] On Venator and Ferrybridge see Adams and Del Punta in Adams, 3; on Peter of Mantua see Perreiah, 3, p. 52 ff.

[13] The best introduction to the work of this school is in Clagett, p. 199 ff. For references to Swyneshed as well as other members of this school in logic see Spade, 3, 4. For Heytesbury see Wilson and Howell, pp. 32–55. For trends in 14th century English logic before Ockham, see Pinborg, 3.

[14] See Seigel, p. 128 and Sr. M. Brown, 1, and Boh, 3, 4.

[15] See Ashworth, 6, p. 4 ff.

[16] See below note 29.

[17] See Jardine, p. 153. On the general background of Humanism in relation to Scholasticism see Kristeller, 1, Gilbert, 1 and Perreiah, 7. Another aspect of medieval logic is its relationship to rhetoric; for there are important connections between issues of logical form and those of rhetorical style. These become critical in an area such as dialectic which is shared by both logic and rhetoric. The best treat-

ments of medieval rhetoric are: Murphy, McKeon, Erickson, Howell and Seigel.

18 For anti-Scholastic satire in the *Praise of Folly* see Erasmus, pp. 150–155.

19 See More, p. 20 ff. For an interpretation of *Utopia* as anti-Scholastic satire see Wooden. Professor De Rijk has recently constructed from manuscript sources the contents of logic manuals in 15th century Cambridge and Oxford. These reconstructions are quite similar to the *Logica Parva*. See De Rijk, 8, 9. Professor Ashworth has shown the influence of the *Logica Parva* on the *Logica* printed in Oxford ca. 1483 by Theodoric Rood. See Ashworth 9.

20 See Vives, p. 85 ff.

21 See for example the work of Moody, 2, Boh, 1–4 and Ashworth, 6.

22 See Davidson and Harman, 1 and 2. Davidson's article, "Semantics for Natural Languages", and Harman's article, "Logical Form", are especially useful.

23 On medieval grammar see Hunt. On Speculative Grammar see Pinborg, 2; Bursill-Hall, 1, 2 and Trentman, 3.

24 Professor Nuchelmans in Nuchelmans has already initiated this study.

25 See Davidson, "Truth and Meaning", in Davidson and Harman, 1. Whether and how the criteria for evaluating theories of logical form could be modified to take into account the medieval theories remains an open question. See Harman, "Logical Form" in Davidson and Harman, 2.

26 On the importance of such methods see Chomsky.

27 Paul of Venice, 1.

28 See Mengus Bianchellus.

29 See the references to each author. For Juan Hidalgo see Muñoz Delgado. Manuscripts of additional commentaries are: Casale Monferrato, Seminario Vescovile, II e 7, Antonius de Ymola, *Compendium super quattuor tractatus logice Pauli Veneti* 79 fols. not numbered; I d 23, Hieronymus de Mutina, *Expositio super summulas Pauli Veneti*, 177 fols. 1510; Florence, B. Riccardiana, 895, Anonymous commentary on *obligationes* and *insolubilia*, ff. 108–114; Modena, B Estense, Lat. 92 (Alpha S. 9, 5) D. Magistrii Dominici Bondii *In logicam Pauli Veneti*, 58 chapters; Siena, B Comunale, Azzoni K x 9, Anonymous, *Brevis explanatio Pauli Veneti*, not numbered; Turin, B Nazionale, 989 (G.III.29) 483 fols. Vatican City, Codex Vaticanus Latinus 2141, Incerti auctoris *Quaestiones in Pauli Veneti Logicae parvae partem I*, fols. 2v–25r.

30 With regard to influences on the doctrines of the *Logica Parva* too little is known or published at present to render a final judgment. For example, I have determined from commentaries available only in manuscript that Chapter I has a great deal to do with views held by Arabic logicians. With respect to Chapter II, I have found at least one other manuscript in Padua which contains the unique divisions of supposition presented in the *Logica Parva*; but this lone text is anonymous. Concerning Chapter III, I suspect that the major influence is Ralph Strode; but I want to wait until further evidence is published by Professor Alfonso Maierú before deciding this. For Chapter IV

Professor Ashworth has suggested the importance of Billingham; but I have not had an opportunity to establish this. In the notes to Chapter V, I have recognized the importance of Roger Swyneshed; but I have found in the meantime several manuscripts on *obligationes* and *insolubilia* in Florence and Mantua which lead me to defer a final decision. In Chapter VI, I have noted the influence again of Roger Swyneshed as well as William of Heytesbury; but final attributions would require careful study of the manuscripts just mentioned. Finally, I believe that Chapters VII and VIII are to some extent borrowed from other authors and to some extent Paul's own doing; though, of course, all of the argumentation throughout the eight chapters of the *Logica Parva* is Paul's original work. For all of these reasons I have decided that final judgment about the outside sources of the *Logica Parva* must await further research.

Introduction

Termini

While the question whether medieval logic was a formal logic in the modern sense remains controversial to this day, there is considerable evidence that the logic of the Middle Ages made valuable contributions to the theory of logical form.[1] What is the difference between a formal logic and a theory of logical form? A formal logic codifies the possible forms of rational discourse as such. A theory of logical form examines the structures inherent in a given language used by ordinary persons in a particular time and place. A formal logic is normally developed as a formal system with axioms, theorems and rules for the manipulation of uninterpreted signs. A theory of logical form need not be presented as a formal system. Rather it pictures a natural language as itself a formal system and shows how the potentially infinite sequences of statements in that language are generable according to rules from a finite stock of expressions. A formal logic may be pursued apart from the details of expression, meaning, truth and even of inference which are present in a particular language. A theory of logical form must account for the factors of expression, meaning, truth and inference in some language. The *Logica Parva* contributes much less to formal logic as such than it does to the theory of logical form.

To explain the nature and functions of a language a theory of logical form pays careful attention to the component parts of that language. (1) It inventories the basic elements from which the larger segments of the language are composed. (2) It offers methods for settling questions of meaning including synonymy, ambiguity, and amphiboly within the language. (3) It gives rules for the replacement of one sentence by another and for inference between sentences. (4) It establishes procedures for determining those conditions under which sentences of the language are decidably true or false. These diverse kinds of information about a language take on a systematic character because the rules pertaining to meaning, to truth and to deduction (items 2, 3, 4) are keyed to a definite group of basic elements set forth in (1). Thus, to achieve the aims of a theory of logical form, the *Logica Parva* takes a compositional view of language. The larger unities of the language, i.e., the arguments, are seen as combinations of propositions. Propositions in turn are viewed as combinations of terms.

Terms themselves are classified into several fundamental types. Conversely, the typology of terms provides an index to the rules of meaning, the rules of truth-conditions and the rules of inference. In addition to these doctrines covered in the first half of the *Logica Parva*, the second half of the work offers instruction in several areas important for medieval education: these include rules for dialectical exchange and for oral examinations in logic. Finally, in the last two chapters of the work the rules expounded in Chapters I and III are submitted to criticism; and by answering these criticisms, the *Logica Parva* seeks to justify many of the rules which are central to the theory of logical form itself.

This essay examines the contents of Chapter I.[2] It introduces the reader to the basic concepts appealed to throughout the remaining eight chapters. With a slight reorganization of the text we discuss in succession the three main components of Paul of Venice's theory of logical form. Here is a topical outline.[3]

I. Terms
    A. Various distinctions: Significative/Non-significative; Natural/Conventional; Categorematic/Syncategorematic; Prime Intention/Second Intention; Prime Imposition/Second Imposition; Complex/Incomplex (Sections 1–4)
    B. Nouns/Verbs   (Sections 2, 3)
    C. Statements   (Sections 4, 5*)
    D. Predicables   (Section 15*)
    E. Categories   (Section 16*)

II. Propositions
    A. Types: Categorical/Hypothetical (Section 6*)
    B. Hypotheticals: Conditionals (Section 12*), Conjunctives (Section 13*), Disjunctives (Section 14*)
    C. Various properties of propositions: Affirmation/Negation; Truth/Falsity; Necessity/Contingency; Possibility/Impossibility; Quantified/Unquantified; Modal/Non-modal;   Composite Sense/Divided Sense (Sections 6*, 7*)

III. Arguments
    A. Immediate Implications: Oppositional Square (Sections 8* and 9*) Equivalence (Section 10), Conversion (Section 11)
    B. Mediated Implications: Syllogisms (Section 17*)

We will now study these topics in detail. A conclusion will relate each of them to later chapters of the *Logica Parva*.

I. Terms

Starting with the ultimate subject of all knowledge – individual things and their properties and relations – the *Logica Parva* divides rational discourse into three domains.[4] (1) Mental language which immediately signifies the world is comprised of the term *(terminus)*, the proposition *(propositio)* and the argument *(syllogismus)*.
(2) Spoken language which signifies mental language includes correspondingly the word *(dictio* or *terminus vocalis)*, the statement *(oratio* or *propositio vocalis)* and the inference *(consequentia vocalis)* expressed orally.
(3) Written language which signifies spoken language embraces in like manner the word *(terminus scriptus)*, the statement *(propositio scripta)* and the consequence *(consequentia scripta)* expressed in writing. Having neatly delineated these three domains Paul of Venice indifferently applies the words "term" *(terminus)*, "proposition" *(propositio)* and "inference" *(consequentia)* to the corresponding units in all three domains.

With this picture before us the distinctions introduced in Chapter I should become clear. The first division of terms is into "significative and non-significative".[5] This distinction marks a difference between terms which have some positive signification or meaning and those which do not. A term signifies if it calls something to the mind of a person who hears or sees the term. Words like "man" or "dog" are significative; words like "buf" or "baf" are not. Secondly, terms are divided into those which signify naturally *(naturaliter)*, i.e., mental terms and those which signify by convention *(ad placitum)* i.e., the expressions of spoken or written language.[6] Thirdly, terms are divided into those which signify something both by themselves and with other terms and those which signify only with other terms.[7] This distinction corresponds to the traditional one between categorematic and syncategorematic terms; and we will return to it by and by. Fourthly, terms are divided into prime intentions *(primae intentionis)* which signify things outside the mind and second intentions *(secundae intentionis)* which signify other mental terms.[8] "Socrates" and "man" in the proposition "Socrates is a man" would be examples of terms of prime intention. "rational animal" in the proposition "man is the rational animal", exemplifies a second intentional term because it does not signify any existing man but rather the concept "man" in the mind. The fifth division of terms is that into prime and second imposition; this distinction simply replicates the foregoing one with regard to spoken or written expressions.[9] The sixth and last distinction is between incomplex and complex terms.[10] The former is a word like "stone" or "cross" which is not further analyzable into significant parts; the latter is a phrase like "white man" which is further analyzable into significant parts. The later distinctions which Paul draws between nouns (Section 3) and verbs (Section 4) are based on the fact that the first signify apart from temporal conditions; whereas the second signify only within temporal conditions. This distinction becomes important in Chapter II in connection with the doctrines of supposition, ampliation, restriction and appellation; but it need not detain us here.

Because they play a prominent part in the later analyses of propositions and of arguments, we should clarify further Paul's distinctions between categorematic and syncategorematic terms.

Syncategorematic terms are used primarily to classify propositions so that their meaning, truth and inferential connections with other propositions may be discerned. Hence, we will examine syncategorematic terms later in discussing propositions. Categorematic terms are those terms which provide the content of the language. They are represented in a natural language by all of the words which describe the world. As an Aristotelian, Paul of Venice teaches that all such words fall into one of ten categories. Thus, the words of a natural language will express either Substance (e.g., "man", "dog", "tree"), Quantity (e.g., "1", "2", "3"), Quality (e.g., "red", "smooth", "crooked"), Relation (e.g., "...to the right of..."), Place (e.g., "on the street", "in the house"), Time (e.g., "at 1:00 p.m."), Position (e.g., "above", "below"), Action (e.g., "running", "barking"), Passion (e.g., "being killed", "being hit"), State (e.g., "crowned", "armed"). The doctrine of the categories is thus an exhaustive classification of non-complex terms. As will become evident in Chapter II, terms resulting from the use of quotational expressions will have a special place with the doctrine of the categories.[11]

When categorematic words are combined into sentences, the predicates of those sentences relate to their subjects in several discernable ways. The doctrine of the predicables defines the relationships which predicates have to subjects. After Porphyry there were said to be five predicables: Genus, Species, Difference, Property and Accident.[12] The predicates of many statements of ordinary discourse express some non-essential feature or "accident" of their subject: for example, the predicate "sitting" in "Socrates is sitting". In some cases, a predicate may express an essential property of the subject; for instance, "capable of laughter" in the sentence "Socrates is capable of laughter". In specialized contexts a predicate may give the definition of the subject: e.g., in "man is the rational animal", "animal" describes the genus and "rational" describes the "difference". The genus plus the "difference" defines the species. Although the doctrine of the predicables was used to analyze the relationships between subjects and predicates in the ways which we have shown, it had still another and more important use in the logical theory of the *Logica Parva*.

A category in the *Logica Parva* is "a coordination of many terms divided into higher and lower levels" (Section 16).[13] This definition implies that the descriptive terms of a natural language are arranged in a hierarchical order extending from terms of the highest level to those of the lowest level. Between the highest and the lowest there are several intermediate levels of terms. The highest level of term is said to be "the most abstract", and the lowest level of term is called "the most concrete". Furthermore, the *Logica Parva* states this rule: "In any category where a word signifying the concrete is posited, there the same word can be posited in its abstract form and conversely."[14] For example, in the same category where one posits "man" in the concrete one can posit the abstract expression "humanity". The vocabulary which the *Logica Parva* deploys to describe the various levels of terms in this hierarchy is taken from the traditional theory of the predicables. Here is an analysis of the levels of terms within the category of Substance :

Most general genus:	SUBSTANCE
Differences:	Corporeal – Incorporeal ↓
Subaltern genus:	BODY ↓
Differences:	Animated – Unanimated ↓
Subaltern genus:	LIVING ↓
Differences:	Sensible – Insensible ↓
Subaltern genus:	ANIMAL ↓
Differences :	Rational – Irrational ↓
Most special species:	MAN ↓
Individuals:	Socrates, Plato et al.

Note that this scheme has two boundary concepts: the most general genus is that concept which has none other above it, and the most special species is that which has below it no other species but only individuals. Each generic concept is divided by two differentiating concepts; and the generic concept plus one of the differentiating concepts defines the subalternate genus. In the above example, the *differentiae* on the left combine with the generic concepts above them in order to define the subalternate genus below them. Additional genera could be defined by taking the *differentiae* on the right. Schemes similar to this can be found in each of the categories analyzed in Chapter I.[15] The two conceptions, (a) that the descriptive terms of a natural language fall into categories and (b) that the terms within each category are located somewhere in a hierarchy divided into higher and lower levels were important ideas throughout the Middle Ages. In the *Logica Parva* they have important ramifications for Paul of Venice's approach to the structure of language and especially for his doctrines of supposition and of inference.

II. Propositions

The *Logica Parva* defines a proposition as "an indicative statement *(oratio)* signifying what is true or false". (Section 5)[16] It is important to note that the same proposition, i.e., the same concatenation of terms, may signify different things when expressed at different times, or by different persons or under different conditions of use. Thus, the statement, "I am sitting" signifies what is true when it is used by me to describe my bodily position while typing. Used by the person standing next to me to describe his physical position it is, of course, false. In both cases, however, the statement qualifies as a proposition; for "it is an indicative statement signifying what is true or false". As noted earlier, syncategorematic terms have the primary function of indicating the logical type of the statements in which they occur; and because of this they figure prominently in classifying propositions and in discussing their properties. Propositions fall into two groups: categorical and hypothetical.[17] The former are composed of three parts: a subject, a predicate and a copula which joins the two "extremes", i.e., the subject and the predicate. In the proposition,
(P) Man is an animal.
"Man" is the subject, "animal" is the predicate, and "is" is the copula. A hypothetical proposition is one with two or more categorical propositions as principal parts. For example,
(P) Socrates is running and Plato is sitting,
is analyzable into three components: "Socrates is running", "Plato is sitting", and the syncategorematic term "and". These definitions imply that the categorical proposition is primitive in the system, and this point is generally reflected throughout the *Logica Parva*. In addition, most of the properties which propositions themselves may have, e.g., "Truth", "Necessity" etc., are defined in the first instance with respect to categorical

propositions. For that reason we will discuss the various kinds first of hypothetical propositions and second of categorical propositions.

There are three species of hypothetical proposition. Each is defined by the presence in it of certain syncategorematic expressions.

Hypothetical Propositions:

Conditional:	"if ... then ..." , e.g.,	"*If* Socrates runs, *then* Socrates moves".
Conjunctive:	"...and ...",	e.g., "Socrates runs *and* Plato sits".
Disjunctive:	"... or ... ",	e.g., "Socrates runs *or* Plato sits".

With regard to conditionals, the proposition prefaced by "if" *(si)* is called the antecedent *(antecedens)*; that which follows "then" *(igitur, ergo* etc.*)* is called the consequent *(consequens)*. The two propositions which make up the conjunctive are called conjuncts *(propositiones conjunctae)*. Those which comprise the disjunctive are known as disjuncts *(propositiones disjunctae)*.

Categorical propositions fall into several types depending upon the presence or absence of certain syncategorematic expressions. They are first of all divided into unquantified and quantified. Exclusive propositions like "only Socrates runs" as well as exceptive propositions like "everyone except Socrates runs" are considered unquantified. Quantified propositions are sorted according to the kind of syncategorematic expression which governs their subject term. A proposition with no quantifying sign immediately before its subject-term is said to be "indefinite", e.g., "man runs". Those definite quantifying signs are of three types:

Categorical Propositions:

Universal:	"Every ... is ...",	e.g., "every donkey runs".
Particular:	"Some ... is ... ",	e.g., "some donkey brays".
Singular:	"Brunellus is ... ",	e.g., "Brunellus is a donkey".

There are, of course, many expressions equivalent to the quantifying expressions illustrated here. The most frequently used are: universal signs "all" *(omnis)*, "any" *(quilibet)*, etc.; particular signs "some" *(aliquis)*, "a certain" *(quidam)*, "one" *(unus)*, etc.; singular signs "Socrates" *(Sortes)*, "this man" *(iste homo)*, etc. We note that where the singular term is expressed through the demonstrative pronoun plus the common noun the two must agree in number and gender with the object or objects which they signify. We should note also that the principal parts, which are called the

23

"extremes", of a categorical proposition may be structured in special ways. For instance, a subject or predicate may be composed of conjoint or disjoint terms as in "Socrates and Plato dispute" or "Socrates or Plato runs". Moreover, categorical propositions may be themselves complex having both principal and dependent clauses. Because of the presence in these propositions of expressions like "that" *(qui, quae, quod* etc.*)* which are said to exercise some "office" over the clauses which follow them these are called "officiable propositions". Their logical features and truth-conditions are discussed in Chapters II and IV.[18]

We have been speaking largely about the fundamental kinds of propositions and their various subtypes. Now we must take up the properties which propositions may have. It is convenient to divide this discussion into two parts: the first will examine properties which are shared by both hypothetical and categorical propositions; the second will treat those properties found only in categorical propositions.

Both kinds of proposition, it is clear, may be either affirmative or negative. The examples we have given all illustrate affirmative forms. Their corresponding negatives may be constructed in several ways: the basic rule of negation, however, is to preface the entire proposition with the sign of negation, "no" *(non)* or its equivalents. Here are the resulting forms:

Negative Hypotheticals:

Negative Conditional: "Not: if . . . then . . . ",
e.g., "it is not the case that if Socrates runs, then Socrates moves".

Negative Conjunctive: "Not: . . . and . . ."
e.g., "it is not the case that Socrates runs and Plato sits".

Negative Disjunctive: "Not: . . . or . . ."
e.g., "it is not the case that Socrates runs or Plato sits".

Negative Categoricals:

Negative Exclusive: "Not: only . . .",
e.g., "it is not the case that only Socrates runs".

Negative Exceptive: "Not: every . . .",
e.g., "it is not the case that everyone except Socrates runs".

Negative Unquantified: "Not: ...",

                    e.g., "it is not the case that man runs".

Negative Quantified:

Universal:	"No . . . is . . .", e.g., "no donkey runs".
Particular:	"Not: some . . . is . . .", e.g., "it is not the case that some donkey brays".
Singular:	"Not: Brunellus is . . .", e.g., "it is not the case that Brunellus is braying".

In addition to governing the entire proposition, of course, the sign of negation may operate over one or another part of a proposition; in other words, terms as well as propositions may be negated. The rules for negation and for the mutual replacement of propositions containing negations are treated in the section on equipollent propositions.[19]

Although the *Logica Parva* distinguishes between "modal and nonmodal" propositions, every proposition is modal in some sense. For by definition every proposition signifies what is true or false; and truth and falsity are modes of propositions. Hence, every proposition is modal in some sense. Both hypothetical and categorical propositions may share in one or more of six modalities: truth/falsity, necessity/contingency, possibility/impossibility.[20] We will elaborate on these properties pertaining first to hypotheticals and then to categoricals. Hypothetical propositions possess modal properties according to the following definitions: I. An affirmative conditional is true if and only if the opposite (i.e., the negation) of its consequent is repugnant to its antecedent. The notion of "repugnance" is defined in this way: one proposition is repugnant to another if the one does not "stand with" *(stat cum)* the other without a contradiction. For practical purposes this means that the conjunction of the two propositions creates a false proposition. Further complexities in the *Logica Parva's* treatment of truth for conditionals have evoked considerable controversy. These will be discussed in connection with Chapter III, so they need not detain us here.[21] Conjunctive propositions are true if and only if both of their conjuncts are true. Disjunctive propositions are true if at least one of their disjuncts is true. All of these definitions of truth apply to affirmative hypotheticals. Negative hypotheticals are adjudged true or false by comparison with their corresponding affirmatives. The properties of necessity and contingency are defined: a proposition is necessary if, being true or false, it cannot be otherwise; a proposition is contingent if, being true or false, it can be otherwise. A proposition is possible if there is some instance in which it, or a proposition like it, is true; otherwise it is impossible. A true conditional proposition is said to be necessary; a false conditional impossible. A conjunctive is "necessary" if both of its conjuncts are necessary; otherwise it is contingent. Again, it is said to be possible if both parts are possible and neither is incompossible (i.e., not possible together) with the other. A conjunction is impossible if any of its parts is impossible. A disjunctive proposition is necessary if one of its parts is necessary; if neither part is necessary, it is contingent. A disjunctive proposition is possible if one of its parts is possible and is not incompossible with another part: it is impossible if both of its parts are impossible or are incompossible. All of these properties of hypothetical propositions were important in medieval logic, science, philosophy and theology. But we should not lose sight of the fact that the first pair of properties – truth or falsity – are by far the most important for general discussions of the structure of natural language.

Categorical propositions are divided into two types: modal and non-modal. A non-modal categorical is also called a proposition of "existence in" *(de inesse)* because it expresses the idea that what the predicate signifies "exists in" some subject. Modal categoricals by contrast express the manner in which the signification of the predicate exists in a subject or the manner in which the signification of an entire proposition applies to what it is about. The former are called modal propositions in the divided sense *(sensus divisus)* e.g., "Socrates contingently runs"; the latter are modal propositions in the composite sense *(sensus compositus)*, e.g., "contingently Socrates runs". The distinctions between divided and composite sense apply to the four modal auxiliaries – necessity/contingency and possibility/impossibility and to their adverbial forms. These are amply discussed and illustrated in the text.[22]

As we observed earlier, the categorical proposition is basic to Paul of Venice's account of the structure of natural language. This observation is confirmed by the fact that the truth or falsity of hypotheticals is defined in function of the truth or falsity of their component categoricals. The definition of truth for categoricals is fundamental. A categorical proposition is true if and only if "its primary and adequate significate" is true; otherwise it is false. "The primary and adequate significate" of a proposition is "the customary significate".[23] This is said to be "that significate which is like the signification of the statement but in the infinite and conjunctive sense". The adequate significate of "Socrates runs", may be expressed in either direct or indirect discourse: "Socrates runs", *(li Sortes currit)* adequately signifies *either* (1) Socrates runs *(Sortes currit)* or (2) It is thus that Socrates runs *(Ita est quod Sortem currere)*. Where (1) is simply the categorical proposition actually used by someone, (2) employs the Latin construction of accusative plus infinitive to say the same thing. Both forms express the adequate significate.[24] Where this expression signifies what is in fact the case, the original proposition is true; where this is not the case, the proposition is false. Paul's definition of the predicate "true" for categorical propositions may be summarized:

"S is P" is true if and only if S is P. [25]

Thus, on Paul of Venice's account the predicate "true" systematically maps the significations of propositions onto the object or objects signified by those propositions.

III. Arguments

A theory of logical form must give, as we have said, an account of the implicational relationships between sentences. This is important not only because it clarifies the relation of a given sentence to others of the same or different forms. It is important also in connection with the modal auxiliaries and especially with regard to the properties of truth and falsity. For once the implicational relationships between sentences have been defined and formulated into rules, it is easy to see how the properties of truth or falsity attached to any one sentence are transmissable or communicable to other sentences throughout the language. Hence, along with the theories of meaning and of truth, the theory of argument is essential to the theory of language. An argument in the *Logica Parva* is understood to be a sequence of sentences in which from one or more sentences another sentence follows. This definition is very general and covers two systems of implication whose rules are elaborated in the *Logica Parva*. Let us place these rules into two groups: rules of immediate implication and rules of mediated implication. Rules for both immediate and mediated implications between hypothetical propositions are treated in Chapter III. Rules for both types of implication between categorical propositions are presented in Chapters I and III. Rules for immediate or one-step implications apply to propositions having like subjects, predicates and copulas. This restriction entails that the categorematic terms of the propositions involved must match in number and gender and that adjustments must be made for variations of case. Moreover, the copulas of the sentences involved must be of the same quantity and have an appropriate tense. Specific rules are given in the sections on Equipollence, on Conversion, on Contraposition and on the Square of Opposition (including rules for contradiction, contrariety, subcontrariety, subimplication, and superimplication).[26]

The principal kinds of mediated implications treated in Chapter I are those governed by the rules of syllogism.[27] In every valid syllogism two propositions are so related that a third proposition follows from them. Since the theory of syllogistic is familiar, we will take this opportunity to underscore those features of syllogistic reasoning which are important in Paul of Venice's approach to logical form. Consider this example of a syllogistic form.

Major premise: Every _____ is _____ .

Minor premise: Every _____ is _____ .

Conclusion: Every _____ is _____ .

In order for the conclusion to follow validly from the premises several conditions must be met: (1) the argument must contain three and only three unambiguous categorematic terms. By definition, the MAJOR TERM is the predicate of the conclusion. The MINOR TERM is the subject of the conclusion. And the MIDDLE TERM occurs twice in the premises and not in the conclusion. (2) No term in the conclusion may exceed the quantity (universal or particular) which it has in the premise. (3) At least one premise must be affirmative. (4) The middle term must be universal in at least one of its occurences. From the viewpoint of a theory of logical form it is important to recognize that this and the (eighteen) other valid forms of syllogistic reasoning warrant the deduction of conclusions from premises just in case the formal conditions of syllogistic reasoning are satisfied. In other words, it makes no difference which categorematic terms come to occupy the blanks: so long as the formal requirements are met, the conclusions follow from the premises. Of course the premises may be either true or false, as we have seen. If they are true, the conclusion will be true as well. If one or both are false, the conclusion will be false. Nonetheless, as part of the theory of logical form syllogistic sets forth the major ways in which syncategorematic terms of certain types function to connect some sentences of the language with others.

Conclusion

Chapter I of the *Logica Parva* presents the rudiments of a theory of logical form for that part of medieval Latin used for discursive purposes. (1) It catalogues the basic kinds of terms from which propositions of the language may be composed and it describes the behavior of those expressions. Particularly important in this regard is the distinction between categorematic and syncategorematic terms. (2) By reference to the syncategorematic terms which they contain it classifies the basic forms of sentences which can be composed in the language and explains some of the salient properties of those sentences. Most notably, (3) it gives a general account of truth and falsity for propositions. Finally, (4) it sets down rules for implicational relationships between sentences of the forms recognized in (2), and it prepares the way for the fuller treatment of implication relationships to be given in Chapter III. The systematic character of this approach to natural language results from the connections between these three determinants of logical form: TERMS, PROPOSITIONS and ARGUMENTS. For the syncategorematic terms or logical words not only supply the key for classifying propositions. They are crucial in establishing truth-conditions, and they are the main structural factors in the rules of implication. Hence, the typology of terms welds the separate accounts of meaning, truth and inference into one comprehensive theory of the logical form of the language under investigation. By the end of Chapter I, however, only the groundwork has been laid. The theory is far from complete.

Roughly speaking, the *Logica Parva* may be divided into two parts. The first four chapters deal with the analytical side of a theory of logical form. The last four chapters address the dialectical dimension – how the various components of argument function in actual situations of argumentation as well as how a number of distinctions and rules are to be justified. Chapter II on Supposition pursues some additional issues of logical form; in particular it offers a method for assigning a single logical form to each sentence of the language. Chapter III continues the unfinished business of Chapter I by specifying more than four dozen rules of inference. Chapter IV elaborates the theory of truth conditions for the sorts of propositions recognized in Chapter I. Chapters V and VI go beyond the sphere of logical theory and lay down a number of rules for dialectical exchange and for oral examinations in logic. Chapters VII and VIII attempt to justify by the indirect method (i.e., *reductio ad absurdum*) many of the rules set forth in Chapters I and III.

Notes

[1] Many scholars have alluded to the concept of "logical form" in connection with medieval logic. For example, Fr. Bocheński writes: "[W]e find ... logic limited to concern with *logical* form, which leads to an exact definition of formal logic when this form is equated with the syncategoremata. Scholastic practice is wholly in accord with this definition in its cultivation of the corresponding theory of logical form." (Bocheński, 2, pp. 156–157). Other authors are less precise about what they mean by "logical form".

In these essays "theory of logical form" is a collective term distantly related to recent work on the logical structure of natural languages. Although the list of contributors to this theory would be long and would include the names of major logicians and philosophers of the past century, Professors Donald Davidson and Gilbert Harman have discussed the general features of such a theory in several articles and two volumes published jointly by them. See Davidson and Harman 1, 2. For a statement of what a theory of logical form includes see Davidson, 2. For one view about how to evaluate theories of logical form see Harman, 1.

As will become clear, the *Logica Parva* does not attempt to analyze the structures inherent in the whole of the Latin language but rather only those in that part of late medieval Latin which was used for discursive purposes. This includes the Latin employed in everyday thought as well as in the Sciences, Philosophy and those parts of Theology which were amenable to rational expression and scrutiny (an ever expanding domain of Theology in this period). Although this is admittedly an idiom of late medieval Latin used mainly by professors and other professionals it qualifies as a "natural" as opposed to an "artificial" or "parified" language because it is understood to express the concepts, judgments and reasonings of rational persons.

2   Paul of Venice, *Logica Parva*, the 1472 Venice Edition reprinted by Georg Olms Verlag, 1970, Hildesheim—New York. All page references are to this edition, pp. [1]—[30].

3   Sections designated by starred numbers contain materials which are submitted to dialectical discussion and justification in Chapters VII and VIII.

4   The best discussions of the components of rational discourse are: Boehner, 6, pp. 201—232; Loux, 1, p. 1 ff.; Ashworth, 6, pp. 42—43. For an excellent history of the theory and the development of the later terminology see Nuchelmans, p. 139 ff. For comparison with views in the *Logica Magna* see Nuchelmans, p. 266 ff.

5   On the distinction "significative/non-significative" see Aristotle, *De Interpretatione*, Chapter 1 ff. and Boehner, 6, pp. 201—232; Loux, 2; Ashworth, 6, pp. 26—76; Trentman, 2.

6   On the distinction "naturally/by convention" see Aristotle, *De Interpretatione*, Chapters 1 and 2 and the references in note 4.

7   On the distinction "categorematic/syncategorematic" see Aristotle, *Categories* and *De Interpretatione*, 1, 16a 1 ff. Also, see Boehner, 6, p. 222 ff.; Bocheński, 2, p. 156 ff.; Ashworth 6, pp. 49—52: O'Donnell, Kretzmann, 3; Mullally, 2.

8   On the distinction "first and second intention" see: Boehner, 6, p. 222 ff.; Loux, 2. Fr. Bocheński has suggested that the scholastic distinction between first and second intention corresponds to the modern one between the expressions of an object language and those of a meta-language. Bocheński, 2, p. 154 ff. This is a very loose correspondence, however, see Kneale, p. 229 ff.

9   On the distinction "first and second imposition" see the references to note 8.

[10] On the distinction "incomplex and complex" see Aristotle, *De Interpretatione*, Chapters 1–3 and Nuchelmans, pp. 195–208.

[11] The effect of the signs of quotation introduced in Chapter II is to shift the signification of a term from its ordinary or normal significate to itself or its like as a language sign. See Chapter II.

[12] On the predicables see: Aristotle, *Categories*, Chapters 2–5. Also, Eleonore Stump, "Differentia and the Porphyrian Tree". As Ms. Stump points out, "In the *Topics* Aristotle makes use of four predicables: definition, property, genus and accident... In the *Isagoge*, Porphyry discusses five predicables, omitting one of Aristotle's (definition) and adding two which Aristotle mentions but does not examine in detail (species and differentia), so that for Porphyry the predicables are genus, species, property, accident and differentia", pp. 238–239. See also, Bocheński, 2, pp. 135–136.

[13] *Logica Parva*, pp. [23]–[26].

[14] *Logica Parva*, p. [26], p. [221]. Here is evidence that Paul of Venice recognizes a difference between concrete and abstract terms and that the latter may be formed out of the former. The notion of an abstract term occurs in the *Logica Magna* doctrine of simple supposition *(suppositio simplex)*. See Paul of Venice, *Logica Magna* Treatise on Suppositions, edited and translated in Perreiah, 3, pp. 43–81.

[15] *Logica Parva*, pp. [23]–[26].

[16] See Aristotle, *De Interpretatione*, Chapter 4. For a history of the definition see Nuchelmans, p. 132 ff. For a comparison with views of the proposition in the *Logica Magna* see Nuchelmans, p. 266 ff. and Adams and Del Punta, p. 80 ff. See also Kretzmann, 3 and Ashworth, 6, p. 47 ff. and 3.

[17] In medieval logic, the term "hypothetical" designates three kinds of compound statement: namely, conditionals, disjunctions and conjunctions.

[18] See *Logica Parva* on "Appellation of Form", p. [63] ff. and "Officiable Propositions", pp. [86]–[90].

[19] See *Logica Parva*, p. [12]. An excellent treatment of negation is in Prior, 1, pp. 126–156.

[20] See Kneale, pp. 117–128.

[21] See *Logica Parva*, pp. [65]–[66].

[22] See *Logica Parva*, pp. [6]–[10] and pp. [92]–[95].

[23] See *Logica Parva*, p. [6].

[24] In addition to the adequate significate Paul of Venice expounds the concept of the principal significate which is important in connection with solutions to the paradoxes. The differences between the two types of significate are:

a. The adequate significate of "Socrates runs", is: Socrates runs or it is thus that Socrates runs.

b. The principal significate of "Socrates runs", is: Socrates runs or it is thus that Socrates runs *and* "Socrates runs" is true.

For a fuller discussion of the principal significate and its use in re-solving insolubles see Chapter VI. For treatments of the nature of the adequate significate of a proposition see: Bocheński, 2, pp. 110–111; Kneale, pp. 138–158; Nuchelmans, p. 22 ff.; Ashworth, 6, pp. 55–62; Adams and Del Punta, p. 80 ff.

25 Because of its central place in a theory of logical form, the theory of truth in Scholastic logic must be more fully understood. Good historical introductions may be found in Boehner, 6, pp. 174–200; Moody, 2, pp. 30–63; Kneale, pp. 138–158; Nuchelmans, p. 273 ff. A basic issue is, of course, whether an approach to truth like that in the *Logica Parva* satisfies Professor Tarski's "Convention T" which sets a standard, or criterion of adequacy for a definition of truth. For brevity we quote Professors Davidson and Harman on the import of convention T:

Suppose now that the object language is L and the metalanguage is M, and that M contains the predicate "is true-in-L". Then convention T says that a defini-tion of "is true-in-L" is an adequate definition of truth for L if it has as a con-sequence every sentence of the form

s is true-in-L if and only if p

where "s" is replaced by a standardized description of a sentence of L and "p" is replaced by a translation of "s" into M ("s" may be replaced by s itself if the object language is part of the metalanguage). The definition must also entail that only sentences are true.

Davidson and Harman, 1, Introduction, p. 5 ff. An excerpt from Alfred Tarski's "The Concept of Truth for Formalized Languages", may be found in Davidson and Harman, 1, pp. 152–197.

Discussions of the definition of truth in medieval logic have arisen mainly in connection with treatments of the semantical paradoxes. Thus, the remarks in Moody, 2, p. 11 ff.; Prior, 2; Scott, 1, p. 49 ff. and Ashworth, 6, pp. 55–66, do not address the question directly whether the medieval theories they discuss satisfy Tarski's convention T. Only Professor Spade confronts the issue head on, and his judg-ment is that medieval definitions of the truth of a proposition like that in the *Logica Parva* do not meet Tarski's test. See Spade, 1, pp. 1–3. We should note, however, that Professor Spade's remarks concern only one aspect of such definitions of truth, viz., that which is deployed in solving sophisms and insolubles. That is the part which concerns the principal significate of a proposition. The entire de-finition of truth, however, must include the concept of the adequate significate which we have presented as basic. In that respect, the theory has not been evaluated. In the *Logica Parva* it is clear that Paul of Venice is more interested in expounding rules for the use of the predicate "true" and the other modal auxiliaries than he is in elaborating a complete theory of truth. Yet even this interest requires him to devote a great deal of attention to the aspects of logical form which are relevant to the conception of truth. For comparisons with views in the *Logica Magna* see Adams and Del Punta, 3, p. 4 ff.

26 Aristotle, 1, *De Interpretatione*, Ch. 6 ff. For a general introduction to these topics see: Prior, 2, pp. 103–125; Ashworth, 6. For an interesting discussion of the square of opposition see Veatch.

27 There are many good introductions to the theory of syllogism. See Prior, 2, pp. 103–125; Bocheński, 2, pp. 210–264; Kneale, pp. 67–81; Ashworth, 2, 6, p. 187 ff., pp. 224–252.

Suppositiones

The theory of supposition is generally thought to be a unique invention of late medieval logic.[1] There is nothing like it in any of the ancient sources whether Aristotelian, Stoic or Boethian. Nor does it appear in medieval logic prior to the 12th century.[2] Its importance may be inferred from the fact that in recent years, apart from the theory of consequences, no other part of medieval logic received more scholarly attention than supposition theory.[3] Yet despite this work there is still no commonly accepted interpretation of supposition theory. There is not even agreement on what kind of theory it is. Various authors place the theory in one or another area of Semiotic. Some say that it is a theory of reference and is part of the medieval method for determining the truth or falsity of propositions.[4] Read in this way, supposition theory would be part of Semantics. Others claim that it is an incipient theory of quantification; and thus it would be part of Syntax.[5] Still others regard it as a theory about how expressions are used in context, and hence it would be a contribution to Pragmatics.[6] Finally, echoing a theme stated by Fr. Bocheński, " 'Supposition' covers numerous semiotic functions for which we now have no common name", several scholars have parcelled out various segments of supposition theory into different departments of Semiotic.[7]

Viewed as part of a theory of logical form the nature of supposition theory becomes clear. For the *Logica Parva* approaches the logical form of natural language by way of three theories: (1) Terms, (2) Propositions and (3) Arguments. To say that supposition is reference would be to place it within the theory of propositions and specifically within that part of the theory which deals with the truth or falsity of propositions. But the *Logica Parva* treats these matters in the theory of proof *(probatio)* (Chapter IV) where the uniform effects of terms on the truth or falsity of propositions are examined in detail, and where the distinctions pertaining to supposition are taken as already established. To claim that supposition is a part of quantification theory would be to locate it within the theory of deduction. But the rules of supposition are not themselves rules of deduction, and the discussions of deductive principles in the *Logica Parva* either make no mention of the rules of supposition (Cf. the Chapter I treatment of Syllogism) or assume beforehand the rules of supposition (Cf. the Chapter III doctrine of inference). It follows that supposition theory belongs neither to the theory of propositions nor to the theory of arguments, but rather to the theory of terms. The medieval texts themselves are nearly unanimous in declaring that "supposition is a *property of categorematic terms* in the context of a proposition".[8]

The purpose of the theory of supposition becomes even clearer when we consider the phenomenon of ambiguity in natural languages.[9] Where "ambiguity" is that property of a term which has more than one meaning, the language studied by medieval logic afforded ample room for ambiguity. On the view elaborated earlier that terms within each category fall into a hierarchical order it is noteworthy that the same expression, e.g., "man" could represent now a genus, now a species or now again an individual depending on the sentence in which it occurs. Moreover, there are the normal problems of ambiguity. Although the same expression "man" occurs in all of these sentences,

I   Every man runs,
II   Man runs,
III   This man runs,
IV   Man is the rational animal,
V   Man is a three-letter word,

its signification differs markedly from one sentence to another. What does it signify in each case? Are the significations interrelated? And, if so, how are they interrelated? To answer these questions the theory of supposition performs three tasks: (a) it makes explicit the significations of the categorematic terms, (b) it traces their relationships to the significations of other categorematic terms and (c) it locates these significations within a hierarchy of terms having signification. By making precise the significations of their component terms, and by showing their position within a hierarchy of terms, the theory of supposition articulates for each sentence of a language a basic logical form. If a sentence admits of more than one form, the theory specifies alternative forms. It should be clear that the task of assigning basic logical forms to sentences must be accomplished before their truth or falsity can be decided and before inferential operations can be performed on them.

To the extent that it renders explicit the logical forms of sentences the theory of supposition performs a role very much like that of a modern system of conceptual notation.[10] Modern notational systems make a clear division between the non-logical and logical components of a language. Next, among the logical units they distinguish between those which operate over entire statements and those which govern the parts of statements. Logical components are further grouped into types, levels and modes of operation. Conventions for punctuation are adopted in order to avoid ambiguity in the formulas of the system. As a medieval system of conceptual representation supposition theory employs a terminology which is rich in spatial metaphors and figures of speech. With its talk of "higher and lower", of "descent and ascent", of "impeding and non impeding", of "mobility and immobility" supposition theory helped the medievals to picture visually their discoveries about linguistic structure. But the most remarkable difference between modern notational systems and their medieval counterparts lies in the fact that the former are designed for the printed page whereas the latter were devised originally for spoken discourse. Before the advent of printing the logical forms delineated by supposition theory were recorded in the memories of students who heard them expressed orally far more frequently than they were read or written down in manuscripts or school copybooks. If the formulas of supposition theory transcribed into the written word strike us today as clumsy and awkward, we should see that modern systems of symbolic notation would prove no less cumbersome if they were reexpressed and confined to the spoken word. Hence, the vocabulary of supposition theory provides for the Middle Ages a technical medium within which the logical forms of sentences in a natural language can be studied and represented.[11]

The following sections of this essay will discuss in greater detail: (1) the definitions, divisions and rules of formal supposition, (2) the theory of material supposition as a nascent theory of quotation for a natural language and (3) some extensions of supposition theory for determining the logical forms of sentences containing special expressions. The reader will note a generous proliferation of paradoxical theses throughout the text. A conclusion will comment on the purpose of these sophisms.

I. Formal Supposition

Logic manuals of the later Middle Ages speak of three properties of terms: (1) Signification, (2) Supposition and (3) Verification.[12] The first, as we saw in Chapter I, is that property whereby a term calls something to mind. The third, as we shall see in Chapter IV, is not, strictly speaking a property of terms but rather of propositions. However, because a proposition is proved true or false by reduction to singular propositions and a singular proposition is one in which a categorematic term is predicated of some thing, verification is said to be a property of a term. Nonetheless, supposition theory falls midway between the other two theories: the *Logica Parva* defines "supposition" *(suppositio)* as "the acceptance *(ac-*

ceptio) of a term in a proposition for *(pro)* some thing or things".[13] This definition calls for clarification. If the theory of signification analyses the proposition into its elementary parts, the theory of supposition regards those same elements as interdependent parts of a unified whole. To "accept" a term is to recognize that it is one of several constitutive factors in a single proposition.

The word "supposition" *(suppositio)* and its various forms, e.g., "has supposition for" *(habet suppositio pro)* or "stands for" *(supponit pro)* or *(stat pro)* has an obscure origin.[14] In the *Logica Parva* "supposition" is one of three species in the category of relation: superposition *(superpositio)*, supposition *(suppositio)* and equiparity *(equiparantia)*[15] The present spelling of the term seems to have come from "subpositio" by the development of "b" into "p". The occurrence of the term "supposition" in discussions of the category of relation provides some clues about the property of supposition itself. It suggests, first of all, that supposition is the status or stance of a term relative to other terms. The prefix *"sup"* along with those of the other expressions *(super-* and *equi-)* suggest that a term said to have supposition stands beneath some other term, presumably one having superposition. The particle *"pro"* suggests that the term stands with respect to some thing or things. As we shall see, these are called the *"supposita"* of the term said to have supposition. In short the terminology of supposition suggest that supposition is that property of a categorematic term whereby it is stationed within a hierarchy of other categorematic terms which are, figuratively at least, "above", "below" and "on a par with" it. As we shall see on closer examination, the distinctions, definitions and rules of supposition theory confirm this initial insight.

Supposition theory embraces both a general method for determining the supposition of terms and particular patterns for deciding this in special cases. The method of suppositional analysis requires first of all a decision about the kind of signification a term has. If a term stands for its normal or formal meaning, it is said to signify "personally". If it can signify formally but in fact signifies itself only as a language sign it is said to signify "materially". Of course, many words of a natural language can have both kinds of signification, and this is a principal source of ambiguity. By calling for a decision about the kind of signification a term has the theory of supposition makes a first step toward eliminating unwanted ambiguity.

The method of suppositional analysis can best be illustrated by considering three cases in which terms are said to supposit or to have supposition:

I.   Discrete Supposition
     (1) This man runs.

37

II. Determinate Common Supposition
   (1) Some man runs.
   (2) These are all men (man$_1$, man$_2$, man$_3$).[16]
   (3) This man$_1$ runs or that man$_2$ runs or that man$_3$ runs.
III. Distributive Common Supposition
   (1) Every man runs.
   (2) These are all men (man$_1$, man$_2$, man$_3$).
   (3) This man$_1$ runs and that man$_2$ runs and that man$_3$ runs.

A cursory examination of these cases will reveal that Discrete Supposition (Case I) where the subject-term of the proposition represents a singular object is the centerpiece of suppositional analysis: for Cases II and III simply show how an original proposition whose subject term is not singular may be reduced to a concatenation — disjunctive or conjunctive — of propositions with singular subject-terms. In Chapter I we noted that terms within any one category may be distinguished by means of the predicables into generic and specific. The terminology of supposition theory reflects those distinctions by dividing terms into higher and lower levels *(terminus superius vel terminus inferius)*. In the foregoing cases, "man" in Case I is said to be at "the lowest level" for it is not further divisible into species, and it has "beneath it" only individuals. In Cases II and III "man" in (1) is called a higher-level term in relation to "man $_1$, $_2$, $_3$" in (2) and (3). Not surprisingly, "man $_1$, $_2$, $_3$" in (2) and (3) are said to be on a lower level than "man" in (1). The passage from (1) to (3) in each case is called a "descent" *(descensus)*; and that from (3) to (1) an "ascent" *(ascensus)*. A term which admits such passages is said to be "mobile" *(mobilis)*; one which does not is "immobile" *(immobilis)*. The purpose of the rules of supposition is to govern the passages from propositions with terms of one type to those with terms of another type.

A syncategorematic term which has the power to effect certain kinds of supposition on terms following it is said "to confound" *(confundere)* or "to have the force of confounding" *(habere vim confundendi)*. Syncategorematic terms are principally divided into affirmative and negative. Sometimes a later syncategorematic term alters the power of an earlier syncategorematic term to fix the supposition of a categorematic term. In this case the second term is said "to impede" *(impedire)* the first. A categorematic term which is affected by a syncategorematic term having the force of confounding *(vim confundendi)* is said to be "confused" *(confusa)*. Some categorematic terms are "confused" in a distributive way; others are said to be "merely confused" *(confusa tantum)*. "Man" in (1) of Case III above is confused in a distributive way. To say that a term is "merely confused" means that its relationships to other categorematic terms is underdetermined and that the term is "frozen" within the hierarchy of terms with no passage to other terms permitted. In this case the term is "merely confused immobily" *(confusa tantum immobile)*. Sometimes a term is said to be "merely confused mobily" *(confusa tantum mobile)*; this means that strictly no passage from or to the term is permitted; but *if* one should be permitted, *then* it would be in the way indicated.

Here follows a brief list of rules which tell how syncategorematic terms of various sorts cause certain types of supposition in the categorematic terms which follow them:[17]

(1) Every universal affirmative sign confounds a term immediately following it in a confused and mobily distributive way; and it confounds a term mediately following it in a merely confused way.

(2) Every negative sign confounds distributively and mobily terms following it whether immediately or mediately.

(3) All terms expressing the comparative or superlative grade (e.g., "as much...so much...", "the strongest...") as well as certain verbs (e.g., "I want ...", "I need ...") confound a term following them in a mobile distributive way.

(4) An exclusive expression, e.g., "only", "alone", confounds a term following it immediately in a merely confused and mobile way.

(5) An exceptive expression, e.g., "except", "save" confounds a term following it in a merely confused way.

(6) A reduplicative expression, e.g., "... insofar as ...", confounds the term following it in a merely confused and immobile way.

(7) Terms expressing acts of the mind such as "I know ...", "I believe...", "I doubt..." confound terms following them immediately in a merely confused and mobile way.

(8) Adverbial modifiers such as "twice", "thrice" confound terms following them immediately in a merely confused and mobile way.

(9) Modal terms such as "necessarily", "possibly" in the composite sense confound in an immobile way the terms which follow or precede them.

(10) The verbs "begins", "ceases" confound terms following them in several special ways.

(11) Intentional verbs like "I promise", "I owe", etc. confound the terms following them in a merely confused and immobile way.

(12) Any sign of a condition, e.g., "if" confounds all of the non-distributed terms following it in a merely confused and immobile way.

These rules call for several comments. First of all, the text makes no attempt to justify them as it will attempt to justify the rules of syllogism, the rules of inference and even some of the rules for proving terms, i.e., showing general conditions for the truth or falsity of propositions. Secondly, the rules apply to categorematic terms in both subject and predicate position. As a method for analyzing the position of a categorematic term relative to other categorematic terms of different levels within any one category, supposition theory applies to predicates equally as well as to subjects. Thirdly, although normally a syncategorematic term operates over terms follwing it either immediately or mediately (i.e., later in the sentence) some syncategorematic terms govern terms preceding them. See for example Rule 9.

In sum, the rules of supposition perform the following tasks. (1) They tell how to distinguish between the kinds of signification (formal or material) a term may have. (2) They show how to locate a given term within a hierarchy of terms of the same category. (3) They define basic relationships between the subject and predicate terms of a proposition. By performing each of these tasks the theory of supposition achieves its major aim: that is, articulating the basic logical forms of the sentences to which it is applied.

II. Material Supposition

The definitions and rules of material supposition closely parallel those of formal supposition. This is apparent in a comparison of the divisions of the two types of supposition:

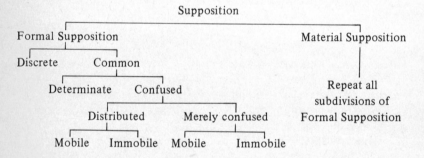

From a theoretical viewpoint, one or the other of these divisions is redundant. If Paul of Venice were primarily concerned with theoretical elegance he would have retained only one set of divisions and simply distinguished between two kinds of significate. In practice, however, he does just this. The parallel treatment of material and personal supposition seems to have a pedagogical justification. Teaching the two types of supposition in tandem confirms the fact that the same subdivisions are common to both types and reminds the student that a term must retain the same type of

40

supposition throughout any one context. Learning them in this way, the student is trained to detect any alteration in the supposition of a term within a single context.

Apart from its value in uncovering ambiguites in the language, the theory of material supposition is most useful because it provides a theory of quotation for the natural language. That is: it offers a system of definitions and rules by which the logical forms of sentences containing quoted expressions may be determined. By so doing it prepares those statements for the application of rules of deduction or of truth-conditions. Modern theories of quotation have been developed principally with regard to written discourse; the medieval theory of material supposition was applied initially to expressions in spoken discourse and only later to those in written discourse. Another important difference between modern and medieval theories is this. Most modern theories of quotation construe expressions within quotational signs as names for those same terms without quotational signs. Thus, within quotation marks an expression becomes a new kind of linguistic entity. On the medieval view, quotational signs operate like syncategorematic terms which signal a special use of the categorematic terms which they govern.[18] The precise quotational devices used were expressions like, "this term", "this word" or the definite article adopted from Old French, *"Ly"* or *"Li"*.[19] When a word, phrase or sentence is preceded by any of these expressions it indicates that the speaker or writer is calling special attention to them as language signs. Thus, the *Logica Parva* does not conceive the function of quotation marks as mapping expressions onto names of those expressions. Rather it treats quotation as a special use of ordinary discourse: the quoted expression is a special use of the ordinary expression, and the quotational devices merely call attention to its status as a language sign.

The rules of material supposition are quite complicated, and this introduction will not be able to give a complete elaboration of them. There are both general principles and specific rules. Moreover, separate sets of rules are worked out for terms of first and second intention as well as for first and second imposition. For the sake of simplicity we speak only about the general principles and those rules which apply to terms regardless of whether they are thought (intention), spoken or written (imposition). Two general principles apply:

I. Any term which is not verifiable of itself without a sign of materiality [i.e., "this term", *"ly"*, *"li"* etc.] has both a formal and a material significate.

II. Any term which is verifiable of itself without a sign of materiality has only a formal significate.[20]

For a term to be "verifiable of itself" it must be predicable of itself in a true affirmative statement, e.g., "this is a man" where the demonstrative pronoun "this" points to the predicate term "man". The falsity of such a statement shows that "man" has both a formal and a material significate and hence it is not verifiable of itself without a sign of materiality. Some expressions are predicable of themselves in true affirmative sentences, e.g., "a term is a term", *(terminus est terminus)*. Such expressions do not have both a formal and a material significate: they have a formal supposition unless there is some reason, expressed or implied, to take them otherwise. If a term is ambiguous between its formal and its material signification a sign of materiality is needed to show that its material significate is the one the speaker has in mind. If no sign of materiality is given, the term is taken to signify its formal significate. As a general rule of thumb any proposition containing terms whose supposition is not clear is to be interpreted in a way which would render the proposition true.

III. Extensions of Supposition Theory

The last four sections of Chapter II discuss several types of term whose supposition is special. These are terms represented in the natural language by relative, possessive and reflexive pronouns and by other expressions which behave like them. Previous discussion has concentrated on the supposition of subject or predicate terms joined by a copula in the present tense. Section 8 addresses the question of the supposition of terms when the copula is in past or future tense and when certain modal expressions govern the copula. Section 9 on Appellation examines the supposition of predicate terms in statements with copulas in past or future tense or which have modal auxiliaries or terms expressing mental acts.

Relative terms are those in apposition to other terms in a proposition. The supposition of relative terms is affected systematically by the terms to which they are in apposition. In turn, relative terms govern systematically the supposition of other terms. Relatives are divided broadly into two groups: relatives of substance and relatives of accident. Each of these types of relative term is subdivided into relatives of identity and of diversity. Relatives of identity of accident would be terms like "of such", "of such a kind" *(talis, qualis)* and of diversity "of another kind" *(aliusmodi)*. Relatives of diversity of substance are words like "another" *(alius)* or "other" *(alter)*. By far the most interesting group of relatives is relatives of identity of substance. These are divided into non-reciprocals, e.g., "that", "who", "which", "what" *(ille, qui, quae, quod)* and reciprocals, including possessives, e.g., "my", "yours", "his" *(meus, tuus, suus)* and non-possessives "of its" ("*sui*" in the genitive case). In general, a relative term acquires its basic kind of supposition (i.e., formal or material) from its apposite term. Beyond that, the particular type of supposition is fixed by each type of relative according to rules like the following:

(1)   Relatives of diversity of substance and relatives of possession do not stand for that for which their antecedents stand.

(2)   Non-possessive relatives of identity (of substance) stand for that for which their antecedents stand.

(3)   A relative of identity of accident stands for its like or what is equal to that for which its antecedent stands.

(4)   A relative of diversity of accident stands for what is dissimilar to that for which its antecedent stands.

(5)   A relative of diversity of accident stands for a supposit different from that of its antecedent.[21]

A more specialized set of rules along with examples may be found in the text. In the light of our earlier discussions, it is clear that the treatment of relative terms in the *Logica Parva* attempts to locate them within a hierarchy of terms according to the kind of supposition which they exhibit. Some stand for the very same significates which their apposite terms stand for. Others stand for the siginificates like or unlike their apposites. Still others stand for significates which are categorically different from those of their apposite terms.

That part of supposition theory which deals with sentences of past and future tense is called ampliation. When the tense of a sentence like "every man is running", is changed from present to past tense, "every man was running", this alteration causes a change of supposition on the part of the subject term. Thus, the original sentence is said to be "ampliated" into a sentence with a disjunct subject term:

"Whoever is or *was* a man was running."

Again, a future tense proposition such as "every man will be running", is analyzed: "whoever is or *will be* a man will be running". The examples of propositions made notorious by the Humanist critics of Scholasticism arise in this context. "A whore will be a virgin", is analyzed: "One who is or will be a whore will be a virgin".[22] This would be true in the sense that one who will become a whore in the future will have been previously a virgin. In addition to the ampliation of terms caused by changes in tense, a term may be ampliated by the occurrence in a sentence of verbs like "happens" *(contingit)*, "able to be" *(potest esse)*, "begins" *(incipit)*, and "ceases" *(desinit)* and by adjectives such as "imaginable" *(imaginabilis)*, and "possible" *(possibilis)*. In all of these cases, the theory of ampliation discloses the logical form of the proposition containing the ampliational term. For example, in "white can be black", the subject-term is understood to have supposition for "that which is or *can be* white"; and on this interpretation the proposition can be true. Again, in the sentence, "I know a rose", "rose" is taken to signify formally and thus to have supposition for "a rose which is or can be or can be imagined". Hence, the theory of ampliation extends supposition theory by showing how the supposition of subject-terms is affected by the occurrence of verbs of various special kinds.

The doctrine of appellation elaborates on the supposition of predicate-terms in propositions containing special temporal, modal or mental expressions, e.g., "was", "will be", "begins", "ceases", "able to be", "I understand", "I know" etc. Terms following a past or future tense verb are said "to appell" past or future time. This means that the signification of predicate-terms is extended to include the time span indicated by the tense of the verb. This is called "temporal appellation". When a subject-term is ampliated by a verb of mode or of time, such as "begins" or "ceases" the predicate-term also is said "to appell" whatever the subject-term signifies. This is called "ampliational appellation". Finally, when a term signifying a mental act such as "I know" or "I understand" is used in a sentence the predicate term following it is said "to appell" the form signified by the term. This doctrine claims that in any statement expressing a mental act the subject-term is always conceived under some aspect or with regard to some concept and the predicate-term is said "to appell" that concept. For example, "I know a rose" is analyzed: "I know something *as (sub ratione qua)* a rose". Or "I know something under the aspect of rose". Once a term following a mental expression has been introduced into a context under a determinate concept, the term must retain the same supposition here called "appellation of form" throughout the context. This entails that in any substitutions or inferences involving the predicate-term within the context, the same supposition must be preserved.[23]

Conclusion

The Chapter on Supposition concludes with a number of paradoxial theses.[24] These are remarkable in two respects: on the one hand, the two propositions which make up the thesis appear to contradict one another; and on the other hand, both theses are duly supported by "proofs" which appeal to the doctrines previously expounded. Close inspection of these proofs will reveal, however, that the two propositions are not mutually contradictory. Although their terms and even their significations may be the same, the terms of the two propositions will differ in supposition and hence the propositions will differ in logical form. It follows, of course, that the inferences derivable from the two propositions as well as the truth-conditions appropriate to each will be different. Puzzles of this sort were widely used in the teaching of medieval logic. They abound in Chapter IV of the *Logica Parva* and in the second half of the work. They afforded at once sentences which could be easily committed to memory as well as ones whose associated proof would be relatively easy to recall from memory. Like all paradoxes, however, their apparently contradictory character is dissolved when their component propositions are analyzed carefully according to the rules previously expounded.

The theory of supposition is thus a system for the elucidation and representation of the logical forms of sentences in natural language. Although the doctrine has been interpreted as either a theory of inference or a theory of truth the *Logica Parva* presents the theory in neither of these ways. Rather it introduces supposition theory as the fuller elaboration of term theory. The theory of signification (Chapter I) defines and classifies terms outside the context of a proposition. The theory of supposition (Chapter II) analyzes terms as interdependent parts of propositional wholes. By displaying the relationships of each term in a proposition *both* to other terms inside the proposition *and* to other terms within a hierarchy of terms, suppositional analysis renders precise the logical form of the proposition in question. The spatial metaphors which pervade supposition theory betray the fact that it served originally in an oral tradition as a system of conceptual representation. When the logical doctrines of the Middle Ages were retained chiefly in the memories of masters and students the language of supposition theory was an invaluable tool for symbolizing the logical features of language. When the logical doctrines of the Middle Ages came to be recorded in manuscripts and later in printed books — when the written symbol surpassed the spoken word as an instrument for expressing logical functions — the original utility of the language of supposition theory was lost. As a framework for exhibiting the logical forms of sentences, however, the theory of supposition is taken for granted in the *Logica Parva's* approach both to the rules of inference and to the rules for truth-conditions of propositions.

Notes

[1] Bocheński, 2, p. 162 ff.
[2] On the early history of supposition see: Bocheński, 2, p. 162 ff.; Kneale, pp. 246–274, De Rijk, 1, Vol. II, Pt. 1, Henry, 1. On supposition in the 13th century see: Mullally, 1, Kretzmann, 1, Steele, Alessio and De Rijk, 1. For the 14th century see: Boehner, 3, 4, 7,

pp. 232–267, Moody, 1, 2, 4, 5, and De Rijk, 1, 5, 6, 7. Also, note studies of supposition in particular authors. For Burleigh see: Boh, 1, 2. For Ockham see Boehner, 2, 3, 5, 6, 7, and Adams, 2. On the relationship between Burleigh and Ockham on supposition see S. Brown, which also contains references to the relevant secondary literature. For background on supposition theory in Paul of Venice see Perreiah, 2 and Trentman, 1, 4. For the period after Paul of Venice see Ashworth, 6, p. 77 ff. and Ashworth, 1.

[3] For a critical review of several major approaches to supposition-theory see Perreiah, 2.

[4] This alternative is discussed in Perreiah, 2, pp. 390–398. The present author adopted the semantical interpretation for his translation of the *Logica Magna* Treatise on Suppositions; but he now regards that reading of the theory as questionable. For his reasons see the next note.

[5] Of all the interpretations given to supposition-theory in the past 30 years, the syntactical ones seem to have held the greatest sway. From Boehner, 3, 7, to Bocheński, 2, Moody, 2, this should be evident. Even Geach, and Henry, 2, presuppose a syntactical framework for their basically semantical understandings of supposition-theory. The syntactical reading has been questioned by Swinarski, Matthews, 2, and Perreiah, 2. In fact the syntactical reading would seem to have come full circle in Professor Matthews, 1, and 2. For the first article presents a syntactical interpretation of supposition, and the second article shows that such an interpretation is not feasible. In his review of recent literature on the subject Professor Spade calls for "a rethinking of just what purpose the theory of 'modes of supposition' was meant to serve". (Spade, 5.) The present essay argues that supposition provided a language within which the basic logical forms of propositions could be assigned. Hence, it operated like a system of representation or conceptual notation in an oral tradition. It is easy to see how such a theory could have given rise to the variety of interpretations tried in the 20th century: for both syntactical and semantical issues are related to the logical forms of propositions and supposition-theory was designed to articulate those forms.

[6] Professors Kneale and De Rijk have stressed the pragmatical aspects of supposition-theory. See Perreiah, 2, pp. 398–403.

[7] See for example, Scott, 1.

[8] See Peter of Spain in Mullally, 1.

[9] Insofar as it has a bearing on the later theory of signification and supposition, Professor Henry's work on Anselm should be consulted; for the theory of paronymy in Anselm and the theory of supposition are both concerned with the elimination of unwanted ambiguity. See Henry, 2 and Nuchelmans, p. 201. On the topic of ambiguity within the theory of logical form see Davidson and Harman, 1,2.

[10] See Frege and Professor Geach's essay in Geach, 1, pp. 127–162. Of course Frege attacked the "traditional" conception of a proposition as analyzable into subject and predicate, and he sought to establish the function-argument analysis of the proposition in its stead. In Geach, 2, and 3, pp. 1–13, and in other papers Mr. Geach has vig-

orously attacked the subject-predicate analysis of the proposition which was current among some late 19th century British logicians. Dubbed the "two-name" theory of predication by Mr. Geach the doctrine has also been revived by the 20th century Polish logician Stanisław Leśniewski. Professor Henry has interpreted some medieval views of predication along the lines of Leśniewski's analysis. Trentman has ably discussed these views in Trentman, 1, 2, 3, and in several other articles. One point to be learned from Geach's writings, however, is his insistence on the importance of a symbolism or a system of representation within which the prominent logical features of a language may be articulated. The theory of supposition provided such a system for medieval logicians. See also Ong, pp. 53–91.

11 It is a fact of medieval logic that the same terminology, the same theories, and often the same subdivisions of supposition-theory are found alike in authors whose views on issues in syntax, semantical and even pragmatics differ widely. For instance, the same language of supposition is found in both nominalists and realists. When supposition-theory is understood as a system of conceptual representation, as a common linguistic framework within which the basic logical structures of sentences can be articulated and discussed this perplexing phenomenon becomes intelligible. See Ong, p. 69 and Perreiah, 8.

12 See Ashworth, 6, pp. 26–101; Boehner, 6, 7, Bocheński, 2, pp. 162–179; Kneale, pp. 246–274.

13 *Logica Parva*, p. [30].

14 See De Rijk, 1, Vol. 2, Pt. 1, entire and 5, 7. Also, see Henry, 1. For a useful history of some of the terminology employed in supposition-theory see De Rijk, 1, Vol. 2, Pt. 1, p. 589 ff.

15 *Logica Parva*, p. [24].

16 This premise is required for the inference to be valid. It is called "the due mean" or "the constancy of singulars". See Ashworth, 6, pp. 216–221.

17 *Logica Parva*, pp. [45]–[50].

18 Mr. Christensen argues in Christensen that the "use-mention" distinction where expressions mentioned are construed as "names" is dispensable. Moreover, he claims that it is incorrectly applied to the medieval conception of *suppositio materialis*.

19 See *Logica Parva*, pp. [33]–[34]. For the origin of this quotational device see Boehner, 7, p. 270. For further references see also De Rijk, Vol. 2, Pt. 1, p. 125.
P. Geach has stated in Geach, 2, ix: "The lack of a definite article in medieval Latin means that no 'theory of definite description' may be looked for in medieval writers." I have argued in Perreiah, 4, that John Buridan did have and employ a conceptual machinery to effect singular descriptions. Apart from the fact that *"li"* was the definite article in Old French, was borrowed by medieval thinkers and was ubiquitous in later medieval Latin texts, most colloquial languages of the Middle Ages existing side by side with medieval Latin had definite articles, e.g., *"gli"* (Italian), *"die"* (German), "the" (English), etc. In her otherwise excellent work on the articles in traditional philo-

sophy, E.M. Barth seems to have overlooked these prominent features of medieval language and logic. See Barth.

20 *Logica Parva*, p. [33].
21 *Logica Parva*, pp. [51]–[58].
22 Appellation is the relating of the signification of one term to that of another. It is discussed in modern contexts as a contribution to the theory of connotation. For the distinction between appellation and ampliation see: Ashworth, 7, pp. 89–97; Bocheński, 2, pp. 173–177, Kneale, pp. 246–274, and Scott, 1, pp. 42–49.
23 See Scott, 1, pp. 42–49.
24 On the background of logical paradoxes in medieval education see: Spade, 2, and De Rijk, 1, Vol. 1 and Vol. 2, Pt. 1, pp. 126–176 and pp. 491–512. After the introduction of Aristotle's work *De Sophisticis Elenchis* into the Latin West the interest in and importance of such paradoxes grew steadily. See below Chapter VI.

Consequentia

A theory of logical form shows how the sentences of a language are generable from a finite stock of elements. Chapter I examined terms outside the context of a proposition and gave an account of the varieties of propositions together with their fundamental properties, viz., truth/falsity, possibility/impossibility, necessity/contingency. Chapter II treated terms within the context of a proposition; by the method of suppositional representation it clarified the meanings of those terms and showed how to establish the basic logical forms of sentences. Chapter III continues this program by showing how the sentences of a language are relatable one to another in virtue of their fundamental logical form. Because it presents the rules for systematically relating sentences the theory of consequences holds a very important place in the *Logica Parva*. Its importance is evident in the fact that Chapters III and VIII (which also examines the rules of consequence) together comprise almost one third of the entire work. Paul of Venice canvasses more than five dozen rules of inference. Allowing that some of these are alternative formulations of the same basic principles while others are rejection rules, the final version lays down approximately four dozen rules with corollaries to account for the most common inferential connections between sentences.[1]

This introductory essay does not discuss all of Paul's rules. Not only is their total number great; but most of them give rise to issues in logical theory which would be impossible to treat in summary fashion. Thus, we have concentrated on the main contributions of Chapter III. These are discussed in two sections: I. clarifies the general notion of consequence in the *Logica Parva* and organizes the rules of consequence into seven groups; II. illustrates the nature of each type of rule by selecting examples from every group. A full listing of all of the rules together with symbolic formulations of them appears in the appendix.[2]

A consequence *(consequentia)* is defined as "the delivery" or "inference" *(illatio)* of a consequent *(consequens)* from an antecedent *(antecedens)*.[3] The antecedent is "the proposition preceding the sign of the inference" *(notam rationis)*; the consequent is "that which follows [the sign of the inference]". Signs of inference are: "therefore" *(ergo)* or "thus" *(igitur)*. In all of this it is important to note the difference between propositions and *sequences* of propositions; or more familiarly, the difference between propositions and arguments. For consequences are conceived as sequences of propositions; and though there are some comparisons between, for example, conditional propositions and some types of consequences, the theory of consequences contributes to the theory of argument and not to the theory of propositions or of terms.

To mark these differences an entirely new terminology is introduced to describe the possible relationships between an antecedent and a consequent. A consequent is said "to follow from" or "not to follow from" *(valet* or *non valet)*, "to stand with" or "not to stand with" *(stat cum* or *non stat cum)*, "to hold" or "not to hold" *(tenet* or *non tenet)* with its antecedent. Moreover, the expressions *bona* and *mala* (and their adverbial forms *bene, male*) are introduced to indicate inferences which do or do not follow according to accepted rules of consequences. The translation and hence the understanding of these terms is, of course, crucial; and scholars have read them in several ways. Some have translated the terms literally as "good" and "bad" without offering any explanation.[4] Others have employed the vocabulary of validity by translating the terms as "valid" /"invalid".[5] But there are problems with this approach. "Valid"/"invalid" are used today to signify the property of formal validity alone; but in the middle ages the terms *bona* and *mala* were used equally as well of material inferences. Still others have resorted to the terms "sound" and "unsound".[6] But in modern parlance "soundness" implies the truth of premises; and in the Middle Ages a *bona consequentia* could have false premises. Thus *bona* and *mala* suggest something more than mere formal validity and something less than soundness. Some insight into the genuine sense of these terms might be gained from the observation that the participants in a disputation routinely characterize one another's arguments as *bona* or *mala* and one another's acts of inference as *bene* and *male*. Moreover, it is not unreasonable to suppose that this way of speaking about inferences originates, and is nurtured by, the practices of the opponent in judging the performance of a respondent in the medieval school exercise of the *obligatio*.[7] In that context, the terms *bona* and *mala* and their adverbials *bene* and *male* express primarily the opponent's approval or disapproval of the respondent's reply. By extension they could signify as well those *types* of inference which were generally accepted or rejected by the community of language users. For the term "solid" the *Oxford English Dictionary* records this definition: "Of arguments, reasons, etc.: Having a sound or substantial foundation; based upon sound principles or indisputable facts."[8] Not only is this sense of the term early (1615), but it conveys adequately the sense which the term *bona* has in the context of medieval dialectic. For these reasons we have translated the terms *bona* and *mala* as "solid" and "unsolid".

The definition of a solid consequence *(bona consequentia)* remains a controversial topic to this day. Paul of Venice defines a solid consequence as "that in which the opposite of the consequent is repugnant to the antecedent".[9] The notion of "repugnancy" calls for clarification. Paul attempts to define it by reference to "imaginability", a term in the 14th century which meant "conceivability" or "capability of being thought". As a matter of verbal definition this is clear enough; but there remain problems about which propositions are "conceivable" or "inconceivable". These ideas will become clearer, I believe, when we examine the various types of inference.

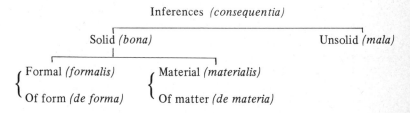

Inferences *(consequentia)*

Solid *(bona)*   Unsolid *(mala)*

{ Formal *(formalis)*   { Material *(materialis)*
 Of form *(de forma)*   Of matter *(de materia)*

A solid formal inference *(bona consequentia formalis)* is "that in which the opposite of the consequent is repugnant formally to the antecedent". The two sentences are "repugnant formally" when the antecedent and the consequent are "not imaginable to stand at the same time without a contradiction *(non sunt ymaginabilia stare simul sine contradictione)*".[10] For example, "you run; yet you do not move". A solid material inference *(bona consequentia materialis)* is "that in which the contradictory of the consequent is materially repugnant to the antecedent". The two propositions are "materially repugnant" when they cannot *in fact* stand at the same time; yet one can imagine them to stand together without any contradiction, for example, the propositions, "God is not" and "some man is". Because Paul of Venice regards the first as impossible and the second as true their conjunction in "God is not and some man is", is itself an impossible proposition because it is a conjunction one of whose parts is impossible. Nonetheless, the two propositions are not *mutually* contradictory or "incompossible". For that reason although they cannot *in fact* stand together; they "can be imagined" together. An inference solid of form *(bona de forma)* is "one similar in form to any other solid inference". Inferences similar in form are those having like or comparable categorematic and syncategorematic ingredients and structured like formal inferences. An inference solid of matter *(bona de materia)* is one which is

51

solid only in virtue of the meanings of its categorematic terms. For example, this inference is solid: "you are not a man; therefore, you are not an animal". Yet another inference of apparently the same type is not solid: "this is not a donkey (pointing to a donkey); therefore, this is not an animal". Hence, an evaluation of these inferences would depend on a correct understanding of the meanings of their component terms. According to Paul's rules by the addition of an appropriate premise many solid material inferences can be converted into solid formal inferences.

In the midst of his discussion of the nature of inference, Paul of Venice sets down two general principles:

(1)   From the impossible (i.e., an impossible proposition) any proposition follows.

(2)   The necessary (i.e., a necessary proposition) follows from any proposition.[11]

Paul of Venice does not comment on these two principles which in contemporary logic are called the "paradoxes of strict implication". To call them paradoxes, however, in the present context is misleading; for Paul of Venice clearly thinks that they specify two general patterns for solid inference. Their theoretical importance is eclipsed in the *Logica Parva* by discussion of the rules of inference themselves.

There are approximately four dozen rules of solid inference which are organized into several groups according to the types of propositions to which they apply.[12]

Group:			Propositional Domain:
I.	8	Universal Rules of Formal Inference (Section 2)	Unquantified propositions including some modal propositions.
II.	6	Universal Rules of Formal Inference (Section 3)	Quantified propositions having higher and lower-level terms.
III.	6	Particular Rules of Formal Inference (Section 4)	Quantified propositions having higher and lower-level terms.
IV.	7	Rules of Inference (Section 5)	Propositions containing exceptive and exclusive terms.
V.	7	Rules of Inference (Section 6)	Propositions containing "pertinent" and "non-pertinent" terms.
VI.	10	Rules of Inference (Section 7)	Propositions containing various provable (i.e., exponible, officiable and describable) terms.
VII.	7	Rules of Inference for Hypothetical Propositions (Section 8)	Hypothetical propositions.

It is noteworthy that all of these rules apply to inferences in virtue of the formal features of terms and propositions which were discussed in Chapters I and II and which will be discussed in Chapter IV. More than half of the rules (all in groups II through V) apply to propositions only after the status (higher or lower position in a hierarchy) of their component terms has been fixed. The rules of two groups (VI and VII) presuppose the analyses of a later chapter, i.e., Chapter IV. We will now explore the character of rules in each of these groups as they relate to standard cases of inference.

Each rule of inference in the *Logica Parva* is a specification of one or another inferential principle for sentences in definite contexts. Many of the general principles are quite familiar: e.g., *Modus Ponens, Modus Tollens* and *Hypothetical Syllogism*. The patterns of these principles are easily recognizable:

Modus Ponens	*Modus Tollens*	*Hypothetical Syllogism*
P → Q	P → Q	P → Q and Q → R
P	Not Q	Therefore, P → R.
Therefore, Q.	Therefore, Not P.	

Rules 1.2, 1.3, 1.7 and 1.8 are various formulations of the principle of *Modus Ponens*. For example, rule 1.2, "if an inference is solid and the antecedent is true, the consequent is true", or again, rule 1.3, "if an inference is solid, and the antecedent is necessary, the consequent is necessary". rule 1.7, "if an inference is solid and is known by you to be solid and its antecedent is conceded, its consequent must also be conceded". And finally, rule 1.8, "if an inference is known by you to be solid and the antecedent is also known by you, the consequent is known by you". The first two of these (1.2 and 1.3) relates *Modus Ponens* to sentences having the properties of truth and necessity. The third (1.7) relates *Modus Ponens* to sentences in dialectical contexts wherein sentences are either conceded, denied or doubted. The fourth (1.8) specifies a version of *Modus Ponens* for intentional contexts, i.e., those in which the sentences are governed by words expressing a mental act, e.g., "knows", "believes", "hopes" etc. In a similar manner, rules 2.1 and 7.1 are versions of the principle of *Modus Tollens*. Respectively, "if an inference is solid, and the consequent is false, the antecedent is false", and "if a consequent is to be denied by you, the antecedent also should be denied". The former specifies the *Modus Tollens* pattern for sentences having the property of falsity. The latter does the same for sentences in a dialectical context. The general pattern of Hypothetical Syllogism is evident in rules 5.1, "if an inference is solid and something follows from the consequent, the same follows from the antecedent", and 5.2, "in a chain of propositions when all of the intermediate inferences

are solid, formal and invariant, an inference from the first antecedent to the last consequent is formally solid". Group I also contains some rules which specify acceptable inferences to or from propositions consistent or inconsistent with antecedents and consequents. And finally, it contains some rejection rules or those which define several patterns of "unsolid" inference.

Group II sets forth six rules which govern inferences between propositions containing higher and lower order terms. It is assumed that the locus of a term within a hierarchy has been exhibited in each case in the schematic manner discussed in Chapter II.[13] Rule 2.1 states that from a lower-level term to its corresponding higher-level term where no sign of distribution (i.e., "all", "every" etc.) and no "confounding sign" (i.e., "no" — the sign of negation) are involved there is a solid inference. Thus where "man" is a term on a lower level than "animal", the inference from "some man is running", to "some animal is running", is solid. Rule 2.3 says, "from a lower-level term to its corresponding higher-level term with a sign of negation placed after the term and with a due mean (i.e., an additional proposition needed to yield the consequent) there is a solid inference". For example, from "some man does not run", together with the premise, "all men are animals", it follows solidly: "some animal does not run". Rule 2.3 warrants the inference from a higher-level term to its corresponding lower-level term with a sign of negation placed in front of the higher-level term. E.g., using the same terms as above, "no animal is running", solidly yields "no man is running". The appendix lists also the three rejection rules from this group.[14]

Group III gives the rules for inferences between various kinds of quantified propositions. The first of these warrants inferences which parallel some implicational relationships already discussed. For example, 3.1 allows the inference from a superimplicant to a subimplicant (see the earlier discussion of the Square of Opposition).[15] The remaining rules of solid inferences give the patterns of inference between certain quantified propositions. These rules justify a number of deductive patterns which were employed earlier in the discussion of supposition.[16] For instance rule 3.3, "from a universal affirmative [proposition] to all of its singulars collectively or divisively and with a due mean there is a solid inference and conversely taken [collectively]". Again, rule 3.4, "from a universal negative to any of its singulars there is a solid inference and conversely with a due mean". Rule 3.5, "from a particular to its indefinite there is a solid inference and conversely". And finally, rule 3.6, "from a particular or indefinite to all of its singulars taken disjunctively and with a due mean there is a solid inference". The presence of each of these rules in the Chapter on Inferences is additional confirmation of the claim made earlier in connection with supposition theory; namely, that supposition theory itself does not constitute a theory of deduction.[17]

Group IV presents four accepted and three rejection rules for solid inferences. These rules apply to propositions containing exclusive or exceptive particles. The first rule, 4.1, "from an exclusive proposition to its corresponding universal with the terms transposed there is a solid inference and conversely", is illustrated in the following way. From (a) "only men run", we may infer (b) "every running thing is a man". Note that the converse would not be recognized as a valid move under ordinary circumstances; it would be allowed only in a situation where it was already known in the context that (b) had been inferred from (a). Again, rule 4.2 regulates the inference from a negative exceptive proposition to its corresponding affirmative exclusive: from "no one except man runs", it follows: "only men run". Rule 4.3 applies to inferences from propositions containing lower-level terms to those containing higher-level terms: "from a lower-level term to its corresponding higher-level term on the part of the subject with an exclusive added to it there is a solid inference". For instance, from "only man runs", it follows "only animal runs". Rule 4.6, "from a confused and distributed term to a determinate term there is a solid inference", endorses the move from a sentence like, "you differ from man", therefore, "you differ from some man".

Group V rules control inferences between propositions having so-called "pertinent" and "non-pertinent" terms. These are terms which have a semantical relationship such that the one can be substituted for the other without loss of meaning. Synonyms such as "man" and "rational animal" would be examples. Another type of pertinent term is the correlative term, i.e., that which has a determinate relationship to some other term, e.g., in "2:4:4:8", "2" is correlative to "4", and "4" is correlative to "8" because each has an exact relationship to the other, viz., the ratio of one-half. Non-pertinent terms are by contrast those which are not substitutable the one for the other without loss of meaning: these are examples, e.g., "man"/ "donkey", "white"/"black" etc. Especially important in this group of rules are those covering inferences between interchangeable propositions or between propositions whose subjects and predicates are interchangeable without any alteration in their denomination. Rule 5.2, "from one of a pair of propositions whose subjects and predicates are interchangeable while remaining the same in denomination to the other there is a solid inference", and rule 5.3, "from one interchangeable proposition to the other there is a solid inference and conversely". Where "P" and "Q" contain interchangeable subjects and predicates the first rule allows that "if P implies Q", then "Q implies P" and conversely. The second rule repeats the same principle for unanalyzed propositions which are interchangeable with one another. Examples in the text also make clear that the subject and predicate terms mentioned in the formulation of rule 5.2 are interchangeable in virtue of features essential to the meaning of the subject term; whereas the subject and predicate terms mentioned in rule 5.3 are not interchangeable in virtue of any features essential to the meaning of the subject term. The remaining rules should be clear from the text.

Group VI comprises nine rules of solid inference plus one rejection rule. These rules apply to sentences containing various types of syncategorematic terms each of which calls for special analysis. A typology of these terms and the appropriate methods for analyzing them are elaborated in Chapter IV, "On the Proofs of Terms".[18] The notion of "proof" is familiar. To prove a proposition in the context of a theory of logical form is to exhibit the truth conditions for that proposition in virtue of the terms which it contains. Recalling our earlier discussion of the concept of truth, we saw that the truth-conditions of some propositions are evident immediately: for example, (P) "this runs" is true just in case the subject-term of that sentence in a definite context indicates some object to which the predicate term also applies. Such a proposition is said to be "immediate" because its truth may be established without recourse to any other proposition. The truth of some propositions, however, cannot be shown in this direct manner. These are so-called mediate propositions which must be reduced to a concatenation of immediate statements in order to establish their truth-values. The classification of these types of proposition is founded on the five basic kinds of syncategorematic term which have a principal place in them: (1) Resoluble propositions are indefinite, particular and singular propositions without a demonstrative pronoun in subject position. (2) Exponible propositions are either universal propositions or propositions having various other terms such as comparatives, exceptives, exclusives and reduplicatives. (3) Officiable propositions are those containing relative clauses introduced either by a modal term or a term signifying an act of the mind, e.g., "knows", "believes" etc. (4) Describable propositions are those containing a term which signifies a mental act followed by a singular term, e.g., "I know Socrates". (5) Provable propositions are those which have several "causes of truth", i.e., several immediate propositions taken disjunctively. In 13th-century science a number of terms such as "begins" *(incipit)* and "ceases" *(desinit)* were thought to be of this kind. Propositions in each of these classes must be analyzed according to a standard procedure designed to lay bare the immediate propositions which establish their truth or falsity.

The model which underlies all five patterns of analysis is the following:

Analysandum (probandum) ⟷ *analysans (propositiones probantes)*

"P" ⟷ "(Q . R . S . . .)"

The expression on the right reveals the complex logical structure of the expression on the left. For example, the resoluble proposition, "some man runs", is analyzed into "this is a man and this runs". This analysis may be expressed in the form of a conditional:

"*If* some man runs, *then* this is a man and this runs".

The immediate propositions are, in turn, expressed in the antecedent of a conditional:

"*If* this is a man and this runs, *then* some man runs".

Clearly, the conjunction of these two conditionals is equivalent to the biconditional:

"Some man runs if and only if this is a man and this runs".[19]

Of course, the nature and logical order of the base propositions varies in each case according to the type of provable propositions whose truth conditions are analyzed. We are now in a position to see the importance of Group VI rules of inference. They state the acceptable inferential moves between *analysans* and *analysanda* in these patterns of analysis. For a fuller discussion of this group of rules the reader should consult Chapter IV.

The last group of inference rules which Paul of Venice takes up in the *Logica Parva* are those which apply to hypothetical propositions. Several of these are versions of principles of implication which we have already discussed. But in each case the rules discussed earlier are specifications of principles for various contexts, e.g., *Modus Ponens* was defined for a dialectical situation in the following way: "If an inference is solid and is known by you to be solid and its antecedent is conceded, its consequent must also be conceded". Group VII rules specify how some of the same principles may be applied directly to propositions of the various hypothetical forms, viz., conditional, conjunctive or disjunctive. Here are some of the rules. (7.6) *Modus Ponens*: "From an affirmative conditional with its antecedent to its consequent there is a solid inference". (7.7) *Modus Tollens:* "From an affirmative conditional with the contradiction of the consequent to the contradiction of the antecedent there is a solid inference". In addition, there is the common principle known as "disjunctive syllogism" (7.3): "from an affirmative disjunctive proposition with the destruction of one of its parts to the other part there is a solid inference". The rule of adjunction is similarly recognized (7.2): "from the principal part of an affirmative disjunctive to the total disjunctive proposition there is a solid inference; but not conversely". The rule of simplification is treated as an inference rule and not as a rule of replacement (7.1): "from an affirmative conjunctive to either of its principal parts there is a solid inference; but not conversely unless owing to the matter, [i.e., the specific categorematic terms which may warrant the converse inference in a particular case]". Lastly, rules 7.4 and 7.5 give two versions of the so-called "De Morgan Laws": "from a negative disjunctive to an affirmative conjunctive made from the contradictory parts of the [negative] disjunctive there is a solid inference and conversely". All of these rules are commonly accepted in modern logic.

Conclusion

To conclude this introductory chapter, we should like to underscore two respects in which the *Logica Parva's* approach to reasoning differs *toto caelo* from recent approaches to the same subject matter.

The first feature is the *Logica Parva's* recognition of a fundamental difference between deduction and inference. The syllogistic rules discussed in Chapter I are rules of deduction *sensu stricto*. They are rules which apply to statements regardless of their component categorematic terms and regardless of varying contexts of use. The rules of inference treated in Chapter III do not set forth alone what is possible formally. Not only do they specify rules of material inference and rules for inference which are "like" formal and material inferences, they tell what transformations are permissable in actual contexts of inference. They prescribe those generally approved rational operations which are carried out or are capable of being carried out by actual reasoners in typical contexts of reasoning. In a word, deduction is impersonal; it is the mere transformation of expressions in function of their ingredient signs. Inference is intrinsically personal: it involves an act of mind passing from one proposition to another according to a rule in an actual context. This difference between deduction and inference is manifest in the simple fact that while you can do other persons' deductions for them you cannot draw their inferences for them.

The second salient feature of the *Logica Parva's* approach to reasoning is its recognition of the difference between a theorem and a rule. A theorem (or a metatheorem) is by definition a thesis demonstrable from one or more axioms according to a rule. A rule is a specification of the structure of some accepted rational principle. The practice (prevalent in scholarship on medieval logic over the past thirty years) of re-writing medieval rules of inference as theorems or metatheorems within a deductive system (however loosely and imperfectly conceived) has obscured the fundamental character of the medieval rules of consequences as rules of inference. While several authors have sought to show that one or another medieval logician conceived of the rules of consequences as derivable *more geometrico* from a few axioms, almost no attention has been paid to the ways in which those rules are employed in actual contexts of use. By treating the rules of consequences not as theorems or metatheorems but rather as rules of inference we have sought to overcome these deficiencies.

In these introductory essays and in the translation which follows we have sought to recognize the fact that the medieval theory of consequence is first and foremost a theory of inference rather than a theory of deduction and that the medieval rules of consequences are rules rather than theorems or metatheorems derivable from axioms. In a word we have sought to show that the interpretation of the *Logica Parva*'s contribution to the theory of consequences makes much more sense when viewed as component in the theory of logical form than in the theory of formal logic in the strict sense. Our discussions of remaining chapters will continue to support this thesis.

Appendix A*

Group I. Universal Rules of Formal Inference (Section 2)

Rule 1.1 If the contradictory of its antecedent follows from the contradictory of its consequent, an inference is solid.

$(\sim Q \rightarrow \sim P) \rightarrow (P \rightarrow Q)$

* 1.1.1. If the contradictory of its antecedent does not follow from the contradictory of its consequent, an inference is not solid.

$* \sim (\sim Q \rightarrow \sim P) \rightarrow (P \rightarrow Q)$

Rule 1.2 If an inference is solid, and the antecedent is true, the consequent is true.

$[(P \rightarrow Q) \ \& \ T \ `P'] \rightarrow (T \ `Q')$

1.2.1. If an inference is solid and the consequent is false, the antecedent is false.

$[(P \rightarrow Q) \ \& \ F \ `Q'] \rightarrow (F \ `P')$

* 1.2.2. If the antecedent is true and the consequent is false, the inference is not solid.

$*(T \ `P') \rightarrow (F \ `Q')$

Rule 1.3 If an inference is solid and the antecedent is necessary, the consequent is necessary.

$[(P \rightarrow Q) \ \& \ \square P] \rightarrow \square Q$

* 1.3.1. If the antecedent is necessary and the consequent is contingent, the inference is not solid.

$* (\square P \rightarrow \Diamond Q) \rightarrow \sim (P \rightarrow Q)$

Rule 1.4 If an inference is solid and the antecedent is possible, the consequent is possible.

$[(P \rightarrow Q) \ \& \ \Diamond P] \rightarrow \Diamond Q$

* 1.4.1. If the antecedent is possible and the consequent is impossible, the inference is not solid.

$* (\Diamond P \rightarrow \sim \Diamond Q) \rightarrow \sim (P \rightarrow Q)$

60

Rule 1.5   If an inference is solid and something follows from the consequent the same follows from the antecedent.

$$[(P \rightarrow Q) \& (Q \rightarrow R)] \rightarrow (P \rightarrow R)$$

1.5.1.   Whatever implies the antecedent also implies the consequent.

$$[(P \rightarrow Q) \& (R \rightarrow P)] \rightarrow (R \rightarrow Q)$$

1.5.2.   In a chain of propositions when all the intermediate inferences are solid, formal and invariant, an inference from the first antecedent to the last consequent is formally solid.

$$\{[(P \rightarrow Q) \& (Q \rightarrow R)] \& [(R \rightarrow T) \& (T \rightarrow S)]\} \rightarrow (P \rightarrow S)$$

Rule 1.6   If an inference is solid and something is consistent with an antecedent the same is consistent with the consequent.

$$[(P \rightarrow Q) \& (P^o R)] \rightarrow (Q^o R)$$

1.6.1.   Something inconsistent with the consequent is inconsistent with the antecedent.

$$[(P \rightarrow Q) \& (Q \phi R)] \rightarrow (P \phi R)$$

Rule 1.7   If an inference is solid and is known by you to be solid and its antecedent is to be conceded, its consequent must also be conceded.

$$[(P \rightarrow Q) \& K (P \rightarrow Q) \& C \text{ 'P'}] \rightarrow (C \text{ 'Q'})$$

1.7.1.   If the consequent is to be denied by you, the antecedent also should be denied.

$$[(P \rightarrow Q) \& (D \text{ 'Q'})] \rightarrow (D \text{ 'P'})$$

* 1.7.2.   If the antecedent is to be conceded by you, but the consequent is to be denied by you, that inference is not solid.

$$*[(C \text{ 'P'}) \rightarrow (D \text{ 'Q'})] \rightarrow \sim(P \rightarrow Q)$$

Rule 1.8   If an inference is known by you to be solid and the antecedent is also known by you, the consequent is known by you.

$$\{ [K (P \rightarrow Q)] \& K \text{ 'P'} \} \rightarrow (K \text{ 'Q'})$$

K – knows
C – concedes
D – denies

61

Appendix B

Group II. Universal Rules of Formal Inference (Section 3)

Rule 2.1.   From a lower-level term to its corresponding higher-level term without a sign of distribution and without a confounding sign there is a solid inference.

M i R → A i R

*Rule 2.2.   From a lower-level term to its corresponding higher-level term with a sign of distribution or a confounding sign there is not a solid inference.

* M a R ↛ A a R

Rule 2.3   From a lower-level term to its corresponding higher-level term with a sign of negation placed after the term and with a due mean there is a solid inference.

[(M o R) & (M a A)] → A o R

*Rule 2.4.   From a higher-level term to its corresponding lower-level term in affirmative propositions and without a sign of distribution there is not a solid inference.

* A i R ↛ M i R

*Rule 2.5.   From a higher-level term to its corresponding lower-level term in a distributed affirmative proposition the inference is not solid except with a due mean.

* A i R ↛ M a R

2.5.1.   [(A i R) & (M a A)] → M a R

Rule 2.6.   From a higher-level term to its corresponding lower-level term with a sign of negation placed in front of the higher-level term there is a solid inference.

A e R → M e R

M − man
R − rational
A − animal

Appendix C

Group III. Particular Rules of Formal Inference (Section 4)

Rule 3.1. From a universal to its particular or indefinite there is a solid inference.

$$Asp \rightarrow Isp \qquad Esp \rightarrow Osp$$
$$Asp \rightarrow I'sp \qquad Esp \rightarrow O'sp$$

*Rule 3.2. From a particular or indefinite to its universal there is not a solid inference except owing to the matter.

$$Isp \rightarrow Asp \qquad I'sp \rightarrow Asp$$

Rule 3.3. From a universal affirmative to all of its singulars collectively or divisively and with a due mean there is a solid inference and conversely [taken collectively].

$$[\,Asp \,\&\, (S_1, S_2, S_3 \text{ are all singulars)}\,]\,\leftrightarrow$$
$$(As_1 p \,\&\, As_2 p \,\&\, As_3 p)$$

Rule 3.4. From a singular universal negative to any of its singulars there is a solid inference and conversely with a due mean.

$$[\,Esp \,\&\, (S_1, S_2, S_3 \text{ are all singulars)}]\,\leftrightarrow$$
$$(Es_1 p \,\&\, Es_2 p \,\&\, Es_3 p)$$

Rule 3.5. From a particular to its indefinite there is a solid inference and conversely.

$$Isp \rightarrow I'sp$$

Rule 3.6. From a particular or indefinite to all of its singulars taken disjunctively and with a due mean there is a solid inference.

$$[\,Isp \,\&\, (S_1, S_2, S_3 \text{ are all singulars)}]\,\rightarrow$$
$$(As_1 p,\, V\, As_2 p\, V\, As_3 p)$$

$$[\,I'sp \,\&\, (S_1, S_2, S_3 \text{ are all singulars)}]\,\rightarrow$$
$$(As_1 p,\, V\, As_2 p\, V\, As_3 p)$$

I = particular affirmative	O = particular negative
I' = indefinite affirmative	O' = indefinite negative

Appendix D

Group IV. Rules of Inference (Section 5)

Rule 4.1.   From an exclusive to its corresponding universal with the terms transposed there is a solid inference and conversely.

$$<M> i R \longleftrightarrow R a M$$

Rule 4.2.   From a negative exceptive to its corresponding affirmative exclusive there is a solid inference.

$$(\overline{M}) e R \rightarrow <M> a R$$

Rule 4.3.   From a lower-level term to its corresponding higher-level term on the part of the subject with an exclusive added to it there is a solid inference.

$$M i R \rightarrow <A> i R$$

Rule 4.4.   From a lower-level term to its corresponding higher-level term on the part of the predicate with an exclusive expression added to the subject there is not a solid inference.

$$* M i R \rightarrow <M> i O$$

Rule 4.5.   From a merely confused or determinate term to a confused distributed term there is not a solid inference.

$$* \ll M \gg i R \rightarrow M a R \quad \text{or} \quad M i R \rightarrow M a r$$

Rule 4.6.   From a confused and distributed term to a determinate term there is a solid inference.

$$M a R \rightarrow M i R$$

Rule 4.7.   From a merely confused term to a determinate or distributed term there is not a solid inference.

$$* \ll M \gg i R \rightarrow M i R \quad \text{or} \quad \ll M \gg i R \rightarrow M a R$$

$\overline{M}$ = non-man
$<>$ = sign of exclusive term
$(\ )$ = sign of exceptive term
$\ll \gg$ = sign of merely confused term

Appendix E

Group V. Rules of Inference (Section 6)

Rule 5.1. From an affirmative proposition with one disparate [predicate] term to a negative proposition with another disparate [predicate] term there is a solid inference; but not conversely.

$S A P \rightarrow S e \overline{P}$

Rule 5.2. From one of a pair of propositions, whose subjects and predicates are interchangeable while remaining the same in denomination to the other there is a solid inference.

$(P \leftrightarrow Q) \leftrightarrow (Q \leftrightarrow P)$

Rule 5.3. From one interchangeable proposition to the other there is a solid inference; and conversely.

$(P \leftrightarrow Q) \rightarrow (Q \leftrightarrow P)$

Rule 5.4. From one of two correlatives to the other there is a solid inference.

$A a R \rightarrow A a \overline{t}$

Rule 5.5. From a privative term to an infinite term there is a solid inference; but not conversely.

$A a B \rightarrow A a \overline{s}$

Rule 5.6. From an affirmative proposition with a privative or infinite predicate to a negative proposition there is a solid inference; but not conversely.

$A a \overline{B} \rightarrow A e B$

Rule 5.7. From a negative proposition with a finite predicate to an affirmative proposition with an infinite predicate with the due mean there is a solid inference; and conversely.

$(A e B) \ \& \ (\text{There are A's}) \leftrightarrow A a \overline{B}$

R = running	B = blind	$\overline{B}$ = non-blind
$\overline{t}$ = not sitting	$\overline{s}$ = not seeing	

Appendix F

Group VI. Rules of Inference (Section 7)

Rule 6.1. From all of the exponents of a proposition — taken simultaneously — to the exponible proposition there is a solid inference; and conversely.

Rule 6.2. From an exponible proposition to *each* of its exponents [i.e., taken separately] there is a solid inference; but not conversely except in virtue of matter.

Rule 6.3. From any contradictory of an exponent, the contradictory of the exposited proposition follows; but not conversely.

Rule 6.4. From a resoluble proposition to its resolvent[s] there is a solid inference; but not conversely.

Rule 6.5. From an officiable proposition to its officiates there is a solid inference; but not conversely.

Rule 6.6. From a description to its described proposition there is a solid inference; and conversely.

*Rule 6.7. From a proposition in the composite sense to one in the divided sense and conversely there is not a solid inference.

Rule 6.8. From one cause of truth to a proposition having that cause of truth there is a solid inference; but not conversely.

Rule 6.9. From an active proposition to a passive proposition there is a solid inference and conversely.

Rule 6.10. From a three-termed proposition to a two-termed proposition without a distracting term there is a solid inference.

Appendix G

Group VII. Rules of Inference for Hypothetical Propositions

Rule 7.1.   From an affirmative conjunctive to either of its principal parts there is a solid inference; but not conversely unless owing to the matter.

$$[(P \& Q) \rightarrow P], [(P \& Q) \rightarrow Q]$$

Rule 7.2.   From the principal part of an affirmative disjunctive to the total disjunctive proposition there is a solid inference; but not conversely.

$$[P \rightarrow (P \vee Q)], [Q \rightarrow (P \vee Q)]$$

Rule 7.3.   From an affirmative disjunctive proposition with the destruction of one of its parts to the other part there is a solid inference.

$$\{ [(P \vee Q) \& \sim P] \rightarrow Q \} \ , \{ [(P \vee Q) \& \sim Q] \rightarrow P \}$$

Rule 7.4.   From a negative conjunctive to a disjunctive made from the contradictory parts of the affirmative conjunctive there is a solid inference [and conversely].

$$[\sim (P \cdot Q) \leftrightarrow (\sim P \vee \sim Q)]$$

Rule 7.5.   From a negative disjunctive to an affirmative conjunctive made from the contradictory parts of the [negative] disjunctive there is a solid inference and conversely.

$$[\sim (P \vee Q) \leftrightarrow (\sim P \cdot \sim Q)]$$

Rule 7.6.   From an affirmative conditional with its antecedent to its consequent there is a solid inference.

$$\{ [(P \rightarrow Q) \cdot P] \rightarrow Q \}$$

Rule 7.7.   From an affirmative conditional with the contradiction of the consequent to the contradiction of the antecedent there is a solid inference.

$$\{ [(P \rightarrow Q) \cdot \sim Q] \rightarrow \sim P \}$$

Notes

1. For background on the medieval theory of consequences see: Łukasiewicz, Dürr, Boehner, 1, 3, 6, Bocheński, 2, pp. 189–209; Boh, 1, 2, 3, 4, 5; Kneale, pp. 274–297; Moody, 1, 2, 4, 5; Ashworth, 4, 6, p. 118 ff. Professor Otto Bird has discussed the relationship between medieval doctrines of the topics and the medieval rules of consequences. The present study would seem to confirm a connection between the two theories at least with respect to those rules of consequences which depend on the prior distinction of terms into higher and lower levels, for that doctrine is rooted in the theories of the categories and the predicables and the latter are fundamental to the notion of a topic as a "seat of argument". See Stump and Bird, 1,2. For the teachings of particular authors see: Boehner and Moody on Ockham, Hubien on Buridan, Boh on Burleigh, Sr. Mary A. Brown on Paul of Pergula, etc. Although Professor Moody cites some rules of consequences from Paul of Venice's *Logica Parva* in Moody, 2, (he cites the Venice, 1544 edition) and though Professor Bottin alludes to some of the rules in Bottin, 1, which is devoted to the rules of consequences in the *Logica Magna*, Appendices A through G contain the first catalogue all of Paul's inference rules in the *Logica Parva*.
2. See appendices pp. 60–67.
3. *Logica Parva*, p. [64] ff.
4. This practice is followed by Adams and Del Punta in Adams, 3.
5. This practice is widespread; it is followed by Professors Boh, Ashworth and others.
6. For an example of this way of describing consequences see Mates and occasionally Kneale, e.g., p. 277.
7. See Chapters V and VI below.
8. *The Oxford English Dictionary*, Volume X, Oxford. The Clarendon Press, 1961, p. 399. Of all the commentators only Professor Kneale seems to respect the character of these rules as rules of inference or entailment. He attributes to Abelard, Robert Kilwardby and Pseudo-Scotus the view that *bona* and *mala* express approval or disapproval. Kneale, p. 277.
9. *Logica Parva,* p. [65].
10. For an excellent discussion of the notions involved in Paul of Venice's definitions of a solid consequence see Ashworth, 6, pp. 126–130. Note especially on p. 127 where Melanchthon is cited as defining a valid consequence as "one which did not violate the precepts of dialectic". If the present interpretation is correct this is not so very far from Paul of Venice's own view for the notions of "imaginability" and "conceivability" must be understood in a dialectical context like that of the *obligatio*. Also see Murdoch, 3, p. 681 ff. For the problems to be encountered in teaching conditionals see Bedell.
11. *Logica Parva*, pp. [65]–[66]. See Ashworth, 6, 1, p. 134.
12. See above Appendices A through G, pp. 60–67.
13. See pp. 143–167.
14. Note that all rules preceded by an asterisk are rejection rules.
15. See p. 27.

[16] This confirms, again, the fact that supposition-theory is not *per se* a theory of deduction.

[17] See p. 55.

[18] *Logica Parva*, pp. [134]–[158].

[19] This example is much simplified deliberately for the sake of illustration here. Notably, the example would be valid for a universe of one individual and for a specified time. In standard (more complicated) cases like Paul discusses the universe of discourse would be specified to include, for example, three men and the inferences from determinate to singular propositions or vice versa would be permitted only under the condition of a "due mean" *(debito medio)*, viz. "These are all the men there are: man_1, man_2, man_3". (Chapter II, [40] and Chapter IV, [81])

For example,

(1) Some man runs.

(2) These are all men (man_1, man_2, man_3).

(3) Therefore, $this_1$ is a man and $this_1$ runs or $this_2$ is a man and $this_2$ runs or $this_3$ is a man and $this_3$ runs.

And conversely,

(1) $This_1$ is a man and $this_1$ runs or $this_2$ is a man and $this_2$ runs or $this_3$ is a man and $this_3$ runs.

(2) These are all men (man_1, man_2, man_3).

(3) Therefore, some man runs.

Clearly, the conjunction of these two conditional sequences justifies the biconditional. Where Paul seems to reject the second conditional needed for the biconditional in a rule of inference for resoluble propositions (Chapter III, [81]), he does so only for a context where the time at which the original determinate proposition is true has been left unspecified. Finally, it is noteworthy that the fundamental form to which propositions are reduced in order to establish their truth or falsity is a biconditional. See the Chapter I discussions of "truth".

Probationes

The procedure called "proof" *(probatio)* is a prominent feature of Paul of Venice's method in the *Logica Parva*. Not only are the expressions "it is proved" *(probatur)* and "it is clear" *(patet)* found on practically every page of the work; but it is the central topic of Chapter IV "On the Proofs of Terms" *(De probationibus teminorum)*[1] If, as we have claimed, an account of truth is essential to a theory of logical form, the concept of proof is basic to the theory of truth. Proof is nothing more than the analysis of a proposition in order to lay bare those conditions under which it is decidably true or false. But truth and falsity are properties of whole statements, and proof concentrates on the analysis of terms. How are these two points to be reconciled? As we saw in Chapters I and II complete statements – the proper vehicles of truth and falsity – are composed of terms, and the truth and falsity of those statements is a function of the number, kind and order of the terms which they contain. Hence, to prove a statement one must disclose the logical properties of its component terms.

Prior to the application of any method of proof, Paul of Venice divides terms broadly into two groups: "mediate terms" and "immediate terms".[2] This division corresponds to the common difference between singular and nonsingular terms. In accord with the kind of terms which it embodies, a proposition is called either "mediate" or "immediate". An immediate proposition contains in subject-position only terms which are singular in number. A mediate proposition is one whose terms require reduction to a concatenation of immediate propositions before their truth or falsity can be established. Medieval verification theory requires, therefore, that the truth or falsity of any statement be established by inspection of the truth or falsity of its elementary or primitive propositions which are singular in form.

The medieval theory of verification is elaborated according to the standard model of analysis. The proposition to be analyzed is called the *analysandum*. The analysis itself is the *analysans*. More precisely, the former is called the proposition to be proved *(probandum)* and the latter are known as the proving propositions *(propositiones probantes)*. The proof *(probatio)* consists in showing (a) the elementary propositions to which the original

70

proposition is reducible and (b) the correct form of the concatenation of those elementary propositions. Because the proved propositions express the truth-conditions of the proposition under examination and because the provable proposition may, in turn, be inferred from the proved propositions, an equivalence *(equipollens)* exists between the two sides of the analysis.[3]

The *Logica Parva* designs four methods of proof according to this model. The various methods are necessary in order to accomodate the diverse kinds of terms which may occur in propositions. The names of the methods are: (1) Resolution, (2) Exposition, (3) Officiation and (4) Description. In each case the pattern of proof gives an accepted procedure for explicating the proposition in question by reducing, if necessary, a mediate proposition to a properly ordered concatenation of immediate propositions. Section I of this essay examines each of the four methods of proof. Section II devotes further attention to several special terms as well as to terms which may be analyzed by more than one method. Throughout Chapter IV the reader will note — and probably be vexed by — the large number of paradoxes which are posed. Once Paul has elaborated a new doctrine, he commonly expounds sets of propositions whose members appear, at least, to be mutually contradictory. This practice is all the more disturbing since the seemingly contradictory theses are applications of the doctrines just expounded. What is the nature and function of these paradoxes in the *Logica Parva*? The conclusion will offer an answer to this question.

I.a Resolution

Resolution is a method for analyzing the truth-conditions of statements of three kinds: indefinite, particular and singular statements without a demonstrative pronoun.[4] An indefinite statement is one which has no explicit syncategorematic term governing its subject-term; for example, "man runs", A statement is particular when its subject-term is modified by the expression "some" *(aliquis)* or its equivalent. A singular statement without a demonstrative pronoun is ordinarily a statement with a proper name in subject position, e.g., "Socrates runs". In addition to these features resoluble propositions may be either affirmative or negative. To show its truth conditions, the resoluble proposition is first of all divided into subject and predicate. Next, two singular propositions are presented: in the subject position of each of these there is a singular demonstrative pronoun, "this" *(iste, ista, istud)* in the predicate position of the first proposition goes the predicate of the original proposition, and in the predicate position of the second proposition goes the subject of the original proposition.

Resoluble proposition: Resolvent propositions:
"Socrates is running."   ⟷   "This is running and this is
                                              Socrates."

Because the proposition on the right can be checked immediately against an existing state of affairs it is said to express the truth-conditions of the original. Conversely the truth or falsity of the proposition on the left follows from the truth or falsity of the proposition on the right. Hence there is an equivalence relationship between the two. This example applies to affirmative propositions. Negative propositions call for one additional step: they are provable through their contradictories. For example, "No chimera is a man" is true because its contradictory "Some chimera is a man" is false. The latter is seen to be false by exhibiting its truth conditions:

"Some chimera is a man" ⟷ "This is a man and this is a chimera".

These methods of resolution are extended to include statements with verbs in the past or future tenses as well as those with complex subject or predicate terms and those with singular or plural subject terms.

I.b Exposition

Exponible propositions comprise the largest class of provable propositions.[5] They include affirmative and negative statements with a variety of syncategorematic expressions: viz., universals, e.g., "every man runs"; exceptives, e.g., "every man except Socrates runs"; exclusives, e.g., "only man runs" and reduplicatives, e.g., "man insofar as he is man is not a donkey". In addition this class embraces propositions containing phrases of comparison of either the comparative or the superlative grade: e.g., "Socrates is stronger than Plato", "Socrates is the strongest of men". Certain expressions which have a negative force such as "differs from", "not other than" as well as adverbs like "immediately", "necessarily", "contingently" are also factors which make a proposition exponible. Other expressions which had a great importance in medieval physics and theology such as "from eternity" *(ab aeterno)*, "always" *(semper)*, "all" *(totus)*, and "infinite" *(infinitus)* also turn propositions into exponibles. Because of the large number of expressions in this group it will be impossible to illustrate them all. Following Paul's example Section I will treat only a few of the most important kinds; Section II will look at several others. In each case the modes of exposition will vary according to the exigencies of the type of proposition under examination. But the basic goal is the same: namely, to produce a concatenation of immediate propositions whose truth or falsity is clear through inspection.

Exposition

Exponible Proposition:
Universal:
"Every man runs." ⟷ "Man runs and nothing is man unless it runs."

Exclusive:
"Only man runs." ⟷ "Man runs and nothing not-man runs."

Exceptive:
"Every man except Socrates runs." ⟷ "Socrates does not run and every man who is not-Socrates runs."

Reduplicative:
"Socrates insofar as he is man is animal." ⟷ "Socrates is man; and Socrates is animal; and if something is a man, the same thing is animal."

Later we will take up the grades of comparison as well as the modal auxiliaries together with several special problematic expressions.

I.c Officiation

Officiable propositions are those with dependent or relative clauses which follow either a modal term or a term expressing a mental act. Modal terms are those canvassed in Chapter I. Mental terms are ones like these: "I know" *(scio)*, "I doubt" *(dubito)*, "I will" *(volo)*, "I do not will" *(non volo)*, "I understand" *(cognosco)*, etc. This list is not exhaustive; moreover, the method of officiation applies also to the participial forms of these verbs. These propositions are called "officiable" because the modal or mental terms which open the subordinate clause exercise some office or governance over the expressions which follow them. An expression following a sign of officiation is called the dictum and it is ordinarily in the Latin construction with a noun in the accusative case plus an infinitive. Regarding modal auxiliaries, it is important to discern whether the modal expression operates over the entire sentence (composite sense) or only over part of the sentence (divided sense).[6] The latter may be analyzed as *either* an exponible *or* a resoluble proposition. Only modal propositions in the composite sense are treated as officiable.

Officiable proposition:

Modal in composite sense:
"It is possible that Socrates   ⟷   "This proposition is possible,
runs."   'Socrates runs', which adequately
                                                 signifies Socrates to run."

Mental proposition:
"I know Socrates to run."   ⟷   "This proposition is known by me,
                                                 'Socrates runs' which adequately
                                                 signifies Socrates to run."

"I doubt that Socrates runs."   ⟷   "This proposition is doubted by
                                                          me, 'Socrates runs', which ade-
                                                          quately signifies Socrates to run."

It is clear that these propositions have a great importance for any complete account of language. For such a theory must cover not only direct but indirect discourse as well. It is important to note also the need for quotational devices in order to carry out this analysis, and thus, the distinction between formal and material supposition introduced in Chapter II is important for the theory of Chapter IV.[7]

I.d Description

We have seen that the mental expressions in officiable propositions operate over clauses. Such expressions are also said to be complex. Describable propositions are those containing mental terms which operate over noncomplex expressions only. There are two types of noncomplex expressions: (1) genuinely noncomplex and (2) apparently noncomplex which signify, nonetheless, a complexum. These are illustrated and analyzed respectively:

Description

Describable propositions:
"I know Socrates."   ⟷   "I know someone as Socrates."

"I know proposition *A*."   ⟷   "I know the adequate significate of
                                                proposition *A* which I know is
                                                adequately signified through
                                                proposition *A*."

Since describable propositions are interchangeable with their descriptions one may infer from right to left or left to right. The method of description is especially useful when an ambiguous statement is tendered with no specification of the conditions under which its ambiguity is to be settled. The method of description allows one to interpret an ambiguous statement in a particular way so that it is no longer ambiguous. Statements with intentional expressions are notorious candidates for such ambiguities; and it was to these that the medieval method of description was primarily applied. The traditon which Paul of Venice follows on these matters stems at least from John Buridan who held that expressions within intentional contexts retain all of the properties of signification and truth which they might have outside of those contexts.[8] But in addition such statements always involve a larger conceptual field in which they are posed. In fact every expression governed by an intentional term is introduced under some higher-order concept. The method of description affords a way to make explicit just that concept under which the statement is tendered. Such expressions need not, therefore, remain   irretrievably ambiguous. Nor are they forever "opaque". Inferential operations may be performed on them just so long as these are always done under the same concept which governed the statement in the first place. Because most sophisms play on the fact that a clause or sentence is conceivable under more than one concept, the method of description was an important tool in the medieval arsenal for dealing with sophisms and insolubles.[9]

II. Further Applications

This section discusses in greater detail first some expressions which call for special analysis under one of the four methods of proof. These are: (a) the comparative of equality, the comparative of inequality and the superlative grade of comparison (Sections 6, 7, 8); (b) the expression "it differs" (Section 9), (c) the expressions "immediately" and "immediate" *(immediate)* (Section 13), (d) the expressions "begins" and "ceases" (Section 14). Next, we will show how some expressions may be submitted to more than one method of analysis (Section 5). Finally, we will show how it is possible to construe some words either syncategorematically or categorematically and how those interpretations affect the truth or falsity of statements in which they occur. In the last two cases we will select illustrations from Sections 15 through 18.

Adjectives used in the context of a comparison are divided into three groups.[10] Section 6 treats comparatives of equality where two items are thought to be equal in some respect. Section 7 deals with the ordinary comparative of inequality where one item is thought to exceed or to excell another in a certain respect. Section 8 presents the doctrine of superlatives.

All comparatives are treated as exponible propositions. Here are examples of the three types:

The comparative of equality:
"You are as strong as some man in the world." $\longleftrightarrow$ "You are strong, and some man is strong; and it is not the case that some man in the world is stronger than you."

The comparative of inequality:
"Socrates is stronger than Plato." $\longleftrightarrow$ "Socrates is strong, and Plato is strong; and Plato is not as strong as Socrates."

The superlative grade of comparison:
"You are the strongest of these." $\longleftrightarrow$
(a) "You are strong and these are strong, and it is not the case that some of these are stronger than you."
or
(b) "You are strong and these are strong and it is not the case that some of these are as strong as you."

All of these methods of analysis may be extended to sentences with past and future tense verbs as well.[11]

The expression "it differs" was commonly used in all of medieval logic, science and philosophy. This was in part due to the emphasis placed in traditional science on definition, and definition always requires the statement that a thing differs *in certain respects* from other things of the same kind. Because of its connection with negation, the expression had important ramifications for truth-conditions. Propositions including it as a verb were treated as exponibles which can be analyzed into three exponents.

"You differ from man." $\longleftrightarrow$ "You are, and man is; and you are not man." This analysis is also extended to past and future tense sentences. In these cases there were special problems when the sentences included terms which did not represent any actual object, e.g., the term "Antichrist" in "You differ from Antichrist". For if the above pattern were followed in this case it would produce as the second exponent the false statement: "Antichrist will be". Hence there is an alternative analysis: "You will be, and Antichrist will be when you will be, yet you will not be Antichrist."

The expression "immediately" was very important for medieval analyses of time and motion; hence its logical properties and their relationship to truth conditions were very important.[12] Statements including the expression "immediately" are treated as exponibles, to be analyzed in the following way:

"Immediately before A you were." $\longleftrightarrow$ "Before A you were, and there was no instant before A unless between that and A you were."

Again,

"Immediately after B you will be." $\longleftrightarrow$ "After B you will be; and no instant will be after B unless between that and B you will be."

And in a similar way one treats negative sentences which follow "immediately".

"Immediately before this you were not white." $\longleftrightarrow$ "Before this you were not white, and there was not an instant before this unless between that and this you were not white."

When the word "immediately" is itself preceded by a negation sign, the proposition is proved to be true or false by discerning the truth or falsity of its contradictory.

The expressions "begins" *(incipit)* and "ceases" *(desinit)* were very important in the language of medieval physics; and because of this the *Logica Parva* offers a full discussion of the logical features of these two expressions.[13] Incidentally, Paul of Pergula's *Logica* does not treat these as exponibles; rather it locates these expressions along with two other types under a special category of "provable" propositions.[14] A proposition with the term "begins" as the auxiliary verb is expounded in the following two ways:

"Socrates begins to be white." $\longleftrightarrow$ "Socrates now is white, and immediately before this present instant he was not white."

or again,

$\longleftrightarrow$ "Socrates now is not white, and immediately after this present instant he will be white."

On a similar format "ceases" is expounded in two ways:

"Socrates ceases to be white." ⟷ "Socrates now is not white; and
immediately before the present
instant he was white."

or alternately,

⟷ "Socrates now is white, and
immediately after the present
instant he will not be white."

Having presented the four methods of analysis, the *Logica Parva* points
out that some expressions are subject to more than one method of analysis.
This is best illustrated in the case of modal auxiliaries. Although there are
six standard expressions, "true", "false", "possible", "impossible", "contingent" and "necessary", we will use for the sake of illustration the terms
"contingent" and "necessary" and their adverbial forms, "contingently" and
"necessarily". The election of which method to use in analyzing these
expressions depends on the place where the modal auxiliary occurs in
the sentence to be analyzed. When the nominal or adverbial expression
occurs either at the beginning or at the end the sentence and is thought
to operate over the entire sentence it is said to be in the compositional
sense *(sensus compositus)*. We saw earlier when it is in the nominal form,
it is treated as an officiable term. When it is in the adverbial form, it is
treated as an exponible, e.g.,

"Necessarily man is animal." ⟷ "Men are and animals are and no
things are men unless they are
animals."

or

"You run contingently." ⟷ "You run and you can not-run."

When the modal auxiliary occurs between the subject and the verb or
between the verb and the predicate, the sentence is said to be in divided
sense *(sensus divisus)* and then it is treated as a resoluble proposition:

"Man necessarily is animal." ⟷ "This necessarily is animal,
and this is man."

again,

"Socrates is contingently running." ⟷ "This contingently is running
and this is Socrates."

Closer study of the examples in the text will reveal many other cases of
terms which can be analyzed according to more than one method.[15]

The last group of expressions whose truth-conditions are studied in the *Logica Parva* have wide usage in medieval logic, cosmology, metaphysics and theology. They are treated in Sections 15 through 18, and include "whole" *(totus)* (Section 15), "always" *(semper)* (Section 16), "from eternity" *(ab aeterno)* (Section 17), "infinite" *(infinitus)* (Section 18) and their opposites. These expressions have uniform effects on the truth conditions of sentences in which they occur. The first and fourth of these expressions may be used in either of two senses: either syncategorematically or categorematically. For example, "whole" is taken categorematically in the sentence "Socrates is a whole man", and in this case "whole" is interchangeable with the term "Socrates". In the sentence, "the whole Socrates runs", it is used syncategorematically and then it is convertible only with one or more of the parts of Socrates, viz., those parts which are running. Again, "infinite" may be taken in either of two senses: categorematically it means the same thing as "without beginning and end" and it is normally taken in this sense when it occurs alone in subject or predicate position as in "something is infinite" or "A is infinite".[16] In some cases, however, "infinite" is taken in a syncategorematic sense: "infinite body is". This is expounded in the following way: "a body of some size is: and there is no finite body of some size greater than that". Further extensions of these doctrines for past and future times are also developed. The expression "always" is generally convertible with the expression "for all time" *according to the exigencies of the verb* in the sentence in which it occurs. Thus, "always man was", is equivalent to "for all past time man was", which is analyzed as: "once man was, and there was not any time save when man was". The special condition attached to the convertibility of "always" with "for all time" is to prevent anomalies in the language such as this one. If "always" in "always God was", were interchangeable with every time absolutely this statement would be false; since it would imply "if God was in all time and the present time is time, then in the present time God *was*". But this is false because the *present* time never *was*. Hence, the expression "always" is interchangeable with "for every time" according to the exigencies of the verb of the sentence in which it occurs. The last expression which calls for special analysis is "from eternity" *(ab aeterno)*. This expression may be used either nominally, or adverbially as in "from eternity *A* was", or "eternally God was", respectively. In the first case the expression is convertible with "from some eternity" in the latter case it means "from all eternity". The former is a resoluble proposition, "this was *A*, and this is or was eternal". The latter is an exponible proposition, "before some finite time God was, and there was no finite time save before that God was".

Conclusion

In addition to the instruction which they give on the various methods of proof all of the sections of Chapter IV offer an ample supply of an entirely new ingredient not encountered previously in the *Logica Parva*. Each section concludes with a collection of controversial "theses" or paradoxes which were called "sophisms" *(sophismata)* in the Middle Ages.[17] Here are some examples, "an old man will be a boy" (Section 1), "everything which was, is" (Section 2), "I want to give you my horse; yet no horse of mine do I want to give you" (Section 3), "the one approaching I know; however, I do not know the one approaching" (Section 4), and so forth. Section 1 contains one dozen such statements; and Sections 2 through 18 present no less than seven dozen of them. Many had been passed down from the ancient world but many more still were invented in the medieval world itself. These statements are remarkable for at least two reasons; first, each is proved to be true from the rules which Paul has just explained in each case; second, each seemingly contradicts some obviously true statement, e.g., "no old man will be a boy", "nothing which was, is", etc. And several seem to contradict even themselves. All of these statements are strangely ambiguous and hence are unacceptable as they stand. How may their ambiguity be removed?

The equivocation which infects these sentences becomes manageable when we carry the analytic process a step or two beyond the point at which Paul's proofs leave us. To continue with the first example, "an old man will be a boy", is proved or reduced to its truth-conditions:

"This will be a boy; and this is or will be an old man."

This conclusion itself is a sentence with a disjunct predicate term. It may be analyzed further into a disjunction of two conjunctive propositions:

"*Either* this will be a boy and this is an old man *or*
this will be a boy and this will be an old man."

Now just as the first of these conjunctions is false, the second is true. Hence, the original sentence is equivalent to a disjunctive proposition one of whose members is true. Therefore, the entire disjunction is true. Further, analytic procedures of the appropriate kind may be applied to any of the dozens of paradoxes which are collected in this chapter in order to show that their paradoxical character is only apparent.

What is the purpose of listing these paradoxes in the Chapter on Proof? Many answers could be given to this question. Primarily they are capsule summaries of the doctrines to which they are annexed. The presence of a large number of such statements in the *Logica Parva* makes sense when that text is viewed as the written record of a tradition which was first and foremost an oral one. For each of these formulas is not only attractive, easily remembered and ready to recall on a moment's notice. Any of them could just as easily suggest the steps necessary to clarify it and thus to settle any controversy which it might provoke. As memorable capsule summaries of doctrines these paradoxes served a useful pedagogical purpose during the Middle Ages when instruction in logic was primarily oral and before the age when written texts were readily available.

Notes

1 *"probatio"* (from *probare*, "to try", "to inspect", "to examine") is translated as "proof", "demonstration". Literally, the terms *"probatur"* or *"probo"* in the *Logica Parva* signal the fact that Paul is initiating a proof or demonstration of the proposition in question. On occasion, however, the term *"patet"* (meaning "it is clear" or "it is evident") is said of a proposition and this will, in turn, be followed by a proof. There are four species of proof in the *Logica Parva*: (1) Resolution, (2) Exposition, (3) Officiation and (4) Description. In addition to each of these specialized conceptions of proof, Paul recognizes the broad division of proof into direct and indirect. The former is simply the reduction of a proposition to a concatenation of singular propositions which lay bare the conditions of its truth. The latter involves the assumption of the contradictory of the proposition in question and the subsequent reduction of the assumed proposition to absurdity. The best discussions of the medieval approach to proof are in Boh, 3, pp. 85−86 and Pinborg, 2 p. 103 ff. For a contrast with modern approaches to proof see Bocheński, 2, pp. 280−284.

2 An "immediate term" in subject-position renders the proposition in which it occurs true or false by direct inspection of the circumstances in which the proposition is used. A "mediate term" requires a further reduction of the proposition in question to a concatenation of propositions each of which has as subject an immediate term.

3 Note that the predicate "is true" is sayable of a proposition if the propositions into which it is analyzed are true; otherwise it is false. On pp. [90]−[91] Paul seems to deny this principle by distinguishing between describable and exponible propositions, on the one hand, which are replaceable by their descriptents or exponents and resoluble and officiable propositions, on the other hand, which are not replaceable by their resolvents or officiants. The Group VI inference rules of Chapter III also place restrictions on inferences involving resoluble and officiable propositions. See above Group VI Rules 6.4. and 6.5. Although Paul does not explain completely how these two kinds of proposition fit into the basic *probatio* framework or how such propositions are to be verified in all cases, his practice clearly indicates that the *probatio* format is useful in clarifying their truth-conditions.

4   For brief treatments of resoluble propositions see Pinborg, 2, p. 106
    and Boh, 3, p. 185.
5   The best critical treatment of exponible propositions is Ashworth,
    5. The reduplicative proposition, e.g., "Socrates insofar as he is man
    is animal", was a very important form used in the medieval expression
    of law-statements. See the reference in Boh, 3, p. 73, note 15. For
    applications to medieval science, see Murdoch, 4.
6   On the distinction between "composite and divided sense" see above
    p. 26. Also, Bocheński, 2, pp. 224–231. Professor Wilson elaborates
    no less than eight senses of these terms as distinguished by Heytesbury,
    see Wilson, pp. 12–18.
7   It is important to note that with regard to truth-conditions Paul of
    Venice treats in a similar way all propositions including elements of
    indirect discourse: thus propositions including quoted expressions
    as well as those having subordinate clauses introduced by mental or
    modal expressions are all to be analyzed as officiable propositions.
    For an excellent analysis of several kinds of these propositions and a
    comparison with modern approaches to the same material see Moody,
    3. Also, Scott, 1, p. 42 ff.
8   On this point see Moody, 3, p. 586 ff. and Scott, 1, pp. 42–60.
9   See Scott, 1 and below Chapters VI, VII and VIII.
10 Also see Wilson, pp. 29–87 and Murdoch, 4, p. 130, which discusses
    views in the *Logica Magna*.
11 See Reichenbach, p. 311 ff., especially p. 315.
12 The expression "immediate" in the Latin text is ambiguous between
    the adjective *(immediatae)* and the adverb *(immediate)*. Paul of
    Venice's discussion of the term brings out these differences and the
    analyses appropriate to each. See also Murdoch, 4, p. 130.
13 On this topic in Heytesbury see Wilson, pp. 29–56. On the topic
    in several other authors see Kretzmann, 4 and Murdoch 4.
14 See Sr. Mary Brown, 1, pp. 79–83.
15 *Logia Parva,* pp. [80]–[118].
16 On the term, "infinite" and its two senses see Murdoch, 3, p. 285
    and note 60.
17 On the *sophismata* tradition see Scott, 1, on Heytesbury's *Sophismata*
    all but three of which are included in Paul of Venice's *Sophismata
    Aurea,* see Wilson, pp. 153–168. Also see Chapter II, pp. 59–64 and
    Chapters VI-VIII., pp. [142]–[230]. On the use of *sophismata* in the
    scholastic tradition see Ong, p. 37 ff. and Gilbert, 2.

Obligationes

Medieval treatises on obligations *(Tractati de obligationibus)* first appear in the Terminist logic manuals of the early 1200's.[1] Variously called *Tractatus de obligationibus, Tractatus obligatoriae artis, Tractatus de obligatione, De arte exercitativa*, these tracts retain a central place in the logical literature well into the 16th century.[2] Their importance can be inferred from the fact that they constitute an essential chapter in every elementary and advanced logic text throughout the period. Yet despite their prominence it may be surprising to learn that they have been neither thoroughly studied nor properly understood. Even a cursory review of modern opinions on them reveals a great diversity of views about their purpose, form and content.[3] In this essay and in the following one, I have assumed that the rules of obligation and of insolubles govern the interchange between a teacher and a student carried out for the purpose of exercise or of examination.[4] In the following sections we examine: (a) the general nature of an obligation, (b) the rules of obligations and (c) some simple illustrations of obligatorial exchanges. A conclusion will comment on the importance of the obligation for medieval education in the field of logic.

a. In general an obligation is an exchange between two persons wherein one party consents to respond to statements proposed by the other party; and both agree to do this relative to an original statement and within a time limit. There are two basic types of obligation: position *(positio)* and deposition *(depositio)*. In the former both parties agree to carry out their verbal exchanges on the assumption that the original thesis is accepted. In the latter they agree to the successive proposing and responding to statements on the assumption that the original thesis is rejected. These two species of obligation are practically mirror images of one another; and the rules for each type of obligatory exchange reflect this fact. Both forms of obligation admit of systematic variation. One of these is called "conversion" where the initial thesis is said to be convertible or interchangeable with some other statement; and this operation agreed to by both parties is present in all subsequent exchanges between them. Another variant on the basic obligation may be called "similation" or "dissimilation". In these two cases the original thesis is said to be "similar to" or "dissimilar from" some other statement; and this operation agreed to by both parties is evident in all subsequent discourse.

b. Having given a general outline of the obligation, together with its basic types and variations, we must now develop in greater detail some basic terms, rules and examples of *obligationes*.

The term "obligation" *(obligatio)* applies generally to the entire exchange between the two parties. Precisely, it names the initial statement which is posed for examination. This statement is composed of two parts the sign of the obligation, e.g., "I pose to you" *(pono tibi...)* in a deposition "I reject to you", *(depono tibi...)* and something posited or obligated *(positum vel obligatum)* (in a deposition this is called the *depositum*), e.g., "every man runs". Once admitted the obligation is the fulcrum, the Archimedian point, around which the entire interchange is to take place, for all proposals and all replies to proposals are to be judged in reference to it. The two parties in the obligatory exchange are called the opponent *(opponens)* and the respondent *(respondens)*. To accentuate our claim that the medieval *obligationes* are examination arguments, I will use instead the terms "examiner" and "examinee" respectively. The examiner initiates the obligation by posing a sentence which the examinee either admits or does not admit. The time of the obligation lasts from the moment the examinee admits the sentence until (a) the examinee concedes a proposition which either directly or indirectly contradicts the original sentence or (b) the examiner calls off the obligation by declaring, "let the time of the obligation stop!" *(Cedat tempus!)* or (c) the examiner goes on to some other matter. To admit an original thesis posited is for the examinee "to put himself under an obligation" to respond to the succeeding series of statements proposed by the examiner in relation to the initial statement. It is, in effect, to consent to be examined on all other propositions which may have a bearing on the original one.

The medieval rules of obligation provide the examinee with some guidelines to be followed in giving his responses to statements proposed to him. The examinee is said to admit *(admitto)* the original thesis. All subsequent statements proposed to him within the time of an obligation he either concedes *(concedo)*, denies *(nego)* or doubts *(dubito)*. Paul of Venice gives the following rules of obligation:[5]

Rule I. Everything possible which is posited to you is to be admitted by you.

(Omne possibile tibi positum est a te admittendum.)

Rule II.   Everything posited to you and admitted by you [and] proposed within the time of the obligation is to be conceded by you.

(Omne tibi positum et a te admissum infra temporis obligationis propositum est a te concedendum.)

Rule III.   Everything following *per se* from what is posited and admitted or from what is posited together with one or more conceded [sentences] and proposed within the time of the obligation is to be conceded.

(Omne sequens ex posito admisso per se aut ex posito cum concesso vel cum concessis infra temporis obligationis est concedendum.)

Rule IV.   Everything inconsistent with what is posited together with a conceded sentence or conceded sentences taken collectively or separately is to be denied.

(Omne repugnans posito cum concesso vel concessis collective vel divisive est negandum.)

Rule V.   Everything following from what is posited together with the opposite or opposites of what has been proposed and denied within the time of the obligation is to be conceded.

(Omne sequens ex posito cum opposito bene negati vel oppositis bene negatorum infra temporis obligationis est concedendum.)

Rule VI.   Everything inconsistent with what has been posited together with the opposite or opposites of what has been correctly denied within the time of the obligation is to be denied.

(Omne repugnans posito et opposito bene negati vel bene negatorum infra temporis obligationis est negandum.)

Rule VII.   To every irrelevant proposition one is to respond according to its quality. That is: if it is true, it is to be conceded. If it is false, it is to be denied. If it is doubtful, it is to be doubted.

An irrelevant proposition I call one which neither follows from nor is inconsistent with [another proposition].

(Ad omne impertinens est respondendum secundum qualitatem. Id est si est verum concedendum. Si est falsum negandum. Si est dubium dubitandum. Impertinens vero est quod non sequitur nec repugnat.)

Rule VII.   Corollary:
Every false proposition that does not follow is to be denied, and every true proposition that is not inconsistent is to be conceded.

(Corollaria. Omne falsum non sequens est negandum et omne verum non repugnans est concedendum.)

Rule VIII. Because a possible thing is posited, an impossible is not to be conceded nor is a necessary thing to be denied. For nothing inconsistent is to be conceded nor is something following to be denied.

(Propter possibile positum non est impossibile concedendum; nec necessarium negandum quia nullum repugnans est concedendum; nec aliquod sequens est negandum.)

Rule IX. When every part of a conjunctive proposition is conceded the conjunction of which they or similar sentences are principal parts is to be conceded. And when one part of a disjunctive proposition is conceded, the disjunction of which it is a principal part [is to be conceded].

(Qualibet parte copulativae concessa concedenda; etiam copulativa cuius ille vel similis sibi sunt partes principales. Et una parte disjunctivae concessa concedenda est illa disjunctiva cuius ista est pars principalis.)

Rule I, of course, is basic; by applying it, the examinee allows the obligation to start. It is presupposed by all of the other rules. In tendering propositions to the examinee, the examiner may simply repeat the original statement posited. If so, Rule II requires that the examinee must concede the proposition wherever it is proposed. In an effort to trip up an examinee the examiner may propose certain statements which are irrelevant to *(impertinens)* the original statement. An irrelevant statement is defined as one which neither follows from nor is inconsistent with the original sentence. Rule VII guides the examinee with respect to irrelevant propositions: he should either concede, deny or doubt them depending on whether they are true, false or doubtful. The remaining rules apply to propositions which are relevant *(pertinens)* to the original statement. A relevant proposition is defined as one which either follows from or is inconsistent with the original sentence. Now, a proposition may follow immediately *(per se)* without additional premises or mediately with additional premises. Rule III requires the examinee to concede any statement following immediately from earlier statements. Rules IV, V and VI tell the examinee how to respond to sentences which follow from or are inconsistent with statements already conceded or denied. Rule VIII pertains generally to the concession or denial of necessary and impossible propositions. Finally, Rule IX directs the response of an examinee who is confronted with conjunctive or disjunctive propositions. Especially important in the application of all of these rules is, of course, the *order* in which an examiner proffers his statements. For instance, an examinee who has conceded "P or Q" need not concede either "P" or "Q" separately. And while an examinee may deny "P and Q" when first proposed; he might indeed be compelled to concede "P and Q" where he has earlier conceded "P" and "Q" separately.

c. The rules of obligation both suggest the possible strategies of an examiner and govern the possible answers of an examinee. Although actual obligations, of which we have facsimilies in the *Logica Parva* are exceedingly complex, it will be useful to consider some simplified illustrations of obligatorial exchanges. To show how the rules of obligation apply to obligations themselves, we now turn to some examples:

A. 1. Exr: I pose to you "Every man runs".
2. Exe: I admit and I concede "Every man runs".   Rule I
3. Exr: I propose to you "Some man does not run".
4. Exe: I deny "Some man does not run".   Rule IV
5. Exr: I propose to you "Some man runs".
6. Exe: I concede "Some man runs".   Rule III
7. Exr: I propose to you "Every man runs".
8. Exe: I concede "Every man runs".   Rule II
9. Exr: Let the time of obligation stop!

B. 1. Exr: I pose to you "No man sits".
2. Exe: I admit and I concede "No man sits".   Rule I
3. Exr: I propose to you "Some man sits".
4. Exe: I deny "Some man sits".   Rule IV
5. Exr: I propose to you "Some man does not sit".
6. Exe: I concede "Some man does not sit".   Rule III
7. Exr: I propose to you "Every man sits".
8. Exe: I deny "Every man sits".   Rule VI
9. Exr: I pose to you "No man runs".

C. 1. Exr: I pose to you "Some man runs".
2. Exe: I admit and I concede "Some man runs".   Rule I
3. Exr: I propose to you "No man runs".
4. Exe: I deny "No man runs".   Rule IV
5. Exr: I propose to you "Whoever runs moves".
6. Exe: I concede "Whoever runs moves".   Rule VII
7. Exr: I propose to you "Some man moves".
8. Exe: I concede "Some man moves".   Rule V
9. Exr: Let the time of the obligation stop!

D. 1. Exr: I pose to you "Every man runs".
2. Exe: I admit and I concede "Every man runs".   Rule I
3. Exr: I propose to you "Every man is a donkey".
4. Exe: I deny "Every man is a donkey".   Rule VIII
5. Exr: I propose to you "Every man runs or every man sits".
6. Exe: I concede "Every man runs or every man sits".   Rule IX
7. Exr: I propose to you "Every man sits".
8. Exe: I deny "Every man sits".   Rule VII
9. Exr: I pose to you "A stick stands in the corner".

E. 1. Exr: I pose to you "Every man runs".
2. Exe: I admit and I concede "Every man runs".   Rule I
3. Exr: I propose to you "Every man sits".
4. Exe: I concede "Every man sits".   Rule VII
5. Exr: I propose to you "Every man runs and every man sits".
6. Exe: I concede "Every man runs and every man sits".   Rule IX
7. Exr: I propose to you "Some man does not run".
8. Exe: I concede "Some man does not run". (!)   ! Rule VI
9. Exr: You respond poorly *(male)*.

These simple exchanges may begin to illustrate the ways in which the rules of obligation guide the answer of the examinee in the obligation. In each case, the step taken is justified by one or more rules of obligation. It is noteworthy that in all cases except the last the examinee responds well: in that case we note the customary assessment given for an examinee's performance: "You respond well *(bene)* or poorly *(male)*".

A deposition *(depositio)* contrasts with a position *(positio)* in virtue of whether the initial statement proffered by the examiner is to be accepted or rejected. In deposition we find all of the elements seen before except a special set of rules for the deposition. There are two participants, the examiner and the examinee. There is an initial statement. There is a sequence of sentences proposed by the examiner and in turn either conceded, denied or doubted by the examinee. The time of the obligation is set as usual by the examinee's consistent declarations or by the examiner's decision. The examinee's performance is similarly rated good *(bona)* or bad *(mala)*. The key words "I reject to you..." *(Depono tibi...)* signal the opening of a deposition. If the examinee admits that the original sentence is rejected, the deposition begins, and the examiner in turn proposes other sentences for consideration. Within the time of the obligation the examinee is bound to tell whether he concedes, denies or doubts each subsequent sentence. In this case, he is guided by the rules of deposition which call for him to answer on the assumption that the original statement is *rejected*. That is: *as if* the original statement were false. Here are Paul of Venice's rules of deposition:[6]

Rule I.   Everything rejected *(depositum)* and admitted within the proposed time of the obligation is always to be denied.
(Omne depositum et admissum infra temporis obligationis propositum semper est negandum.)

Rule II. Everything that implies what is rejected, either *per se* or together with one or more conceded opposites of what has been correctly denied always is to be denied.

(Omne per se antecedens ad depositum aut cum concesso aut cum concessis aut cum opposito bene negati vel oppositis bene negatorum semper est negandum.)

Rule III. Everything inconsistent with what is rejected and every proposition following from that inconsistent proposition either *per se* or together with one or more conceded opposites of what has been correctly denied is to be denied.

(Omne repugnans deposito et omne sequens ex illo repugnante per se aut cum concesso vel cum concessis vel opposito bene negati vel oppositis bene negatorum est concedendum.)

Rule IV. Everything inconsistent with the contradictory of something rejected either *per se* or together with one or more conceded opposites of what has been correctly denied is to be denied.

(Omne repugnans contradictorio depositi per se aut cum concesso aut cum concessis vel cum opposito bene negati vel oppositis bene negatorum est negandum.)

Rule V. With regard to every proposition following from the rejected and with regard to every irrelevant proposition one is to respond according to its quality.

(Ad omne sequens et ad omne impertinens ad depositum respondendum est secundum sui qualitatem.)

It is rather easy to see that these rules of deposition are like the rules for position. However, there are some differences. The first rule of deposition combines the cases covered under Rules I and II of position. Again, the fifth rule of deposition combines the cases covered under Rules V and VII of position. Finally, the rules of deposition contain no instructions about responding to impossible propositions (Position Rule VIII) or to conjunctive or disjunctive propositions (Position Rule IX). Presumably, attention to these kinds of proposition in the case of deposition would have complicated matters beyond belief. Here we might credit the Scholastics with not carrying a good thing too far.

To illustrate the rules of deposition here are two examples:[7]

F. 1. Exr: I reject to you "Every man runs".
   2. Exe: I admit and I deny "Every man runs".   Rule I
   3. Exr: I propose to you "Some man does not run".
   4. Exe: I concede "Some man does not run".   Rule III
   5. Exr: I propose to you "You are a man".
   6. Exe: I concede "You are a man".   Rule III
   7. Exr: I propose to you "You do not run".

| 8. Exe: | I concede "You do not run". | Rule III |
| 9. Exr: | Let the time of the obligation stop! | |

G. 1. Exr: I reject to you "No man runs".
   2. Exe: I admit and I deny "No man runs".   Rule I
   3. Exr: I propose to you "Every man runs".
   4. Exe: I doubt "Every man runs".   Rule V
   5. Exr: I propose to you "Some man runs".
   6. Exe: I concede "Some man runs".   Rule III
   7. Exr: I propose to you "You are a man".
   8. Exe: I concede "You are a man".   Rule III
   9. Exr: I propose to you "You do not run".
   10. Exe: I concede "You do not run".   Rule III
   11. Exr: I reject to you "A stick stands in the corner".

In reading through these exchanges it is evident that the examinee must keep constantly in mind the fact that the original statement is *rejected*. This could be tedious business if his examination should include a mixture of positions and depositions.

Another variation of the basic obligation is the practice of conversion. This occurs where a statement posited initially is said to be converted or interchanged with some other statement also posited at the beginning. Then throughout the obligatorial context the examinee must respond to the implicants of either statement in the same way and to both in relation to the original statement. For example, the examiner may say "Let the sentence 'A stick stands in the corner', be interchanged with 'The sun rises' ". Then one must respond to all statements subsequently proposed as if the statements were equivalent. Often two sentences said to be interchanged were mixed as to their qualities: for instance, the chief instance of a necessary statement, "God exists", might be interchanged with the chief instance of an impossible statement, "a man is a donkey". Once the initial statement is admitted by the examinee, he must respond only after systematically interchanging these two propositions wherever and whenever they occur. His goal, as usual, is to avoid conceding or denying any statement which would imply the contradictory of the original statement. Here are Paul of Venice's rules for interchangeable propositions:[8]

Rule I.   Whenever two propositions are posited to be interchangeable thus signifying adequately of which one is necessary and the other one impossible the case is not admitted, because then from the necessary the impossible would follow.

(Quandocunque ponitur duas propositiones converti adequatae significando quarum una est necessaria alia impossibilis non admittatur casus iste quia tunc ex necessario sequeretur impossibile.)

90

Rule II.   Whenever two propositions thus signifying adequately are posited to be interchangeable of which the one is possible and the other impossible the case is not admitted.

(Quandocunque ponitur duas propositiones converti sic adequate significando quarum una est possibilis et alia impossibilis non admittatur casus.)

Rule III.   Whenever two propositions are posited to be interchangeable thus signifying adequately of which one is necessary and the other contingent, the case is not admitted.

(Quandocunque ponitur duas propositiones converti sic adequate significando quarum una est necessaria et altera contingens non admittatur ille casus.)

Rule IV.   Whenever two contingent propositions are posited to be interchangeable thus signifying adequately, of which the one is contradictorily inconsistent with the other, the case is not admitted.

(Quandocunque ponitur duas propositiones contingentes converti sic adequate significando quarum una alteri contradictoriae repugnat non admittatur ille casus.)

Rule V.   Whenever two contingent propositions are posited to be interchanged, thus signifying adequately, of which neither is inconsistent with the other the case is admitted.

(Quandocunque ponitur duas propositiones contingentes converti sic adequate significando quarum una alteri non repugnat admittatur casus iste.)

Rule VI.   Whenever two propositions, either contingent or non-contingent, are posited to be interchanged, not making mention of the adequate significate the case is admitted. And when they are proposed, with respect to conceding and denying, one may respond within [the time of the obligation] just as [one does outside the time of the obligation]. But if the first is conceded to be true or necessary; then the second is treated in the same way. If, however, the first is false or impossible the second is taken in the same way.

(Quandocunque ponitur duas propositiones converti sive sint contingentes sive non contingentes non faciendo mentionem de adequato significato admittatur casus. Et ipsis propositis quo ad concedere vel negare respondeatur intra sicut extra. Sed si prima conceditur esse vera vel [necessaria et secunda similiter. Si autem falsa vel impossibilis] et secunda similiter.)

The key to the rules of responding to interchanged propositions is to respond according to the conditions which pertain to the first statement with which the second statement is interchanged. Each of these rules mentions

the phrase "thus signifying adequately". In the *Logica Magna* a great a-
mount of disputation wages over the definition of "the adequate significate" of a proposition.[9] Fortunately, the *Logica Parva* defines "the adequate significate" as "the customary significate"; and the entire problem
is bypassed by one simple sentence. Moreover, the student is simply instructed by the rules of conversion to gear his response to a proposition solely
on whether "there is mention of the adequate significate" without paying
attention to what that might be. Rules I through IV tell which interchanged
propositions are not to be admitted. Rules V and VI describe those which
are to be admitted. Here is an example of an obligation involving interchanged propositions:

H. 1. Exr: I pose to you "God is" and "A man is a donkey"
          are interchanged.
   2. Exe: I do not admit "God is" and "A man is a donkey"
          are interchanged.   Rule I
   3. Exr: I pose to you "You are a man" and "A man is a
          donkey" are interchanged.
   4. Exe: I do not admit "You are a man" and "A man is a
          donkey" are interchanged.   Rule IV
   5. Exr: I pose to you "You are a man" and "You run" thus
          signifying adequately are interchanged.
   6. Exe: I admit "You are a man" and "You run" are
          interchanged.   Rule V
   7. Exr: I propose to you "You are a man".
   8. Exe: I concede "You are a man".   Position Rule II
   9. Exr: I propose to you "You run".
 10. Exe: I concede "You run".   Position Rule II
 11. Exr: Let the time of the obligation stop!

It is evident that the main purpose of the conversion or interchanging of
propositions in the obligation is to test the student's skills at substitution.
It is to discover how well the student can judge the admissability of any
proposition relative to some original on the condition that the proposition
in question substitutes for some other proposition.

Another experience in mental dexterity is the last variation on the
obligatio. That is the concept of similar and dissimilar propositions. Here
we find the ordinary format for an obligation except that the examiner
declares that the initial proposition is true or false and he also tells whether
two statements introduced initially are similar or dissimilar with regard to
truth or falsity. Then as usual a sequence of propositions is given for an
examinee's responses. Here are Paul of Venice's rules for similar propositions:[10]

92

Rule I. Whenever two propositions are posited to be similar, and no mention is made of the adequate significate, one may respond to them by conceding, denying or doubting within the time of the obligation just as he would outside of the time of the obligation.

(Quandocunque ponuntur duas propositiones esse similes non faciendo mentionem de adequato significato respondeatur ad easdem concedendo negando vel dubitando infra temporis sicut extra.)

Rule II. Whenever two propositions are posited to be similar, and no mention is made of the adequate significate, with respect to the truth or falsity of the first proposition one may respond as he would outside of the time of the obligation and with regard to the truth or falsity of the second proposition he may respond in a consistent manner.

(Quandocunque ponuntur duas propositiones esse similes non faciendo mentionem de adequato significato ad primam propositionem esse veram vel falsam respondeatur infra sicut extra et ad secundam consequenter.)

Rule III. Whenever two propositions are posited to be similar thus signifying adequately, of which the one is contradictorily inconsistent with the other, the case is not to be admitted.

(Quandocunque ponuntur duas propositiones esse similes sic significando adequate quarum una alteri contradictoriae repugnat non admittendus est casus.)

Rule IV. Whenever two propositions are posited to be similar thus signifying adequately of which one or each follows from the contradictory of the other, those propositions are similar in truth; and wherever and whenever they are proposed they are to be conceded.

(Quandocunque ponuntur duas propositiones esse similes sic adequate significando quarum una vel qualibet sequitur ad contradictorium alterius, illae sunt similes in veritate et ubicunque et quandocunque proponuntur sunt concedendae.)

Rule V. Whenever two propositions thus signifying adequately are posited to be similar and one follows from the opposite of the other, they are similar in falsity; and whenever one is posited it is to be denied.

(Quandocunque ponuntur duas propositiones esse similes sic adequate significando ex quarum una sequitur oppositum alterius ille sunt similes in falsitate et quandocunque ponitur aliqua est neganda.)

93

Rule VI.   Whenever two propositions thus signifying adequately are posited to be similar, of which each is irrelevant to the other, they can be similar in truth or falsity, and they may be conceded or denied.

(Quandocunque ponuntur duas propositiones esse similes sic adequate significando quarum quaelibet est alteri impertinens possunt esse similes in veritate et in falsitate et concedendae et negandae.)

Dissimilar propositions are those which differ as to truth and falsity; hence two propositions are "dissimilar" if one is true and the other is false. In an obligation an examiner may declare that two statements posited initially are dissimilar: and the examinee will respond to subsequent propositions according to the rules for dissimilar propositions:[11]

Rule I.   Whenever two propositions are posited to be dissimilar without any mention of an adequate significate one may respond to either of them when proposed, by conceding or denying it within the time of the obligation just as he would outside of the time of the obligation.

(Quandocunque ponuntur duas propositiones esse disimiles non faciendo mentionem de adequato significato ad quamlibet propositionem concedendo negando respondeatur infra temporis sicut extra.)

Rule II.   Whenever someone posits two propositions to be dissimilar without any mention of an adequate significate, with regard to the truth or falsity of the first one proposed one may respond within the time of the obligation just as he would outside of the time of the obligation. And to any other proposition, he may respond in the opposite way.

(Quandocunque ponuntur duas propositiones esse disimiles non faciendo mentionem de adequato significato ad primam propositionem esse veram vel falsam respondeatur infra sicut extra et ad aliam disimiliter.)

Rule III.   Whenever two propositions thus signifying adequately are posited to be dissimilar of which each is interchangeable with the other, this case is not to be admitted.

(Quandocunque ponuntur duas propositiones esse disimiles sic significando adequate quarum qualibet altera convertitur non admittendus est casus.)

94

Rule IV.   Whenever two propositions thus signifying adequately are posited to be dissimilar of which one is necessary and the other contingent, then the necessary one is always to be conceded and the other one denied.

(Si ponuntur duas propositiones esse disimiles sic adequate significando quarum una est necessaria et alia contingens necessaria semper est concedenda et alia neganda.)

Rule V.   If two contingent propositions thus signifying adequately are posited to be dissimilar of which one implies the other but not vice versa, the antecedent wherever it is proposed always is to be denied, and the consequent is to be conceded.

(Si ponuntur duas propositiones contingentes esse disimiles sic adequate significando quarum una antecedit ad reliquam et non e contra, antecedens ubicunque proponitur est negandum et consequens concedendum.)

Rule VI.   If two propositions thus signifying adequately are posited to be dissimilar of which each one is irrelevant to the other, one may respond to the first one proposed within the time of the obligation just as he would outside of the time of the obligation and to the other in the opposite way.

(Si ponuntur duas propositiones esse disimiles sic adequate significando quarum qualibet alteri set impertinens ad primam propositam respondeatur infra sicut extra et ad aliam disimiliter.)

Thus, the rules for the similarity and the dissimilarity of propositions are designed to guide the student in responding to propositions put to him. Here are two examples of how these rules work:

I.   1. Exr: I pose to you " 'You are in Paris' and 'You are in Rome', signifying adequately are similar". And let this be true: You are in Paris.
     2. Exe: I admit the case posited.   Sim. Rule I
     3. Exr: I propose to you "You are in Paris", thus signifying adequately.
     4. Exe: I concede "You are in Paris".   Sim. Rule IV
     5. Exr: I propose to you "You are in Rome".
     6. Exe: I deny "You are in Rome".   Sim. Rule V
     7. Exr: Let the time of the obligation stop!

J.   1. Exr: I pose to you " 'You are a man' and 'You are white', signifying adequately are dissimilar".
     2. Exe: I admit the case posited.   Dissim. Rule VI
     3. Exr: I propose to you "You are a man".
     4. Exe: I concede "You are a man".   Dissim. Rule VI

95

5. Exr: I propose to you "You are white".
6. Exe: I deny "You are white".   Dissim. Rule VI
7. Exr: I pose to you "God is" and "Man is a donkey".
8. Exe: I admit and I concede "God is" and I deny
    "Man is a donkey".   Dissim. Rule I
9. Exr: I propose to you "No God is".
10. Exe: I deny "No God is".   Dissim. Rule II
11. Exr: Let the time of the obligation stop!

These exchanges will serve to illustrate the ways in which the rules for similar and dissimilar propositions are to be applied in the obligation. The key component in most of the rules is the concept of "signifying adequately"; where this is not mentioned explicitly by the examiner the examinee is instructed either to reject the case posited, or to deny the statement proposed or to answer as he would outside the time of the obligation. This factor of "signifying adequately" plays an important part in some dilemmas which Paul of Venice turns up in his discussion of obligations.

Conclusion

We have claimed that the medieval obligation is a pedagogical device: its main purpose is to examine the student's command of logic. What skills specifically does it test? A good response to the questions put to him would demonstrate several things about the student's knowledge. It would display (1) his grasp of the logical as distinct from the grammatical forms of sentences (2) his command of the rules of deduction as these apply to each statement under consideration (3) his skill in substituting one sentence for another and (4) his recognition of the truth-conditions for any one statement specified by the original statement accepted or rejected *plus* or *minus* all subsequent statements whether conceded or denied.[12] Of these various activities the fundamental one seems to be that of determining the prominent logical features — logical form, inferential consistency, and truth — of a given statement relative to other statements in a context. All of these tasks may seem fairly elementary in an age where logical functions are commonplace. But it must be remembered that the examinees in the medieval *obligatio* were youngsters of 12 or 13 years of age, the equivalent of our modern high school freshman.

The interpretation of the *obligatio* offered in this paper is consistent with one point noted by Professor Spade: namely, that we have no texts of actual *obligationes*.[13] If the Rules of Obligation were in fact rules for oral examinations in logic, we should not expect them to have been written out, nor should we hope to find written evidence of them. Yet we do know that *obligationes* texts were required reading for students. Moreover the sets of rules for Obligations varied somewhat from university to university.[14] Is it not reasonable to infer that students were examined on these same subjects? Perhaps, the only written records we will ever have in connection with the *obligatio* practice are those lists of students who passed or failed their requirements in Logic.[15]

Notes

[1] For the background of *obligatio*-theory see De Rijk, 1, Volume 2, Part 1, pp. 128–176 and pp. 595–596. On the 13th century see De Rijk, 8 and Green.

[2] For the 14th century developments in the theory of *obligationes* see Weisheipl, 1 and 2. Regarding the treatises of particular authors see Spade, 3, 6, 7. Especially important for the background of Paul of Venice's *Logica Parva* tract on Obligations is Spade's edition of the treatise of Roger Swyneshed in Spade, 4 and the references to William of Heytesbury in Spade, 3. For the views of Paul of Pergula (15th century) see Sr. Mary Brown, 2 and Angelelli.

[3] The *obligatio* has been interpreted as: (1) a "game": see Hamblin, pp. 125–133, De Rijk, 10 and Angelelli; (2) a format for debate or disputation: see Kneale, pp. 233–234; (3) an axiomatization of formal logic: see Boehner, 3, pp. 14–15; (4) a contribution to deontic logic: see Dumitriu, Volume II, p. 167; (5) a contribution to "possible world" semantics: see Spade, 4, p. 246; (6) a format for exercise in disputation: see Sr. Mary Brown, 2 and Green. Each of these views is examined critically in Perreiah, 5.

[4] The origin of the rules of *obligationes* is in Aristotle's *Topics* and *On Sophistical Refutations*. See Aristotle, 4, and Perreiah, 5.

[5] See *Logica Parva*, pp. [118]–[122].

[6] See *Logica Parva*, pp. [138]–[140].

[7] In these sample exchanges "you" refers throughout to the student or the respondent.

[8] See *Logica Parva*, pp. [131]–[134].

[9] See *Logica Parva*, p. [131], p. [162]. For the *Logica Magna* doctrine on the adequate significate see Adams and Del Punta in Adams, 2, pp. 284–285.

[10] See *Logica Parva*, pp. [135]–[137].

[11] See *Logica Parva*, pp. [137]–[138].

[12] Professor Spade in Spade, 4, has distinguished two traditions in the *obligationes* literature, the *"antiqua responsio"* and the *"nova responsio"*. The former held that the student's replies in the subsequent stages of an *obligatio* were to be determined by the original *positio plus* what followed from or was inconsistent with it. The latter held that the student's replies were to be determined by what followed from or was inconsistent with the original *positio* alone. Thus, the *"antiqua responsio"* held that once parts of a conjunction are conce-

ded, the whole conjunction is to be conceded; and that once part of a disjunction is conceded, the entire disjunction is to be conceded. Whereas the *"nova responsio"* held that one can concede both parts of a conjunction yet not concede the whole conjunction: and one can concede a disjunction though neither part is conceded. Finally, although the order of concessions or denials is important in the *"antiqua responsio"* this is not so with the *"nova responsio"* where each step in effect starts all over. In the *"antiqua responsio"* tradition Professor Spade lists the anonymous *obligationes Parisienses* edited by De Rijk as well as works by Albert of Saxony, Peter of Ailly and Paul of Pergula. To this list we add the *Logica Parva* by Paul of Venice. In the *"nova responsio"* tradition Spade reckons Roger Swyneshed and Richard Lavenham.

It is one of the virtues of the interpretation proposed in this essay that it is consistent with both of these traditions. Moreover, the interpretation of the *insolubilia* rules of Chapter VI claims that they are rules to guide the student in responding to statements posed to him initially in the *obligatio*. Where these statements are insoluble *simpliciter* they are not even to be admitted by the respondent. Where they are insoluble *secundum quid*, however, they are admissible; and this implies that they are possible and true in some respect. The *"nova responsio"* rules would allow the student to explore those propositions which are consistent with the original statement alone, without regard to any subsequent affirmations or denials. So far as I know none of the interpretations cited in note 3 can explain or justify the two responsive traditions.

13 See Spade, 4, p. 245. There are difficulties, of course, in seeking written records of exchanges which were carried out in an oral tradition and which were actually spoken. Nonetheless, the *Logica Parva* contains numerous examples of explicit *obligationes*. Having laid down his rules, Paul of Venice says, "so that the truth of these rules may be grasped more firmly, against each of them I will formulate an obligation" *Logica Parva*, p. [122]. In addition Paul alludes to an *"implicit obligatio"*. *Logica Parva*, p. [194]. When both explicit and implicit *obligationes* are taken into account, the *Logica Parva* alone is replete with examples of *obligationes*.

14 For references to statutes and required readings in later medieval universities see Thorndike, pp. 244–247, p. 279, p. 297.

15 We have claimed that the *obligatio* rules served primarily a pedagogical purpose: to exercise and to examine the student's command of basic principles and rules of logic. In the context of a theroy of logical form they may also be seen to serve a purpose akin to "the rules of conversational implicature" elaborated by Professor Paul Grice. See Professor Grice's article in Davidson and Harman, 2.

Insolubilia

Although some of the rules of obligations pertain to the admission or non-admission of statements posited initially most of them apply to statements proposed in the course of the *obligatio* once the initial statement has been admitted. Here is where the Chapter on Insolubles extends and complements the Chapter on Obligations.[1] For it offers additional instruction concerning the admission or non-admission of initial statements. Just as an examiner may intermingle propositions of various kinds in the course of the exam, e.g., relevant and irrelevant, interchangeable and non-interchangeable, similar and dissimilar etc., so he may posit initially statements which are normal or soluble alongside those which are insoluble. The former, of course, do not of themselves lead to contradiction: whereas the latter of themselves do lead to absurdity. The rules of insolubles are designed to guide the student in deciding whether to admit or not to admit these initial statements. Once an insoluble is admitted, however, the Rules of Obligations provide all of the guidance necessary for conceding, denying or doubting them.

The *Logica Parva* offers a three-step decision procedure for dealing with insolubles: (1) Identification, (2) Admission and (3) Solution. First, insoluble propositions must be identified. Since they may be interspersed with normal or soluble ones, the student must recognize the several types of insoluble propositions by their distinguishing marks. Second, insoluble propositions may be wholly false or only partially false. The former lead straightaway to contradiction and must not be admitted into the *obligatio*. The latter yield contradictions only under certain conditions. The student must know the exact conditions under which insoluble propositions lead to absurdity and, if he admits one into an *obligatio*, he must be careful subsequently to deny such a proposition. Third, an insoluble is admitted *into* an *obligatio* because it is possible; but it is to be denied *within* the *obligatio* because it is false. In a solution *(solutio)* the student exhibits those respects in which the insoluble proposition is possible yet false. The following three sections will examine each of these steps in greater detail. A conclusion will comment on the importance of exercises including insolubles for medieval training in logic.

a. Identification

To identify an insoluble, one must keep in mind the definition of an insoluble as well as several distinctions and divisions. An insoluble is a proposition assertively signifying itself to be false.[2] Now, insolubles may signify themselves to be false in one of two ways: Some do so immediately, e.g., in the sentence "this proposition is false", where the demonstrative points to the very proposition in question. Others signify themselves to be false mediately, i.e., through other propositions. For example, from "this proposition is not true", it does not follow that the same proposition is false unless there is a minor premise, "that (pointing to the first proposition) is a proposition". For according to the rules of syllogism an affirmative conclusion cannot follow from a negative premise without the addition of an affirmative minor premise. Moreover, insolubles are divided into two groups with respect to their origin: some originate in our own act, e.g., Socrates' statement, "Socrates says something false". Others originate in some property of their expression, e.g., "this proposition is false" (pointing to itself). Finally, insolubles are divided into two groups with respect to kind: Some statements are insoluble simply *(simpliciter)*; others are insoluble according to a condition *(secundum quid)*. The former is always introduced with a case; and when the case is admitted, a contradiction follows. The latter is also introduced with a case; yet when the case is admitted, no contradiction follows.

Next, Paul turns to the examination of actual insolubles. He classifies them into two groups: (A) Apparent insolubles *(insolubilia apparens)* which refer explicitly to their own truth or falsity and (B) Non-apparent insolubles *(insolubilia non apparens)* which make no mention of their own truth or falsity but which are posited in a context which establishes their truth-conditions. Here is a catalog of the kinds of insolubles which Paul of Venice canvasses in the *Logica Parva*:[3]

A. Apparent
  1. Categorical
     a. Singular (A) "Socrates says something false."
     b. Particular (A) "Some particular proposition is false."
     c. Universal (A) "Every universal proposition is false."
     d. Exclusive (A) "Only Socrates says something true."
     e. Exceptive (A) "Nothing except Socrates says something true."
  2. Hypothetical
     a. Conjunctive (A) "God exists and no conjunctive proposition is true."
     b. Disjunctive (A) "No God exists or no disjunctive proposition is true."

B. Non-apparent
   1. (A) "Socrates will not have a dime."
   2. (A) "[Socrates] will not cross the bridge."

Considering the number of pages devoted to each item, it is notable that Paul spends five-sixths of his Chapter examining apparent insolubles and only one sixth on non-apparent insolubles. Thus, the first of Paul's three-step procedure for responding to insolubles is complete. If the examiner's technique includes the intermixing of insoluble with soluble statements, it is paramount that the examinee learn to identify which propositions tendered to him are insoluble. The sentences themselves and the cases associated with them contain the clues. The definitions, divisions as well as the classification itself are all aids in the initial task of detection.

b. Admission

The second step of Paul's procedure is to decide whether to admit a statement into the *obligatio* context. This step is crucial. By admitting an initial statement, a student consents to be examined on subsequent statements relative to the first one; and as we have seen, his aim is to concede or to deny no statement subsequently which would contradict the original statement. Now, if the original statement itself should be self-falsifying or otherwise logically vicious it would lead to absurdity; and if admitted into the *obligatio*, it could make the student fail the exam. But not all propositions lead to absurdity in the same way. Some as we saw, are false absolutely *(simpliciter)*; others are false only relatively *(secundum quid)*. Moreover, some propositions are introduced alone; while others are tendered along with a statement of conditions called a "case". Here are two very general rules to guide the student:[4]

Case Rule I.   Never admit a case from which an insoluble simply originates.

Case Rule II.   Always admit a case from which an insoluble according to a condition originates.

It is plain that the insoluble statement must be assessed along with its case in order for the examinee to make a decision concerning admission or nonadmission.

Every case will contain at least one of three conditions.[5] These are expressed in clauses which I call: (1) Uniqueness, (2) Existence and (3) Preciseness. The first stipulates that the statement in question, e.g., (A) "Socrates says something false", is the one and only proposition which

Socrates utters. It is the requirement that "one such be every such" or "that (A) is every proposition". This condition limits the universe within which the insoluble proposition is to be considered. The second condition which may be specified is that the proposition, i.e., the insoluble, is understood by someone, in this case Socrates. The third condition certifies that the proposition in question, i.e., (A), "signifies precisely as the terms indicate". Where (A) is "No proposition is true", condition (3) states that "its terms do not signify *save* that no proposition is true". Because the condition can be phrased in this way the Preciseness Clause is sometimes called "the sign of exclusion". With these three conditions in mind we are prepared to examine Paul of Venice's rules for the admission or non-admission of cases associated with actual insoluble propositions.

Paul's first five rules apply to categorical propositions of various kinds. Rule I concerns a singular insoluble without a demonstrative pronoun, for example a sentence like (A) "Socrates says something false". If this statement is presented with a case in which all three clauses are specified, it is an insoluble simply and is not to be admitted.

Insoluble Rule I. Every singular insoluble without a demonstrative arising from our own act, in order that it be an insoluble simply, requires three conditions. The first condition is that one such be every such. [Uniqueness Clause] The second condition is that one says or understands such a proposition and no other. [Existence Clause] The third is that it signify precisely as the terms indicate. [Preciseness Clause].[6]

Rule II governs the same type of insoluble, i.e., a singular insoluble without a demonstrative pronoun; but if the examiner omits the Preciseness Clause, the statement is an insoluble according to a condition and by Admission Rule II, it is to be admitted.

Insoluble Rule II. Every singular insoluble without a demonstrative pronoun arising from our own act in order to be an insoluble according to a condition requires the same conditions [as Insoluble Rule I] except for the exclusive expression [i.e., the Preciseness Clause].[7]

Since any insoluble according to a condition is in some respect possible, it may be admitted into the *obligatio*. Then a decision must be made to concede, to deny or to doubt it. But more about this later.

The third rule of insolubles governs all singular insolubles with demonstrative pronouns and all non-singular insolubles (i.e., Universals, Particulars or Indefinites as well as Exclusives and Exceptives), arising from our own act. Such statements are insoluble simply when the examiner states only the Existence and Preciseness Clauses, i.e., (2) and (3) above.

Insoluble Rule III. Every non-singular insoluble or every singular insoluble with a demonstrative pronoun arising from our own act, in order that it be an insoluble simply, requires only two conditions.[8]

In other words, if the case does not state that (A) is unique, then (A) is insoluble simply, and by Admission Rule I is not to be admitted. Again, the same types of proposition would be insoluble according to a condition if the examiner should state clauses (1) and (3) but omit (2), i.e., the Existence Clause. By Admission Rule II, then, such an insoluble should be admitted. The next rule applies to insolubles which arise from the property of an expression:

Insoluble Rule IV. Every insoluble arising from the property of an expression requires only two conditions or only one condition.[9]

This rule is obviously incomplete. In practice it has four possible variations. First, a proposition of this kind is insoluble simply if the examiner stipulates only conditions (1) and (3) and omits (2). For example, (A) "Some proposition is false", given in a case with only Uniqueness and Preciseness Clauses but omitting the Existence Clause, is an insoluble simply and so is not to be admitted. Second, an insoluble arising from the property of an expression is an insoluble according to a condition if the Uniqueness Clause alone is included in the case. Then, by Admission Rule II, it is to be admitted. Third, insolubles arising from the property of an expression are insoluble simply if the examiner states only the Preciseness Cause along with the insoluble: e.g., (A) " 'This proposition is false', thus signifying adequately". In this case we have an insoluble simply and so one which is not to be admitted. Fourth, a proposition such as "This proposition is false", stated by itself without a case is an insoluble according to a condition and so is to be admitted. Propositions of the last kind constitute a special variety which Paul has in mind when he tells us that some propositions are stated with a case and some without a case.[10]

With respect to those which must be stated with a case, however, if the examiner should neglect to specify the case sufficiently, the proposition is subject to

Insoluble Rule V. Every insoluble which is not an insoluble without a case, when one sets aside some required condition is thoroughly doubtful.[11]

Aristotle's teaching on the Examination-Argument which is the model for the medieval *obligatio* recognizes several alternatives for the student confronted with a statement which is underdetermined. He may ask for clarification or a fuller elaboration of the thesis tendered by the examiner. Or he may merely state the sense in which he admits the proposition in question. Or he may judge the proposition in question just as he would outside the context of the examination. Or he may simply register his doubt. In dialectical practice Paul of Venice disports all of these; but the *Logica Parva* Chapter on Insolubles rarely invokes Rule V. The insolubles examined there are decidedly admissible or non-admissible, and then they are routinely denied. Before going into that aspect of the procedure we need to review several additional rules.

The first five rules dealt with categorical propositions of various kinds: the following rules apply to hypothetical insolubles or propositions in hypothetical form which are insoluble.[12] The topic is divided into Conjunctive and Disjunctive propositions. We will consider the rules affecting each one in turn. The three rules for conjunctive propositions are:[13]

Conjunctive Insoluble Rule I.

> With respect to a conjunctive insoluble one of whose parts is necessary *per se*, if in the case all of the conditions along with the sign of exclusion i.e., [Preciseness Clause] are added to it, it is an insoluble simply; and the case is not to be admitted.

Conjunctive Insoluble Rule II.

> With regard to a conjunctive insoluble one of whose parts is possible or contingent, by adding to it all conditions with the sign of exclusion [Preciseness Clause], it is an insoluble according to a condition; and the case is to be admitted.

Conjunctive Insoluble Rule III.

> Every conjunctive insoluble is insoluble according to a condition by adding to it all of the conditions except the sign of exclusion [Preciseness Clause]; and the case is to be admitted.

Thus, the rules for conjunctive insolubles are divided into those for conjunctives with modal operators (I and II) and without modal operators (III). Note the special importance of the Preciseness Clause: its presence or absence from a case can easily determine whether the insoluble proposition is to be admitted.

The three rules for disjunctive propositions are similarly set forth:[14]

Disjunctive Insoluble Rule I.

> A disjunctive insoluble one of whose parts is impossible
> *per se*, if in the case all of the conditions with the sign
> of exclusion [Preciseness Clause] are added to it, is
> insoluble simply.

Disjunctive Insoluble Rule II.

> A proposition appearing to be a disjunctive insoluble
> one of whose parts is contingently false is an insoluble
> according to a condition, by adding to it in the case all
> conditions with the sign of exclusion [Preciseness Clau-
> se].

Disjunctive Insoluble Rule III.

> Every disjunctive insoluble is insoluble according to a
> condition by adding to it in the case all conditions ex-
> cept the sign of exclusion [Preciseness Clause].

Again, the rules for disjunctive insolubles are divided into those for disjunctives with modal operators (I and II) and without modal operators
(III). We note also the central feature of the Preciseness Clause whose
addition or deletion from the case usually determines whether or not an
insoluble is to be admitted.

The *Logica Parva* treatment of non-apparent insolubles, i.e., those which
contain no explicit reference to their own truth or falsity, is simply an
extension of the approach described thus far.[15] For these need to be
identified as insolubles, and a decision concerning their admission or non-
admission must be made. Examples of such insolubles are: "(A) "Socrates
will not have a dime", or (A) "[Socrates] will not cross the bridge". Insolubles of this type are always presented with a case; and, as usual, the
student must scrutinize the case before responding. The three clauses —
(1) Uniqueness, (2) Existence and (3) Preciseness — are the main conditions relative to the question of admission or non-admission. If an examiner should posit a proposition of this sort together with a case which
omits the Preciseness Clause, the statements are insoluble according to a
condition and so are to be admitted. Admission of an insoluble proposition,
into the context of an *obligatio* is only the second step in Paul's three-part
procedure.

c. Solution

The third step is solution *(solutio)*. Before explaining this part of the method it will be instructive to reflect on some of the implications of previous
discussions. To be subject to solution a statement must be an insoluble

according to condition. For only such an insoluble is possible, and only propositions which are possible can be admitted into an *obligatio*. Recall obligation rule I: "Everything *possible* which is posited to you is to be admitted by you".[16] Thus, to be a candidate for solution, an insoluble must already have passed the tests previously discussed. And many insolubles do not pass these tests. It follows that solutions will be called for in a relatively limited number of cases. This point is important; for much of the literature has overemphasized solution and neglected the other aspects of Paul's treatment of insolubles.[17]

Paul of Venice's method for solving insolubles rests on the principle that every insoluble proposition has both a surface and a deep structure, and that its deep structure always has a greater degree of complexity than its surface structure. He says in several places that an insoluble proposition has a conjunctive form: "It signifies a conjunctive proposition just as any insoluble does."[18] And later, "any insoluble according to a condition signifies conjunctively...".[19] This principle implies the following. An insoluble statement (A) "(A) is false" is not, as it first appears, simple and categorical in form. It is rather hypothetical and conjunctive; for every such statement has a statement conjoined to it: namely, "(A) is true". And the same applies to insolubles which first appear complex and hypothetical in form. For example, the conjunctive insoluble (A) "God exists and no conjunctive proposition is true", has conjoined to it "(A) is true". The significate of the insoluble given first in each of these examples is called "the adequate significate". The significate of each of the insolubles conjoined with the statement of its truth is called "the principal significate". In general, we may say that Paul of Venice's practice implies that any insoluble with a surface complexity of degree X has a deep complexity of degree X+1. Is this principle justified? It is, I submit, a direct consequence of the first rule of obligations: "Everything possible which is posited to you is to be admitted by you."[20] A proposition must be *possible* in order to qualify for admission into the positive obligation *(positio)*. To paraphrase Paul's teaching, with regard to its adequate significate an insoluble is possible; with regard to its principal significate it is impossible.[21] For a respondent in admitting an insoluble proposition (A) to state "and (A) is true" is nothing more than to express his belief that (A) is possible. It is, of course, the prerogative of the respondent to specify the sense in which he admits or does not admit a proposition.

By definition, however, an insoluble falsifies itself and so is *eo ipso* false. Hence, the insoluble proposition conjoined with a statement that it is true will always produce a false conjunctive proposition. But according to obligation rule VIII: "Because a possible thing is posited, an impossible is not to be conceded nor is a necessary thing to be denied. For nothing in-

consistent is to be conceded nor is something following to be denied."[22]
Or again to paraphrase the text, an insoluble is to be admitted because its adequate significate is possible; it is to be denied because its principal significate is impossible. In other words, once admitted into the *obligatio*, the insoluble proposition is to be denied. And this is just what Paul of Venice routinely does.

To illustrate how the method works, consider the following example:

(A): (A) is false.

Here is a proposition which asserts itself to be false. Hence it meets the definition of an apparent insoluble arising from the property of an expression. (See Definition, Distinctions and Classification.) Moreover, it need not be presented with a case; and it is an insoluble according to a condition. (See insoluble rule IV, fourth variation.) For all these reasons the proposition is to be admitted. (See admission rule I.) Because it is an insoluble, however, it is admitted with the added stipulation that it is true. (See obligation rule I.) Thus, we get:

(A): (A) is false and (A) is true.

The first conjunct is true because this proposition is possible "Every (A) is false" and this (A) (pointing to the above) is some (A). The second conjunct is false because it contradicts the first conjunct. But a conjunction one of whose conjuncts is false is false; and thus it is to be denied. (See obligation rule VII.) From the denial of a false proposition, however, nothing absurd follows. Hence, by this method of responding to insolubles posited initially the examinee is saved from contradiction.

Conclusion

We have presented Paul of Venice's three-step procedure for dealing with insolubles. (1) IDENTIFICATION: The various definitions, distinctions and classifications are designed to help the examinee detect among all statements posited to him initially those which are insoluble. (2) ADMISSION: The rules of admission assist the examinee in distinguishing those statements which are insoluble simply from those which are insoluble according to a condition. The former are not to be admitted; the latter are to be admitted. For an insoluble according to a condition is true in one respect, false in another. (3) SOLUTION: The third step of the method consists in specifying the sense in which an insoluble is true and the sense in which it is false. An insoluble is to be admitted into an *obligatio* with respect to its truth; it is to be denied within the context of the *obligatio* with regard to its falsity. It is important to note that the Chapter on Insolubles sets forth formal rules only for the first two steps in the procedure. The rules for solution — if one may so call them — are not presented formally in Chapter VI. They are inferred from Paul of Venice's practice and remarks as well as Chapter V's Rules of Obligations.

Notes

1 For the background of medieval *insolubilia* see Spade, 2, De Rijk, 3. Concerning the 14th century see Roure, Scott, 1, 2, Burge and Weisheipl, 1, 2. On the later tradition (after 1400) see Ashworth 3 and 7 and Bottin, 2. Fr. Weisheipl notes, "the intimate relation between *insolubilia* and *obligationes*", in Weisheipl, 2, p. 166. For an interpretation of this relation see Perreiah, 6.

2 *Logica Parva*, p. [142] ff. Professor Spade notes that the phrase "falsifies itself" betrays the influence of Roger Swyneshed. See Spade, 3, Item 6 XIII.

3 For apparent insolubles see *Logica Parva*, pp. [143]–[149]. For non-apparent insolubles see *Logia Parva*, pp. [159]–[163].

4 *Logica Pava*, p. [146].

5 *Logica Parva*, p. [143].

6 *Logica Parva*, p. [143]. Professor Spade notes that the phrase "signifying precisely as the terms pretend", derives from Heytesbury. See Spade, 3, Item LXIX and additional references there.

7 *Logica Parva*, p. [144].

8 *Logica Parva*, pp. [144]–[145].

9 *Logica Parva*, p. [145].

10 *Logica Parva*, p. [146].

11 *Logica Parva*, p. [145].

12 *Logica Parva*, p. [155].

13 *Logica Parva*, p. [155]–[156].

14 *Logica Parva*, pp. [157]–[158].

15 *Logica Parva*, pp. [159]–[163].

16 *Logica Parva*, p. [118], emphasis added.

17 Three authors have offered interpretations of Paul of Venice's method for solving insolubles (1) Fr. Bocheński in 1, 2, pp. 237–251, and 3; (2) Professor Bottin, 2; (3) Professor Ashworth, 7, especially pp. 77–81. Each of these interpretations is examined critically in Perreiah, 6.

18 *Logica Parva*, p. [144].

19 *Logica Parva*, p. [147].

20 See above note 16.

21 *Logica Parva*, p. [162].

22 *Logica Parva*, p. [121].

Dialectica

The preceding six essays have stressed the didactic side of Paul of Venice's teaching. They have sought to elaborate and to explicate the central ideas in each chapter. Careful reading of the text, however, will reveal in Paul's approach still another side to which we have alluded only in passing. That is the practice of dialectical argumentation. It is one thing to set forth a doctrine — in this case the definitions, distinctions and rules of a theory of logical form. It is quite another to defend one's views against opposition or to justify them in the face of criticism. While dialectical argumentation occurs here and there in the first half of the work, it is ubiquitous in the second half. But Paul of Venice does not engage in dialectical reasoning in a merely haphazard manner. He recognizes definite forms of dialectical reasoning and each of these is consciously employed in the *Logica Parva*. What are those forms? Where do they occur in the work? And how are they to be understood? These are the central questions of the present essay.

The study is divided into two sections. The first surveys the types of dialectical reasoning recognized in the later Middle Ages and identifies each of these in the eight chapters of the *Logica Parva*. The second investigates various techniques of argumentation which are used by Paul of Venice. A conclusion will comment on the purposes of dialectical reasoning in this work.

I. Background

Aristotle defines reasoning *(sullogismus)* as a discourse in which from certain propositions laid down other propositions follow of necessity.[1] Thus, in Aristotle's text reasoning may be done by ordinary persons no less than by specialists; and among specialists it may be performed by the rhetorician and the poet as well as by the scientist and the philosopher. By the early 13th century Aristotle's fourfold division of reasoning *(sullogismus)* in the *Topics* was familiar:

A philosopheme *(philosophema)* is a demonstrative inference; an epichireme *(epichirema)* is a dialectical inference; a sophism *(sophisma)* is a conten-

tious inference; an aporeme *(aporema)* is an inference that reasons dia-
lectically to a contradiction.[2]

Each of these forms of syllogism is distinguishable from the others by (a)
the nature of its premises, (b) the characteristics of its internal structure,
(c) the features of its conclusion and (d) the purpose to which it is put. A
philosopheme is an inference performed on premises which are universal
and necessary: and if done according to the rules of formal deduction, it
yields a conclusion which is equally universal and necessary.[3] This form
of reasoning is demonstration in the strict sense and it is used primarily
in the acquisition of scientific knowledge. The sophism by contrast is a
spurious form of reasoning.[4] It begins with premises which are true or
which might be granted by a hearer, and it appears to conform to the
canons of rational thought; but it concludes with a statement which is
manifestly false and unacceptable. Because valid reasoning cannot yield
a false conclusion from true premises, every sophism masks a mistake of
one sort or another in reasoning. The epichireme is a form of argument
which begins with any premises granted by a respondent.[5] It is important
to note that these premises need be neither true nor necessary. Proceeding
according to accepted rules of inference, the epichireme produces a conclusion which may be either true or false. Normally this form of argument
is called into play in order to examine some controversial topic and to show
that the views held by an adversary are false. It is thus the primary instrument for examining any topic with respect to which scientific knowledge
is not possible and it is a ready tool for the refutation of an opponent.
Finally, the aporeme begins with premises which are granted by a respondent, proceeds according to convential rules of inference and arrives at a
conclusion which is contradictory either in itself or in relation to other
acceptable propositions.[6] All of these forms of dialectical reasoning are
found in the *Logica Parva* but chiefly the latter two types.

Taken by themselves Chapters I and III offer straightforward exposition
of the doctrines of logical form propounded in them. Read together with
Chapters VII and VIII the earlier two chapters take on an entirely new
dimension: for the main postulates of the earlier two chapters become the
controversial topics subjected to epichiremic argument in the later two
chapters. Just how this comes about as well as some details of these dialectical exchanges will be explored in Section II. Of all the Chapters of the
Logica Parva Chapter II is remarkable for the fact that it contains almost
no trace of dialectical reasoning. Nor are its central doctrines of supposition submitted anywhere in the work to dialectical scrutiny and criticism.
Chapter IV, as we saw, introduces sophisms at the end of each section,
and these accumulate to a total of more than seven dozen. Chapter V

illustrates the theory of obligations by actually engaging the hearer or reader in a number of *obligationes*. Similarly, Chapter VI produces some insolubles in order to illustrate its central doctrines. But the fundamental form of dialectical reasoning which operates in the *obligatio* (of which the insolubles may be a part) is the aporeme.[7] Recall that the respondent in the obligation agrees to be exercised or examined on some thesis which he either accepts or rejects, and that the purpose of the opponent is to elicit premises which would lead to the opposite of the respondent's view. Because the aim of the opponent is to produce a conclusion which contradicts the thesis held by the respondent, the underlying dialectical structure of the *obligatio* (with or without the insoluble) is the aporeme. The respondent who fails to block the progress of his opponent falls clearly into a state of perplexity which is the appropriate mental state for a respondent whose reasoning has led to a contradiction. Since we have already said a number of things about the scientific syllogism (philosopheme), the sophism and the aporeme, we will concentrate in the next section on the epichireme and in particular on Paul of Venice's techniques of argumentation in Chapters VII and VIII.

II. Applications

The practice of dialectical argumentation in a medieval text is shot through with a technical organization and vocabulary which are foreign to most modern readers. Yet to follow these texts one must know not only what an author says and means but how his language is deployed in actual instances of dialectical reasoning. We could select a segment from almost any part of the *Logica Parva* which exhibits dialectical as opposed to didactic argumentation; but for simplicity's sake, we begin with the two main paragraphs of Chapter VII, Section 1:[8]

(1) First, against the definition of a proposition i.e., "a proposition is an indicative expression signifying what is true or false", one can argue in this way.[9] (2.a) "Antichrist were white" *(Antichristus esset albus)* is a proposition; (2.b) yet it is not indicative. (2.c) Therefore, the definition of a proposition is not sufficient. (3) The inference is solid with regard to the minor premise; and I prove the major premise. (4.a) For every antecedent of a conditional is a proposition, (4.b) but "Antichrist were white", is an antecedent of a conditional; (4.c) therefore, it is a proposition. (5) This conclusion is valid because this is a syllogism in the third mood of the first figure. (6) And the major is also clear because a conditional proposition is that in which many categorical propositions are joined together by

means of a sign of a condition. (7) I prove the minor premise; for the antecedent of this conditional proposition, "if Antichrist were white, Antichrist would be colored", is that expression, "Antichrist were white".

(1) recalls Paul of Venice's definition of a proposition from Chapter I, and announces an argument against it. (2) pictures in outline the opposing argument:

(2.a) "Antichrist were white", is a proposition,   (Major premise)
(2.b) "Antichrist were white", is not indicative,   (Minor premise)
(2.c) Therefore, some proposition is not indicative.   (Conclusion)

This is an argument by counter-example that (2.c) contradicts Paul's definition. The force of (2.c) is put in this way: "The definition of a proposition is not sufficient." (3) allows that the passage from (2.c) is an acceptable inference insofar as it depends upon the minor premise (2.b). (2.b) is taken to be evidently true and so needs no argument. (4) offers a proof of the major premise (2.a):

(4.a) Every antecedent of a conditional is a proposition.   (Major Premise)
(4.b) "Antichrist were white", is an antecedent of a conditional.
      (Minor Premise)
(4.c) Therefore, ["Antichrist were white"] is a proposition.   (Conclusion)

Again, (5) admits that the passage from (4.a) to (4.c) is a valid inference because it is an instance of a syllogism in Barbara. (6) offers additional evidence in defense of (4.a): namely, the definition of a conditional proposition as "that in which many categoricals are joined together by means of a sign of a condition". Finally (7) gives a proof of (4.b):

(7.a) Any proposition which precedes the sign of the condition
     is the antecedent of that conditional.   (Major Premise)
(7.b) But in "If Antichrist were white, Antichrist would be colored",
     "Antichrist were white", precedes the sign of the conditional.
      (Minor Premise)
(7.c) Therefore, "Antichrist were white", is the antecedent of
     a conditional.   (Conclusion)

Note that (7.a) is not expressed in the text; but it is assumed. (7.b) is explicit in the text and (7.c) is interchangeable with (4.b). In summary, the objection to Paul's definition is expressed in the principal argument (2.a) − (2.c). Where the minor premise is taken to be true without argument, the major premise is backed by a subordinate argument (4.a) − (4.c). In this subordinate argument the major premise (4.a) is confirmed by the definition of a conditional proposition and the minor premise (4.b) is again backed by a subordinate argument (7.a) – (7.c).

Every objection which is raised against a point in Paul of Venice's theory is met by a response; and we shall examine Paul's reply to the objection outlined above.[10]

(8) One may respond by conceding the definition of a proposition; but I deny that this expression, "Antichrist were white", is a proposition. (9) And then with regard to the argument I deny this major premise, "every antecedent of a conditional is a proposition". (10) And when this is proved through a definition of a conditional viz., "a conditional proposition is that in which many categoricals are joined together by means of a sign of a condition", I say that this definition is false taken in virtue of expression *(de virtute sermonis)*.[11] (11) For it means that a conditional is that in which either many categorical (propositions) are joined together or many expressions are related through a categorical mode *(se habentis per modum categoricae)*. (12) However, in the conditional proposition in question not many categorical [propositions] but rather many expressions are related through a categorical mode. (13) Whence this expression, "Antichrist were white", is not a categorical proposition, but an expression related through a categorical mode. (14) For it has its principal parts through the mode of subject, of predicate and of copula.

(8) States Paul's acceptance of his opponent's definition of a proposition as well as Paul's denial of (2.a) " 'Antichrist were white' is a proposition", the major premise of the principal argument, (4.c) which is interchangeable with (2.a), follows from (4.a); and (9) attacks (4.a). According to Paul (4.a) is false because it follows from a faulty interpretation of a conditional proposition as "that in which many categoricals are joined together by means of a sign of a condition". On Paul's analysis this formula is ambiguous: "categoricals" may be *either* (1) "categorical propositions" *or* (2) "expressions related through a categorical mode". (12), (13) and (14) state Paul's contention that the counter example cited in the objection is a categorical only in sense (2). In this sequence of objections and replies Paul's strategy is first to recount the opposing argument in some detail and then to attack the major premise on which the conclusion of that argument rests. His own counter argument consists in showing that the premise is ambiguous as it stands, and that when its ambiguities are sorted out, the objection to his original definition is not sustained.

For a somewhat different example of dialectical reasoning we turn to an argument midway through Chapter VIII. It concerns the second rule from Group IV, "From a negative exceptive proposition to its corresponding affirmative exclusive proposition there is a solid inference".[12]

(1) Against this rule one argues in this way. (1.a) This inference does not follow: "No man except Socrates runs; therefore, only Socrates runs." (1.b) And this is argued according to the rule. (1.c) Therefore, the rule is false. (2) This inference holds with respect to the minor premise because it does not seem to be other than an exceptive proposition. (3) the major premise is proved because in a possible case posited the antecedent is true, and the consequent is false. (4) This is proved: for I posit that Socrates runs and no other masculine being runs: however, many women run. (5) With this posited, the antecedent is true through its exponents, and the consequent is false because some non-Socrates runs; therefore, it is not the case that only Socrates runs.

(6) One may respond that this exclusive proposition does not correspond to that exceptive proposition; but rather this proposition, "only Socrates is some man running", according to what was stated concerning the proofs of terms in the section on exceptive propositions where this rule was declared.[13]

(1) states in brief the objection to the rule. It offers an inference from one negative exceptive proposition to an exclusive proposition, and asserts that this inference follows the rule. Here is the pattern of the principal objection:

(1.a) This inference does not follow: "No man except Socrates
       runs; therefore, only Socrates runs."   (Major Premise)
(1.b) This (1.a) is argued according to the rule,   (Minor Premise)
(1.c) Therefore, the rule is false.   (Conclusion)

(2) acknowledges that (1.b) is true, i.e., that the statement "no man except Socrates runs", is an exceptive proposition. It will comment on the exclusive, "only Socrates runs", in a moment. Then, the criticism turns to the task of supporting (1.a). (3) says that in a possible case posited the antecedent is true, and the consequent is false. (4) presents the possible case. Consider a universe within which Socrates runs but no other masculine being runs; however, many women run. In such a universe, the antecedent, "no man except Socrates runs", will be true; but the consequent, "only Socrates runs", will be false. And this is just what (5) declares.

Paul's reply to this objection takes issue with the conclusion of the example cited in the case.[14] "Only Socrates runs", is not the exclusive which corresponds correctly to the negative exceptive, "no man except Socrates runs". The exclusive which correctly corresponds to that exceptive is rather: "Only Socrates is some man running." And in support of this analysis he refers us to the section on exceptive propositions.[15]

As a third example of Paul's dialectical practice we select an objection and reply from Chapter VIII near the end of the entire work. It is the criticism of the third rule of inference from Group VII. (7.3) "From an affirmative disjunctive proposition with the destruction of one of its parts to the other part there is a solid inference."[16] Here is the text:

(1) Against the rule one argues in this way: (1.a) This inference does not follow: "You are a donkey or you are not a donkey: but you are not a donkey; therefore, you are a donkey."[17] For the antecedent is true, and the consequent is false, as is clear. (1.b) Yet it is argued according to the rule. (1.c) Therefore the rule is false.

(2) One may respond that it is not argued according to the rule because in the second part of the antecedent the contradictory of the first part of the disjunctive proposition occurs; (3) or the second part of the disjunctive expression follows if the opposite of the first part is assumed. It is clear that this [objection] is not argued according to the rule because the other part is not implied, namely, "you are not a donkey". And with that implication, the inference and the conclusion is conceded. (4) If, however, one says that for the second part of the antecedent there is another disjunctive expression implying a different [proposition] one responds that it is not argued according to the rule. (5) For its contradictory ought to be taken in this way: (5.a) "You are a donkey or you are not a donkey; (5.b) but you are a donkey; (5.c) therefore, you are a donkey." (6) However, the minor premise is denied.

(1) Introduces this objection to the rule.
(1.a) This inference does not follow: "You are a donkey or you are not a donkey; but you are not a donkey, therefore, you are a donkey." For the antecedent is true and the consequent is false.

(Major Premise)
(1.b) Yet it is argued according to the rule.   (Minor Premise)
(1.c) Therefore, the rule is false.   (Conclusion)

Far from being an application of the principle of Disjunctive Syllogism, this objection rests on a fallacy. The correct form of Disjunctive Syllogism is:

$$[(P \vee Q) \cdot \sim P] \to Q$$

Here is the argument carried out according to the rule:

I.   You are a donkey or you are not a donkey.
II. But you are not a donkey.
III. Therefore, you are not a donkey.

(2) and (3) say this in so many words. (4) sums up the objection and (5) offers an argument by *reductio ad absurdum* to the same conclusion.

I.   You are a donkey or you are not a donkey.
II. But you are a donkey.
     (= It is not the case that you are not a donkey.)
III. Therefore you are a donkey.

This argument is valid, but it is unsound. The conclusion is false because one of the premises, "you are a donkey", is false. Hence, the original rule is sustained; for the objection against it is seen to be fallacious.

Conclusion

As we have noted Chapters VII and VIII are devoted respectively to the systematic criticism of many of the definitions of Chapter I and to most of the rules of Chapter III. But that should not lead us to think that the last two chapters of the *Logica Parva* serve exactly the same purpose.

Chapter VII begins with a statement of its purpose: "In order that the knowledge of [Chapter I] may be committed to memory, I present certain objections against its rules and definitions, and the solution of these will bring out new clarity."[18] This strongly suggests that Paul's purpose is not primarily logical but rather pedagogical. By considering the arguments *pro et contra* the student is able to see the clear sense of the master's teachings and thus is better able to commit them to memory. This idea echoes that given in the earlier Chapters where dialectical arguments are introduced. For example, sophisms are used in Chapters I and IV to illustrate the subject at hand and to challenge the student to resolve those sophisms by calling into play the definitions, distinctions and rules propounded. Where he engages in the aporematic form of dialectical argumentation in Chapters V and VI it is clearly, again, for the purpose of illustrating his doctrines.[19] Moreover, it affords the student an opportunity to confront an aporematic form of argument first hand and to deal with it according to the prescribed rules.

Chapter VIII begins with a markedly different statement of purpose: "Having understood the objections against [Chapters I and VII] here follows last as was stated in the beginning: namely, the material to strengthen the rules of inference."[20] The subsequent discussions of objections to the rules as well as Paul's resolutions of them allude to "*the* sense of the rule" (my italics). In addition to repeating the pedagogical aim, this statement suggests another way to view the dialectical arguments of Chapter VIII. That is to see them as so many indirect proofs or proofs by *reductio ad absurdum* of Paul's original rules. From this perspective, the objections to Paul's rules amount to so many efforts to show that they lead to ab-

116

surdity. If they do indeed imply absurd consequences the hearer or reader would be justified by the method of *reductio ad absurdum* in rejecting the rules from which those absurdities follow. But, by the same token, if Paul's replies effectively refute those objections, so far from constituting proof against them, they offer additional evidence for their truth.

Whether Paul's purpose in advancing dialectical arguments is primarily logical or pedagogical, there is no question that he has a legitimate purpose. He is not arguing merely "for the sake of argument". Nor is he spawning dialectical arguments simply to confuse a hearer or reader. He has a serious, as opposed to a sophistic, purpose. The specimens of dialectical reasoning chosen for this essay are of a medium degree of complexity. Some arguments in the text are less difficult; still others are more so. However, the general patterns of objection and reply, of principal argument and supporting argument are found throughout. And the issues of solidity of reasoning as well as truth or falsity of premises must be settled in each case. Paul strives to give *both* the customary typical objection to the doctrines he holds *and* the strongest replies which he has at his disposal. In some cases, as in some of the texts examined above, his counter arguments may not impress us. We may feel that he has presented a weak objection to a questionable thesis. Or that he has given a shaky reply to a strong objection. On occasion we might think that his reply borders dangerously on a quibble. But the content of these exchanges is not nearly so important as the form of them. Dialectical argumentation of any variety is instructive because it exposes the mind to the pros and cons of any proposition tendered for acceptance or rejection. And only by becoming involved in such arguments can the student come to have a clearer knowledge and a better command of the ideas which he seeks to understand.

Notes

1. Aristotle. 2. 24a, 18.
2. Aristotle, 4, *Topics* III, 11, 162a, 8 ff. While the history of dialectical reasoning has not yet been written there are a number of works worth consulting in this regard. On Plato see Robinson and Ryle, 2. On Aristotle Evans and Owen. On the Stoics see Long, "Dialectic and the Stoic Sage", in Rist. On Augustine see Jackson. On Boethius see Stump. On Abelard see De Rijk, 1, pp. 91–92 and 4. On John of Salisbury, see Salisbury. On the later tradition see Vives. Good general discussions may be found in Kneale, pp. 7–16.
3. Aristotle 2, 3. See also, Kneale, pp. 64–100.
4. Aristotle, 4; Kneale, p. 12 ff.; Evans, p. 8 ff. Professor Scott offers a useful distinction between three kinds of problem sentences in later medieval logic: *insolubilia, impossibilia* and *sophismata*. "An

insoluble was a proposition arrived at by apparently valid forms of reasoning, which nonetheless implies its own contradictory. An impossible was a proposition whose contradictory is evident, so that it cannot be demonstrated.... The sophisms designated simply *sophismata* were characterized more broadly as propositions seeming to follow from well-established rules, which yet are somehow unacceptable or present special problems." Scott, 1, p. 5.

5   Aristotle, 2. See also Stump, pp. 159–178.
6   Aristotle, 2, *Topics* VIII. While essential to Aristotle's method of instruction in the *Metaphysics*, the work *On the Soul* and the *Nicomachean Ethics* the aporeme is the neglected member among the four species of syllogism distinguished above. The best treatment of this form of argumentation is in Owens, pp. 211–258.
7   See Chapters V and VI, pp. 214–256.
8   *Logica Parva*, p. [163].
9   The definition of a proposition was presented earlier. See *Logica Parva*, pp. [4]–[5].
10 *Logica Parva*, p. [163].
11 To take a term or proposition "in virtue of expression" is to understand it in an unqualified or improper or metaphorical sense. The phrase "in virtue of expression" *(de virtute sermonis)* has an important history in the Middle Ages. For an interesting discussion of its meaning see Boehner, 6, pp. 248–254.
12 *Logica Parva*, p. [210]. For the statement of the rule see *Logica Parva*, p. [74].
13 *Logica Parva*, p. [74].
14 *Logica Parva*, p. [210].
15 *Logica Parva*, p. [44].
16 *Logica Parva*, p. [227]. For the statement of the rule see *Logica Parva*, p. [79].
17 *Logica Parva*, p. [227].
18 *Logica Parva*, p. [162].
19 See Chapters V and VI, pp. 214–256.
20 *Logica Parva*, p. [189].

Paul of Venice

Logica Parva

Chapter I
Terms, Propositions and Arguments

[1] Looking at the range of books in which the great number of students find mental tedium, not to mention the other books whose excessive brevity includes practically no theory, and wanting to hold the mean and the essence of either extreme, I composed a useful compendium divided into several chapters for young students. Of these *summulae* the first treats the term *(noticiam)*. The second expounds the matter of supposition. The third examines the doctrine of inferences. The fourth instructs on the ways of proving terms. The fifth teaches the rules of obligations. The sixth gives the way of solving insolubles. The seventh objects to the first chapter adding a responsive solution. The eighth indeed strengthens through argument the third chapter. Since, therefore, any doctrine takes its beginning from more common things, as the Philosopher says in the first book of the *Physics*, the first chapter begins by defining the nature of a term.[a]

Section 1 – Term

A term *(terminus)* is a sign which makes up a statement *(oratio)* as a proximate part of it. Examples: "man", "animal". And note that it says "proximate part" because a statement *(oratio)* has proximate and remote parts. A proximate part is called an expression *(dictio)*. A remote part is called a letter or a syllable. An expression *(dictio)* is a term and not a letter or a syllable of it.

The first division of terms is that into significative and non-significative.[b] A term *per se* significative is that [2] which taken by itself *(per se)* represents something, e.g., man or animal. A term which is non-significative *per se* is that which taken by itself represents nothing: e.g., "every" *(omnis)*, "no" *(nullus)*, and the like.

The second division of terms is that into terms which signify naturally *(naturaliter)* and terms which signify by convention *(ad placitum)*. A term which signifies naturally is one which is representative of the same for everyone: e.g., "man", "animal" in the mind *(in mente)*. A term which signifies by convention is one which is not representative of the same for everyone: e.g., the term "man" *(homo)* in speech or in script which among us signifies men and among certain other nations signifies nothing, for example among those who are Greeks or Hebrews.

The third division of terms is that into categorematic and syncategorematic. A categorematic term is that which *per se* as well as with another [term] has a proper significate: e.g., "man". Whether it is put in a statement *(oratione)* or outside of it, it always signifies men. A syncategorematic term is that which has a function which taken *per se* is significative of nothing: e.g., universal signs "every", "no" and the like. Also particular signs: e.g., "some", "certain", etc., and prepositions, adverbs and conjunctions. Distributive signs, then, have functions because they determine distributively and particular [signs] particularly. Prepositions determine in a certain case; adverbs modify the verb, and conjunctions have the function of joining terms and statements *(orationes)*.

The fourth division of terms is into terms of prime and second intention. A term of prime intention is a mental term [3] signifying what is not a term: i.e., signifying a thing which is not a term, given that it should exist. Thus "man" signifies Socrates and Plato neither of which is a mental term. Nor can they be a term. A term of second intention is a term signifying only a term or a proposition: e.g., the mental term "noun" *(nomen)*, "verb" *(verbum)*, "participle", "proposition", "statement" *(oratio)*.

The fifth division of terms is that into prime imposition and second imposition. A term of prime imposition is a vocal or written term signifying not a term but a thing *(rem)*; "man", "animal" in speech or in script would be examples. A term of second imposition is a vocal or written term signifying as well a term or a proposition; these are vocal or written terms: "noun" *(nomen)*, "verb", "participle".

The sixth division of terms is into complex and incomplex. A complex term is a phrase *(oratio)* like "white man" or "God to be". An incomplex term is a term which is called an expression *(dictio)* like "stone", "wood", and the like.

Section 2 – Noun

Because the logician principally considers nouns and verbs from which a statement *(oratio)* and a proposition *(propositio)* are composed here are some definitions. A noun is a term significative without time. No part of a noun signifies something separate: for example, man. This definition places it in the genus of a term; because every noun is a term; but not every term is a noun. Secondly, it says "significative" because those terms which are not significative are not nouns according to the logician; but they are nouns according to the grammarian; for example, "every", "no" and the like. Thirdly, [4] it says "without time" in order to differentiate it from verbs and participles which signify with time. Fourthly, it says "no part of which signifies something separate" *per se* in order to differentiate it from a statement whose parts signify objects separate [from it].

Section 3 — Verb

A verb is a term significative temporally and unitive of extremes.[a] No part of a verb signifies something separate; for example, "runs" and "disputes". It says "significative temporally" first to differentiate it from a noun which signifies without time. Secondly, it says "unitive of extremes" in order to differentiate it from a participle which signifies with time; but it does not unite an object *(suppositum)* with an apposite *(apposito)*, as a verb does. The remaining parts of the definition then are just like those in the definition of a noun.

Section 4 — Statement

A statement *(oratio)* is a term some of whose parts signify something separate: for example, "white man", *(homo albus)* and "God to be", *(deum esse)*. The last point is made in order to differentiate it from a noun and a verb whose parts do not signify anything separate. Statements *(orationum)* are perfect or imperfect. A perfect statement is what generates a perfect sense in the mind of a hearer: e.g., "a white man runs". An imperfect statement is that which generates an imperfect sense in the mind of a hearer: e.g., "white man". Among perfect statements, some are indicative like "a man runs", some are imperative like "Peter, teach John", others are optative like "if only I could love God with a pure heart", still others are subjunctive like "if you honor me, I will give you a horse".

Section 5 — Proposition

A proposition *(propositio)* is an indicative statement *(oratio)* signifying what is true or false; for example, "a man runs". First, it says "statement" *(oratio)* [5] just to describe the genus; because every proposition is a statement but not conversely. And it says "indicative" because only an indicative [sentence] is a proposition and not an imperative or an optative or a subjunctive. Lastly, it says "signifying what is true or false" because of propositions like these: "Socrates can", "Plato begins", which though indicative are not propositions because they do not signify what is true or false. Rather they are imperfect statements.

Section 6 — Divisions of the Proposition

Divisions under proposition are the following: First, propositions are divided into categorical and hypothetical. A categorical proposition is one which has a subject, a predicate and a copula as its principal parts, e.g., "a man is an animal", "man" is the subject; "animal" is the predicate, and the copula is always that verb "is" because it conjoins the subject with the predicate. And if someone says "a man runs" *(homo currit)* is a categorical proposition but it does not have a predicate, it can be replied that it has an implicit predicate, viz., "running". This is clear by analyzing *(resolvendo)* that verb "runs" into "I am", "you are", "it is" and its participle. Now the subject is that of which something is said. And the predicate is that which is said of another. But the copula always is the substantive verb, e.g., I am, you are, it is. Later we will talk about the hypothetical proposition which differs from the categorical proposition.[a] [For the principal parts of the hypothetical proposition are not subject and predicate but rather many categorical propositions.]

Secondly, categorical propositions are divided into affirmative and negative. An affirmative categorical proposition is one in which the principal verb is affirmed, e.g., "a man runs". A [6] negative categorical proposition is one in which the principal verb is negated, "a man does not run".

Thirdly, categorical propositions are divided into true and false.[a] A true categorical proposition is one whose primary and adequate significate is true; e.g., "you are a man". This proposition, then, "you are a man" is true because "that you are a man" is true *(te esse hominem est verum)*. I call, then, the primary and adequate significate of a proposition that which is like a statement *(simile orationi)* in the infinite or conjunctive sense: [whence I call "you are a man" *(te esse hominem)* or "you are a man" *(tu es homo)* the primary and adequate significate of] "you are a man" *(tu es homo)*. Further, then, it signifies you to be an animal, you to be a substance and the like. These others are called "secondary significates" and with regard to them that proposition is not said to be true or false. A false categorical proposition is one whose adequate significate is false: e.g., "you are a donkey".

Fourthly, categorical propositions are divided into possible and impossible. A possible categorical proposition is one whose primary [and adequate] significate is possible, e.g., "you run". An impossible categorical proposition is one whose primary [and adequate] significate is impossible: e.g., "a man is a donkey".

Fifthly, categorical propositions are divided into contingent and necessary. A contingent categorical proposition is one whose primary and adequate significate is contingent: e.g., "you are in Rome". I call that significate "contingent" which indifferently can be true or false. A necessary categorical proposition is one whose primary and adequate significate is necessary: e.g., "God is".

Sixthly, categorical propositions are divided into those of some quantity or those of no quantity. A categorical proposition of some quantity is a proposition which is either universal, [7] particular, singular or indefinite. A universal categorical proposition is one in which a common determinate term is subjected to a universal sign: e.g., "every man runs". A common term in the present work I call an appellative name or a plural pronoun. Universal signs are these: "every", "no", "either", "neither", "any", "however many", "whoever" and the like. A particular proposition is one in which a determinate common term is subject to a particular sign: e.g., "some man runs". Particular signs, then, are: "a certain", "some", "one", "another", "other" *(quidam, aliquis, alter, ceter, reliquus)* and the like. An indefinite proposition is that in which the subject is a common term without some sign: e.g., "man runs", or "man is animal". A singular proposition is that in which a discrete term or a common term with a demonstrative pronoun [singular in number] is subject: e.g., "Socrates runs", "this man disputes". I call then a discrete or singular term a proper name or an appellative [word] with a demonstrative pronoun [singular in number]: e.g., "this" (masculine, feminine, neuter), "that" (masculine, feminine, neuter). From which one can see that there may be a categorical proposition of no quantity; and it is said to be that which is neither universal, nor particular, nor indefinite, nor singular. Exclusive and exceptive propositions are cited as examples: sc., "Only man runs". "Every man except Socrates runs".

With regard to the first, the second and the last divisions [remember] this verse:

Que ca vel hyp
Qualis ne vel af
V quanta par, in, sin.

In this verse the first part is understood to be an answer to the question [8] about the types of proposition, viz., categorical or hypotherical. The second asserts that in reply to a question about quality one answers: affirmative or negative. But in the third, to the question about quantity one responds: universal, particular, singular or indefinite. And these answers depend on the proposition which is proposed [in the question].

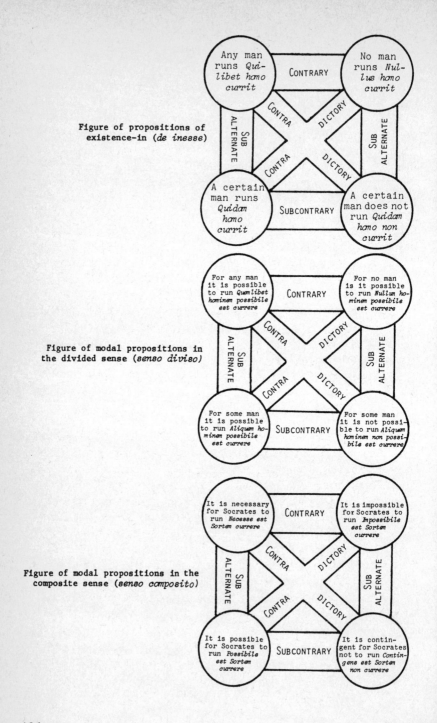

Figure of propositions of existence-in (*de inesse*)

Figure of modal propositions in the divided sense (*senso diviso*)

Figure of modal propositions in the composite sense (*senso composito*)

Section 7 – Two Additional Divisions

Beyond the above divisions two others are given. The first sets off categorical propositions of existence-in *(de inesse)* [i.e. assertoric propositions] from those which are modal.[a] A categorical proposition of existence-in is that in which no mode is posited: "a man runs", "man is animal". A categorical modal proposition is that in which some mode is posited: e.g., "it is possible that man runs" *(possibile est hominem currere)*. The modes then are six: possible, impossible, contingent, necessary, true or false. The second division is into modal propositions in the divided and the composite sense. A modal proposition in the divided sense is one in which the mode falls between the accusative case and the infinitive verb: e.g., "[for] Socrates it is possible to run" *(Sortem possibile est currere)*. A modal proposition in the composite sense is one in which a mode totally precedes or finally follows a statement: e.g., "[for] God to be is necessary" or "it is impossible [for] man to be a donkey". From these divisions come three figures: The first pertains to relations between propositions of existence-in. The second concerns modals in the divided sense having themselves the mode of the first figure. The third also relates to modals in the composite sense with respect to the other figures. These declarations are illustrated in the [preceding] diagram. [9]

Section 8 – Figures of the Propositions [10]

For the first as well as the second figure, then, there are these general rules. The first rule: a universal affirmative and a universal negative with like subjects, copulas and predicates standing for precisely the same thing or things are contraries in the figure. Example: "Any man runs" and "no man runs". The second rule: a particular affirmative and a particular negative with like subjects, copulas and predicates standing for precisely the same thing or things are subcontraries in the figure. Example: "A certain man runs" and "a certain man does not run". The third rule: a universal affirmative and a particular negative or a universal negative and a particular affirmative of like subjects, copulas and predicates standing precisely for the same thing or things are contradictories on the figure. Example: "Any man runs", and "a certain man does not run" or "a certain man runs" and "no man runs". The fourth rule: a universal affirmative and a particular affirmative as well as a universal negative and a particular negative of like subjects, copulas and predicates standing for the same thing or things are subalternates on the figure. Example: "Any man runs" and "a certain man runs" or "no man runs" and "a certain man does not run". From these state-

127

ments it follows that these are not contraries: "every *(omnis)* man runs" and "no *(nullus)* man runs". Nor are these contradictories: "every *(omnis)* man runs" and "a certain *(quidam)* man does not run". Because these terms do not stand for precisely the same thing or things. Nor are these [11] subalternates: "every man *(omnis homo)* runs" and "a certain man *(quidam homo)* runs" because always in one the terms stand for either sex; whereas in the other they stand for the masculine [sex] only.[a]

Section 9 — Nature of Propositions

Just as propositions are situated in the figure by four rules, in like manner the law and nature of them is understood by four other [rules]. The first: it is not possible that two contraries be simultaneously true; but they may well be simultaneously false. The first part of the rule is clear inductively to all; the second is proven because these statements are simultaneously false: "any man is white" and "no man is white". And similarly, "every animal is a man" and "no animal is a man". The second rule: it is not possible for two subcontraries to be simultaneously false but they may well be simultaneously true. The first part of the statement is clear by checking individual sentences, and the second part is proven because these statements are simultaneously true: "some man is white" and "some man is not white"; or "some animal is man" and "some animal is not man". The third rule: it is not possible for two contradictories to be simultaneously true or simultaneously false. This rule is clear by checking through individual contradictory sentences. The fourth rule: if a universal is true, then a particular and an indefinite subalternate is true but not conversely. Whence if this is true; "any man runs", this also is true, "a certain man runs", but not conversely because now *de facto* this is true, "some man runs", but this is not true: "any man runs". And one should speak in a similar way about all propositions having a subalternate.

Section 10 — Equipollent Propositions [12]

There are three rules of Equipollents. The first: a sentence with a negation posited before it is equipollent with the contradictory of the sentence. For "not: every man runs", is equipollent with "a certain man does not run". And "not: no man runs" is equipollent with "a certain man runs". The second rule: [a sentence with] a negation posited after it is equipollent with the contrary of the proposition. Proof: "any man does not run" is equipollent with "no man runs". And "no man does not run" is equipollent

128

with "any man runs". The third rule: [a sentence with] a negation posited before it and a negation posited after it is equipollent with the subalternate of the proposition. "not: any man does not run" is equipollent with "a certain man runs". And "not: no man does not run" is equipollent with "a certain man does not run". Thus the verse:

> Prae/contradic [it].
> Post/contra [riantur].
> Prae/postquam subalter [nantur].

This rule applies not only to the first and second figures but to the third figure as well. And I call a negation "posited before" when the negation is placed before the mode *(modo)* or the mode is placed before the entire sentence or is placed after the entire sentence. And I call it "posited after" when the negation is joined to a verb of infinitive mode. Example of the former: "it is not possible [for] Socrates to run" *(non possibile est Sortem currere)* or "[for] Socrates to run is not possible"*(Sortem currere non est possibile)*. Example of the latter: "it is possible [for] Socrates not to run" *(possibile est Sortem non currere)* or "[for] Socrates not to run is possible" *(Sortem non currere est possibile)*. This, therefore, "it is not possible [for] Socrates to run" is equipollent with "it is impossible [for] Socrates to run" *(Non possibile est Sortem currere equipollent isti impossibile est Sortem currere)*. This follows by the first rule. And "it is impossible [for] Socrates not to run" is equipollent with "it is necessary [for] Socrates to run". This follows by the second rule. And this may be said of any similar propositions. [13]

Section 11 – Conversion

Conversion is the transposition of a subject into a predicate and conversely; for example, "man is animal" and "animal is man". And conversion is divided into simple, accidental and contrapositional. Simple conversion is the transposition of a subject into a predicate and conversely – the quality and quantity of the proposition remaining: "no animal runs" and "no running thing is an animal". Accidental conversion is the transposition of a subject into a predicate and conversely with the quality remaining the same but with a reduction in quantity: for example, "every man is animal" and "a certain animal is a man". Contrapositional conversion is the transposition of a subject into a predicate with the quantity and quality of the proposition remaining the same but with a change of the finite term into infinite terms: for example, "a certain animal does not run", "a certain non-running thing is not non-animal". In order then to learn that propositions are converted in these ways there is a verse:

Feci simpliciter convertitur.
Eva per acci[*dens*].
Asto per contra[*positionem*].
Sic fit conversio tota.

In this verse there are four vocal letters, a, e, i, o. "A" signifies a universal affirmative. "E" signifies a universal negative. "I" signifies a particular or indefinite affirmative. "O" signifies a particular or indefinite or singular negative. The verse says *feci simpliciter* because a universal negative is converted simply into a universal negative, and a particular affirmative is converted simply into a particular affirmative. *Eva per acci*[*dens*] means that a universal negative and a universal affirmative are converted *per accidens*. *Asto per contra* says that a universal affirmative and a particular or [14] indefinite or singular negative are converted through contraposition. Of these, then, simple conversion is the more useful because universally if a converse is true, its convertend is also true and conversely. But accidental conversion and contrapositional conversion are not as useful. For in a conversion *per accidens* the converse is false, and the convertend is true; for example, "every animal is a man", (this is false) but its convertend is true: "a certain man is an animal". In contrapositional conversion the converse is true, and the convertend is false. For this is true, "some rose is not a substance" (assuming no rose exists). But this is false: "some non-substance is not non-rose". It is false because its contradictory is true; namely, "every non-substance is non-rose".

Against what was said concerning conversion one can argue. This is true: "no man is a woman" *(nullus homo est mulier)* and this is false "no woman is man" *(nulla mulier est homo)*. Secondly, this is true: "no house is in a man", however, this is false: "no man is in a house". Third, this is true: "no blind man sees being". However, this is false: "no being sees a blind man".

To the first, I reply that the sentence proffered is not the proper convertend but rather this: "no woman is some man" *(nulla mulier est aliquis homo)*, and this proposition ought to be similar in quantity in both the converse and the convertend. To the second, I reply that the sentence is not the proper convertend: but rather this, "nothing existing in a man is a house", and the terms of this proposition ought not to change in grammatical case. To the third, I reply that it is not [a conversion] of the subject into the predicate: because the predicate is not "being" but "seeing being" and this readily converts into "no seeing being is a blind man". [15]

Section 12 – Hypothetical Propositions

A hypothetical proposition is that which contains several categorical propositions joined by a sign *(notam)* of a condition, of a conjunction or of a disjunction or of signs equivalent to these. Example: "you are a man, and you are an animal". Thus there are three species of hypothetical proposition which are not equivalent in their signifying function; namely, conditional, conjunctive and disjunctive. Other conditions, namely local, causal and temporal are not hypothetical but categorical.[a]

A conditional proposition is that in which several categorical propositions are joined by a conditional sign; e.g., "if you are a man, you are an animal" *(si tu es homo, tu es animal)*. Conditional propositions are divided into affirmative and negative. An affirmative conditional proposition is that in which the sign of a condition is affirmed: e.g., "if you are a man, you are an animal". A negative conditional proposition is that in which the sign of a condition is negated; e.g., "not: if you are a man, you are a donkey". And this proposition is proved through its affirmative form.[b] For the truth of an affirmative conditional it is required and it suffices that the opposite of the consequent is repugnant to the antecedent; e.g., "if you are a man, you are an animal". The antecedent is that which immediately follows the sign of a condition; and it precedes the principal verb. The consequent is the second part of the expression or it is that proposition which follows the principal verb in the conditional or what is inferred from the antecedent. It is clear in this example, "you are a man" is the antecedent, and "you are an animal" is the consequent. For the falsity of an affirmative conditional it is required and suffices that the opposite of the consequent [16] stand with *(stet cum)* the antecedent; e.g., "if you are a man, you are sitting". Because these propositions stand at the same time "you are a man" and "you are not sitting", the above conditional is false. The same thing does not apply to propositions which are possible, impossible, necessary or contingent; for every conditional which is true is necessary and every conditional which is false is impossible. No conditional, then, is contingent.[a] These rules apply to conditionals containing *(denominata a)* "if" *(si)* and not to conditionals containing "unless" *(nisi)*.

Section 13 – Conjunctive Hypothetical Propositions

A conjunctive proposition is that which includes several categoricals joined by a sign of conjunction. Example: "you are a man and you are sitting". Conjunctive propositions are either affirmative or negative. An affirmative conjunctive proposition is that in which the sign of conjunction is affirmed:

131

e.g., "you are a man and you are sitting". A negative conjunctive proposition is that in which the sign of conjunction is negated: e.g., "not: you are a man and you are a donkey". And a negative is proved through its affirmative. For the truth of an affirmative conjunctive it is required that each *(quilibet)* of the principal parts be true: "you are a man and you are an animal". For the falsity of an affirmative conjunctive it is required and it suffices that one part be false; e.g., "you are a man and you are a donkey". For the possibility of an affirmative conjunctive it is required and it suffices that any of its principal parts be possible and no part be incompossible with another, e.g., "you are a man and you are sitting". For the impossibility [of an affirmative conjunctive] it suffices that one part be impossible or incompossible with another part. Example of the former: "you are running and you are a donkey". Example of the latter: "you are and you are not". For the necessity [17] of an affirmative conjunctive it is required that each of its principal parts be necessary: e.g., "man is animal and God exists". For the contingency of an affirmative conjunctive it is required and it suffices that one part be contingent and that the other part not be impossible or incompossible with the first. Example: "you are running and you are a man" or "God exists and you are running etc.".

Section 14 – Disjunctive Hypothetical Propositions

A disjunctive proposition is that in which several categorical propositions are joined by a sign of disjunction; e.g., "you are a man or you are a donkey". Disjunctive propositions are either affirmative or negative. An affirmative disjunctive is that in which the sign of disjunction is affirmed; e.g., "you are a man or you are a donkey". A negative disjunctive is that in which the sign of disjunction is negated; e.g., "not: you are a man or you are a goat". And this type of proposition is always proved through its affirmative form; for it would not be negative if there were not a negation posited before it; e.g., "you are not a donkey or you are not a goat". This is an affirmative proposition in which neither of the negations goes over into the sign of the disjunction. For the truth of an affirmative disjunctive it is required and it suffices that one of the parts is true; e.g., "you are a man or you are a donkey". For the falsity of an affirmative disjunctive it is required that both parts be false; e.g., "you are running or no stick is standing in the corner". For the possibility of an affirmative disjunctive it suffices that one part be possible; e.g., "a man is a donkey or a stick is standing in the corner". For the impossibility of an affirmative disjunctive it is required that both parts be impossible: e.g., "a man is a donkey or God does not exist". For the necessity of an affirmative disjunctive it suffices that one of its parts is necessary or that the parts mutually *(invicem)* contradict. Example [18] of the former: "God exists or Socrates is moved". Example of the latter: "you are or you are not". For the contingency of [an affirmative disjunctive] it is required that both parts be contingent and that no part be repugnant to another or be mutually contradictory: e.g., "Antichrist is white, or this runs". The last condition is stated because this disjunctive is necessary, viz., "you are not a man or you are an animal". However, no part of this proposition is repugnant to the other part, and both parts are contingent. But here is a proposition whose contradictory parts are repugnant: "you are a man or you are not an animal". Or it can be said – and it is better to say – that for the necessity of a disjunctive it is required and it suffices that the conjunction made from the contradictory parts of the disjunctive be impossible; e.g., "you are not running or you are moving"; "you are running and you are not moving". And for the contingency of [a disjunctive] it is required that the conjunction made from the opposite parts be contingent. This proposition, then, is necessary: "you are not running or you are moving", because this conjunction is impossible: "you are running and you are not moving". And this is contingent: "you are running or you are not moving", because this conjunction is contingent: "you are not running and you are moving", according to the rules for conjunctive propositions given above.

Section 15 – Predicables

A predicable is taken in two senses: commonly and properly. A predicable taken commonly is a term suited *(aptus natus)* to be predicated of something. And a singular term as well as a common term or a complex as well as an incomplex term is called a predicable. But properly speaking a predicable is defined as a simple univocal term suited *(aptus natus)* to be predicated of many; thus no singular term [19] and no transcendental or composite term is called a predicable or a universal, which is the same thing, since no such term is univocal. But a univocal term is a simple term signifying many things according to one concept *(secundam unicam rationem)*. In this way the term 'man' signifies Socrates, and Plato and all of its significates and it does this according to this concept *(rationem)*: rational animal. From this it follows that a simple term is not a composite term. And since the definition says "signifying many things" it excludes singular terms. Again, since it says "according to one concept" it excludes transcendent terms, e.g.; "being", "something", etc. An equivocal term is a simple term signifying many things according to diverse concepts *(diversas rationes)* as this term "dog" which signifies the dog capable of barking, the dogfish or the constellation, and it does this under different concepts *(diversis rationibus)*. A predicable taken properly is divided into five universals: genus, species, difference, property and accident.

A genus is an incomplex univocal term predicable *in quid* of many things different in species with regard to *what* [they are] *(in eo quod quid)*; as "animal" is predicated of man and donkey which differ in species with regard to what [they are]. "With regard to what" *(in eo quod quid)* is added because to the question asked by using "what" *(quid)* as in "what is man?" one responds, "animal". Genus is divided into two domains, for there is a most general genus and a subaltern genus. A most general genus is a term which is a genus in such a way that it cannot be a species, as is the term "substance". A subaltern genus is a term which is a genus [20] which can be a species; e.g., "animal". For it is a genus with respect to man and to donkey but it is a species with respect to body.

A species is a non-supreme univocal term predicable *in quid* of many things different in number; e.g., "man" is predicated of Socrates and of Plato with regard to what they are because to the question made by using "what", e.g., "what is Socrates or Plato?" one responds, "man". "Species" is divided into a most special species and a subalternate species. A subalternate species is a term which, although it is a species, can be a genus, e.g., "animal". A most special species is a univocal term predicable *in quid* of many things different only in number. And notably it is said "only in number", because "animal" is not a most special species; however, it is a univocal term predicable *in quid* of many things different in number because it is predicable of Socrates and of Plato. But it is not predicable of things different "only in number" because it is predicable also of things different in species, e.g., of a man and of a lion, etc.

Difference is a univocal term predicable of many things in an essential quality; e.g., "rational" is predicable of Socrates and of Plato insofar as their essential quality *(quale essentiale)* is concerned because to the question about essential quality *(quale essentiale)*, e.g., "how is Socrates?" one replies, "rational".

Property is a univocal term predicable of many things insofar as their accidental quality is converted, e.g., "risible", which is predicated of Socrates and of Plato insofar as their quality is concerned because to the question concerning how, e.g., "how is Socrates?" one normally responds that he is risible. [21] And the main reason why it is predicable of that is because it ["risible"] is a proper feature *(passio)* of the term "man" with which it is converted.

An accident is a univocal term predicable of many things with regard to non-convertable accidental quality; e.g., "white" is predicable of man insofar as it is a non-convertable accidental quality; because to the ques-

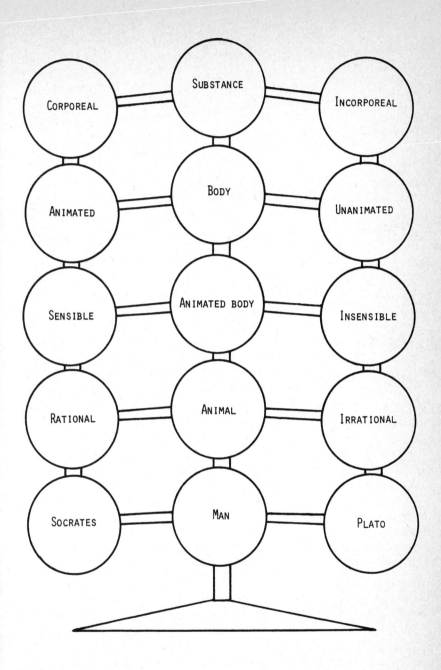

tion concerning how, e.g., "how is Socrates?" either "man" or "donkey" normally can be said in reply because he is white, and he is this non-convertibly because "white" does not convert with those other terms. It is sufficient that predicables have these modes: Every universal is predicable either essentially or accidentally. If essentially, then it is predicable either in the sense of "what" *(in quid)* or in the sense of "how" *(in quale)*. If in the sense of "what" then [if it is predicable] of many things different in species, it is a genus. Or [if it is predicable] of many things different in number alone, it is a species. If in the sense of "how", this is the concept of a difference. If, indeed, it is predicable accidentally, it will be either as a convertible accidental quality, and that is a property; or it will be predicable as a non-convertible accidental quality, and that is an accident. From what has been said it can be concluded that predication is either direct or indirect and either essential or accidental. A direct predication is that in which a higher-level term is predicated of its lower-level term, e.g., "man is animal". An indirect predication is that in which a lower-level term is predicated of its higher-level term, e.g., "animal is man". An essential predication is that in which a higher-level term is predicated of its lower-level terms or their differences. For that reason it is said that an accidental predicate is that in which a property or an accident is predicated of a genus, of a species or of a difference [22] or of its individual and conversely. An example of the former: "man is risible", or "animal is white". An example of the latter: "risible is man", or "white is animal", and conversely. A similar point can be made concerning the individual and the differences. Again, it may be said that an essential predication is a predication of different terms in the same category; e.g., "man is animal". An accidental predication, however, is a predication of different terms and of different categories: e.g., "man is white". A term on a higher level than another is said to be that which contains it [i.e., the lower-level term] and not conversely; e.g., "animal" with respect to this term "man"; because it signifies whatever this is and with this [signification] something beyond it and not conversely. A term on a level lower than another is said to be that which is contained by another and not conversely, e.g., "Socrates" with respect to the term "man".

Section 16 – Categories

[23] A category is a coordination of many terms divided into higher and lower levels. There are ten categories. The first is the category of substance *(substantia)* whose most general genus is substance. Beneath substance falls body, beneath body animated body, beneath animated body animal, be-

neath animal the most special species, e.g., man or donkey; and beneath these species there are individuals, e.g., Socrates and Plato, Brunellus and the like.

The second category is the category of quantity *(quantitas)* whose most general genus is the category of quantity; beneath it there are two subaltern genera of which neither is on a level higher than the other: namely, continuous and discrete. Of the first these are the species: "line", "surface", "body", ["time" and "place",] of which these are the individuals: "this line", "this surface", "this body", "this time", and "this place". Of the second there are an infinite number of species: "two", "three", "four", etc. Of the latter, there are these individuals: "this two", "this three", and thus of singulars.

The third category is the category of quality *(qualitas)* whose most general genus is quality, beneath which there are four subaltern genera which are not divided into higher and lower levels. The first is function *(habitus)* or disposition. The second is natural power or non-power. The third is passion *(passio)* or sufferable quality. The fourth is form or figure surrounding something. Of the first kind these are the species: "grammar", "logic", "rhetoric", etc.; the individuals beneath these are "this grammar", "this logic", "this rhetoric", etc. Of the second kind these are the species: "hard", "soft", of which these are the individuals: "this hard", "this soft", etc. Of the third kind these are the species: "sweetness", "bitterness", "hot", "cold", "dry" [24] of which these are the individuals: "this sweetness", "this bitterness", "this hot", "this cold", etc. Of the fourth kind the species are: "circle", "triangle", "quadrangle", and the like. The individuals of these are: "this circle", "this triangle", "this quadrangle", etc.

The fourth category is the category of relation *(relatio)* whose most general genus is relation or "to something" *(ad aliquid)*, beneath which there are three subaltern genera which are not divided into higher and lower orders. The first is equiparity *(equiparatio)*. The second is superposition. The third is supposition. Of the first kind the species are "near", "equal", and "like"; the individuals of these are: "this near", "this equal", "this like". Of the second kind these are the species: "father", "lord", "master" and these are the individuals: "this father", "this lord", "this master". Of the third kind the species are: "son", "servant", of which the individuals are: "this son", "this servant", etc.

The fifth category is the category of action *(actio)* whose most general genus is action: beneath this there are six subaltern genera which are not divided into higher and lower orders, namely, "to generate", "to corrupt", "to increase", "to diminish", "to alter", and "to move in space". Of the first and second kind the species are: "to generate a man", "to corrupt a horse"; the individuals of these are "to generate a man in this way", "to corrupt a horse in this way". Of the third and fourth kinds the species are: "to increase in length", "to diminish in width", of which the individuals are: "to add thus in length", "to diminish thus in width". Of the fifth kind the species are: "to heat", "to cool"; of these the individuals are: "to heat thus", "to cool thus". Of the sixth [25] kind the species are: "to move over", "to move under", of which the individuals are: "to move over in this way", "to move under in this way".

The sixth category is the category of "being acted upon" *(passio)* whose most general genus is "being acted upon" and similarly it has six subalternate genera which are not divided into higher and lower orders; namely, "to be generated", "to be corrupted", "to be increased", "to be diminished", "to be altered" and "to be moved in space". Of the first and second genera, the species are "man to be generated", "horse to be corrupted" of which the individuals are: "this man to be generated", "this horse to be corrupted". Of the third and fourth genera the species are: "to be increased in length", "to be diminished in width", of which the individuals are: "to be increased in length in this way", "to be diminished in width in this way". Of the fifth genus the species are: "to be heated [in this way]", "to be cooled in this way". Of the sixth genus the species are: "to be moved over", "to be moved under".

The seventh category is the category of place *(ubi)*, whose most general genus is place. Beneath this there are subaltern genera, viz., "in place", "in space"; the species of these are: "in a house", "in a street". The individuals of these are "in this house", "in this street", "here" or "there" *(ibi)*.

The eighth category is the category of time *(quando)* whose most general genus is when *(quando)*. Beneath this there are subaltern genera, viz., "in time", "in the past", "in eternity". The species of these are "today", "yesterday", "tomorrow", etc.; the individuals of these are: "then", "now", "in that day", or ["in that instant"], etc.

The ninth category is the category of situation *(situs)* whose most general genus is situation or position: beneath this are these species: "to stand", "to sit", "to fall". [26] The individuals under these are: "to stand in this way", "to sit in this way", "to fall in this way".

The tenth category is the category of state *(habitus)* whose most general genus is "state". Beneath this are these species: "ringed" *(annulus)*, "crowned", "to be armed", or "to be shod". Of these the individuals are: "this ringed", "this crowned", "to be armed in this way", "to be shod in this way".

It is noteworthy that in any category where a word signifying the concrete is posited, there the same word can be posited in its abstract form and conversely.[a] Thus in the same category in which one posits "man", one

138

posits "humanity". In the same category in which one posits "white", one posits "whiteness". And let these remarks suffice for the topic of categories.

Section 17 — Syllogisms

A syllogism is a discourse *(oratio)* in which after something is posited and conceded it is necessary that something else come from *(evenire)* those things which were posited or conceded.[b] An example: "every man runs; Socrates is a man; therefore, Socrates runs". And it is to be understood that every syllogism contains three terms: a major, a minor and a middle. The middle term is that which is posited twice before the conclusion, and it does not occur in the conclusion, e.g., "man". The major term is that which is posited in the major proposition with the middle term, e.g., "running". The minor term is that which is posited in the minor proposition with the middle term, e.g., "Socrates". Second, it is to be noted that the figure of a syllogism is the disposition or arrangement of terms. It is threefold: in the first figure the middle term is the subject of the first proposition and the predicate of the second proposition.[c] In the second figure the middle term is the predicate of both propositions. In the third figure the middle term is the subject of both propositions. Example of the first figure: "every animal is [27] a substance; every man is an animal; therefore, every man is a substance". Example of the second figure: "no stone is a man; every risible thing is a man; therefore, no risible thing is a stone". Example of the third figure: "every man is an animal; every man is risible; therefore, a certain risible thing is an animal". Thus the verse:

Sub prae prima.
Bis prae secunda.
Tertia sub bis.

Third, it is to be noted that a conclusion can be direct or indirect. A direct conclusion is that in which the major term is predicated of the minor term in the conclusion; e.g., "every man is an animal; Socrates is a man; therefore, Socrates is an animal". An indirect conclusion is that in which the minor term is predicated of the major term in the conclusion; e.g., "every man is an animal; Socrates is a man; therefore, a certain animal is Socrates". Fourthly, it is to be noted that from all these figures there are nineteen moods of the syllogism: The first nine pertain to the first figure; the four following to the second figure and the remaining six to the third figure. All are brought together in this verse:

Barbara, celarent, darii, ferio, baralipton.
Celantes, dabitis, fapesmo, frisesomorum.
Cesare, camestres, festino, baroco, darapti.
Felapton, disamis, datisi, bocardo, ferison.

And all of these have direct conclusions except the last five of the first figure. In these moods, then, there are four vocal letters, viz., a, e, i, o. The first signifies a universal affirmative; the second signifies a universal negative; the third a particular affirmative, the fourth a particular [28] or indefinite or singular negative. Secondly, a syllogism ought to be constituted by the location of these letters in the mood. In Barbara the letter 'a' is put three times since every proposition in this mood is a universal affirmative. And because in Celarent "e" is posited first, then "a" and finally "e", the first and third propositions are universal negatives, and the second is a universal affirmative. If, then, someone asks what Barbara is, you should say that it is made from two universal affirmative propositions concluding directly to a universal affirmative. Celarent is composed out of a universal negative and a universal affirmative concluding directly to a universal negative. Fifth, it is to be noted that the first four expressions of the first verse begin from these consonants: b, c, d, f, and similarly every following expression; and through this is understood that all other moods beginning with 'b' ought to be reduced to the first mood of the first figure. And all moods beginning with 'c' ought to be reduced to the second mood of the first figure. And all moods beginning with "d" ought to be reduced to the third mood of the first figure. And all moods beginning with "f" ought to be reduced to the fourth mood of the first figure. Further wherever "s" is expressed it denotes in these verses that the proposition understood through the immediately preceding vocal sign *(vocalem)* ought to be converted simply. And through "p" it ought to be converted *per accidens*. And through "m" it becomes transposed in the premise so that the major becomes the minor and conversely. And through "c" that it is reduced *per impossibile*. An example of the first may be seen by reducing [29] Fapesmo to Ferio; e.g., "every man is an animal; no stone is a man; therefore, a certain animal is not a stone". It is reduced in this way: "no man is a stone; a certain animal is a man; therefore, a certain animal is not a stone". This reduction is reached by converting the major proposition *per accidens*, the minor simply; by which conversions the premises are transposed; and a similar thing holds for all similar arguments. How, then, treat the mood where "c" is posited? It is reduced *per impossibile*. For in these two moods alone "c" occurs, namely, *Baroco* and *Bocardo*. Indeed two moods only are reduced *per impossibile* to Barbara. An example of the former: "every man is an animal; some stone is not an animal; therefore, some stone is not a man". This is reduced to Barbara *per impossibile* by taking the contradictory of the conclusion with the major and by inferring the opposite of the minor; e.g., "every man is an animal; every stone is a man; therefore, every stone is an animal". An example of the latter: "a certain man is not a stone; every man is an animal; therefore, a certain animal is not a stone". This may be reduced to Barbara *per impossibile* by assuming the contradictory of the conclusion with the minor and thus inferring the opposite of the major; e.g., "every animal is a stone; every man is an animal; therefore, every man is a stone". Thus there is a verse:

> *Simpliciter verti vult s p vero per acci.*
> *M vult transponi c per impossibile duci.*

From the foregoing statement it follows that no syllogism is composed entirely of particular propositions nor entirely of negative propositions; and if either of the premises should be particular or negative, the conclusion will be particular or negative. And let these discussions suffice for syllogism. [30]

Notes

[1]$_b^a$ Aristotle, *Physics* I.

The distinction between "significative and non-significative" marks the difference between a term which calls some signification or intelligibility or meaning to the mind of a person hearing it e.g., "man", "animal" and a term which does not, e.g., "buf", "baf". The gloss which follows the distinction in the present text is important for understanding the difference between categorematic and syncategorematic terms. See below the "third division of terms". On the historical background of the theory of signification see De Rijk, 1, Vol. 2, Pt. 1, pp. 177–220 and Boehner, 6, pp. 201–232.

[4]^a The extremes of a proposition are the subject and the predicate of the proposition. The subject is that which the proposition is about; the predicate is that which is said of the subject.

[5]^a See below Sections 12, 13, 14, pp. [15]–[19]

[6]^a The "adequate significate" of a proposition is discussed below p. [6]. It is appealed to again in several of the rules of *obligationes* in Chapter V, [130]. At [131] Paul says, "I mean by the expression 'thus signifying adequately', the customary significates." It is a crucial part of Paul's rules for solving *insolubilia* in Chapter VI, p. [143] ff. For some references in the *Logica Magna* to "the adequate significate" of a proposition see Adams and Del Punta in Adams, 3, pp. 284–285. Also see Perreiah, 3, p. 79.

[8]^a A proposition of "existence in" *(de inesse)* is one which states that some property *exists in* some thing. A modal proposition is one which contains at least one of the six modal auxiliaries: "true",

141

"false", "possible", "impossible", "necessary", "contingent" or their adverbial forms.

[11]^a The rules of logical inference and replacement apply only to propositions having the same terms or terms comparable in number *and* gender. The fact that Paul of Venice stresses in his writings the factor of gender may indicate that it was often neglected by other writers. See Perreiah, 3, p. 89 ff.

[15]^a Some authors distinguished several kinds of conditional, e.g., local, causal and temporal. See Lambert of Auxerre's *Logica* in Alessio, pp. 16–17.

b To "prove" a proposition is to exhibit the conditions under which it is true. In the present case the negative, "Not: if you are a man, you are a donkey", is true just in case, "If you are a man, you are a donkey", is false. See Chapter IV, p. [80]–[119] for a full discussion of the various methods of exhibiting truth-conditions.

[16]^a These properties of conditional statements are of interest primarily in logical theory; and Paul of Venice discusses them further in Chapter III, p. [65] ff.

[26]^a This passage indicates that in the *Logica Parva* Paul recognizes a distinction between concrete and abstract terms. The *Logica Magna* presents a type of supposition called "simple" *(suppositio simplex)* to account for the logical form of statements including abstract terms. See also below p. [221] and Perreiah, 3, p. 43 ff.

b This is the generic sense of "syllogism" *(sullogismus)*. See Aristotle, 2, 24a 18.

c Only three figures are recognized because the major and minor terms were defined with respect to their position in the premises and not with respect to their position in the conclusion.

Chapter II
On Suppositions

Section 1 – Supposition – Definitions and Divisions

Supposition is the acceptance of a term in a proposition for some thing or things. Example of the former: "Socrates runs". Example of the latter: "Socrates and Plato run". In the first the subject stands for some thing. In the second the subject stands for *(supponit pro)* some things, and note that it says "in a proposition" because outside of propositions a term does not "stand for" although it may well signify. Thus "man" signifies in a proposition as well as outside of a proposition; however, it never stands [for] *(supponit [pro])* unless it is posited in a proposition. Supposition is divided into two kinds: material and personal.[a] Material supposition is the acceptance of a term in a proposition for its material significate, e.g., " 'man' is a noun". It is clear that "man" does not stand for [anything] unless for itself or for its like which are the material significates of this term "man". Personal supposition is the acceptance of a term in a proposition for its formal significate, e.g., "Man is an animal" it is clear that "man" stands for Socrates or for Plato which are the formal significates of this term "man".

To support these definitions it must be understood that there is a difference between the formal and the material significates of a term. For the formal significate is that which the term signifies, and through the same object it is verifiable affirmatively [i.e., in an affirmative sentence] without the addition of a material sign.[b] Thus Socrates and Plato are the formal significates of the term "man"; because of Socrates and Plato "man" is verified in an affirmative sentence without the addition of a material sign. For these are true: "Socrates is a man"; [31] "Plato is a man". The material significate of a term is that which the term signifies; however, through that the term is not verifiable in an affirmative sentence without the addition of a sign of materiality. Thus the term 'man' and any terms like it is the material significate of the very same term 'man' because it signifies itself and any term similar to it; however, it is verifiable of no such object without a sign of materiality. For this is false: "the term 'man' is man". But this is true: "the term 'man' is 'man' ". Or it may be said more briefly that the formal significate of a term is that of which the term is verifiable affirmatively by means of a demonstrative pronoun without the addition of a sign of materiality. An example: Socrates is the formal significate of the term "man" because this is true by pointing to Socrates: "this is a man". But the material significate of a term is that of which no term is verifiable affirmatively unless through the mediation of a sign of materiality. Thus the term "man" is the material significate of itself because this is not true: "this is a man", while pointing to the term "man". But this is true: "this is a 'man' ", while pointing to the term "man".

From which it follows that any term which is not verifiable of its very self without the means of a sign of materiality has a two-fold significate, viz., formal and material. Thus the term "man" (as well as the terms "wood", "animal", "stone", and the like) signifies man or Socrates formally, and it signifies itself or its like materially.

Secondly it follows that any term [32] which of its very self is verifiable without a material sign has only one significate and that is formal; and it signifies formally, e.g. the terms, "being", "something", "name", "term" and the like. For this proposition is true: "being is being", and this is true: " 'being' is a being". Moreover, this is true: "name is a name" and this is true: " 'name' is a name".

Thirdly, it follows that just as some term of prime intention or imposition has only a formal significate and some has both kinds of significate, likewise some terms of second intention or imposition have only a formal significate; while others have both kinds of significate. The first part is clear: because "being" as well as "man" are terms of prime intention or imposition; however, "man" has either kind of significate, and "being" has only the formal significate. The second part is proved because "name" and "proposition" are terms of second intention or imposition; yet "name" has a formal significate only because this is true: " 'name' is a name". And "proposition" has either significate because this is not true: " 'proposition' is a proposition" but any of these is true: "an affirmative proposition is a proposition", and "a negative proposition is a proposition". Similarly, this term "syllogism" has either significate because this is not true: " 'syllogism' is a syllogism", but any of these is true: "A is a syllogism", and "B is a syllogism", given that A is a syllogism in the first figure and B [is a syllogism in the] second figure.

Fourthly, it follows that just as some term of prime intention or imposition can stand materially; and some term can stand personally; so also some term of second intention or imposition can [33] stand personally, and some can stand materially. The first part is clear; and the second part is proved: for by saying "name is a term", "name" stands personally because it stands for its formal significate. And the same applies to "a proposition or a syllogism is a statement". But by saying "proposition is a simple term", or "syllogism is a name", "proposition" as well as "syllogism" stands materially and for its material significate.

Section 2 – Material and Personal Supposition

In order to make known when terms stand materially and when they stand personally special rules are assigned.

First, every term having only a formal significate is capable of standing *(supponibilis)* only personally. This is clear because such a term never stands unless it stands for its formal significate. E.g., terms of prime intention or imposition like the terms "being", "quality", "something". Example of a term of second intention or imposition: "term", "name", and the like.

The second rule is this: Every term having both significates, if a sign of materiality be added to it in a proposition, stands only materially. It is clear that it does not stand unless for its material significate by reason of being limited by a sign of materiality. An example of a term of prime intention or imposition: " 'man' is 'man' ", " 'animal' is 'animal' ", "man" as well as "animal" stands materially. Example of a term of second intention or imposition: " 'proposition' is 'proposition' ", " 'syllogism' is 'syllogism' ", "proposition" as well as "syllogism" stands materially because these refer only to their material significates. Signs of materiality are these: "*li*", [34] "this proposition", "this statement", "this utterance"; but the most powerful is "*li*".

The third rule: In any proposition whose extremes are terms of prime intention or imposition to which a material sign is not added, the subject as well as the predicate stands personally; e.g., "man is animal", "Socrates runs". And notably it says "if a material sign is not added", because by that addition a term standing personally would stand materially according to the second rule.

The fourth rule: In any proposition whose extremes are terms of second intention or imposition in which the subject has only a formal significate and the predicate both (i.e., formal and material) the subject as well as the predicate stands personally – provided a material sign is not added to the predicate: "proposition is a sign" *(signum est propositio)*, "syllogism is a term" *(Terminus est syllogismus)*.

The fifth rule: If the extremes of a proposition are terms of second intention or imposition and the subject has either type of signification and the predicate has either type of signification as well or only formal signification, no general rule is given because at one time *(interdum)* either of them stands personally, at another time *(interdum)* either of them stands materially, e.g., "proposition is a statement" *(propositio est oratio)*. Both extremes have either significate; yet both stand personally; and if someone says, "proposition is a name" *(propositio est nomen)*, the subject has either significate, and the predicate only a formal significate; however, the subject stands materially because otherwise the proposition would not be true. Further, if it is said, "proposition is an incomplex term" *(propositio est terminus incomplexus)*, both extremes have both significates; however, the subject stands materially because otherwise the proposition [35] is false.

The sixth rule: Of any proposition whose predicate is a term of prime intention or imposition and whose subject is [a term] of second intention removed from every impediment of a sign of materiality, the subject as well as the predicate stands personally. E.g., "species is man" *(species est homo)*, "some genus is animal" *(aliquod genus est animal)*.

The seventh rule: In any proposition whose subject is a term of prime intention or imposition which does not signify itself formally and whose predicate is a term of second intention or imposition is removed from the impediment or limitation of a material sign, the subject stands materially and the predicate [stands] personally; e.g., "man is a name", "*Sortes* is nominative case", and it should be noted that the example says "man is a name", "*Sortes* is nominative case", not signifying itself formally because if some term should signify itself formally it would stand personally according to the first rule, e.g., "being is a transcendent term". Further the rule says, "without the impediment of a limiting sign", because a universal or particular sign limits the word itself to personal supposition; e.g., "some man is a species", "no animal is a genus". Both "man" and "animal" stand personally because of the limitation of a sign. From which it follows that the subalternate of this proposition, "man is a species", is not this, "every man *(omnis homo)* is a species", but this, "every man *(omne homo)* is a species". Nor is its particular this: "some man *(aliquis homo)* is a species", but this "some man *(aliquod homo)* is a species". Nor is its singular: "this man *(iste homo)* is a species", or "this man *(ista homo)* is a species", but this: "this man *(hoc homo)* is a species". Furthermore, the contradictory of "man is a species" [is not, "nothing which is man *(nihil quod est homo)* is a species"], or "no man *(nullus homo)* is a species", [36] because then two contradictories would be simultaneously true; but the contradictory is this, "no man *(nullum homo)* is a species". Moreover, its subcontrary is [neither, "some man *(aliquis homo)* is not a species", nor "something which is man *(aliquod quod est homo)* is not a species", but rather,] "some man *(aliquod homo)* is not a species". The reason why some of these are placed in the figure and some are not is this: in some of them the same supposition is found while in others the same supposition is not found; thus propositions existing in the figure ought to have in general similar supposition.

And if someone asks why material supposition requires a sign neuter in kind, I reply that all terms standing materially are neuter signs and indeclinable nouns; and this is according to the grammarians. Whence the verse:

An expression *(dictio)* taken materially
is neuter in kind and an indeclinable noun.

Out of the last two rules it follows that this is not a valid conversion: "man is a species; a species is man" because "man" in the first is posited materially and in the second formally. But "man is a species", is converted in this way: "a species is 'man' *(li homo)*". Nor is this a valid conversion *per accidens* "no name *(nullum nomen)* is a man"; therefore, "man is not a name". But this follows: "something which is man is not a name".

Section 3 — Material Supposition

Material supposition contains many divisions. First it is divided into discrete and common.[a] Discrete material supposition is the acceptance of a term standing materially with a demonstrative pronoun, e.g., "this man is a species", or "this term animal is a genus". Common material supposition is the acceptance of a term standing materially [37] without a demonstrative pronoun, "man *(homo)* is nominative case", "Peter is a proper noun", since "Peter" taken personally is a discrete term and a proper noun. But taken materially it is a common term predicable of many, as for example this term "Peter" in the mind *(in mente)* in the utterance *(voce)* or in the inscription *(scripto)*. Similarly, "you is a pronoun". The subject here is not a pronoun, but it is an indeclinable noun taken materially and having similarly many referents.

Secondly, common material supposition is divided into determinate and confused *(confusa)*. Determinate material supposition is the acceptance of a common term standing materially beneath which one descends *(contingit descendere)* to all of its referents disjunctively: e.g., "man is a common term and these are all terms man; therefore, this 'man' *(hoc homo)* is a term or this 'man' *(hoc homo)* is a common term and thus of singulars".

From the above it follows that this proposition is true: "man *(homo)* is not nominative case" as well as this proposition, "man *(homo)* is nominative case". For these are two indefinite subcontraries the first of which has a subject indicated through the term "man" which is in the dative case or the accusative case taken materially; and the second has a subject [like the first] but indicated through the term "man" in the nominative case. In this way, it is conceded: "I love is a verb" and "I love is not a verb", "reading is a participle", and "reading is not a participle". "You is a demonstrative pronoun" and "you is not a demonstrative pronoun", because these are not two contradictories; rather they are subcontraries. For that reason I do not concede: "I love is a verb", and "not: I love is a verb", [38] and "you is a pronoun", and "not: you is a pronoun", because they are contradictories.

Confused material supposition is the acceptance of a common term standing materially beneath which one does not descend to all of its referents disjunctively. But if one should descend, he must do so in disjuncts; e.g., "Only man is a name, and these are all terms man; therefore, only this 'man' *(hoc homo)* is a name or this 'man' *(hoc homo)* is a name and thus of singulars". In this case the antecedent is true, and the consequent is false.

The third division of confused material supposition is into merely confused and distributively confused.

The fourth division of merely confused material supposition is into mobile and immobile. Merely confused mobile supposition is the acceptance of a term taken materially beneath which one descends to all of its referents in disjuncts; e.g., "Only man is a name; and these are all terms man; therefore, only this 'man' *(tantum hoc homo)* or this 'man' *(hoc homo)* and thus of singulars is a name". Merely confused immobile supposition is the acceptance of a common term standing materially beneath which one does not descend; but if one should descend, he must do so in disjuncts. For example, in "necessarily man is a species", "man" stands merely confused immobily, and it is not legitimate to descend. Thus, it does not follow: "necessarily man is a species, and these are all terms man; therefore, necessarily this 'man' *(hoc homo)* or this 'man' *(hoc homo)* is a species and thus of singulars". For the antecedent is true, and the consequent is false. However, if one happens to descend he should descend in the way stated.

The fifth [39] division of distributive material supposition is into mobile and immobile. Mobile distributive material supposition is the acceptance of a common term standing materially beneath which one descends to all of its referents conjunctively. E.g., "every 'man' *(omne homo)* is a term; and these are all terms 'man'; therefore, this 'man' *(hoc homo)* is a term, and this 'man' *(hoc homo)* is a term and thus of singulars". Immobile distributive material supposition is the acceptance of a common term standing materially beneath which one does not descend to all of its referents. But if one should descend, he must descend conjunctively: e.g., in "necessarily every man is a species", 'man' stands materially and immobily distributive because it is not possible to descend. For it would not follow: "necessarily every 'man' *(omne homo)* is a species, and these are all terms 'man'; therefore, necessarily, this 'man' *(hoc homo)* is a species, and necessarily this 'man' *(hoc homo)* is a species and thus of singulars". For the

148

antecedent is true, and the consequent is false. It is true, however, if one should happen to descend he should do so in the mode previously discussed [i.e., in disjuncts].

With regard to this discussion note that this expression "and" has two basic senses: in conjuncts and conjunctively. It is taken in conjuncts when it conjoins terms: e.g., "Socrates and Plato run". It is taken conjunctively when it conjoins propositions: e.g., "Socrates runs and Plato disputes". Similarly, this expression "or" has two senses: in disjuncts or disjunctively. It is taken in disjuncts when it disjoins terms. It is taken disjunctively when it disjoins propositions. Example of the former: "Socrates or Plato disputes". An example [40] of the latter, "Socrates runs or Plato disputes".

Section 4 – Personal Supposition

It is convenient to state here some rules of personal supposition.[a] First, personal supposition is divided into discrete and common. Discrete personal supposition is the acceptance of a singular or common term with a demonstrative pronoun standing personally, e.g., "Socrates runs", or "this man disputes".

From this definition follows this rule: Every discrete or singular term or common term with a demonstrative pronoun existing as part of a proposition stands personally whether a distributive sign precedes it or not. Thus in this proposition, "no donkey are you" just as in that proposition, "you are a man" "you" stands discretely. Common personal supposition is the acceptance of a common term standing personally without a demonstrative pronoun, e.g., "a man runs" *(homo currit)*.

Secondly, common personal supposition is divided into determinate and confused. Determinate supposition is the acceptance of a common term standing personally beneath which one descends to all of its singulars disjunctively, e.g., "man runs and these are all men; therefore, this man[1] runs or this man[2] runs and thus of singulars".

With respect to this supposition there are two rules. First, any particular or indefinite subject stands only determinately – whether affirmative or negative and whether in material supposition or in personal supposition.

Second, every common term which is preceded by none other than a particular sign stands determinately, [41] e.g., in this proposition "man is animal" the subject as well as the predicate stands determinately. However, if a sign of particularity were added to either of these, it would not impede this kind of supposition.

Common confused supposition is the acceptance of a common term standing personally beneath which one does not descend disjunctively as

149

in "only man is risible", ["man" stands confusedly; and one ought not to descend disjunctively, as will be clear].

Thirdly, confused personal supposition is divided into merely confused and distributively confused.

Fourthly, merely confused personal supposition is divided into mobile and immobile.

Common mobile personal supposition which is merely confused is the acceptance of a common term standing personally beneath which one descends to all of its referents in disjuncts, as in "every man is animal and these are all animals; therefore, every man is this animal or that animal and thus of singulars".

With respect to this supposition there are some rules: First, in every universal affirmative proposition, if the predicate is a common term removed from every impediment, the predicate stands merely confused mobily. And notably I say, "if it is a common term", because if it were a discrete term, it would stand discretely. And also I say, "without impediment", in order to exclude other signs: for by saying "every man is every animal", "animal" is the predicate of a universal affirmative, and it is a common term; however, it does not stand merely confused but distributively [confused] as will be clear.

The second rule: In every exclusive proposition of the first order (where the sign of exclusion is not negated) if the subject is a common term removed from every impediment, the subject stands merely confused mobily, e.g., "only man runs", or [42] "only man does not run"[a] In both of these propositions "man" stands merely confused mobily.

Merely confused personal supposition which is immobile is the acceptance of a common term standing personally beneath which one does not descend; but if one should descend, he must do so in disjuncts. E.g., in "necessarily man is animal", "man" refers in the way previously stated, i.e., immobily because with no due mean it follows, "therefore, necessarily this man *(ille homo)* or that man *(illa homo)* and thus of the others is an animal". Here the antecedent is true and the consequent is false. However, if one should descend in that way, three rules apply.

The first rule is this: Every affirmative conditional with a common term removed from impediment by another sign stands merely confused immobily; e.g., in "if man is animal is", "man" as well as "animal" stands merely confused immobily.

The second rule: In any reduplicative affirmative where the predicate is capable of confusion *(predicatum si fuerit capax confusionis)*, and it does not have some impediment, the predicate stands merely confused immobily; e.g., in "Socrates insofar as he is man, is animal", "animal" stands in this way [i.e., merely confused immobily].[b]

150

The third rule: In any modal proposition in the composite sense having a non-distributed common term that term stands merely confused immobily; e.g., "necessarily man is animal", "it is impossible for man not to be", because one cannot descend [to the singulars,] as is clear.[c]

The fifth division is this: personal distributive supposition is divided into mobile and immobile. [43] Mobile distributive [personal] supposition is the acceptance of a common term standing personally beneath which one descends to all of its referents conjunctively; e.g., "every man runs and these are all men"; therefore, "this man *(iste homo)* runs and this man *(ista homo)* runs and thus of singulars". Whereby one concludes that "man" stands confused distributively and mobily. To these propositions I add these rules: first, in any universal affirmative the subject stands confused and distributive mobily. E.g., in "every man runs", "any man disputes", "any animal is moved", "man" as well as "animal" stands confused mobily distributively.

Second, in every universal negative proposition in the ordinary mode of speaking *(de consueto modo loquendi)* the subject as well as the predicate stands mobily and distributively confused provided it is an unimpeded common term. E.g., in "no man is a donkey", "man" as well as "donkey" stands mobily distributively confused. And note that I say, "in the ordinary mode of speaking", because in this kind of negative proposition, "every man is not an animal", *(Omnis homo animal non est)* "animal" which is the predicate does not stand distributively confused but merely confused.

Third, in every particular, indefinite or singular negative proposition in the ordinary mode of speaking (provided the predicate is a common term removed from the impediment of another sign) the predicate stands confused and mobily distributive. [E.g., "some man is not a donkey", "an animal is not a stone", "Socrates is not a goat". In these the predicate stands confused and mobily distributive.] But with the impediment of another sign it would not stand in that way. For example, by saying "Socrates is not every man", "man" does not stand distributively and determinately as was pointed out.

Fourth, [44] every first order exclusive proposition (provided the predicate is a common term removed from the impediment of another sign) the predicate stands confused and mobily distributive; e.g., in "only animal is man", "man" stands confused and mobily distributive.

Immobile distributive personal supposition is the acceptance of a common term standing personally beneath which one does not descend; but if one should descend, he must do so conjunctively. For example from "necessarily every man is animal", it does not follow with the due mean, "therefore, necessarily this man is animal and thus of singulars", because the antecedent is true, and the consequent is false.

Concerning these suppositions, here is the first rule: in every conditional proposition with a distributive term that term stands immobily and distributively confused, and it does this in relation to the total conditional; e.g., "if every animal runs, every man runs", "man" as well as "animal" stands immobily and distributively confused because one cannot descend in relation to the total conditional.

Second, in every proper exceptive statement (whether affirmative or negative) that expression by which it is an exceptive stands confused in an immobily distributive way because it is not valid to descend. E.g., in 'Every man except Socrates *(praeter Sortem)* runs", "no animal except man *(praeter hominem)* is rational", "man" as well as "animal" stands immobily and distributively because it is not legitimate to descend.

Third, in every modal proposition in the composite sense having a distributive term, that term stands confused and immobily distributive; e.g., "necessarily every man is animal", "[for] every man to be an animal is known by me", because it is not valid to descend. Where, however, one could [45] descend it would be due to the matter involved because by chance the opposite of the consequent would be repugnant to the antecedent.

Section 5 – Confounding Terms

To lend greater support to the foregoing statements, I offer some rules of terms having the force of confounding *(vim confundendi)*. The first: every universal affirmative sign confounds a term *immediately* following itself in a confused and mobily distributive way; and it confounds a term *mediately* following it (provided the term is capable of a confusion), *(si fuerit capax confusionis)* mobily and in a merely confused way, provided also that the term is removed from the impediment of another sign. Example: "every man is animal", or "every man an animal is not" *(Omnis homo animal non est)* in both "man" stands in a confused and distributive way, and "animal" in a merely confused way. And notably it is said, "provided it is capable of a confusion" first because of singular terms which are commonly not able to stand *(possunt supponere)*. Second, because of propositions like these: in "seeing every man is an animal", "a donkey of any man runs", neither "animal" nor "runs" is confounded because the power of the sign [of confusion] does not operate constantly on the predicate, since it is part of the whole subject. Secondly, the rule says, "removed from the impediment of another sign" because in this proposition, "not every man is animal", "man" does not refer distributively but determinately according to one rule pertinent to this matter, viz., whatever mobilizes the immobile, immobilizes the mobile. That is: If any sign having the power to distribute some term finds again the same term undistributed, the sign makes the term stand distributively; and if the sign finds again the same term distributed, the sign makes the term stand without distribution, i.e., it makes it stand determinately or merely confused. [46] An example: in "man runs", the subject of this proposition stands non-distributively. By saying, however, "every man runs", it stands distributively. For that reason with the addition of another sign congruently it will stand non-distributively, i.e., "not every man runs". Further, it is to be noted that if two distributive signs fall over the same term, they make it stand determinately; e.g., "you differ from every man". And, furthermore, if one should be affirmative and the other negative, they make these stand determinately — "you do not differ from man", or "not any man runs". And if both are negative and [the two distributive signs] fall *immediately* over the same term, they make that term stand determinately, e.g., "not no man runs".[a] If, on the other hand, they fall *mediately*, given that a distributive term mediates, they make the same stand merely confused, e.g., "no man does not run". It is clear that "running" is confused only *(confusa tantum)* because this proposition is equivalent to this' "any *(quilibet)* man runs", where "running" stands merely confused. Similarly, by saying "not some man is not animal", "animal" stands merely confused because its equivalent is clear: "any *(quilibet)* man is animal", where "animal" stands merely confused *(confusa tantum)*.

The second rule: Every negative sign which is not impeded confounds distributively and mobily a term *mediately* following it as well as a term *immediately* following it, provided this term will be capable of a confusion, e.g., "not: man runs and no man disputes", the subject as well as the predicate confounds confused mobily and distributively. But in this proposition, "a donkey of no man is an animal", "animal" does not stand distributively because [47] it is not capable of confusion by a sign. For there is a limitation made on the part of its subject.

The third rule is this: Every comparative and superlative grade, "as much ...so much..." *(tam...quam...)*, "...other than..." *(... aliud...)*, "not the same as" *(non idem)*, "so" *(ita)*, "as" *(sicut)*, and "differs from" *(differt)* and these verbs: "I want", "I need" and the like confound mobily and distributively a term immediately following them provided it is a term capable of a confusion, and every other impediment is removed. E.g., "you are a stronger man", "you are the strongest man", "you are just as strong as some man", "you differ from a man", "you are other than a man", or "you are not the same as a man", "I want or I need money", and thus of others. In all of these the term immediately following (the confounding term) stands confused, and it is distributed mobily.

But it is to be noted that the comparative grade confounds of itself a term in a mobily distributive way in the nominative case because of the nature of a comparison. An ablative, however, confounds in a merely confused way a term in the nominative case because of the nature of an excess. Example: "I am taller than you by a length of one forearm", "by a length" refers in a confused way. Further, none of these terms confounds distributively unless it does so to a term of itself in the nominative case placed after it. Thus, by saying "a man is stronger than a horse", or "from a man a donkey differs", neither "horse" nor "donkey" stands distributively but only determinately.

The fourth rule: An exclusive expression confounds merely confused mobily a common term following it immediately. It confounds one following it mediately in a mobily and distributively confused way. In, "only man is animal", "man" stands merely confused mobily; and "animal" stands distributively confused mobily.

The fifth rule: An exceptive expression confounds its term according to the case *(casuale)*, [48] if it is a common term, in a merely confused mobile way. E.g., in "no animal except man runs", "every animal except man runs", "man" stands merely confused mobily.

The sixth rule: A reduplicative expression confounds according to the case what is related to it in a merely confused mobile way, and the predicate confounds in a merely confused immobile way; e.g., in "Socrates insofar as he is man is animal", "man" stands merely confused mobily and "animal" [merely] confused immobily. Because under the first one descends in disjuncts but not under the second.

The seventh rule: Terms concerning an act of the mind as "to know", "to believe", "to will", "to doubt", and the like confound merely confused mobily terms following them immediately; e.g., in "I know some proposition", "proposition" stands merely confused mobily because it validly follows: "I know some proposition, and these are all propositions; therefore, I know this [proposition] or that proposition and thus of singulars".

The eighth rule: All adverbial numerals like "twice", "thrice", "four times" and the like confound a term immediately following them in a mobile but merely confused way; in "twice I ate bread", "thrice I drank wine", "bread" and "wine" stand merely confused mobily; for just as I ate bread or drank wine at this time *and* at that time with an interruption of time, so I ate bread and drank wine at this time *or* at that time.

The ninth rule: Modal terms taken nominally or adverbially in the composite sense confound in a merely confused immobile way every common term not distributed which either follows or precedes it; e.g., "necessarily man is animal", or "[for] man to be animal is necessary".

The tenth rule: The verbs "begins", "ceases", confound common non-distributed [49] terms following them in a merely confused immobile way. And they confound a term immediately included in them in a [merely confused] mobile way. E.g., in "you begin or cease to know some proposition", "proposition" stands merely confused immobily because it is not valid to descend beneath the proposition into those in which it is immediately included. Again, in "immediately before this I knew some proposition", "proposition" stands merely confused mobily; but this will be understood more clearly by seeing the treatise on the proofs of terms.[a]

The eleventh rule: These verbs "I promise", "I bind", "I owe", and the like confound merely confused immobily; e.g., in "I promise you a dime", "dime" stands immobily because one cannot validly descend.

The twelfth rule is this: Every sign of a condition or of a reason confounds all of its non-distributed terms in a merely confused immobile way. And this applies also to the entire hypothetical proposition; e.g., "if man is, animal is", "If man runs, animal runs".

It is to be noted first that no distributive term may have distributive force over a preceding term; however, it well has the force of confusion over that term, and it can make it stand in a merely confused way. This is not the case, however, for every term but only for that which indifferently determines before or after itself the verbal composition. Hence these terms "every", "none" and the like do not confound in some way a term preceding them because in all of these "some man is every animal", or "some man is no animal", "man" always stands determinately. Similarly, neither do these verbs "begins", "ceases", "I promise", because in the sentences "man begins to be", or "a dime I promise", "man" as well as "dime" stands determinately. But in these sentences "[for] man to be animal [50] is known by me" *(hominem esse animal est scitum a me)*, or "[for] man not to be is impossible", or "man is animal necessarily", all of the common terms which precede stand in a merely confused and immobile way. The reason: terms making a composite sense determine compositions before them as well as after them. And this is why the rule says, "signs of a condition or of a reason confound before themselves".

Second, it is to be noted that a term having only the force of confounding in a merely confused manner does not impede the distribution of a term although it may impede its descent. For example in "every man is animal", "man" stands distributively and mobily; and it stands in the same way in this proposition: "necessarily every man is animal". But there is a difference because in the first it stands mobily, and in the second immobily owing to the addition of a modal term. I say, therefore, that every term having only the force of confounding immobily impedes the descent, and thus it immobilizes. But others having only the force of confounding merely confused mobily do not impede the descent, and thus they do not immobilize. Hence it follows: "I know all propositions, and these are all propositions; therefore, I know this one and I know that one and thus of singulars".

Third, it is to be noted that if two distributive signs fall over some term of which not anything is assumed *per se*, it falls distributively over the same term, provided none is impeded by another term; e.g., in "Every man is every animal" *(omnis homo omnem animal est)*, "animal" stands distributively — notwithstanding the fact that two distributive signs precede. Because the first taken *per se* would not distribute "animal" but would make it stand merely confused; e.g., "every man is not animal" *(omnis homo animal non est)*. And thus by saying [51] "from Socrates every man differs", *(a Sorte differt omnis homo)* "man" stands distributively — notwithstanding the fact that two distributive signs precede it. The reason is this: the first one would not distribute "man" by saying "from Socrates a man differs" *(a Sorte differt homo)*, because "differs" does not distribute unless a term in the nominative case occurring after it *(a parte post)*, as was said. In a similar way I say in the proposition, "you are stronger than a man", "man" stands confused and distributively. Nor does the first sign impede this because taken *per se* it would distribute only terms in the nominative according to what was said earlier. But by saying "no man is not animal", or "you differ from every man", or "you are whiter than every man", the distribution of the last term is impeded because it is preceded by two signs of which either without the other would distribute that term.

Section 6 — Supposition of Relatives

Next comes the supposition of relative terms where there are certain customary divisions.

The first division is into relatives of substance e.g., *"quis"*, *"qui"*, *"quod"*, *"quid"*, and relatives of accident e.g., *"qualis"*, *"quantis"*, *"qualiter"*, etc.

The second division separates relatives of substance into those of identity e.g., *"qui"*, *"ille"*, *"idem"*, *"ipse"* and the like and those of diversity e.g., *"alter"*, *"alius"*, *"ceter"* and *"reliquus"* and the like.

The third division separates relatives of identity into reciprocals e.g., *"meus"*, *"tuus"*, *"suus"*, etc. and non-reciprocals such as, e.g., *"ille"*, *"ipse"*, *"iste"*, and the like.

156

The fourth division marks off reciprocal relatives into possessives e.g., *"tuus"*, *"suus"* and non-possessives e.g., *"se"*.

The fifth division sets off relatives of accident into those [52] of identity, *"talis"*, *"tantus"* and diversity *"istiusmodi"*, *"aliusmodi"*, *"alteriusmodi"* and the like.

With these divisions in mind, here is the first rule. A relative of diversity of substance and a relative of possession do not stand for that for which their antecedents stand. An example of the first: "if one of two contradictories is true, the other is false". This is clear because "one" stands for one proposition and "the other" stands for another. An example of the second: "Some man runs, and his donkey rests". The antecedent stands for a man, and the relative [pronoun stands for] donkey.

The second rule is this: A non-possessive relative of identity always stands for that for which its antecedent stands in relation to either extreme [i.e., subject and predicate]. An example of a non-reciprocal relative of identity: "some man runs and that one disputes", "that" stands not absolutely for some man; but for some man running. For the second part does not signify absolutely that some man disputes but some running man disputes. Similarly, in the conjunction "some man is a slave, and you are that", the second part does not signify precisely that you are some man because then the conjunction would be true, namely, that you are some man who is a slave. From which it does not follow: "some man is animal and a donkey is that", because the second part signifies affirmatively that a donkey is an animal which is some man. And by the same token this is false: "Socrates is some man and Plato is that". But this is true, ["some man is Socrates and Plato is not that", because Plato is some man who is not Socrates. And conversely, this is true, "some man is not Socrates, and Plato is not that", because Plato (is) some man who is not Socrates, just as Cicero (is some man who is not Socrates). Further, it is conceded: "some man is not Socrates and Plato [53] is that", because Plato is the very one who is not Socrates.] An example of a reciprocal relative of identity: In "every man sees himself", "himself" stands for every man not absolutely which would mean "every man sees every man", but by referring *(referendo)* to each singular thing as in "this man sees himself, and that man sees himself, and thus of singulars".[a] Similarly, "every man having a son loves him", signifies that some man having a son loves the son which he has.

The third rule: A relative of identity of accident always stands for its like or what is equal to that for which its antecedent stands. E.g., in "Socrates is white and such is Plato", or "Socrates is as white as Plato", the relative does not stand for Socrates but for what is similar to Socrates. Likewise, in "Socrates is two cubits and Plato is as much", the relative [stands for] what is equal to Socrates.

157

The fourth rule: A relative of diversity of accident always stands for what is dissimilar to that for which its antecedent stands, e.g., "a swan is white and a raven is of another kind".

From the last two rules the fifth rule follows: a relative of accident, whether of diversity or of identity, always stands for a supposit different from that of the antecedent. The rule is clear from the examples.

Section 7 — Ways of Standing of Relatives

Since we have discussed those objects for which relatives stand, we now go on to point out their mode of standing *(modum supponendi)*.

Here is the first rule: a relative of diversity of substance does not always stand in the same way as its antecedent; but it depends on its sign or position *(sui signi vel situs)*. [54] In some cases the relative stands in the same mode as [its antecedent], e.g., "one man runs and another disputes", "every true proposition is necessary and any other proposition is impossible". In the first the relative and the antecedent stand determinately; in the latter they stand in a distributively confused way. In other cases the antecedent stands in a manner more confused than its relative as in "every true conditional is necessary and some [conditional] is impossible", here the antecedent stands distributively and the relative determinately. In still other cases, on the contrary, a relative of diversity stands in a more confused way than its antecedent as in "some man is black and no other is white". Here the antecedent stands determinately and the relative distributively. Similarly, in "some man reads and only another disputes", the relative stands merely confused, and the antecedent stands determinately.

The second rule: Every relative of identity of substance in the same category as its antecedent always stands in the same way as its antecedent. This is proved inductively: "every man who runs is moved", the relative and the antecedent stand distributively. Again, in "every man is an animal which is rational", [the relative] stands in a merely confused way. In "a man who reads disputes", [the relative] stands determinately. In "Socrates who runs does not sit", the relative stands discretely. The same thing is to be said of reciprocal relatives, whether they are possessives or non-possessives: e.g., in "every man sees himself", "himself" stands confused and distributively. In "some man loves his son", ["his"] stands determinately. In "Socrates' father calls him", "him" stands discretely.

From this rule follows this thesis: There is a universal affirmative categorical proposition having precisely one [55] sign; and the predicate of this proposition stands distributively confused, e.g., "every man is his very own self *(ipsemet)*".

The second thesis is this: The universal sign has the same force of distributing over the predicate as it has over the subject.

The third thesis: When there are two common terms following a universal affirmative sign, and these are not impeded by some other sign, the universal affirmative sign distributes the more remote and not the more proximate. This is clear: in "every man is seeing himself", "himself" stands distributively, and "seeing" stands in a merely confused way. And if against all of these rules, those from the fifth section of this chapter are adduced, I say that they apply outside the matter of relatives.[a]

Against [the third thesis] one argues in this way: given that "himself" will be distributed in the above proposition this inference would follow as well: "every man sees himself: therefore, every man sees every man". And it is said that "himself" stands distributively not absolutely but by referring *(referendo)* to a singular among singulars as in "this man sees himself", and "that man sees himself", and thus of singulars. From this analysis I infer that this inference does not follow: "only Socrates sees himself; therefore, every one seeing himself is Socrates", because "himself" in the first proposition stands discretely and in the second it stands distributively. But it does validly follow: "every one seeing Socrates is Socrates".

The third rule: Every relative of identity of substance hypothetically related to its antecedent standing in a merely confused way does not stand in the same way but determinately by being related to the entire composition of its antecedent. For example, in "every man is an animal and this one is rational", the relative "this one" *(istud)* stands determinately. Thus, the second part is false because it signifies assertively that an animal which every man is is rational, [56] which is false because there is no animal which is every man. Similarly, this is false, "I need an eye for seeing *(ad videndum)* and that I need for seeing" because I need no eye for seeing. Thus, it should be noted that "I need" with its gerund confounds a term in the nominative case coming after it in a merely confused way. And without [the gerund] it confounds in a confused and distributive manner.

The fourth rule: Every relative of identity of substance hypothetically related to its antecedent standing discretely or determinately or distributively stands in the same way in relation to the total composition of the antecedent or to either of the extremes. Thus, any of these is to be conceded: "some man is, and you are that"; "some man is, and you are not that". The rule does not signify that you are not some man who is; but rather that you some man who is are not. And this is true. Further, it is never correct to put its antecedent in the place of a relative unless the same supposition is served. Thus it follows that this is false: "some man is, and every man is that". Where "that" stands determinately the second

159

part signifies that some man is any man. But it is conceded that "every man is animal and the same is capable of laughter". Because "the same" does not stand in relation to the total composition but only in relation to either of the extremes. However, the antecedent stands in a non-distributed way, by having a relation to the total composition.

From this rule these theses follow: First, in a universal affirmative having only one sign whose predicate is a common term the predicate does not stand in a merely confused way but [57] determinately. This is clear from the predicate of the second part of this conjunctive: "some man is and any man is that".

The second thesis is this: When a universal sign is not impeded by some other sign it does not confound in a merely confused way a common term following it mediately in the same category. Nor is this absurd because this does not happen by reason of a sign. But a relative cannot be confounded because of a dependency which it has on its antecedent. Thus none of these theses or preceding statements destroys the rules of the other chapter because either a sign is impeded or a term is not capable of a confusion *(capax confusionis)*.

The fifth rule: A relative of accident, whether of identity or of diversity, does not always stand in the same way as its antecedent but according to the exigencies of its sign or position. Thus, sometimes it stands in the same way as its antecedent, e.g., "some man is white and such is a horse", "every white man reads and no such one disputes". Sometimes the antecedent stands in a manner more confused than its relative, e.g., "every white thing runs and such a one disputes". Sometimes, on the contrary, the relative stands in a manner more confused than its antecedent, e.g., "some man is white and no raven is such", "some man is black, and any Ethiopian is such". In any of these the antecedent stands determinately and the relative in one stands distributively and in the other in a merely confused manner. Further, it is to be noted that a relative of diversity of accident stands occasionally in a manner more confused than its antecedent. "Some man is black and not otherwise is a raven".

The sixth and last rule: Every [58] relative in the world stands in the same way as its antecedent in the basic sense of standing *(supponendi)*. Thus if the antecedent stands materially, the relative does so as well. If [the antecedent stands] personally, the relative stands personally. E.g., "man is a species and that is a name", the relative as well as the antecedent stands materially. But in saying "man is animal and that is capable of laughter" the relative as well as the antecedent stands personally.

The foregoing rules of the modes of standing of relatives ought to be understood in relation to the special modes of standing pertinent to suppositions: viz., discrete, determinate, merely confused, confused and distributive. And let this suffice for the topic of relatives.

Section 8 – Ampliation

Now, we turn to the topic of supposition with respect to diverse times containing the notions of ampliation and appellation. Ampliation is the acceptance of a term assumed temporally beyond the signification of the principal verb or its participle. From this formulation of a definition the first rule follows: every term standing in initial position and with respect to a verb of past time or its participle is ampliated in order to stand for that which is or which was, e.g., in "white was black", "white" does not stand for that which was white precisely or alone for that which is white; but in disjuncts [it stands for] that which is or was white.

From this follows the truth of these propositions: "a virgin was pregnant". It is clear that whoever is a virgin or was a virgin was pregnant. The second proposition: "a boy was an old man". He who is or was a boy was an old man – not certainly when he was a boy [59] [was he an old man] but after he was a boy [he was an old man]. The third proposition: "white was when nothing had whiteness" *(album fuit quando nullam habuit albedinem)*. This is clear because that which is or was white was when nothing had whiteness – given that now there is something white and continuously before this time it was black. Similarly one can treat the participle which is a predicate with respect to the verb "is", e.g., in "some man was dead", "man" stands for a man who is or was, and it signifies this proposition: "a man who is or who was, is dead". And as previously this is conceded: "a virgin was corrupted", because this one who is or who was a virgin was corrupted.

The second rule: Every term standing in initial position with respect to a verb of future time or to its participle stands for that which is or which will be, e.g., in "a man will be generated", "man" stands for only that which is or which will be. Thus it signifies this proposition: "whoever is a man or whoever will be a man will be generated".

From this rule follows the truth of these propositions: (1) "An old man will be a boy". It is clear that whoever is or will be an old man will be a boy. (2) "A whore will be a virgin", because whoever is or whoever will be a whore will be a virgin. (3) "A decapitated person will sing", because whoever is or whoever will be decapitated will sing. Further, we must examine supposition with respect to the participle, e.g., "some man is to be generated". For this proposition signifies that one who is or who will be a man is to be generated.

The third rule is this: Every term standing in initial or in a later position with respect to this verb "happens" *(contingit)* or its participle stands for that which is or happens to be; e.g., "white happens to be black", denotes that that which is white or happens to be white happens to be black. Again, "a sitting thing happens to run" *(sedentem contingens est currere)*.

The fourth rule or thesis is this: Every term standing in initial or later position with respect [60] to this verb "can" *(potest)* or its participles or a verb with terminal 'able' *(bilis* or *bile)* stands for that which is or can be, e.g., "white can be black". This denotes that what is or can be white can be black. From this rule these propositions follow: (1) "a creating one can be God", given that in this case *(ad hoc)* God does not create *in actu* because what is or can be creating can be God; (2) "the hottest thing can be hotter", because what is the hottest or can be the hottest can be hotter; (3) "the least can be less", *(inferius)* because what is or can be the least can be less. The same applies to the participle or the verbals of a term. For that reason it is conceded: "the generated is generable" and "the corrupted is corruptible". The first signifies that that which is generated or can be generated is generable. The second signifies that that which is corrupted or can be corrupted is corruptible.

The fifth rule: Every term standing in initial or later position with respect to these verbs "begins" and "ceases" or their participles stands for that which is or begins or ceases to be. E.g., "white begins or ceases to be", denotes that that which is either begins to be or ceases to be white. And a similar point may be made concerning their participles.

The sixth rule: Every term standing with respect to a verb or participle, having the nature of transcending indifferently what is either imaginable or impossible, whether placed before or after, stands immediately for that which is or can be imaginable or impossible. Thus it is with these verbs: "I understand", "I know" and the like. The significates also "the imaginable" or "the impossible" stand for that which is or can be imagined. When, therefore, someone says, "I understand or I know [61] a rose", it is denoted that I understand or know a rose which is or can be or is imaginable as well. And in this way is understood or known that which is not able to be — namely, as that which is able to be. For I understand a chimera or a golden mountain, neither of which is able to be. And this rule applies to a term in the nominative case relative to an active verb, or to a term in the nominative case relative to a passive verb, placed either before or after it.

From the foregoing rule it follows: First, from a three-term expression to a two-term expression with the predicate of the participle ampliated an argument does not follow.[a] Thus it does not follow: "Adam is dead; therefore, Adam is". "Antichrist is about to be; therefore, Antichrist is".

Second, it follows that this is not a solid conversion: "Antichrist is about to be *(futurus)*; therefore, a certain thing or something about to be is Antichrist".[b] Because in the antecedent "Antichrist" stands in an ampliative way and not in the consequent. Hence, it ought to be converted to "something is or will be Antichrist".

Third, it follows that this syllogism does not follow: "everything about to be is; Antichrist is about to be, therefore, Antichrist is". Because in the conclusion "Antichrist" does not stand in an ampliative way, as it does in the [minor] premise. Further, the [minor] premise ought to be: "what is of the kind of Antichrist is something about to be" *(talis antichristus est aliquod futurum)*, where "about to be" is taken as in the major nominally and not participally. And this is the end of our treatment of ampliation.

Section 9 – Appellation

Appellation is the acceptance of a term in a proposition with respect to the nature of the verb or participle; e.g., "some man is", "man" stands for man – not for any man existing at any time indifferently; but only for a man who is. I will clarify this definition. Note that appellation is divided into temporal appellation, ampliational appellation [62] and appellation of form.

Temporal appellation is the acceptance of a term in a proposition for something or for some things according to the consignification alone of the verb or its participle; e.g., in "white was black", "white" stands indifferently for that which is white or was white; and "black" stands only for that which was black, and its verb consignifies only the past. Thus "black" appells only past time.

The first rule ist this: Every term standing with respect to a verb of present time not ampliated or drawn by an ampliative participle appells the present time whether it stands in initial or in a later position, e.g., "man is animal" or "Socrates runs". Any of these terms, whether subject or predicate, stands only for that which is.

The second rule: Every term following an ampliative verb of past time only or of future time or their participles appells the past or the future, e.g., "this was white", "this will be black". "White" in the first proposition stands precisely for that which was white. In the second proposition ["black"] stands for that which will be black.

Ampliational appellation is the acceptance of an ampliative term taken to be limited through an earlier ampliative term; e.g., in "man can be white", "white" stands in an ampliative way whether it occurs in initial or in a later position. But in initial position "white" does not appell, whereas in a later position "white" appells fully the ampliation.

The first rule is this: Every term standing with respect to some of these verbs "begins", "ceases" or their participles appells an ampliation, e.g., in "Socrates begins to be white", "white" stands for that which is or begins to be white. But posited initially it does not appell because [63] it stands ampliated, yet it does not appell this ampliation. However, posited in a later position it appells because of the limitation of the preceding appellative terms.

The second rule: Every term following some of these verbs: "is able" *(potest)* and "happens" *(contingit)* or their participles appells ampliations of these terms, e.g., in "Socrates happens to be white", "white" is ampliated as well when it occurs after the subject or in the subject. When it occurs after the initial position it appells the ampliations of those verbs which limit it. Yet it does not appell when it is in the initial position because it is not limited by those verbs.

Appellation of form is the acceptance of a term in a proposition limited by a preceding term concerned with a mental act, e.g., in "I understand man", "man" appells its form because it signifies its significate under the very same aspect as that limitation made by a term concerned with a mental act.[a] Thus through the foregoing proposition it is denoted that I understand something under the aspect of *(sub ratione qua)* man. Similarly "I understand a rose", or "I know a rose", i.e., something as a rose; however, in saying "I understand a rose" one need not add that replication, "I understand something as a rose". It suffices that something which is or can be a rose I understand or know. Further, in saying "rose I understand", "rose" stands ampliated only; but in saying "I understand rose", "rose" stands ampliatively and appellatively.

From this definition three theses follow: firstly, "your father I know; however, I do not know your father". This is proved: I posit that Socrates is your father whom I know. However, I do not know who is your father because I am not considering with respect to your father whether you have one or not. That one posited as your father I know because that which is your father I know; I do not know your father, however, because [64] I do not know something under the aspect of *(sub ratione qua)* your father.

The second thesis: "Socrates I want to see; however, I do not want to see Socrates." It is proved: I posit that Socrates is my enemy, and thus that I do not want to see him. And Plato is my friend similar to the Socrates existing in my heart whom I believe to be Plato. Given these conditions, Socrates I want to see because this is Socrates I want to see insofar as, or to the extent that, I hold him to be Plato; however, I do not want to see

Socrates because I do not want to see something under the aspect of *(sub ratione qua)* Socrates.

The third thesis: "A hypothetical proposition you know; however, you do not know some hypothetical proposition." It is proved: I posit that you firmly believe that no proposition is hypothetical; there is, however, some hypothetical proposition which you believe to be categorical [by considering and knowing] its significate. Given these conditions, some hypothetical proposition you know because that which is a hypothetical proposition you know; however, you do not know some hypothetical proposition because you do not know something under the aspect of *(sub ratione qua)* a hypothetical proposition. And consequently, "an affirmative proposition I believe; however, I do not believe an affirmative proposition". Again, "a negative proposition I assent to; yet I do not assent to a negative proposition". Or again, "a necessary proposition I assent to; however, I do not assent to a necessary proposition". "A universal proposition I doubt; yet I do not doubt a universal proposition". And there is an infinity of others which can be considered in the light of the foregoing discussion.

Notes

[30][a] The *Logica Magna* presents a threefold division of supposition into material, simple and personal. Concerning the background of simple supposition see Chapter I, n. [26][a]. The subdivisions of personal supposition are the standard ones. For the *Logica Magna* treatment of material supposition see below n. [36][a].

[b] The material sign is *'li'* or *'ly'*, the definite article borrowed from Old French and present in several vernacular languages in the later Middle Ages, e.g., German *"die"*, English "the" and Italian *"gli"*. See below p. [33] ff.

[36][a] Although the *Logica Magna* does not explicitly subdivide material supposition in direct parallel to personal supposition (as does the *Logica Parva*) it recognizes in practice that terms in material supposition can be further modified by quantifying terms. For example, it says, "as in fact it is true that 'this man is a man' and 'that man is a man', so it is true that 'this 'man' is a 'man', and 'that 'man' is a 'man' ". See Perreiah, 3, p. 67 ff. The usefulness of this recognition is limited, however, because many rules of inference do not apply to statements containing terms in material supposition. "And if one in proving the denied consequence appeals to this rule, i.e., 'from a lower-level term to a higher-level term where no restrictions are involved is a valid inference', as was done above, I say that the rule does not hold in material *suppositio* but only in personal or significative *suppositio*." See Perreiah, 3, p. 33. Of course it is fallacious to reason from a term having one kind of *suppositio* to a term having a different kind of *suppositio*.

[40][a] For personal supposition in the *Logica Magna* see Perreiah, 3, p. 81 ff.

[42][a] The *Logica Parva* divides the exclusive proposition into three kinds. The *Logica Magna* recognizes two additional kinds of exclusives. See below n. [100][a].

b A reduplicative proposition is one containing an expression such as "insofar as" *(inquantum)*. See below Chapter IV, p. [106] ff.

c A modal proposition in the composite sense is one in which the modal auxiliary operates over the entire proposition. See below [87] and [93].

[46][a] One term falls "immediately over" another if no term occurs between the two terms.

[49][a] See Chapter IV, p. [107]ff.

[53][a] This puzzle was much discussed in medieval logic. See Lambert of Auxerre's *Logica* in Alessio, pp. 241–242. Professor Geach has used examples from the medieval texts in writing about reflexive pronouns. See Geach, 3, pp. 112–115.

[55][a] See above Section 5 on "Confounding Terms", pp. [45]–[52] and p. [57].

[61][a] A two-termed proposition *(propositio secunda adjacens)* is a categorical proposition that has only a subject and a copula for its principal parts. For example, "you are". A three-termed proposition *(propositio tertia adjacens)* is a categorical proposition that has a subject, a predicate and a copula for its principal parts. For example, "a man is an animal". Some propositions are of neither the second nor the third adjacent. For a fuller elaboration of the doctrine see Adams and Del Punta, in Adams, 3, p. 266.

b *"futurus"* is the future active participle of the verb "to be". It is almost untranslatable into English. The expression "about to be" is, perhaps, as close a translation as is available. The parallel expression in the past tense is *"praeteritus"* which is even more difficult to translate "passed away" is, perhaps, a close English equivalent. See below note [82][a].

[63][a] For a fuller discussion of terms which "appell" a form see Chapter IV, p. [90]ff.

Chapter III
On Inferences

Section 1 – Definitions and Divisions

An inference is the delivery *(illatio)* of a consequent from an antecedent:
e.g., "man runs; therefore, animal runs".[a] The antecedent I call the proposition preceding the sign of inference *(notam rationis)*; e.g., "man runs".
[65] The consequent I call that which follows: e.g., "animal runs". The
sign of inference or delivery I call "therefore" *(li ergo)* or "thus" *(li igitur)*.
Following the statement of this definition, the first division of inferences
is into solid *(bona)* and unsolid *(mala)*. A solid inference is that in which
the opposite of the consequent is repugnant to the antecedent. E.g., "you
are man, therefore, you are animal". For these two propositions are repugnant: "you are man and you are not animal". Thus the first inference
was solid. An unsolid inference is that in which the opposite of the consequent stands with the antecedent. E.g., "You are man; therefore, you are
sitting", for here, these two propositions stand simultaneously, "you are
man" and "you are not sitting", and therefore, this inference is unsolid.

A second division of solid inferences is into those which are formal
and those which are material. A formal inference is that in which the opposite of the consequent is repugnant formally to the antecedent. E.g., "you
run; therefore, you move". "Formally repugnant" means that these two
propositions are not imaginable to stand simultaneously without a contradiction *(non sunt ymaginabilia stare simul sine contradictione)*; e.g.,
"you run, and you do not move". A solid material inference is that in which
the contradictory of the consequent is materially repugnant to the antecedent. E.g., "God is not; therefore, no man is". Those are said to be
"materially repugnant" which cannot stand simultaneously, yet one can
imagine them to stand simultaneously without any contradiction; e.g., "God
is not, and some man is". For these cannot stand simultaneously because
of the impossibility of the proposition, "God is not", and yet, they can
be imagined to stand simultaneously without any contradiction because
"that God is not" *(quod deus non sit)* and "some man is" *(aliquis homo sit)*
does not seem to imply a contradiction.[a]

Following this definition we lay down two rules.[b] The first rule is:
From the impossible follows anything, i.e. from any impossible proposition
any other proposition follows. [66] E.g., "man is not; therefore, a stick

stands in a corner". The second rule is: The necessary follows from anything, i.e., every necessary proposition follows from any other proposition. E.g., "you are not running; therefore, God is". And these two rules are understood to mean: that inference is solid and material in which the antecedent is impossible or the consequent is necessary, subsuming those under certain other modes by which the inference is made solid and formal. Thus it follows formally: "man is; therefore, animal is". However, the consequent is necessary. Similarly, "man is a donkey; therefore, man is animal". However, the antecedent is impossible.

The [second] division of solid inference is into solid in form *(bona de forma)* and solid in matter *(bona de materia)*. An inference solid in form is that which is such that any inference of like form is solid. E.g., "man runs; therefore, animal runs". This inference is solid, and any similar to it in form is solid", e.g., "white is seen; therefore, color is seen". Those inferences are similar in form which have a mode of arguing similar to a formal inference. More will be said later about these modes and about antecedents and consequents which are similar in form. First, it is to be known that those hypothetical propositions are similar in form in which the categorical expressions and signs are similar in form: e.g., "man runs and an animal is moved". And note that those categoricals are similar in form which are so related that if one is affirmative or negative in a two- or in a three-termed statement the other one is also; and if one is either universal, particular, indefinite or singular, the other one is likewise. Further, if one is exclusive, exceptive, reduplicative or modal in the composite or divided sense, the other one is similarly. Further, if one is of a simple term or of a disjoint, [67] conjoint or conditioned composite, the other one is likewise. Thus these are not similar in form: "man or donkey runs" [and] "man runs", because one is of a composite term and the other of a simple term. Similarly, these are not similar in form. "Each man runs"; and "a donkey moves", because one is universal affirmative, and the other is indefinite. On the other hand, these are similar in form: "man is a donkey", and "man is an animal", notwithstanding the fact that one is necessary, and the other is impossible because they satisfy all of the assigned conditions. From which it follows that these inferences are similar in form: "man runs; therefore, animal runs", "white is seen; therefore, color is seen". For they have a mode of arguing similar to a formal inference since in each of them it is argued affirmatively from a lower-level to a higher-level; and the antecedents of the inferences are similar in form as is clear from the conditions stated. An inference solid in matter is one which is solid, but not any other one like it in form is solid; e.g., "you are not man; therefore, you are not animal". That inference is solid because the contradictory of the consequent is repugnant to the antecedent; yet not any similar to it is solid; e.g., "this is not man — pointing to a donkey; therefore, this is not animal".

From the foregoing it follows that there is a solid and formal inference which is not solid in form *(de forma)*, as the one just mentioned and the following: "only a father is; therefore, not only a father is", "you know yourself to be a stone; therefore, you do not know yourself to be a stone". "You believe precisely that some man is deceived; therefore, some man is deceived".[a]

Section 2 — General Rules of Formal Inference

Here are some universal rules for formal inference. The first: If in some inference the contradictory of the antecedent follows from the contradictory of the consequent, the inference is solid; e.g., "man [68] runs; therefore, animal runs". For it validly follows "no animal runs, therefore, no man runs", or "therefore, nothing which is man runs".

A corollary to the first rule: If in some inference the contradictory of the consequent does not yield the contradictory of the antecedent that inference does not follow. Thus it does not follow: "You are speaking; therefore, you are disputing", because it does not follow: "You are not disputing; therefore, you are not speaking".

The second rule: If in some solid inference the antecedent is true, the consequent also is true; for although the true does follow from the false, from the true none other than the true follows, as Aristotle says in the first book of *Prior Analytics*.

From this rule two other corollaries follow: First, in a solid inference, if the consequent is false, the antecedent is likewise false. "You are a donkey; therefore, you are not a man."

Second, if in some inference the antecedent is true and the consequent is false that inference is unsolid. Thus it does not follow: "a chimera who runs does not move; therefore a chimera runs", because the antecedent is true, and the consequent is false. "You who are God are not man; therefore, you are not man."

The third rule: In a solid inference, if the antecedent is necessary the consequent is necessary also. E.g., "man is; therefore, animal is". From which it follows that if the antecedent is necessary and the consequent is contingent that inference is not solid: e.g., "every man is animal; therefore, you are animal".

The fourth rule: In a solid inference, if the antecedent is possible, the consequent is also possible, e.g., "you are Pope; therefore, you are a high priest". From which it follows that if the antecedent is possible and the consequent is impossible that inference is not solid because it does not follow: "Everything running is man; therefore, this running thing is man" — pointing to a donkey, because the antecedent is possible and the consequent is impossible.

The fifth rule: If some inference is solid, and something follows from the consequent that same thing [69] follows from the antecedent. For it follows validly: "man runs; therefore, animal runs"; from which consequent it follows that "body runs", and thus it must also follow from the antecedent: "Man runs; therefore, body runs". From this rule two others follow.

The first rule is: Whatever implies the antecedent also implies the consequent. Hence this is a solid inference: "man runs; therefore, an animal runs", and since this one "you run" implies the proposition, "man runs", therefore, it also implies the proposition "animal runs". For it well follows: "you run; therefore, an animal runs".

The second rule: In a chain of propositions when all of the intermediate inferences are solid and formal and non-varied, an inference from the first antecedent to the last consequent is formally valid. E.g., "man is; therefore, animal is. Animal is; therefore, body is. Body is; therefore substance is". And thus from the first to the last it follows formally: "man is; therefore, substance is". The intermediate inferences are not varied when the consequent posited in the inference is the antecedent of the subsequent inference, as is the case in the example. If the intermediate inferences should not be solid and unvaried the inference would not be solid. Just as in this example: "no time is; therefore, day is not; day is not, and some hour is; therefore, it is night; night is; therefore, some time is". And yet the inference from first to last, "no time is; therefore, some time is", is not solid because of the variation made; because in the first inference the consequent was "day is not", and it was not the antecedent of the second inference, rather, the conjunctive proposition "day is not and some hour is", was the antecedent of the second inference.

The sixth rule: In a solid inference, where something stands with the antecedent, the same stands with the consequent. E.g., it follows: "every [70] man runs; therefore, [every risible being] runs". With the antecedent stands this one: "Every animal runs" and also "No donkey is moved", and so on. And thus each of these stands with the consequent.

From this rule another rule follows: Anything repugnant to the consequent is repugnant to the antecedent. This is clear by considering all that was said above concerning inferences.

The seventh rule: If some inference is solid and is known by you to be solid and its antecedent is to be conceded, then its consequent must also be conceded. From which two rules follow. First: If a consequent is to be denied by you, the antecedent should also be denied. Second: If the antecedent is to be conceded by you, but the consequent is to be denied by you, that inference is not solid; e.g., "every man is; therefore, Antichrist is".

The eighth rule: If some solid inference is known by you to be [solid] and the antecedent is also known by you, the consequent of the same is known by you; e.g., "you are man; therefore you are animal". And notably it is said, "known by you to be solid" because this inference is solid. "Brunellus is a donkey; therefore, Brunellus is capable of braying *(rudibilis)*". While the antecedent is known by someone, he nonetheless does not know the consequent because he does not know the inference to be solid.

Section 3 — Particular Rules of Formal Inference

Now here are some particular rules of formal inferences which deal with the relationship between logical superiors and logical inferiors.[a] First: from a lower-level term to its corresponding higher-level term affirmatively and without a sign of distribution and without any confounding signs impeding there is a solid inference. E.g., "man runs; therefore, animal runs".

The second rule: From a lower-level term to its corresponding higher-level term with a sign of distribution or of a term merely confused and immobile the inference is not solid. Because it does not follow: "every man runs; therefore, every animal runs". [71] Nor does it follow: "no man runs; therefore, no animal runs". And note that it says, "of a term merely confused and immobile". For it does not follow: "if man is a donkey, man is capable of braying; therefore, if man is animal, man is capable of braying". But by arguing to a term merely confused mobily it is a solid argument. E.g., "every man is animal; therefore, every man is a substance", [where] "animal" has merely confused mobile supposition.

The third rule: From a lower-level term to its corresponding higher-level term, with a sign of negation placed after the term and with a due mean there is a solid argument. E.g., "you are not running, and you are man; therefore, man is not running". And note that it says, "with a due mean" because without that condition the argument would not be solid. Hence it does not follow: "you are not animal; therefore, man is not animal", because the antecedent is possible and the consequent is impossible and because an affirmative does not follow from a negative.

The fourth rule: From a higher-level term to its corresponding lower-level term affirmatively and without a distribution the argument is not solid. For it does not follow: "animal runs; therefore, man runs".

171

The fifth rule: From a higher-level term to its corresponding lower-level term distributed affirmatively the argument is not solid unless with the due mean, because it does not follow: "every animal runs; therefore, every man runs". "You differ from a donkey; therefore, you differ from Brunellus." But with the due mean, the argument is solid, e.g.: "you differ from a donkey; Brunellus is a donkey; therefore, you differ from Brunellus".

The sixth rule: From a higher-level term to its corresponding lower-level term with a sign of negation placed in front there is a solid argument; since it validly follows: "no animal runs; therefore, no man runs". And this rule concerns signs of negation which distribute the higher-level term. Because if the term were not distributed, the argument would not be solid. Thus it does not follow: "not no animal runs; therefore, not no man runs"; nor does it follow: "not every animal is running; therefore, not every man is running". This is clear because in each of these, the contradictory of the consequent stands with the antecedent; therefore, etc.

Section 4 – Rules of Inference Based on Quantity

Here are some rules pertaining to the quantity of propositions. The first rule: From a universal to its corresponding particular [72] or indefinite proposition which is called its subalternate there is a solid argument. E.g., "every animal runs; therefore some animal runs". "No animal runs; therefore, an animal does not run."

The second rule: From a particular or from an indefinite to the corresponding universal proposition the argument is not solid unless owing to the matter. Thus it does not follow: "some man runs; therefore, each man runs". Nor does it follow: ["animal is not running; therefore, no animal is running"]. But sometimes the inference does hold in virtue of matter either because the consequent is necessary or the antecedent is impossible, or because the contradictory of the consequent is repugnant to the antecedent. Hence it surely follows: "some man is; therefore, every man is", "some man is not; therefore, no man is".

The third rule: From an affirmative universal to all of its singulars collectively or divisively accompanied by the due mean there is a solid argument, and conversely. An example of a term taken collectively: "all animals run, and these are all the animals there are; therefore, this animal runs, and that animal runs, and thus for other singulars". An example of a term taken divisively: "every animal runs; this is animal; therefore, this runs". Similarly it follows conversely; "this animal runs and that animal runs and thus of other singulars; and these are all the animals there are; therefore, every animal runs". And notably it is said "with the due mean" because without the due mean the argument is not solid unless owing to the matter; thus it does not follow: "every man runs; therefore, this man runs and so on of other singulars". Similarly, it does not follow: "every man is animal; therefore, this man is animal and that man is animal and thus of other singulars". For the antecedent is necessary and the consequent is contingent, since it is a conjunctive proposition each part of which is contingent and neither conjunct is repugnant to the others. Nevertheless, this inference follows owing to the matter: "every man is a donkey; therefore, that man is a donkey". "every sun lights; therefore, this [73] sun lights", because in the first the antecedent is impossible, and in the second the consequent is necessary.

The fourth rule: From a universal negative to any of its singulars is a solid inference, and it may be argued either with or without a due mean. But conversely, the inference does not hold unless with a due mean, e.g., "no man runs; therefore, this man does not run, nor that one, nor that, and thus of other singulars". But conversely, it does not follow: "this man does not run and that man does not run and thus of other singulars; therefore, no man runs". For after a thousand years the antecedent will be true and the consequent false. But it validly follows with the addition of the due mean: "these are all the masculine men there are".

The fifth rule: From a particular to its corresponding indefinite, affirmative as well as negative, and conversely there is a solid inference; e.g., "animal does not run; therefore some animal does not run" and conversely. Similarly, "some donkey is moved; therefore, donkey is moved".

The sixth rule: From a particular or indefinite proposition to all of its singulars taken disjunctively and with a due mean there is a solid argument: "man runs and these are all the men there are: therefore, this man runs or that man runs and thus of other singulars". Note that the rule says "with a due mean" because without that the argument is not solid, e.g., "man is animal; therefore, this man is animal or that man is animal and thus of other singulars", because the antecedent is necessary and the consequent is contingent: for the consequent is a disjunctive proposition each part of which is contingent, nor is one part repugnant to the other, nor is its contradictory impossible.

Section 5 — Rules of Inference not Based on Quantity

Concerning non-quantitative propositions such as the exclusive, the exceptive and the like, here is the first rule: From an exclusive to the corresponding universal with the terms transposed there is a solid inference. Thus, "only man runs; therefore, every running thing is man"; "only animal runs; therefore, everything which runs [74] is animal". Likewise conversely: 'every animal moves; therefore, that which moves is animal".

The second rule: From a negative exceptive to its corresponding exclusive there is a solid inference. Thus it follows: "nothing except Socrates runs; therefore, only Socrates runs", and conversely; as for example: "only man is capable of laughter; therefore, nothing besides man is capable of laughter". And notably it is said, "to its corresponding exclusive" because this inference is not solid: "no man except Socrates runs; therefore, only Socrates runs". Because this is not its corresponding exclusive but rather this: "only Socrates is some running man etc.".

The third rule is: From a lower-level term to its corresponding higher-level term on the part of the subject with an exclusive expression added to it there is a solid inference. Thus it follows: "only man runs; therefore, only animal runs". Because it is argued from a lower-level term to its higher-level term in a merely confused mobile way.

The fourth rule: From a lower-level term to its corresponding higher-level term on the part of the predicate with an exclusive expression added on the part of the subject there is not a solid argument. Thus, it does not follow: "only man is man; therefore only man is animal". Because it is argued from a distribution, but conversely and with the due mean the inference does hold.

The fifth rule is a corollary following from the aforesaid: From a term standing in a merely confused or in a determinate way to a term standing distributively and confusedly there is not a solid argument; "man is animal; therefore, only man is animal". "You differ from all men; therefore, you differ from man."

The sixth rule: From a term standing in a confused and distributive way to the same one standing determinately there is a solid argument. E.g., "only man is animal; therefore, some man is animal". "You differ from man; therefore, you differ from some man." "You are other than animal; therefore, you are other than [some] animal."

The seventh rule: From a term standing in a merely confused way to the same categorematic term standing determinately with respect to the same syncategorematic term or sign of distribution there is not a solid argument: [75] e.g., "every man is animal; therefore, man is every animal". But with respect to a different syncategorematic term the argument is solid, "only man is animal; therefore, man is every animal".

Section 6 – Rules of Inference Involving Special Terms

Here follow the rules concerning the pertinence and non-pertinence of terms. The first: From the affirmative of one disparate term to the negation of another disparate term there is a solid argument: "you are man; therefore, you are not a donkey". "You are running; therefore, you are not sitting." "You are white; therefore, you are not black." But the converse does not follow because an affirmative does not follow from a negative.

The second rule: Whenever there is a pair of propositions whose subjects and predicates are interchangeable the propositions remaining the same in denomination, there is a solid inference from one to the other. E.g., "you are man; therefore, you are rational animal", and conversely. "You are man or non-man; therefore, you are a being", and conversely. And notably it is said "remaining the same in denomination", because if one should be affirmative and the other negative, they are not converted. E.g., "you are a man and you are not a man". Further, if one were of one quantity, the other of another quantity or no quantity, neither could be converted. E.g., "Every animal is man; therefore, some animal is man", and "only animal is man".

The third rule: From one convertible proposition to another there is a solid inference: "you are man; therefore, you are capable of laughter", and conversely. "Brunellus is capable of braying; therefore, Brunellus is a donkey", and conversely.

The fourth rule: From one of the correlatives to the other in two-termed propositions there is a solid argument: e.g., "double is; therefore, half is", and conversely. And notably it is said "two-termed propositions", because it does not follow: "A is double; therefore, A is half". [76] "A father is bearded; therefore, a son is bearded."

The fifth rule: From a privative term to an infinite term there is a solid inference, but not conversely. E.g., "you are un-just; therefore, you are not just". But it does not follow conversely as in "a stone is not just; therefore, a stone is unjust", because the antecedent is true, as is clear, and the consequent is false; for anything which is unjust can be just, but a stone is not able to be just; therefore, it cannot be unjust.

The sixth rule: From an affirmative with a privative or infinite predicate to a negative there is a solid inference: "you are blind; therefore, you are not seeing". "You are non-man; therefore, you are not man." But conversely the argument is not valid, because from a negative proposition an affirmative one does not follow.

The seventh rule: From a negative proposition with a finite predicate to an affirmative proposition with an infinite predicate and with the due mean, there is a solid inference. E.g., "you are not a donkey; and you are; therefore, you are a non-donkey", etc.

Section 7 — Additional Rules of Inference

With regard to these matters, here are some additional rules. First, from all the exponents of a proposition — taken simultaneously — to the exponible proposition there is a solid inference, and conversely.[a] And this is a general rule applicable to exponible propositions such as [universals], exclusives, exceptives and the like. Thus it follows validly: "man runs and nothing is man unless it runs; therefore, every man runs", and conversely. Likewise, "man runs and no non-man runs; therefore, only man runs", etc.

The second rule: From every exponible proposition to each of its exponents there is a solid inference, but not conversely except in virtue of matter; e.g., "every man runs; therefore nothing is man unless it runs", but not conversely, because from a negative proposition an affirmative one does not follow.[b] Nonetheless, sometimes it holds because of the matter of certain propositions: e.g., "man is donkey; therefore, only man is donkey", because the antecedent is impossible.

The third rule: From any contradictory of an exponent, the contradictory of an exposited proposition follows, [77] but not conversely. Thus it solidly follows: "[some] non-man runs; therefore, not only man runs", but not conversely, because an affirmative does not follow from a negative.

The fourth rule: From resoluble propositions to a resolvent there is a solid inference; but not conversely: e.g., "this is man, and this runs; therefore, a man runs". But it does not follow: "man is running; therefore, this is running and this is man", because after a millenium the antecedent will be true and the consequent false.

The fifth rule: From officiating propositions to their officiates there is a solid inference but not conversely. E.g., "this proposition is true: 'Man is animal', which adequately signifies man to be animal; therefore, man to be animal is true". But the converse argument is not solid because if it were, the antecedent would be necessary and the consequent contingent.[a]

The sixth rule: From a description to the described proposition there is a solid inference and conversely. E.g., "I understand something under the aspect of being a man: therefore, I understand man", and conversely. "I understand man; therefore, I understand something under the aspect of being a man."[b]

The seventh rule: From a proposition in the composite sense to one in the divided sense and conversely there is not a solid inference. E.g., "necessarily man is animal; therefore man necessarily is animal", because the

176

antecedent is true and the consequent false. And it also does not follow: "a white thing can be black; therefore, it is possible for white to be black".

The eighth rule: From one cause of truth to a proposition having that cause of truth there is a solid inference, but not conversely. E.g., "while a man runs, one capable of laughter runs; therefore, by a man running one capable of laughter runs". That inference is solid; but the converse is invalid: "by a man running one capable of laughter runs; therefore, while a man runs one capable of laughter runs". For assuming that nothing runs, the consequent which asserts man to run is false. And the antecedent is true; for its truth is shown through another cause of truth; viz. "if man runs, something capable of laughter runs". It is said, therefore, that a proposition denominated a "consequential ablative" has three causes of truth: viz., conditional, causal and temporal from any of which [78] there is a solid inference to the proposition having these causes; but not conversely.

The ninth rule: From an active proposition to a passive proposition there is a solid inference: e.g., "Socrates loves [Plato] therefore, [Plato] is loved by Socrates".

The tenth rule: From a three-termed proposition to a two-termed affirmative proposition without a distracting term there is a solid inference; e.g., "you are man; therefore, you are". Note that it says "affirmative" because it does not follow: "you are not a donkey; therefore, you are not". And it is said "without a distracting term" because it does not follow: "Antichrist is about to be *(est futurus)*; therefore, Antichrist is", therefore, etc.

Section 8 — Rules of Inference for Hypothetical Propositions

Lastly, here are some rules for the proof of hypothetical propositions: The first: From an affirmative conjunction to either of its principal parts there is a solid inference, but not conversely, unless owing to the matter of the proposition. E.g., "you run and you dispute; therefore, you dispute". But it does not follow: "you dispute; therefore, you dispute and you run". When, however, it holds because of the terms (sc. when the conjunctive is made from two propositions one of which antecedes the other) then from that part to the total conjunction there is a solid inference; e.g., "you are man; therefore, you are man and you are animal". "You run; therefore, you run and you move." And notably, it says "affirmative conjunction" because a negative conjunctive does not allow a solid inference to either of its parts. For it does not follow: "it is not the case that you are a man and you are a donkey; therefore, you are a donkey", because the antecedent is true, and the consequent is false. From this rule it follows that from a proposition with a conjunctive extreme to either part of its extreme the inference is not solid; e.g., "Socrates and Plato sail a boat; therefore, Socrates sails a boat". But if it does follow, it does so owing to the matter of the terms: e.g., "Socrates and Plato run; therefore, Socrates runs".

The second rule: From the principal part of an affirmative disjunction to the total disjunctive proposition there is a solid argument, but not conversely. E.g., "you run; therefore, you run or you are a man". But it does not follow: "You run or you are man; therefore, you run". [79] Sometimes, however, the converse holds because of the matter of the proposition: viz., when a disjunctive proposition consists of two parts one of which follows from the other, then the inference from the proposition to the other part is solid. "You are man or you are animal; therefore, you are animal." Or, "you are white or you are colored; therefore, you are colored". From this rule it follows that from part of a disjunct to a total disjunct there is a solid inference; e.g., "man runs, therefore, man or donkey runs".

The third rule: From an affirmative disjunctive with the destruction of one of its parts to its other part there is a solid inference. "You run or you sit; but you do not sit; therefore, you run."

The fourth rule: From a negative conjunctive to a disjunctive made from the contradictory parts of an affirmative conjunctive there is a solid inference. "It is not the case that you are man and you are donkey; therefore, you are not man or you are not donkey", and conversely. And note that an affirmative conjunctive has two contradictories; one of these is a negative conjunctive in which the negation sign is placed before [the conjunction]; the other one is a disjunctive proposition made from the opposite [i.e., negated] parts of the conjunctive. For this reason it is necessary that a negative conjunctive and an affirmative disjunctive are mutually convertible; e.g., "you are man and you are donkey" has two contradictories of which one is "not: you are man and you are donkey". And the second is: "you are not man or you are not donkey".

The fifth rule: From a negative disjunctive to an affirmative conjunctive made from the contradictory parts of the affirmative disjunctive there is a solid inference and conversely. E.g., "not: you run or you sit; therefore, you do not run and you do not sit", and conversely. The reason is that an affirmative disjunctive gets its contradictory through the negation sign placed in front of the total proposition; or through the conjunction of the opposite [i.e. contradictory] parts. E.g., "you run or you sit", is contradicted by either of these: "not: you run or you sit", or "you do not run and you do not sit".

The sixth rule: From an affirmative conditional with its [80] antecedent to its consequent there is a solid inference. E.g., "if you are man, you are animal; but you are man; therefore, you are animal".

The seventh rule: From an affirmative conditional with the contradiction of the consequent to the contradiction of the antecedent there is a solid inference: "if Antichrist is white, Antichrist is colored; but Antichrist is not colored; therefore, Antichrist is not white". Note that I said, "affirmative" in the statement of both rules; with the negative conditional we do not have the same rules. This is the end of the chapter "On Inferences" usefully collected by the distinguished doctor of arts and sacred theology the great Paul of Venice, of the order of the Hermits of St. Augustine.

Notes

[64]^a The words "antecedent" *(antecedens)* and "consequent" *(consequens)* are properly used to describe the two parts, the protasis and the apodosis, of a conditional statement. Less properly they are used to designate the first and second statement of any compound statement.

[65]^a Because "God is not" cannot be true it is said to be impossible; and since a conjunction one of whose members is impossible is itself impossible, "God is not, and some man is", is also impossible. Despite the fact that it is impossible, Paul allows that the two propositions "can be imagined" together. The notion of "imaginability" was problematic; it seems to involve, minimally, admissibility into the context of a dialectical exchange.

^b These rules state general properties of conditional statements. In modern logic they are called "the paradoxes of strict implication". To call them paradoxes, however, is misleading. On the one hand they express the plainest of tautologies which follow directly from the truth-table definitions of the material conditional. They appear paradoxical only in particular cases when the material conditional so defined is assumed to be the correct translation of a conditional taken from a natural-language context. See Ashworth, 6, pp. 133–136 and Bedell, p. 226 ff.

[67]^a The last of these examples is treated at length in Chapter VIII. See below, pp. [190]–[191].

[70]^a The doctrine of "logical inferiors and superiors" is the view that the categorematic terms of a natural language each have a definite place within a hierarchy of terms extending from the most abstract to the most concrete. This theory is crucial not only in the task of removing unwanted ambiguity from terms and establishing the basic logical forms of propositions. It is important also for the theory of inference because many of the rules of inference are geared to the distinction between higher- und lower-level terms.

[76]^a For a fuller discussion of exponible propositions see Chapter IV., pp. [84]–[87].

   ^b Note that the exponents may be taken together (Rule 1) or separately (Rule 2).

[77]^a For a fuller discussion of officiable propositions see Chapter IV, pp. [86]–[90].

   ^b For a fuller treatment of describable propositions see Chapter IV, pp. [90]–[93].

Chapter IV
On Proving Terms

Section 1 – Resoluble Propositions

How inferential propositions are proved in the present [tense] the doctrine is well known. And first one begins with resolution by which one infers from indefinite or particular propositions singular propositions which have for their subject terms none other than pronominal demonstratives. Each of these three types of proposition is to be inferred in this way: Two demonstrative propositions are taken as the antecedent; in the first of these the predicate of the resoluble proposition is predicated, and in the second the subject of the resoluble proposition is predicated. E.g., "man runs", is thus resolved into, "this runs and this is man; therefore, man runs". An example in an oblique case is resolved in a similar way: "of man is a donkey".[a] "Of this is a donkey and this is man; therefore, of man is a donkey." The same can be said for other cases of singular terms. An example of a plural: "men run; these run and these are men; therefore men run". An example of plural number in an oblique case: "of a pair of contradictories one of the two is true: of these one of the two is true and these are contradictories; therefore, [of a pair of contradictories one of the two is true]". The same can be said of other cases, so that the first demonstrative is always in the same case as the original resoluble; while the second is assumed to be continually in the nominative case. Propositions with an ampliated verb [81] are proved in the same way except that the second demonstrative must be combined with a disjunct predicate with the substantive verb in the present tense and the other verbs of past or future tense or other verbs (e.g., verbs of possibility). For example, "man was running" is resolved in the following way: "this was running and this is or was man; therefore, man was running". Again, "man will be disputing": "this is disputing, and this is or will be man"; therefore, "[man will be disputing]". Thus the substantive verb taken in the second position is always similar in time to the verb of the resoluble proposition. But when the main verb of the proposition to be resolved is "can", "begins", or "ceases", the second proposition will be similar to the second verb, e.g., "man can be white: this can be white and this is or can be man; therefore [man can be white]". Likewise, "white begins to be black: this begins to be black; and this is or begins to be white; therefore, [white begins to be black]". And the same holds with respect to the plural.

A similar point applies to propositions with a conjunct extreme or a disjunct extreme; e.g. "man or donkey runs". If the total disjunct is subject, then the proposition is resolved in this way: "Man or donkey runs: this runs and this is man or donkey; therefore, [Man or donkey runs.]" If, on the other hand, the first part of the disjunct is the subject, then the proposition will be resolved in this way: "man or donkey runs; this runs and this is man; therefore, man or donkey runs". And the same applies to a proposition with a conjunct or conditional subject, e.g., "man and donkey runs", "a proposition, if it is impossible, is false". The same holds for particular and singular affirmative resoluble propositions as well as indefinites; e.g., "some man runs", "Socrates disputes". But a particular or indefinite negative proposition has a double mode of proof: First, it is said, "man does not run": "this does not run and this is man; therefore, man does not run". But where this procedure does not serve the contradictory of the proposition is assumed, [82] as "Chimera is not running". This indefinite proposition cannot be proved by means of two demonstratives, for the second will always be false, i.e., "this is a chimera". Thus in order to judge the truth of that proposition, its contradictory is assumed, i.e., "every chimera runs". And because this is false the other one is true. One can maintain the same view in the case of adverbs where the subject will be an adverb having beneath itself a term, e.g., "at sometime you are: but you are now, and now is at sometime; therefore, [at sometime you are]". Further, "yesterday you were: then you were, and then is or was yesterday; therefore, [yesterday you were]". Further, "before *a* you will dispute: then you will dispute and then is or will be before *a*; therefore, [before *a* you will dispute]". Further, "somewhere you are: in that place you are and in that place is somewhere; therefore [somewhere you are]". And one speaks of past and future in the same way as I said of the present. From this I infer that indefinite and particular propositions with a substantive verb of the present or of the past tense and a participial predicate are to be proved just as propositions with the principal verb of that participle. I want to say that this is to be proved resolubly: "Adam has passed away *(praeteritus)*", just as this one: "Adam was". And this one: "Antichrist is about to be *(futurus)*", as "Antichrist will be"; e.g., "this is and this is or will be Antichrist; therefore, Antichrist is about to be".[a] "Some man was killed" as: "this was killed and this is or was some man; therefore [some man was killed]". "Socrates is able to be *(est potens esse)*"; "this is able to be and this is or can be Socrates. therefore [Socrates is able to be]".

182

From these teachings the truth of many propositions follows: First, "an old man will be a boy". This is proved: "this will be a boy; this is or will be an old man; therefore [an old man will be a boy]", — (pointing to one who is a boy and who will be an old man). Second, the proposition "a boy was an old man". This is proved: "this was an old man — pointing to one old man — and this is or was a boy, therefore, a boy was an old man". Third, "white was when it was not white". [83] This is proved, and I posit that you are white, and continually before this you were black; and this is proved: "this was when it was not white and this is or was white; therefore, [white was when it was not white]". Fourth, "a father will be when he will not have either a son or a daughter". This is proved: "this will be when it will not have either a son or daughter", and this is or will be a father — pointing to a father who will remain after the death of his sons and daughters; therefore, [a father will be when he will not have a son or daughter]". Fifth: "of something taller than you and anything smaller than you you are smaller". It is proved: posited this, "you are smaller than this — pointing to something taller than you — and this is taller than you and anything smaller than you; therefore, [of something taller than you and anything smaller than you you are smaller]". Sixth, "of something smaller than you and anything taller than you you are taller". It is proved: "you are taller than this — pointing to one thing smaller than you — and this is smaller than you and anything taller than you; therefore [of something smaller than you and anything taller than you you are taller]". Seventh, "white can be black". It is proved: "this can be black — pointing to you — and this is or can be white, [therefore, black can be white]". Likewise this proposition is proved: "one who is sitting can run". Eighth, "It is true that the world never was". It is proved: "this is what the world never was" — pointing at this: "you are". And therefore, [this is true: "The world never was]". Ninth, "it is necessary that God never will be". It is proved: "this is what God will never be, — pointing at the world — : this is necessary; therefore [it is necessary that God never will be]". Tenth, "it is possible that nothing was and that nothing will be" . It is proved: "this is what nothing was and what nothing will be" — pointing to the present instant — and this is possible. Therefore, [It is possible that nothing was and that nothing will be]". Eleventh, "a lighted candle was extinguished". It is proved: "this is extinguished — pointing to a candle now extinguished but previously lighted — and this is or was a lighted candle; therefore, [a lighted candle was extinguished]". Twelfth, "a living [thing] is a dead [thing]". It is proved: "this is dead — pointing [84] to Adam —, and this is or was a living thing; therefore, [a living [thing] was a dead [thing]]".

Section 2 – Exponible Propositions

A universal affirmative proposition is proved by exposition through its pre-attached [expressions], and the universal negative corresponding to it. E.g., "every man runs" is expounded in this way: "man runs and nothing is man unless it runs *(quin illud currit)*; therefore, every man runs". An example plural in number: "all men run" becomes, "men run, and no things are men unless they run". Similarly, in the oblique cases except that in the expounding negative proposition the subject of the universal is always in the nominative case and the relative is in the same oblique case as the one which occurs in the proposition to be expounded, e.g., "every man's donkey runs": "a man's donkey runs, and nothing is a man unless his donkey runs *(nihil est homo quin illius asinus currat)*; therefore, [every man's donkey runs]". Further, "of all contradictories one of the two parts is true; and there are no contradictories unless they are such that one of the two parts is true [therefore, of all contradictories one of the two parts is true]". Thus always a relative term follows "unless" *(quin)* and after it comes every term which is on the side of the predicate. Similar remarks apply to the other cases. In a like manner we prove universal propositions with an ampliative verb, except that in the second [sentence of the] exposition a disjunctive word is placed just as in the case of resoluble propositions. E.g., "every man was", expands to "man was, and nothing is man or was man unless it was; therefore, [every man was]". Further, "every white thing will dispute", goes to "a white thing will dispute, and nothing is or will be white unless it will dispute; therefore, [every white thing will dispute]". Further, "every white thing can be black" becomes, "a white thing can be black; nothing is or can be white unless it can be black; therefore, [a white thing can be black]". Further, "every man begins to dispute", is expounded, "man begins to dispute, and nothing is or begins to be man unless it begins to dispute". [85] Therefore, [every man begins to dispute"]. In oblique cases too the analysis is similar by employing the earlier *modus* for the relative words. Similarly, propositions of the present having as a predicate some participle of an ampliative verb, e.g., "every man has passed away", is expounded: "man has passed away *(praeteritus)* and nothing is or was man unless it has passed away *(praeteritus);* therefore, [every man has passed away *(praeteritus)*]". Further, "everything white is to be generated", goes to, "white is to be generated and nothing is or will be white unless it is to be generated, therefore, [everything white is to be generated]". But propositions with a composite subject can be expounded in two ways; according to whether the subject can be the total composite or a part of the composite, e.g., "every man or donkey is a donkey". If the subject is the

184

total disjunct, it is expounded in this way: "man or donkey is a donkey; and nothing is man or donkey unless it be a donkey". If however, the first part of the disjunction is the subject, the second expounding it will be: "nothing is man unless it or a donkey be a donkey". And so the foregoing universal proposition will be false in the first mode and true in the second, the same may be said of others whatever their composition or case may be.

A universal negative proposition, however, is not expounded; it is proved in two ways: Either through its singulars or through its contradictory. E.g., "no man is a chimera", is proved in the first way: "neither this man is a chimera nor that man is a chimera, and thus of other singulars, therefore, [no man is a chimera]". In the second way: This proposition is false: "Some man is a chimera", and this contradicts this, "no man is a chimera"; therefore, this one is true. And it is the same in all other such modes.

From the foregoing way of proving universal affirmative propositions I infer some propositions: First, "everything which was, is". It is proved: "something which was, is; and nothing is what was unless it be; therefore, [everything which was, is]". The major is manifest and the minor likewise because its contradictory is false: i.e., "something is what was, which is not". [86] This, then, is the implication of a contradiction. And in this way one concedes that "what will be, is". "Everything which can be, is." "Everything which is intelligible or imaginable is." Any of these is evident from its exponent propositions in the negative of which one should not posit a disjunctive verb; for the principal verb of the universal is only in the present tense without a participle beneath which some ampliative verb would follow. Second, "everything which was not, is". This is proved: "Something which was not is, such as this present instant; and nothing is which was not unless that thing be; therefore, [everything which was not is]". The second expounding proposition, moreover, is true because its contradictory implies a contradiction, viz., "something is which was not what is not", and consequently it is conceded that "everything which will not be, is". And, "everything which neither could be nor will be able to be, is". Third, "of anything taller than you and anything smaller than you you are smaller". It is proved: "of something taller than you and anything smaller than you, you are smaller". This was proved in another chapter.[a] "Nothing is taller than you and of anything shorter than that you are smaller; therefore, [of something taller than you and anything smaller than you you are smaller]". The minor is clear because its contradictory is false; therefore, [it is proved]. Fourth, "of anything smaller than you and anything taller than you, you are taller". This is proved: "of something smaller than you and of anything taller than you, you are taller; and nothing is smaller than you and anything taller than you unless you are taller than it; therefore, [of anything smaller than you and anything taller than you, you are taller]". The inference is clear; the major is true from what was said in the previous chapter; and the minor is clear because its contradictory is false; i.e., "something is smaller than you and anything taller than you; but you are not taller than it".

Section 3 – Officiable Propositions

An officiable proposition is that whose expression *(dictum)* or infinitive construction *(oratio infinitiva)* is determined by some modal term or a term pertaining to a mental act. Modal terms are these: "true", "false", "necessary", "contingent", "possible", "impossible". [87] Mental terms are: "I know", "I doubt", "I will", "I do not will", "I understand", "I comprehend" and the like and also their participles. These kinds of terms sometimes make a composite sense and sometimes a divided one when they precede totally the dictum or the infinitive phrase or else are placed after it.[a] For example: "it is possible that Socrates run" *(possibile est Sortem currere)*. "That Socrates run is contingent" *(Sortem currere est contingens)*, "you know that God is" *(tu scis deum esse)*, "that God is is known by you" *(Deum esse est scitum a te)*. But when one of these terms is placed between the accusative case and the verb of infinitive construction then it is said to constitute a divided sense: e.g., "God necessarily exists". "Man you know to be an animal", and thus of others. Such a proposition in a divided sense is to be proved according to the exigencies of the preceding term simply and not by reason of a modal term or by reason of another mental term; e.g., "every man can possibly run" *(omnem hominem possibile est currere)*. This is not to be analyzed as an officiable proposition *(officianda)* but rather as an exponible one, according to the doctrine presented on the proof of universal propositions in this way: "[every] man can possibly run; and nothing is or can possibly be man unless it can possibly run; therefore [every man can possibly run]".[b] Further, this is how to resolve the following proposition: "*A* I know to be true": "this I know to be true and this is *A*; therefore, [*A* I know to be true]". On the other hand. a proposition in the composite sense is to be analyzed as an officiable one: "It is possible that Socrates run", goes to: "this proposition is possible: 'Socrates runs', which adequately signifies Socrates to run; therefore, [it is possible that Socrates run]". Further, "it is necessary that God be" *(necessarium est deum esse)*, becomes: "this proposition is necessary: 'God is', which adequately signifies God to be; therefore, [it is necessary that God be]". Similarly, these are proved: "you know Socrates to run", "you doubt that Socrates sits". The first is analyzed as an officiable proposition: "this proposition is known by you: 'Socrates runs', which ade-

quately signifies Socrates to run; therefore, [you know Socrates to run]".
The second is this: "a proposition is doubted by you, 'Socrates sits', which
adequately signifies Socrates to sit; therefore, [you doubt that Socrates
sits]". And this can be maintained of an infinite number of like propositions
containing] [88] a term which makes a composite sense.

From the aforesaid I infer some conclusions: first, "white can possibly
be black and yet it is impossible for white to be black". The first part is
proved: because "this can possibly be black, pointing to you, and this is
or can possibly be white; therefore, [white can possibly be black]". The
consequence is obvious from the resolving to the resoluble. The second
part is proved: for this proposition is impossible: "white is black, which
adequately signifies white to be black; therefore, [it is impossible for white
to be black]". The inference is clear from terms officiating to the officiated.
And in this way this thesis is proved: "a sitting thing can possibly run; yet
it is impossible for a sitting thing to run".

The second thesis: "Every man is contingent to be; yet it is necessary
for every man to be." The first part is proved: because "man is contingent
to be and nothing is or can contingently be man unless it contingently be;
therefore, [every man is contingent to be]". The inference is clear from
exponents to the exposited. The second part is proved: this proposition is
necessary: "every man is, which adequately signifies every man to be;
therefore, [it is necessary for every man to be]". The inference is clear as
previously.

The third thesis: "You know either one of these two to be true, pointing
to these contradictories: a king sits and no king sits; yet neither of these
you know to be true." The first part is clear because this proposition is
known by you: "either of these is true", which adequately signifies either
of these to be true; therefore, ["you know either one of these two to be
true"]. The second part is proved: Neither this one of the two you know to
be true − pointing to the affirmative − nor that one of these two you know
to be true − pointing to the negative; and there are no more than these two;
therefore, ["neither of these you know to be true"]. This is clear by inference from singulars sufficiently enumerated to their universals.

The fourth thesis: "You doubt A to be true; and yet, no A you doubt to
be true." This is proved. I posit that "every A is this one proposition:
'God is' " and let us suppose that you know this proposition to be true
but you doubt whether it is this proposition which is A. Assuming this,
the first part is clear; for this is doubtful to you, [89] "A is true", which
adequately signifies A to be true; therefore, ["you doubt A to be true"].
The second part is proved: "no such proposition 'God is' do you doubt to
be true; but every A is such a proposition; therefore, no A you doubt to be

true". The inference is clear because it is a syllogism in the second mood of the first figure and the antecedent is manifest from the case.

The fifth thesis: "I want to give you my horse; however, no horse of mine I want to give you." This is proved: and I posit that "I promise you my horse which I believe to be in the stable. And let there be around one which presently I believe to be Plato's, and hence not mine, and for this reason I do not wish to give you this horse which I see". This posited, the first part is clear, officiating through the case. And let it be officiated in this way: this proposition is willed by me, "I give you my horse", which adequately signifies me giving you my horse; therefore, ["I give you my horse"]. The inference is valid from the officiating to the officiated. The second part I prove: no horse which I believe to be Plato's do I want to give you; but every horse of mine I believe to be Plato's; therefore, I want to give you no horse of mine. The inference is clear as previously because it is in the second mood of the first figure, etc.

The sixth thesis: "I perceive Socrates speaking, however, no Socrates I perceive speaking." This is proved: I posit that Socrates and Plato are far away; so that I do not know distinctly which is Socrates and which is Plato. However, let Socrates be the one speaking; I recognize well his voice so that I know that it is Socrates and not Plato who speaks. This having been posited, the first part is clear by the case because it follows: I perceive the utterance *(vocem)* of Socrates; therefore, I perceive Socrates speaking. The second part is proved, because it follows: "none of these I perceive to be speaking, [but every Socrates is someone of these; therefore, no Socrates do I perceive to speak". The inference is evident, because it is a syllogism in the second mood of the first figure.]

It is to be noted that these propositions conceded in the Section on resolubles, i.e., "it is true that the world never was", "it is necessary that God never will be", "it is possible that nothing was and that nothing will be" are not provable as officiable propositions. Nor are resoluble and officiable propositions similar in signification, because officiable [propositions] are conjunctive; and resoluble [propositions] are relative.[a]

Section 4 – Describable Propositions

A describable proposition is one in which a mental term [90] mediated by no preceding term determines a noncomplex expression. E.g., "I know Socrates", is described like this: "I know someone as *(sub ratione qua)* Socrates". "You understand man" becomes "you understand something as man". But if mental terms should fall over something [non]complex, which must be signifying a complexum such terms must be described in another way: such words are "to believe", "to doubt", "to know", and the like. E.g., "you know A proposition" is to be described: "you know the adequate significate of proposition A which you know is adequately signified through proposition A; therefore, ["you know A proposition"]. "You believe proposition A" is described: "you believe the adequate significate of proposition A which you believe to be adequately signified by proposition A; therefore, ["you believe proposition A"]. Further, "you doubt propositions A and B", is analyzed: "you doubt the adequate significates A and B of propositions which you know or believe to be adequately signified through A and B propositions". Therefore, ["you doubt propositions A and B"]. Notice that the definition says "mediated by no preceding term" because if a mediate term should precede, then the proposition ought to be proved, because it is always from the first mediate term that the proof of a proposition is to be made.[a] E.g., "every man understands himself". This is to be expounded in this way: "man understands himself, and nothing is man unless that thing understand itself; therefore, [every man understands himself]". Likewise, "men know the future", is resolved: "these know the future and these are men; therefore, [men know the future]".

Concerning what has been said in this chapter and in the preceding ones is should be noted that there is a diversity [of proofs] of the terms preceding any proposition because a describable proposition converts with its description; and a universal affirmative or any other exponibles similarly are converted with their exponents taken together.[b] Hence, it validly follows: "I know man; therefore, I know something as man, and conversely". Further, "every man runs; therefore, man runs and nothing is man unless it runs", and conversely. But a resoluble proposition does not convert with [91] its resolvents, nor an officiable proposition with its officiants. Since it follows: "this is animal, and this is man; therefore, man is animal"; but not, conversely: "man is animal; therefore, this is animal, and this is man", because the antecedent is necessary and the consequent is contingent. For after a millennium it will be just as it is signified by the antecedent, and yet it will not be just as it is signified by the consequent. Further it follows: "this proposition is necessary: 'God is', which adequately signifies God to be; therefore, it is necessary for God to be". But the converse inference is invalid: "It is necessary for God to be; therefore, this proposition is necessary 'God is' which adequately signifies God to be", because the antecedent is necessary and the consequent contingent. Likewise, if no proposition existed what would be signified in one way by the antecedent would not be signified by the consequent.

From these statements I infer some theses. The first: "the one approaching I know; however, I do not know the one approaching". It is proved;

and I posit that someone is at a distance who comes toward me whom I know to be Socrates, and I believe the same not to be moved and I am conceiving of nothing else. This assumed, the first part is clear: "this I know and this is approaching; therefore, the one approaching I know". The second part is clear as well: because I do not know something *as (sub ratione qua)* the one approaching.

The second thesis: "Aristotle knew a God three and one; however, Aristotle did not know a God three and one." The first part is clear: because this Aristotle knew − pointing to God, and this God is three and one; therefore, Aristotle knew a God three and one. The second part is likewise clear: because Aristotle did not know something *as (sub ratione qua)* a God three and one. Therefore, ["Aristotle knew a God three and one; however, Aristotle did not know a God three and one"]. The inference is valid from a description to the described.

The third thesis: "*A* proposition I know; however, I do not know *A* proposition." It is proved and I posit that *A* is this, "God is", which I know and believe not to be something in the world. This posited, "*A* I know", because I know this − pointing [92] to this "God is" and this is *A*; therefore, ["*A* proposition I know"]. However, I do not know *A* because I do not know some significate signified through *A*; whereby I do not know *A* to be; therefore, ["I do not know *A* proposition"].

The fourth thesis: "You see Socrates; however, you do not see Socrates." It is clear, and I posit that Socrates speaks an utterance *(vocem)* you well hear; you believe, however, that there is not some Socrates in the world. This posited, the first part is clear because you perceive this, and this is Socrates; therefore, etc. However, you do not perceive Socrates because you do not perceive this *as (sub ratione qua)* Socrates etc.

Section 5 − The Expressions "Necessarily", "Contingently"

From what is said it is clear that a necessary and a contingent proposition are taken in two senses: namely, resolubly and officiably. But these adverbs viz., "necessarily", "contingently", are proved exponibly.[a] E.g., "necessarily God is", is expounded: "God is and it cannot be but that God is.; therefore, [necessarily God is]". "Necessarily the world was: the world was and it could not be but that the world was; therefore, [necessarily the world was]". Further, "necessarily something will be; something will be, and it could not be but that it will be; therefore, [necessarily something will be]". Thus it is the case that the principal verb of the second expounding proposition is of the same time as the principal verb in the expounded proposition. "Contingently" is expounded in the opposite way. "Contingently you are", is expounded in this way: "you are and it can be that you are not; therefore, [contingently you are]". Further, "contingently you will be": "you will be, and it can be that you will not be". And the same can be said of the past. Here are two important points: First, "necessarily" and "contingently" are sometimes taken in a compositional sense and sometimes in a divided sense just as the terms "necessary" and "contingent". They are taken in a composite sense when they precede totally or succeed finally; e.g., "necessarily man is animal", or "you run contingently". But they are taken in a divided sense when they mediate between a subject and a verb or between a verb and the predicate. An example of the first: "man necessarily is animal". An example of the second: "Socrates is contingently running". The second important point is that no matter how [93] they are taken in a composite sense they are always expounded in the same way, as was said. But when they are taken in a divided sense preceding another mediate sign they are not expounded. A proposition, however, is to be proved according to the exigencies of the preceding term as the foregoing rule states: e.g., "man necessarily is animal". This is not to be expounded nor is it to be proved with respect to this term "necessarily", but it is to be resolved with regard to this term "man". E.g., "this necessarily is animal, and this is man; therefore, man necessarily is animal". The first resolving proposition is to be expounded *(exponenda)* in this way: "this is animal and this cannot not be animal; thus, the "can be" would follow the subject just as "necessarily" or "contingently" also do. From which it follows that that verb "can be" *(potest)* sometimes is taken in the composite sense and sometimes in the divided sense. It is taken in the composite sense when it precedes totally or non-principally, e.g., "it can be the case that you run". It is taken in the divided sense when it is taken principally: e.g., "Antichrist can be".

From these statements I infer some theses. First, "necessarily something is which contingently is". It is proved: something is which contingently is, and it cannot be unless something is which contingently is; therefore, [necessarily something is which contingently is]".

The second thesis: "Your soul necessarily is; yet contingently your soul is." The first part is clear through a resolution, "this necessarily is, and this is your soul; therefore, [your soul necessarily is]".

The second part is proved exponibly in this way: "your soul is, and it can be that your soul is not". For it follows according to the exposition: "you are not; therefore, your soul is not", because an opposite follows from an opposite and it can be just as it is signified in the consequent; therefore, it can be just as it is signified in the antecedent.

The third thesis: "It is necessary for you to have been, yet contingently you were." The first part is clear because this is necessary, "you were", which adequately signifies that you were; therefore, [it is necessary for you to have been]". The second part is clear for "you were, and it could have been that you were not; therefore, [contingently you were]".

The fourth thesis: "It can be that Antichrist is a man who is, yet Antichrist cannot be a man who [94] is." The first part is clear because this is possible, "Antichrist is a man who is". This adequately signifies Antichrist to be a man who is; since "can be" taken non-principally is an officiable term like the term "possible" in the second sentence [is an officiable term]. The reason is clear: if the opposite is considered, i.e., "Antichrist can be a man who is", it follows that Antichrist can be a man and that is *(et ille est)*. Since the consequent is false, the antecedent is also. The inference is clear because "can be" taken principally is an immediate term and "who" is a relative which is resoluble grammatically into that *(ille, illa, illud)* from which it is not impeded through a preceding sign. Here we note that "necessarily" is taken in two senses: in one way nominally in the dative or in the ablative case; in another way adverbially, as was said. In the first way it is not expounded: but it is resolved: e.g., "necessarily you are". This is resolved into "you are, and this is necessary; therefore, necessarily you are". From which it follows that "necessarily you are man; yet contingently you are man"; by taking "necessarily" nominally in the ablative case. Because indeed "you are" (pointing to God) and this is necessary; therefore, [necessarily you are]. By taking "necessarily" adverbially it is the case that this thesis is impossible because of the impossibility of its exponents. Further it is conceded that "necessarily Socrates eats; yet the same Socrates contingently eats", by taking "necessarily" in the dative case. For this Socrates eats − pointing to God − and this is necessary; therefore, "necessarily Socrates eats"]. The second part is also clear by expounding Socrates in this way: "he eats, and he can not eat; therefore, [Socrates contingently eats]".

Section 6 − The Positive Grade of Comparison

Now we turn to the grade of comparison; and first we discuss the comparative. E.g., "you are as strong as some man in the world", it is expounded in this way: "you are strong, and some man is strong, and not: some man in the world is stronger than you; therefore, [you are as strong as some man in the world]. Again, "you were as strong as some man in the world": "You were [95] strong, and some man in the world was strong, and not: some man in the world was stronger than you; therefore, [you were as strong as some man in the world]". And it may be said in the same way of the future in its mode. But it is to be noted that if there

192

should be a comparative with respect to a common term not distributed on the side of the predicate the term cannot be taken in distribution in some of the exponents. E.g., in "you are as white as this man; therefore, you are as white as every man in the world", one ought not to say in the second exponent "every man is white" because this is false, and the exponents [should be] true. It follows, "you are as white as this man; therefore, you are as white as every man". The inference is clear from a lower-level term to its corresponding higher-level term affirmatively without a distribution and without a sign having the power of negation. Thus it ought to be expounded: "you are white and a man in the world is white and not any man in the world is whiter than you", therefore, etc.

From the foregoing mode of exposition I infer some theses: First, "you are as strong as every man in the world; yet you are not as strong as some man in the world". The first part is clear because you are strong, and some man in the world is strong, and not every man in the world is stronger than you; therefore, ["you are as strong as every man in the world"]. The second part is clear similarly because its contradictory is false viz., "you are as strong as some man" because from that these exponents follow: viz., "not some man in the world is stronger than you", which is false.

The second thesis: "An animal which is not as strong as a lion is as strong as every animal in the world." It is proved: "a horse is as strong as every animal in the world, and the same horse is an animal which is not as strong as a lion; therefore, [an animal which is not as strong as a lion is as strong as every animal in the world]". The inference is clear from a resoluble proposition to its resolutions; and the antecedent is clear by expounding and resolving.

The third thesis: "I am as wise as you and God, yet I am not as wise as God". The second part is manifest of itself; and the first part is clear because I am wise, and you and God are wise, and it is not the case that you and God are [96] wiser than I; therefore, ["I am as wise as you and God, yet I am not as wise as God"]. The inference is clear from exponible propositions to their expositions. The first and second parts are manifest. The third indeed is clear because if not, the opposite follows: "you and God are wiser than I; therefore, you are wiser than I". This consequent, however, is false.

The fourth thesis: "You will be as old as you will be: however, in no instant will you be as old as you will be." The first part is clear through its exponents: "you will be old, and never will you be older than you will be; therefore, [you will be as old as you will be]". The second part is clear: because in any instant given in which you will be old in that same instant you will not be as old as you will be because it can be that you will be older; therefore, in no instant will you be as old as you will be. The inference is clear because the contradictory of the consequent is repugnant to the antecedent because of the distribution of this "as" *(sicut)* over a substantive verb. ["Therefore, you will be as old as you will be; however, in no instant will you be as old as you will be."]

Section 7 – The Comparative Grade of Comparison

The comparative grade is similarly expounded through three exponents: e.g., "Socrates is stronger than Plato". "Socrates is strong, and Plato is strong, and Plato is not as strong as Socrates; therefore, [Socrates is stronger than Plato]". Further, "you are stronger than some man". "You are strong, and some man is strong, and some man is not as strong as you: therefore, [you are stronger than some man]". But in this proposition, "you are whiter than every man", the second exponent ought not to be this: "every man is white", because then the exposition would be true, and one of the exponents would be false which is not to be conceded in logic. However, it ought to be expounded in this way: "you are white, and man is white, and not every man is as white as you".

From these statements I infer some theses. The first, "you are whiter than every man, and yet you are not whiter than some man". The first part is clear through its exponents. The second part similarly because the third of its exponents is false, viz., "it is not the case that some man is as white as you", because you are as white as you. Or "any man which is [97] whiter than you is as white as you". i.e., non-precisely.[a]

The second thesis: "Socrates who is not better than God is better than every being in the world." The first part is clear because "Socrates is not better than God", is evident enough. Yet he is better than every being in the world because he is good, and some being in the world is good, and not every being in the world is as good as Socrates; therefore, ["Socrates who is not better than God is better than every being in the world"].

The third thesis: "I am more sensible than you and God; yet I am not more sensible than God." The second part is manifest of itself. The first part is clear through its exponents: "I am sensible; and you and God are sensible; and it is not the case that you and God are as sensible as I".["There-fore, I am more sensible than you and God; yet I am not more sensible than God."] The inference is clear because its opposite, "you and God are as sensible as I", is false.

The fourth thesis: "You will be older than you will be in some instant; yet in no instant will you be older than you will be in some instant." The first part is clear because you will be old, and in some instant you will be old, and not in some instant will you be as old as you will be; there-

194

fore, ["you will be older than you will be in some instant"]. The inference is clear. The second part of the antecedent was proved in another Chapter.[b] The second part of the thesis is clear because if not, the opposite follows: "in some instant you will be older than you will be in some instant and let that be instant A". For it is clear that this is false in instant A: "You will be older than you will be in some instant", because one of its exponents is false, viz., "it is not the case that in some instant will you be as old as you will be in instant A", because in instant A you will be as old as you will be in instant A; and in an infinite number of instances subsequent to A. ["Therefore, you will be older than you will be in some instant; yet in no instant will you be older than you will be in some instant."]

Next, we note how the comparative grade is to be expounded with regard to words like "great", "small" and "as". "I am as strong as you", is expounded: "I am strong and you are strong and you are not as strong as I am; therefore, [I am as strong as you are]". And other theses can be inferred concerning "more" since it is conceded that "an animal which is weaker than a mosquito is as strong [98] as every animal in the world". And "a man who is wiser than every man is less wise than every man", and thus of an infinite number of others.

Section 8 — The Superlative Grade of Comparison

The superlative grade is expounded through three exponents unless one of those coincides with another; e.g., "you are the strongest of these", can be expounded in two ways: either through comparison or through the positive grade taken comparatively. An example of the former, "you are strong, and these are strong, and it is not the case that some of these is stronger than you; therefore, [you are the strongest of these]". An example of the latter: "you are strong and these are strong and it is not the case that some of these are as strong as you; therefore, [you are the strongest of these]". Moreover, "you are the strongest of all men", is expounded in the first way: "you are strong, and men are strong and it is not the case that all men are stronger than you; or it is not the case that every man is stronger than you". In the second way: "you are strong, and men are strong, and it is not the case that every man is as strong as you". One can maintain the same analysis of other statements of past and of future.

From these statements I infer some theses. First, "you are the strongest of these and the weakest of these". It is clear, and I posit that you, Socrates and Plato are equally strong, and with the expression "of these" I point out you three. By this case the first part is clear because "you are strong, and these are strong, and it is not the case that some of these is stronger than you". And the second part is true: "because you are weak and these are weak and it is not the case that some of these are weaker than you; therefore, [you are the strongest of these and the weakest of these]". This conclusion would not be true, however, by expounding it in the second way, [viz. through "as", "just as", *(ita, sicut)*].

The second thesis: "You are the wisest of all men, yet you are not the wisest of some men." The first part is clear through its exponents: "You are wise, and men are wise, and not any man is wiser than you; therefore, [you are the wisest of all men]". The second part is clear because its contradictory is false, viz., "you are the wisest of some men". Furthermore, the third exponent is false by the first mode or the second mode. For this is false: "It is not the case that some man is [99] wiser than you". It is clear and this similarly: "it is not the case that any man is as wise as you" because you are as wise as you.

The third thesis: "You were the hottest of every man; yet you were the coldest of every man." The first part is clear because you were hot, and men were hot, and it is not the case that any man was hotter than you; therefore, it is not the case that every man was as hot as you. The second part is clear in the same way because you were cold, and men were cold, and it is not the case that any man was colder than you; therefore, it is not the case that every man was as cold as you.

The fourth thesis: "Something is the greatest of these which is not the greatest of these." By expounding it positively and comparatively, it is clear. I posit that A is great and B greater and C indeed greater than A and B. With this posited, "B is the greatest of these which is not the greatest of these". It is clear for B is great, and something of these which is not the greatest of these is great, and none of these which is not the greatest of these is as great as B; therefore, ["something is the greatest of these which is not the greatest of these"]. The inference is clear from propositions expounded to their exposition.

Section 9 – The Expression "It Differs"

"It differs" on the other hand is not analyzed in the same way. It is expounded through three exponents; e.g., "you differ from man", is expounded in this way: "you are, and man is, and you are not man; therefore, [you differ from man]". Further, "you differ from every man": "you are, and every man is, and you are not every man; therefore, [you differ from every man]". There is, however, a difference between past and future propositions. For this proposition, "you differ from Antichrist" is not to be expounded in this way: "you will be, and Antichrist will be, and you will not be Antichrist", because the expressions to be expounded are true and their expositions are false. For it follows: "you differ from Antichrist; therefore, you will be at the same time with Antichrist". The consequent is false, as I infer it. It is expounded: "you will be, and Antichrist will be when you will be, yet you will not be Antichrist; therefore, [you differ from Antichrist]". The same applies to the propositions of the past.

From these discussions, I infer some theses: [100] First, "you differ from every man, yet you do not differ from some man". The first part is clear through its exponents because you are, and every man is, and you are not every man; therefore, ["you differ from every man"]. The second part is clear because if not, the opposite follows, viz., "you differ from some man". But this is false because its third exponent is false: namely, "you are not some man".

The second thesis: "You differ from every being which was, which is, or which will be; yet you do not differ from some being which is, which was, or which will be." The first part is clear because you are, and every being which is, which was, and which will be, is; and you are not every being which is, which was, and which will be. The second part also is clear because its contradictory is false since one of its exponents is false, viz., "you are not something which is, which was, and which will be".

The third thesis: "I differ from you and from me; yet I do not differ from me." The first part is clear through its exponents. For I am, and you and I are, and I am not you and I. The second part is clear of itself. And likewise it can be proved: "you differ from man and from donkey; yet you do not differ from man".

The fourth thesis: "You differ from donkey; yet you do not differ from man or from donkey." The first part is clear through its exponents; and the second part similarly. Because if not, its opposite follows: "you differ from man or from donkey". Now, this is false because the third of its exponents is false, viz., "you are not man or donkey". Hence, its contradictory is true, viz., "you are man or donkey". Whatever we have said concerning this verb "differs" applies as well to the analysis of those terms: "another" *(aliud)* and "not the same thing" *(non idem)*.

Section 10 — Exclusive Expressions

Of exclusive expressions some are of first order, some are of second order, and some are of third order.[a] A first-order exclusive is that in which the exclusive sign, e.g., "only", "alone", "in one way", and "precisely", precede the subject as in "only man runs", which is to be expounded: "man runs and nothing not-man runs". ["Therefore, only man runs".] Always the first unit to be expounded is the prefixed exclusive. [101] The second unit is the universal negation of the exclusive subject taken infinitely. A proposition of the past or of the future is exposited in a similar way: e.g., "only Socrates was", "Socrates was; nothing non-Socrates was; therefore, only Socrates was". Again, "only Antichrist will dispute", "Antichrist will dispute, and nothing non-Antichrist will dispute; therefore, only Antichrist will dispute". It is to be noted that an exclusive of the first order is converted with a universal with the terms transposed so that, if one is true, the other is true as well, and conversely. Hence if this is true, "only man is animal", this would be true: "every animal is man", and because the universal is false the exclusive is false.

A second-order exclusive is that in which the exclusive expression *(dictio)* mediates between the subject and the predicate by being placed either before or after the copula e.g., "Socrates only is man", or "Socrates is only man". These are exposited in the same way: "Socrates is man; and Socrates is not non-man". And the same applies to statements of the past and the future.

An exclusive of the third order is that in which the exclusive sign *(dictio)* is posited between the parts of the predicate: e.g., "*A* proposition signifies precisely as it is", which is exposited: "*A* signifies as it is, and *A* proposition does not signify not as it is". Thus the infinite negation always falls over the same term which the exclusive sign falls over in the exposited proposition, as is clear in the examples of this order. Note that if an exclusive sign of some order precedes another provable term one ought not to prove that proposition by reason of the exclusive sign; but [it should be proved] according to the exigencies of the preceding term. Here are examples of each order: "necessarily only man is man", "every man alone is animal", "some proposition signifies precisely as it is". The first is exponible by reason of this term "necessarily"; the second by reason of this term "every"; the third is resoluble because it is a particular affirmative. The opposite of these exclusives is assigned through the negations of the preceding exclusive signs; [102] e.g., "only man runs", whose contradiction is this, "not only man runs". And this has two opposite causes of truth: namely, "nothing which is man runs, or something non-man runs". And if one of these causes is true, the negative exclusive is true. And if either is false the original is false; for an exclusive affirmative is true if both exponents are true; and it is false if one exponent is false. A negative exclusive in which the negation follows the exclusive sign is exponible. The first exponent will be the negative of the subject; the second will be the universal of the subject; the third will be the predicate, e.g., "only man does not run". This is exponded: "man does not run; and whatever is non-man runs". And in this way one exposits any exclusive of the first order. Further, of the second order, e.g., "you only are not a donkey", "you are not a donkey, and you are whatever is not a donkey". There is no negative exclusive of the third order because in such a proposition the negation always follows the principal verb as well as the exclusive expression; e.g. "*A* proposition signifies precisely not as it is". The opposites of these negative exclusive propositions are made with negations preceding the entire propositions. E.g., "only man does not run", the contradictory is: "Not: only man does not run", which has two opposite causes of truth assigned exclusively and negatively to its disjunctive exponents. "Every man runs or some thing non-man does not run." If one is true, this exclusive is true; just as was pointed out above concerning the opposite of an affirmative exclusive.

From these statements I infer some theses: First, "only man is man, yet not only man is animal". The first part is clear through its exponents, and the universals of a transposed term. The second part also is clear [103] because one of its causes is true, i.e., "something non-man is animal", for this is animal (pointing to a donkey) and this is something non-man; therefore, ["not only man is animal"].

The second thesis: "You only are animal; yet not only you are animal." The first part is clear, for you are animal, and you are not non-animal. The second part is true as well because one of its causes of truth is true, viz., ["a donkey which is not you is animal"].

The third thesis: "*A* proposition is precisely signifying as it is; yet *A* proposition is not signifying precisely as it is." The first part is clear, and I posit that *A* is this, "man is a donkey". With this posited, the first part is clear because *A* is signifying as it is, and *A* is not not-signifying as it is. It is clear because the opposite is given: "*A* is not-signifying as it is; therefore, *A* is not signifying as it is". *(A est non significans sicut est ergo A non est significans sicut est.)* The consequent is false; so, "*A* is signifying as it is", because it is signifying man to be. The second part is clear also because of its contradictories one exponent is false, i.e., "*A* proposition is not signifying not as it is", for it signifies "man to be donkey".

The fourth thesis: "*A* proposition precisely signifies what is false and impossible; yet *A* proposition precisely signifies what is true and necessary." The first part is clear through its exponents; for *A* signifies what is false and impossible, and *A* is not not-signifying what is false and impossible. It is clear because the opposite is given: "*A* is not signifying what is false and impossible; therefore, *A* is not signifying what is false and impossible", which is not true. The second part likewise is clear; for *A* signifies what is true and necessary because it signifies man to be, and *A* is not not-signifying what is true and necessary. It is clear because the opposite is given: "*A* is not-signifying what is true and necessary; therefore, *A* is not signifying

199

what is true and necessary". The consequent is false and this inference similarly is clear through the second rule: From an affirmative with an infinite predicate to a negative of finite predicate there is a solid inference.

Section 11 – Exceptive Expressions

Exceptive signs are these: "except *(praeter)*, "without" *(praeterquam)*, and "unless" *(nisi)* and they differ in that *praeter* and *praeterquam* indifferently operate as much in a universal affirmative as in a universal negative; but "unless" *(nisi)* operates only [104] in a universal negative. For one says congruously: "no man except Socrates runs", as well as "every man except Socrates runs". It is not, however, congruous to say "every man unless *(nisi)* Socrates runs". An affirmative exceptive is expounded through two exponents: in the first the predicate is negated of the excepted subject *(a parte extracapta)*: and in the second the predicate is affirmed universally of the assumed subject *(a parte extracapta infinitata)*. E.g., "every man except Socrates runs",: "Socrates does not run, and every man [who is] not Socrates runs". A negative exceptive similarly is expounded through two exponents – the first in which the predicate is affirmed of the excepted subject *(de parte extracapta)* and the second in which it is denied universally of the assumed subject *(a parte extracapta infinitata)*. E.g., "no man except Socrates runs",: "Socrates runs and no man [who is] not Socrates runs". It is to be noted that there are proper and improper exceptives. For a proper exceptive two things are required. First, the expression by which it is an exceptive stands confusedly and distributively. From this it follows that this is improper: "some man except Socrates runs". Second, it is required that the exception phrase *(pars extracapta)* is a term on a level lower than that by which the proposition is an exceptive; from which it follows that this is improper: "every man except man runs", and this is proper: "every man except Socrates runs", because it meets the two conditions, as is clear.[a] Properly, it is to be noted that any negative exceptive is interchanged with its exclusive affirmative in which the subject is an exceptive phrase *(extracapta pars)*, and the predicate is a composite term made from the subject and the predicate of the exceptive thus precisely posited *(supponente)*. Hence it follows, "no man except Socrates runs; therefore, only Socrates is running and conversely". And note that the rule says that the predicate is a term composed from the predicate and the subject of the exceptive because it does not follow: "no animal except man understands; therefore, only man understands". The antecedent is true, and the consequent is false. But well it follows: "therefore, only man is [105] an understanding animal". Also, it says "thus precisely posited", because it does not follow: "no man except Socrates runs; therefore, only Socrates is a man running". But this alone follows: "therefore, only Socrates is some man running". For given that [proposition] under the human species some masculine being would not run unless only Socrates. But with this condition many women may run, and then this would be true: "No man except Socrates runs"; and this similarly "only Socrates is some man running". But this would be false "only Socrates is man running".

From this I infer some theses: First, this inference does not follow: "every man except Socrates runs; therefore, every man except man runs", because the antecedent is an exceptive in the proper sense, and the consequent is not.

The second thesis: "Every animal except Antichrist is animal; yet not every animal except man is animal." The first part is clear through its exponents because "Antichrist is not animal, and every animal [which is] not Antichrist is animal". The second part is clear because, if not, the opposite follows: "every animal except man is animal". It is clear that the first exponent [of this statement] is false, i.e, "man is not animal", and consequently it is an exceptive whose exponent is false. From this conclusion it follows that not every exceptive in the proper sense is repugnant to its prefixed expression *(prejacenti)*. The opposite of this view is commonly maintained. It is clear because any of these is true: "every animal is animal, and every animal except Antichrist is animal".

The third thesis: "You do not differ unless from a donkey; yet you differ from a goat." The second part is manifest; and the first part is clear, "you differ from a donkey, and you do not differ from another apart from a donkey". This is proved: because the opposite is as follows: "you differ from another apart from a donkey; therefore, you are not other than a donkey". The inference is clear from an exposited proposition to one of its exponents.

The fourth thesis: "You see all men who are in this house except Socrates; yet you do not see some man or some men." It is proved, and I posit for the second part of the thesis this point: "In this house are ten men — nine women and one man [106] whom you do not see, but you do see all the women". With this posited, the second part of the thesis is clear; and the first part similarly by appealing to this rule for exceptives: every affirmative proposition which is in part true and in part false can be verified through an exception [of the false part]. With this presupposed this is false: "you see all the men who are in this house precisely except Socrates"; therefore, it can be verified through an exception for Socrates in this way by saying, "You see all the men who are in this house except Socrates".

Section 12 – Reduplicative Expressions

Reduplicatives are expounded through three exponents. In the first a reduplicative term is predicated of a subject. In the second the predicate is predicated of the same subject. And in the third the same thing is posited conditionally of a term reduplicated through a transcendent term: e.g., "Socrates insofar as he is man is animal". "Socrates is man; and Socrates is animal; and if something is man, the same thing is animal". And the same applies to a term taken universally or indefinitely. E.g., "every man insofar as he is animal is substance". "Every man is animal; and every man is substance; and if something is animal, the same thing is substance." A negative reduplicative indeed whose negation follows the sign of reduplication is exponible similarly. E.g., "Socrates insofar as he is man is not donkey", is expounded: "Socrates is man; and Socrates is not donkey; and if something is man, the same thing is not donkey, and thus of others of this kind". A negative reduplicative whose negation precedes the sign of reduplication is not to be expounded. Rather it is to be proved through its opposite, as often is said.

From these statements I infer some theses. First, "some things insofar as they are the same are different". It is clear: some things are the same, and some things are different; and if some things are the same, they are different; therefore, [some things insofar as they are the same are different]. The inference is clear from an exponible proposition to its exposition. The third part of the antecedent is clear because if some things are the same, they are. If they are, they are distinct; and if they are distinct, [107] they are different; therefore, from the first to the last if some things are the same, they are different.

The second thesis: "Any man insofar as he is man is risible; yet not any man insofar as he is animal is risible." The first part is clear through its exponents because any man is man, and any man is risible; and if something is man, the same thing is risible. The second part is clear because, if not, the opposite follows: "any man insofar as he is animal is risible", and it is certain that this is false because its third exponent is false, i.e., "if something is animal the same thing is risible".

The third thesis: "Socrates insofar as he is man is animal; yet Socrates is not, insofar as he is man, Socrates." The first part is clear through its exponents; and the second part similarly. Because, if not, the opposite follows: "Socrates, insofar as he is man, is Socrates". It is clear that this proposition is false because its third exponent is false, viz., "if someone is man, he is Socrates".

The fourth thesis: "You insofar as you are man are not donkey; yet you not insofar as you are animal, are not donkey." The first part is clear because "you are man, and you are not donkey; and if something is man, the same thing is not donkey". The second part is clear because, if it is not granted, the opposite follows: "you, insofar as you are animal, are not donkey". And it is clear that its [third] exponent is false, i.e., "if something is animal the same thing is not donkey". The same teachings apply to the expressions "as great as" *(de quanto et pro quanto)* if they should make a reduplicative proposition.

Section 13 — The Expression "Immediately"

An immediate proposition contains within itself two exponents. The first is set down initially, and the second is a negative corresponding to it according to the exigencies of its verb. E.g., "immediately before A you were", is expounded: "before A you were, and there was no instant before A unless between that and A you were; therefore, [immediately before A you were]". Further, "immediately after B you will be", is expounded "after B you will be; and no instant will be after B unless between that and B you will be". In a similar way one expounds negatives whose negation follows "immediately". E.g., "immediately before this you were not white". "Before this you were not white; and there was no instant before this unless [108] between that and this you were not white." Further, "immediately after the present instant you will not run", is expounded: "after the present instant you will not run, and there will be no instant after the present instant unless between that and the present instant you will not be running". The opposites of these propositions are made by negations preceding "immediately", and such a proposition is not proved unless through the assignment of contradictories.

From these statements, I infer some theses: First "immediately before this you were white, and immediately before this you were black". It is proved. I posit that in any even-numbered part of a past hour you were white and in any odd-numbered part of a past hour you were black. With this posited, one argues in this way: "immediately before this was some even-numbered part; therefore, immediately before this you were white. The inference holds and the antecedent is proved: before this there was some even-numbered part and there was no instant before this unless between that and this there was some even-numbered part; therefore [immediately before this you were white]". Similarly, the other part of the thesis is clear: for immediately before this there was some odd-numbered part; therefore, immediately before this you were black. The inference is clear and the antecedent is proved as previously: before this there was some odd-numbered part and there was no instant before this unless between that and this there was some odd-numbered part; therefore, ["immediately before this you were black"]. The same thesis can be verified of a future statement.

The second thesis: "Two mutually contradictory contradictories immediately before this were true, and immediately before this they were false; yet they were neither simultaneously true nor simultaneously false." It is clear; and I posit that A is this, "you are white", and B is this, "you are not white". Having posited this it is clear that A immediately before this was true. For whenever there was some even-numbered part A was true. But immediately before this there was some even-numbered part; therefore, immediately before this A was true. And also immediately before this A was false, because whenever there was some odd-numbered part A was false; but immediately before this there was some odd-numbered part; therefore, immediately before this A was false. In the same way one can prove that B immediately before this was true and false. That, however, A and B were not [109] simultaneously false or simultaneously true is clear because whenever A was true B was false and conversely. From which it follows, "immediately before this you were white; and immediately before this you were black". The first part is clear and the second is clear as well. For whenever you were black you were not white; but immediately before this you were black; therefore, immediately before this you were not white. And in this way one concedes that "A proposition immediately before this was true; and immediately before this was not true". The first part was proved, and the second is clear for whenever A proposition was false the same was not true; but immediately before this A proposition was false; therefore, immediately before this A proposition was not true.

The third thesis: "Immediately after this there will be an instant which will be not immediately after this." It is proved: for after this there will be an instant which not immediately after this will be and there will be no instant after this unless between that and this there will be an instant which will be not immediately after this. Because whatever instant is given that will be after this and between that same instant and this there will be infinitely many instants none of which will be immediately after this. From this thesis it follows that immediately after this there will be something which will be not immediately after this.

The fourth thesis: "After A you will run; however, not immediately after A you will run", is expounded: "after A you will run, and there will be no instant after A unless before that you will run; yet not immediately after A you will run". It is proved; and I posit that you run today but not tomorrow, and that A will be the middle instant tomorrow, and that you will be running sometime. Having posited this, it is clear that not immediately after A you will run; yet after A you will run, as the case puts

204

it, because before A you will run since today indeed there will be no instant after A unless before that one you will run. Obviously, whoever will run before A will run before any instant which will be after A.

It should be noted that "immediate" is taken in two senses: adverbially and nominally.[a] I was analyzing the adverbial sense. [110] It is taken in the nominal sense, in a statement like this: "the parts in a continuum are immediate", i.e., without any interval between them. This sense of "immediate" is not relevant to the previous discussion.[a]

Section 14 — The Expressions "Begins" and "Ceases"

"Begins" is expounded in two ways: First, through a proposition of the present tense and a denial of the past. Second, through a denial of the present and a proposition in the future tense. E.g., "Socrates begins to be white". In the first way this is expounded: "Socrates now is white, and immediately before this present instant he was not white". In the second way: "Socrates now is not white, and immediately after this present instant he will be white".

"Ceases" is expounded in the reverse manner in two ways: First through a denial of the present tense and a proposition of the past. E.g., "Socrates ceases to be white", is expounded: "Socrates now is not white; and immediately before the present instant he was white; therefore, Socrates ceases to be white". Second, through a proposition of the present tense and a denial of the future. E.g., "Socrates now is white, and immediately after the present instant he will not be white; therefore, Socrates ceases to be white".

From these statements I infer some theses: First "you begin to be white; yet you do not begin to be colored". It is proved, and I posit that you are white now and continously before this [instant] you were black. Having posited this, you now are white and immediately before this present instant you were not white; therefore, you begin to be white; yet you do not begin to be colored. Because now you are colored; and immediately before this present instant you were colored, and immediately after this present instant you will be colored; therefore, [you do not begin to be colored].

The second thesis: "God begins to be in this instant, yet God does not begin to be in any instant." The first part is clear, for God is in this instant, and immediately before this present instant he was not in this instant; therefore, God begins to be in this instant. The second part also is clear, for God is in some instant, and immediately before this present instant he was in some instant and immediately after this [111] present instant he will be in some instant; ["therefore, God begins to be in this instant, yet God does not begin to be in any instant"].

The third thesis: "Everything which is begins to be; yet something which is does not begin to be." The first part is proved because everything which is, is now; yet immediately before this present instant everything which is was not. The second part is proved, for now there is something which is; and immediately before this instant there was something which is; and immediately after this present instant there will be something which is; therefore, ["everything which is begins to be; yet something which is does not begin to be"].

The fourth thesis: "You begin to see men, yet you do not begin to see some men; indeed, you begin to see no men." It is proved, and I posit that continously before this there were none but ten men of whom you saw, you see, or you will see nine; but you will never see the tenth who now first ceases to be through a denial of the present. With this posited, "you begin to see men", because now you see men; yet immediately before this present instant you did not see men because not this tenth one. ["Therefore, you begin to see men."] However, you do not begin to see some men because you now see some men, and immediately before the present instant you saw some men. Also, you begin to see no men because of any one given which you may see or will be seeing the same one immediately before this [present instant] you saw as the case at hand states. ["Therefore, you begin to see no men."]

From this thesis it follows that (1) "you begin to know ten propositions; yet you do not begin to know some propositions", – given that now you know ten, and immediately before this you knew only nine.

Similar theses are conceded in the matter of 'it ceases' *(desinit)*. E.g., "now you cease to run; yet you do not cease to be moved", – given that now you are moved, and you do not run, but immediately before the present instant you ran.

(2) "Everything which is ceases to be, yet something which is does not cease to be."

(3) "God ceases to be in this present instant; yet he does not cease to be in some instant."

(4) "You cease to see men; yet you do not [112] cease to see some man; indeed, you cease to see no man", – given that continously before this present instant you saw every man whom, while you see him, also, a new one now is generated whom you do not see. And in the same way one concedes that "you cease to know ten propositions; yet you do not cease to know some proposition", – given that now you know ten and continuously after this only nine. ["Therefore, you cease to

know ten propositions; yet you do not cease to know some proposition."]

Section 15 – The Particle "Whole"

"Whole" is convertably the same thing with any of its parts when it is taken syncategorematically. E.g., "the whole Socrates is less than Socrates". It is expounded: "some part of Socrates is less than Socrates; yet no part of Socrates but this is less than Socrates". [Therefore, the whole Socrates is less than Socrates.] But when it is taken categorematically, the whole is the same thing as the being made *(perfectum)* from all of its parts. E.g., "Socrates is a whole man", i.e., "Socrates is man made out of his parts". Commonly when "whole" precedes the entire proposition it is taken syncategorematically. When indeed it mediates between a part of the subject or is posited on the part of the predicate it is taken categorematically, e.g., "the whole Socrates is some thing of a man" *(totus Sortes est aliquid hominis)*. In this proposition "whole" is taken syncategorematically. But in saying "being whole animal is moved" *(ens totum animal movetur)*, or "you are whole man" *(tu es totus homo)* this "whole" is taken categorematically.

From these statements I infer some theses: First, "the whole Socrates is something of Socrates; yet the whole of Socrates is not less than Socrates". The first part is proved because part of Socrates is something of Socrates. The second part also is proved because not any part of Socrates is less than Socrates – such as the total body of Socrates. Nor is his intellective soul, which is not a quantity, less than Socrates.

The second thesis: "The whole Socrates is part of Socrates; yet it is not the case that the whole man is part of Socrates." The first clause is clear because any part of Socrates is a part of Socrates. The second clause also is clear because not any part of man is a part of Socrates; for there is some part [of man] which is part of Plato and is not part of Socrates.

The third thesis: "In your eye there is a whole which is in the world; yet no whole which is in the world is in your eye." The first part is proved for in your eye is a being made from its parts; [113] namely, the pupil of your eye. The second part is clear also because not any part of the world is in your eye.

A corollary of these statements is: "In your purse is the whole money of the world, and in your mind is the whole of possible science." The first part is clear because in your purse is a being made from its parts which is the money of the world, given that you have one dime in your purse. The second part also is clear out of the aforesaid where what is in your soul is a being made from its parts which is possible science. From these statements it follows that this proposition is false which is commonly conceded: "an intellective soul is a whole in a whole, and it is a whole in any of its parts; for if it is a whole, it is a being having parts. The consequent is false; [therefore, the antecedent is false]".

Section 16 — The Particle "Always"

"Always" is converted with every time according to the exigencies of the verb added to it. Thus it is the same thing to say, "always man was", as it is to say, "for all past time man was". These are expounded in this way: "once man was *(fuit)*, and there was not any time save when man was, [therefore, always man was]". Further, concerning the future: "something always will be". This is expounded: "once something will be, and there will not be any time save when something will be, [therefore, something always will be]".

From these statements I infer some theses: First, "always something was which was not always". It is proved: "once something was which was not always; and it was not when something (which was not always) was; therefore, [always something was which was not always]".

The second thesis: "Some man always will be who will not be always." It is proved: "once some man will be who will not always be, and he will not be then save when someone who will not always be will be; therefore, [some man always will be who will not be always]".

The third thesis: "There is always this present instant." It is proved: "once this present instant is; and there is not a time save when this present is; therefore, [always this present is]". It is clear also through its convertend: namely, "in every time this present instant is". For the present instant was not in every time. Nor will the present instant be in every time. From the same thesis this corollary follows: "whoever lives always is, and whoever runs or is moved always has that [property]. Although it did not always have it, nor will it always be having it".

Note that the above definition [114] says; "converted with every time *according to the exigencies of its verb*", because if it were converted absolutely with every time this would be false: "always God was", or "the world always will be", because God was not in all time. It is proved: for if God was in all time and the present time is time; then in the present time God was". The inference is clear in the third mood of the first figure in which "time" is ampliated to refer to that which is or was; and the consequent is false. Because the present time never *was*. In the same way this is false: "The world always will be", because it *will* not be in present time.

It is true, however, that the respondent chooses responses which best conform with his own [purposes].[a] For any of these propositions can be sustained. By the second mode of speaking: "once God was not"; and "once heaven will not be"; because then (pointing to the present instant) God was not and then (pointing to the present instant) heaven will not be and then is, or was, or will be at some time; therefore, once God was not; and once heaven will not be.

Section 17 — The Expression "From Eternity"

"From eternity" is expounded in two ways: In one way *nominally* with the determination of a preposition "from" *(a* or *ab)*, and then it is resolved: e.g., "from eternity *A* was". "This was *A*, and this is or was eternal; therefore, from eternity *A* was." Thus "from eternity" taken nominally is converted with "from some eternity". "From eternity" may be taken in another sense, i.e., *adverbially*; and then it is converted with "eternally", and it signifies the same thing as "before all finite time" or "before all or after all finite time". ["From eternity God was"] is expounded in this way: "before some finite time God was and there was no finite time unless before that God was". Similarly, with regard to the future, "from eternity or eternally something will be", is expounded: "after some finite time, something will be; and there is not, or will not be, some finite time unless after that something will be; therefore, [from eternity or eternally something will be]". Again, "after some instant something will be, and there is not nor will there be some instant unless after that something will be". And notably I say "finite" because there was some time before which God was not [115] namely, the infinite time before. Similarly, something will be after time which will be nothing, i.e., the infinite time after.

From these statements, I infer some theses: First, "from eternity you were, yet you were not eternally". The second part is obvious of itself. Because a thousand years before time you were not. The first part is clear; for from this (pointing to God) you were, and this is or was eternal; therefore, from eternity you were. The inference is clear if "from eternity" is taken nominally.

The second thesis: "From eternity you will be; yet you will not be from eternity." This thesis is clear by taking "from eternity" in the first sentence nominally and in the second sentence adverbially; and these statements are not contradictories since both terms are not taken uniformly or univocally.

The third thesis: "From eternity or eternally something was which was not either from eternity or eternally." It is clear: "before some finite time something was which was not either from eternity or eternally. And there is not or was not some finite time unless before that something was which was not from eternity or eternally: therefore, [before some finite time something was which was not either from eternity or eternally]".

The fourth thesis: "Eternally or from eternity some man will be who will not be eternally or from eternity." It is proved: "after some finite time some man will be who will not be eternally or from eternity; and there is not or will not be some finite time unless after that some man will be who will not be eternally or from eternity; therefore, [eternally or from eternity some man will be who will not be eternally or from eternity]". Whatever things are said of this term "eternity" or "eternally" can be said of this term "continuously and in eternity" *(perpetuo et in aeternum)* which can be taken in two senses, nominally and adverbially as just explained.

Section 18 – The Expression "Infinite"

"Infinite" is taken in two senses: categorematically and syncategorematically. Categorematically it is the same thing as "without beginning and end". E.g., "*A* is infinite", [116] i.e., "*A* is without beginning and end". And it is commonly taken in this way when it is posited on the part of the predicate as in the example; or when it is taken in subject position when one says "something infinite is". This limitation occurs when it is taken either adjectivally or substantivally. Taking it [categorematically] one says: "nothing is infinite; nor are some things infinite", because nothing is without beginning and end. But taking "infinite" syncategorematically, it is expounded by two exponents according to the exigencies of a term added to it or according to the proper nature [of the term] either singular or plural in number. E.g., "Infinite body is", is expounded: "a body of some size is; and there is no finite body of some size greater than that; therefore, [infinite body is]". "Infinite body was", is expounded: "a body of some size was, and there is not or was not a finite body of some size greater than this; therefore, [infinite body was]". Plurals are not expounded through "greater" but through "many". "Infinite bodies are", is expounded: "some bodies are and there are not finite bodies unless those are many; therefore, infinite bodies are". Further, of the past, e.g., "infinite men were", is expounded: "some men were; and there are not or were not infinite men unless there were many; therefore, infinite men were". And similarly, concerning the future, "infinite instances will be", is expounded: "some instances will be and there are not or will not be infinite instances unless there are many; therefore [infinite instances will be]". There is, however, another mode of expounding which is commonly done judging in a certain way the nature of singulars. E.g., "infinite body is", is expounded: "body of some size is; and double that, and triple that and so on *ad infinitum*; therefore, infinite body is". Further, the plural number is expounded in this way: e.g. "infinites are", is expounded: "two bodies are, three bodies are and so on *ad infinitum*". Any of these modes of speaking is good for the present; however, the first is more formal and the second is more intelligible.

From these statements, I infer some theses: First, [117] "God can produce infinite body; yet [God] cannot produce an infinite body". The first part is proved because "God can produce a body of some size, and there is not or cannot be a finite body greater than God can produce", or otherwise, "God can produce some body; and double that, and triple that *ad infinitum*". The second part is clear of itself; because God cannot produce a body without end. For out of the nature of body it is the case that it is figured; therefore, it is bounded by a limit or limits, and in consequence it is finite.

The second thesis: "Infinite time has elapsed; yet no elapsed time was infinite." The first part is proved because time of some quantity has elapsed and double that and triple that and thus [ad] *infinitum*. The second part is proved from this: No elapsed time was without end; for it was terminated in some instant. But one can doubt this point for in another chapter it was said that "some time was infinite before; therefore, some elapsed time was infinite". The reference is to where I spoke of the infinite in the sense that it does not have a beginning but an end; just like past infinite time [or of this that does have a beginning and no end] viz. future infinite time.[a] Now, however, I speak of a finite [time] simply which has neither a beginning nor an end.

The third thesis: "An infinite number is finite; however, no finite number is infinite." The first part is clear because any finite number is a finite number and there is no finite number unless a greater than that is an infinite number. The second part is clear because its contradictory is self-contradictory.

The fourth thesis: "Infinites are finite, and yet no finites are infinites." The first part is proved because two are finites, three are finites and thus to infinity. The second part is clear of itself because no finites are beings without end.

The fifth thesis: "There are infinitely many finites [118]; yet no finites are infinitely many." The first part is clear because two finites are many and three finites are many and thus of singulars. The second part is very clear of itself because its opposite is self-contradictory.

The sixth thesis: "There were infinite days and there were infinite years" — given, according to Aristotle, that the world is perpetual and eternal. This thesis is clear however its parts may be expounded. From this thesis it follows that there were no more days than years because both are infinite.

And this brings to an end the fourth treatise which deals with terms.

Notes

[80]^a Medieval grammarians distinguished between the direct *(rectus)* and the oblique *(obliquus)* cases. The former is the nominative and the latter is one of the remaining cases, viz. genitive, dative, accusative, vocative or ablative.

[82]^a *"praeteritus"* is the perfect passive participle of the verb *praetereo* (to pass by). Strictly, it is not translatable into English; however, "has passed away" is near to it in sense.

[86]^a See p. [83] and below p. [95] ff.

[87]^a On the composite and divided senses see below p. [93].
^b See above Section 1, pp. [80]–[84].

[89]^a Officiable propositions are "conjunctive" insofar as they are analyzable into a concatenation of statements joined by "and". Resoluble propositions are "relative" insofar as their analysans includes a subordinate clause with a relative pronoun.

[90]^a The "first mediate term" is the one which occurs first in the sentence to be analyzed. The *Logica Magna* calls this "that most noble rule of all logic": "Where there are many mediate terms in any proposition one always ought to begin the proof of that proposition from the first term. Thus the signification of the prior mediate term ought to be explained before the function of the posterior mediate term is explicated." See Perreiah, 3, p. 105.
^b Earlier discussions of resoluble, exponible, officiable and describable propositions are at p. [76] ff.

[92]^a Note that propositions containing "necessarily", "contingently" and the adverbial forms of other modals are proved as exponibles.

[97]^a "precisely"/"non-precisely" *(praecise/nonpraecise)* modifies the comparative "as...as" and means that the comparative relation is taken either strictly or non-strictly. This is an important factor in Paul's rules for solving insolubles. See below Chapter VI, p. [143] ff.
^b In the previous section p. [96] this proposition was proved: "In no instant will you be as old as you will be." This proposition implies the second exponent of the present proof, viz., "not in some instant will you be as old as you will be."

[100]^a The *Logica Magna* acknowledges two additional kinds of exclusives: "An exclusive proposition of the fourth order is one in which the exclusive term governs only part of the predicate or part of the subject. For example, 'I see only Socrates', 'Proposition A signifies precisely as things are' ". "An exclusive proposition of the fifth order is one in which the exclusive term is placed at the

end. For example, 'you are thus only or precisely' ...'' See Adams and Del Punta in Adams, 3, pp. 259–260.

[104]^a Note that a term which occurs in an exceptive phrase must be on a level lower than the term with respect to which it makes an exception. For example, in "all animals except Socrates run", "Socrates" is on a lower level than "animals".

[110]^a This note underscores the fact that in the Latin text one word *"immediate"* is ambiguous: it can be read as an adverb or as an adjective. Paul's analysis concentrates on the former sense.

[114]^a Note that the disputant can choose to argue either side of a proposition.

[117]^a See p. [115] ff.

Chapter V
On Obligations

Section 1 – Definitions and Rules

An obligation *(obligatio)* is a statement composed of a sign of an obligation and the thing obligated, for instance "I pose to you this 'You are in Rome' ". This whole statement is called an obligation. The signs of obligation are these expressions: "I pose to you this" *(pono tibi istam)*. The thing obligated is this statement: "You are in Rome." There are two species of obligation, i.e. "I pose" *(pono)* and "I reject" *(depono)*. The former is to be pursued first of all by setting out certain general rules.

Rule I.   Everything possible which is posited to you is to be admitted by you.

For example, if I pose to you this, "you are", it is to be admitted, just as its contradictory if posed, "you are not". And likewise of other possible things which are posed.

Rule II.   Everything posited to you and admitted by you [and] proposed during the time of the obligation is to be conceded by you.

For example, I pose to you, "you are in Rome". When this is admitted because it is possible then however many times it is proposed during the time of the obligation it is to be conceded. And notably it says, "during the time of the obligation", because from the cessation of that time the respondent is not obligated further to concede the same thing. And the time of the obligation lasts from the instant [119] of admission until one says "let the time of the obligation stop" or the opponent moves on to another matter.

Rule III.   Everything following *per se* from what is posited and admitted or from what is posited together with one or more conceded [sentences] and proposed under the time of the obligation is to be conceded.

An example of the first kind: I pose to you, "you are in Rome". When this is admitted I propose "you are not in Paris". This is to be conceded, because it is something following *per se* from what is posited. For it validly follows: "you are in Rome; therefore, you are not in Paris". An example of the second kind: I pose to you, "every man is in Rome". When this is admitted, I propose, "you are a man". This is to be conceded because it is true yet irrelevant *(impertinens)*. Next, I propose "you are in Rome" which again is to be conceded because it follows from what was posited together with what was conceded. For it follows: "every man is in Rome; you are a man; therefore, you are in Rome". An example of the third kind: I pose to you, "Every disputing man is in Paris", which having been posited and admitted, I propose to you, "you are a man and you are disputing". Both of these statements are to be conceded because they are true yet irrelevant. Next, I propose, "you are in Paris". This statement ought to be conceded because it follows from what was posited with the two things conceded. For it follows: "every disputing man is in Paris; you are a man; and you are disputing; therefore, you are in Paris".

Rule IV. Everything inconsistent with what is posited together with a conceded sentence or conceded sentences taken collectively or separately is to be denied.

This is clear because two contradictories are not to be conceded by the same person at the same time; but the opposite of any such inconsistent statement is to be conceded because it follows, as the third rule says. Therefore, any such repugnant statement is to be denied. E.g., when this is posited and admitted, "every man runs", and this is conceded, "you are a man", one ought to deny "you do not run", because its contradictory, "you run", follows and is to be conceded.

Rule V. Everything following from what is posited together with the opposite or opposites of what has been proposed and correctly denied under the time of the obligation [120] is to be conceded.

An example of the first kind: I pose to you"every man runs". When this is admitted, I propose, "you run". This is to be denied because it is false and does not follow. Next, "you are not a man". This is to be conceded because it is something following from what is posited together with the opposite of what is correctly denied. Thus, "every man runs; you do not run; therefore, you are not a man". An example of the second kind: I pose "Antichrist is colored". When this is admitted, I propose "Antichrist is white" or "Antichrist is black". Both of these are to be denied because they are false and do not follow. Next, I propose, "Antichrist is colored with a medium color". This is to be conceded. For this follows from what was posited together with the opposite of what was correctly denied. Thus, Antichrist is colored; and he is neither white nor black; therefore, he is colored with a medium color.

Rule VI. Everything inconsistent with what has been posited together with the opposite or opposites of what has been correctly denied within the time of the obligation is to be denied.

For this reason if in the first example [above] the third sentence said, "you are a man" it is to be denied because its contradictory follows. Similarly, if in the second example [above] the third sentence said, "Antichrist is not colored with a medium color", it is to be denied for the same reason; namely, because its contradictory follows.

215

Rule VII. To every irrelevant proposition one is to respond according to its quality. That is: if it is true, it is to be conceded. If it is false, it is to be denied. If it is doubtful, it is to be doubted. An irrelevant proposition I call one which neither follows from nor is inconsistent with [another proposition].

Hence both of these "you are a man" and "you run" are irrelevant to "every man runs", because neither follows from or is inconsistent with it. Indeed, if immediately after that proposition, "every man runs", one proposed "you are a man" it is to be conceded [because it is true and irrelevant], and if one proposes "you run", it is to be denied. A relevant proposition is twofold, i.e. sequent and inconsistent. Whence where you concede "every man runs; you are a man", "you run" is relevant and follows and "you do not run" is relevant and inconsistent. From this rule it follows as a corollary:

Rule VII. Corollary:
> Every false proposition that does not follow is to be denied, and every true proposition that is not inconsistent is to be conceded.

The first [121] part is clear: if that proposition is false and does not follow, therefore, it is irrelevant or inconsistent and consequently it is to be denied. The second part similarly is proved; for if that proposition is true and not inconsistent, then it follows or is irrelevant and consequently according to the above rules it is to be conceded.

Rule VIII. Because a possible thing is posited, an impossible is not to be conceded nor is a necessary thing to be denied. For nothing inconsistent is to be conceded nor is something following to be denied.

But what is impossible at least *per se* is inconsistent with anything and every necessary proposition is something following; therefore, what is impossible is not to be conceded, nor is the necessary to be denied, no matter what possible thing is posited. I conclude, therefore, that under the time of an obligation however many times and whenever someone proposes one of these statements, "God is", "man is a donkey" the first is to be conceded and the second is to be denied. Note that there are two senses of "necessary": *per se* and *per accidens*. A proposition necessary *per se* is that whose adequate significate neither can be nor could be nor will be able to be false, e.g. "God is". A proposition necessary *per accidens* is that whose adequate significate cannot be false [now] but was able to be false, e.g., "you were". Hence it is regularly said that every true affirmative proposition about the past whose truth does not depend on the future is necessary.[a] Similarly, there are two senses of "impossible": *per se* and *per accidens*. An impossible *per se* is that proposition whose adequate significate cannot be and was not able to be and will not be able to be true, e.g., "no God is". An impossible *per accidens* is that proposition whose adequate significate cannot be true but could have been true, e.g., "you were not". Whence always if one of the two contradictories is necessary the other is impossible and vice versa. Therefore, this rule concerns propositions impossible and necessary *per se* because sometimes when a possible proposition is posited, an impossible one is to be conceded and a necessary proposition is to be denied *per accidens*. For example, I posit to you: "this instant was not", – pointing [122] to the present instant. It is to be admitted because it is true. Once that is admitted, it is certain that that instant is past. However, if I propose to you the same proposition it is to be conceded and its opposite is to be denied, despite the fact that it is made impossible *per accidens* and its opposite is made necessary likewise *per accidens*.[a]

Rule IX. When every part of a conjunctive *(copulativa)* proposition is conceded the conjunction *(copulativa)* of which they or similar sentences are principal parts is to be conceded. And when one part of a disjunctive proposition is conceded, the disjunction of which it is a principal part [is to be conceded].

This rule is proven. For just as for the truth of a conjunctive proposition it is required and it suffices that both parts be true and for the truth of a disjunctive proposition that one part be true, so in order for a conjunctive proposition to be conceded it is required and it suffices that both parts be conceded. And for a disjunctive proposition to be conceded it is required and it suffices that one principal part be conceded. E.g., I posit to you, "you are in Rome", which being admitted I propose to you the same proposition. It is to be conceded. Then "you are a man", is to be conceded because it is true and irrelevant *(impertinens)*. Finally, if that conjunctive proposition "you are in Rome and you are a man", is proposed, it also is to be conceded since its parts are conceded. And the same point may be made concerning a disjunctive proposition.

Section 2 – Arguments against the Rules

So that the truth of these rules may be grasped more firmly, against each of them I will formulate an obligation.[b]

Against the first rule, I pose to you every possible proposition. If you do not admit them, I argue in this way. I posit to you every possible proposition, and you do not admit every possible proposition by responding correctly. Therefore, not every possible proposition is to be admitted by you, which violates the [first] rule. If then you admit [every possible proposition] I propose to you these two propositions, "you are" and "you are not". If you concede them you concede two contradictories; therefore,

217

you respond poorly. If you deny one of them, and both of them are proposed to you and admitted by you because they are possible propositions *from all* the possible propositions I proposed to you, therefore, you deny what was proposed to you and admitted by you and consequently [123] you respond poorly. This inference is clear according to the [second] rule. One can respond by not admitting what is posited and then to the argument "I posit to you every possible proposition and you do not admit every possible proposition; therefore, not every possible proposition is to be admitted by you", I deny the argument; just as it does not follow: "I posit to you both of these contradictories 'you are' and 'you are not' and you do not admit both of those contradictories; therefore, neither of those contradictories is to be admitted by you", but rather it follows only that either of those contradictoris is not to be admitted by you. So too in the earlier inference it follows that one is not to admit every possible proposition and this is true since it is consistent with every possible proposition is to be admitted.[a]

Against the second rule, one can argue as follows. I posit to you this: " 'you are in Rome', is posited to you and admitted by you". When this is admitted and conceded, I propose to you this: "you are in Rome". This is to be denied because it is false and irrelevant. Then one can argue in this way: That proposition is to be denied by you, and the same proposition was posited to you and [correctly] admitted by you; therefore, what was posited to you and admitted by you is to be denied. The inference is valid because it is a resolvable syllogism *(syllogismus resolutorius)* and the major was conceded while the minor was indeed posited. One may respond by admitting what was posited; and when "you are in Rome" is proposed, it is denied. And then with respect to the argument, I deny the major premise since it is inconsistent with what was posited. For it follows; "you are in Rome" is posited to you and admitted by you; therefore, "'you are in Rome', is to be conceded by you", which is inconsistent with this proposition " 'you are in Rome' is to be denied by you". However many times, therefore, one proposes "you are in Rome", that proposition is denied. And if someone says that proposition is to be denied by you, that again is denied; and it is conceded that it is to be conceded. And if someone argues in this way: This proposition is to be conceded by you and you deny it; therefore, you respond poorly; one rejects the inference, just as it does not follow: You concede proposition *A* and proposition *A* is false; therefore, you respond poorly — given that *A* is a false proposition that follows. But in all of these inferences one must add to [124] the antecedent, "you are not obligated", which is denied since it is false and irrelevant.[a]

Against the third rule one can argue in this way. I posit to you this proposition, " 'you run and you do not run', is to be conceded by you".

The case is possible, because it is possible that you run, and that the proposition, "you do not run", is posited to you and admitted by you, and consequently it is to be conceded. This case having been admitted, I argue in this way: "you run", is not to be conceded by you: yet "you run" follows from what was posited and admitted according to the rule "from a conjunctive proposition one may infer both of its parts". Therefore, not any proposition following from what was posited and admitted is to be conceded. The inference holds and the first part of the antecedent is proven. For "you do not run", is to be conceded by you according to what was posited. But "you run", contradicts the proposition "you do not run"; therefore, "you run", is not to be conceded by you. The inference holds because if one of two contradictories is to be conceded the other one is to be denied. One may respond by admitting the posited proposition; and then to the argument, I deny the proposition, " 'you run' is not to be conceded by you". And as for the proof, I deny the minor, i.e., " 'you run', contradicts the proposition, "you do not run", − not insofar as it is false but insofar as it is inconsistent with two conceded propositions. For it follows: "you run" is to be conceded by you, and "you do not run" is to be conceded by you: therefore, "you run" and "you do not run", are not contradictories. Nevertheless, if the case should be set up in this way: I posit to you "you run and you do not run", its contradictory, is to be conceded by you; I admit the case, and I concede the proposition, "you run", however many times it is proposed, and I deny that it is to be conceded by me *insofar as it is inconsistent with the second part of the posited conjunction.* For it follows: its contradictory, "you do not run", is to be conceded by you; therefore, "you run", is not to be conceded by you. And if one should argue in this way: "you run", is not to be conceded by you yet you concede it; therefore, you respond poorly, I deny the inference, just as it does not follow: "you deny proposition A, and A is true; therefore, you respond poorly". But one ought to add in the antecedent that "you are not obligated", and this is denied since it is false.

One can argue against the fourth rule [125] by proving that something inconsistent with what is posited is to be conceded by you. And I posit to you "nothing is posited to you". When this is admitted because it is possible, I then propose to you the proposition, "something is posited to you". If you concede it and respond correctly, then I have what I wanted, because that proposition is inconsistent with what was posited. If you deny it, [then] to the contrary: I posited to you the proposition "nothing is posited to you", and that proposition is something; therefore, something is posited to you. I reply by denying "something is posited to you". And then to the argument, I deny the major, i.e., "I posited to you that proposition 'nothing is posited to you' ", insofar as it is inconsistent. For these are inconsistent: "nothing is posited to you" and "I posited to you that [proposition]". And if someone argues that what is posited is inconsistent with what is posited to you; therefore something is posited to you, the antecedent will be denied insofar as it is inconsistent and [so is] any other proposition from which it follows that something is posited to you. One may respond in like fashion, if it is posited, "that you do not exist" *(te non esse)*, by admitting and by conceding the same proposition. And if someone says "you concede this proposition" or "you respond correctly" I deny each such proposition because from it it follows that you exist, which is the opposite of what was posited.

One can argue against the fifth rule. For given the truth of the fifth rule, it follows that having admitted any contingent false proposition any other contingent false proposition is to be conceded. This is proven: and I posit to you this, "you are in Rome". When this is posited and admitted, I propose to you, "you are in Rome and a stick stands in the corner". It is clear that this is to be denied because it is false and it does not follow. Then it is proposed, "no stick stands in the corner". If you deny that proposition, you violate the rule, because it follows from what was posited together with the opposite of what was correctly denied. For it follows, then: "you are not in Rome or no stick stands in the corner. But you are in Rome, according to what was posited. Therefore, no stick stands in the corner". If, therefore, one concedes that proposition, "no stick stands in the corner", I have the conclusion principally to be proved, because just as that proposition is deduced so too any other [false] proposition [may be deduced], provided [126] its opposite is conjoined by means of a conjunction and this conjunctive proposition is proposed immediately after what was posited. One can respond by conceding the conclusion drawn — indeed the same false thing, and any one, can be deduced provided it is posited disjunctively with the opposite of what was posited. E.g., I posit to you, "you run". When this is admitted, I propose to you "you do not run or a stick stands in the corner", or some proposition like "you are Pope or a bishop". This is to be conceded, because it is true and irrelevant. Then when someone proposes, "a stick stands in the corner", it ought to be conceded because it follows from what is posited together with one conceded [proposition]. For it follows "you do not run or a stick stands in the corner; but 'you run', follows from what was posited; therefore, a stick stands in the corner".

One can argue against the sixth rule. I posit to you this disjunctive proposition, "you run or a king sits". When this is posited and admitted, I propose to you this, "no king sits", and it is clear that this proposition is to be doubted because it is doubtful and irrelevant. Next, I propose "you run". This is to be denied because it is false and irrelevant. Then I propose again the proposition, "no king sits". If you deny it or concede it and previously you doubted it, then you respond poorly. The inference holds in virtue of a rule of obligations, because all responses under the time of the obligation are referred back to the same instant. If, therefore, you doubt the proposition and you respond correctly, that proposition is not to be denied by you; yet it is inconsistent with what was posited together with the opposite of what was correctly denied. For it correctly follows, "you run or a king sits; but you do not run; therefore, a king sits". One may respond by admitting what was posited, and when the proposition is proposed, "no king sits", it is doubted. And that proposition "you run", is denied. And when it is proposed again "no king sits", it is denied, because it is inconsistent with what was posited together with the opposite of what was denied. And when it is said that you previously doubted it and now you deny it, therefore, you respond poorly, the argument is not valid. And regarding the rule I say that it applies to inconsistent replies, like conceding and denying.[a] Again, it is conceded in a similar case that some proposition [127] in one place is to be doubted and in another place is to be conceded. E.g., I posit to you this proposition, "you run or a king sits". When this is admitted, I propose "a king sits". This is to be doubted because it is doubtful and irrelevant. Then, "you run"; this is to be denied because it is false and irrelevant. Again, I propose "a king sits". And it is clear that it is to be conceded, because it follows from what was posited together with the opposite of what was correctly denied: "you run or a king sits; but you do not run; therefore, a king sits".

Against the seventh rule one argues by proving that one should not respond to every irrelevant proposition according to its quality. And I pose to you this proposition, "you are in Rome". When this is admitted and conceded, I propose, "you are in Rome in this instant", – pointing to the present instant. If you concede the proposition, I have proved my point. For this proposition is false and irrelevant since it does not follow, nor is it inconsistent [with the posited proposition]. If, on the other hand, it is denied, then to the contrary: everything which is in Rome is in Rome in this instant; but you are in Rome; therefore, you are in Rome in this present instant. The major premise is proved: for everything which is in Rome is in Rome in the present instant. But there is no present instant save this one: therefore, everything which is in Rome is in Rome in this instant.

One may respond by admitting what was posited; and when it is proposed "you are in Rome in this instant", it may be denied. And as for its proof I deny the major because it is inconsistent with what was posited together with the opposite of what was correctly denied. For it follows, "you are in Rome and you are not in Rome in this instant; therefore, not everything which is in Rome is in Rome in this instant". And as for the proof the [former] major I concede that everything which is in Rome is in Rome in the present instant; and I deny the minor premise, i.e., that there is no present instant save this one. For from one conceded proposition and the opposite of what was correctly denied, there follows the opposite of that exceptive. For it follows: "everything which is in Rome is in Rome in the present instant; and not everything which is in Rome is in Rome in this instant. Therefore, there is some instant which is not this instant". This conclusion is inconsistent with that exceptive proposition. And if someone says "what is that [other] instant?", one replies that it can be [128] a [instant] or b [instant]. Nor is such a question to be determined unless disjunctively.

Against the eighth rule one can argue. And I pose to you this proposition, " 'man is a donkey', is posited and admitted by you". Having been admitted and conceded, because it is possible, I propose, "man is a donkey". Either you concede it or you deny it. If you concede it and respond correctly, I have my point, because of a posited possible, a *per se* impossible is to be conceded. If however, you deny it, then to the contrary: everything posited to you and by you admitted is to be conceded by you, but "man is a donkey" is posited to you and is admitted by you; therefore, "man is a donkey", is to be conceded by you. The inference holds, together with its major, because it is a rule; and the minor is clear because it is posited. Then one argues in this way: "man is a donkey" is to be conceded by you and "man is a donkey" is impossible *per se*; therefore, what is impossible *per se* is to be conceded by you. And consequently, what is necessary *per se* is to be denied, because its contradictory is necessary *per se*, i.e., "no man is a donkey". One may respond by admitting what was posited. And when someone proposes, "man is a donkey", it is denied. Then with respect to the argument I concede that "man is a donkey" is to be conceded by you; yet I deny that "man is a donkey" is impossible *per se* insofar as it is inconsistent with a conceded proposition. For it follows "man is a donkey" is to be conceded by you; therefore, "man is a donkey" is not impossible *per se*. And if it is argued in this way: " 'man is a donkey' is to be conceded by you, and you deny that proposition; therefore, you respond poorly", I deny the argument. But it ought to be added "you are not obligated".

Against the last rule one argues in this way. I pose to you this proposition, "you are in Rome". When this is admitted and conceded, I propose to you the conjunctive proposition "you are in Rome and you are a man". This conjunctive proposition is false and irrelevant; therefore, it is to be denied. Nevertheless, each of its parts is to be conceded. Therefore, it is not the case that when each part of a conjunction is conceded the conjunction [itself] is to be conceded, which is against the rule. But it is proved that each part of the conjunction is to be conceded, this is proved for the first part is to be conceded because it is posited and admitted, and the second part [is to be conceded] likewise because it is true and irrelevant. One may respond by admitting what was posited; and when someone proposes the conjunctive proposition, I deny it; and I deny that each of its parts is to be conceded insofar as the second is to be denied. [129] And when someone says that the proposition is true yet irrelevant, I concede that it is true; but it is not irrelevant. Indeed it is inconsistent because its contradictory follows from what was posited together with the opposite of what was correctly denied. For it follows "you are not in Rome or you are not a man; but you are in Rome, by what was posited; therefore, you are not a man". If, however, immediately after the posited it were proposed, "you are a man" I would concede that because it is true and irrelevant; and consequently, I would concede that conjunctive statement "you are in Rome and you are a man", insofar as it follows from its conceded parts.

Again, I argue against the same [i.e., ninth and last] rule. I pose to you this proposition, "every man is in Rome". When this is admitted, I propose "you are a man and you are in Rome". This conjunction is to be denied because it is false and irrelevant. Next, I propose "you are a man". This proposition is to be conceded because it is true and irrelevant. Further, I propose to you the other part, "you are in Rome". And it is clear that this similarly is to be conceded because it follows from what was posited together with a conceded proposition. E.g., "every man is in Rome, and you are a man; therefore, you are in Rome". And thus is made my point, that a conjunctive proposition is to be denied; yet both of its parts are to be conceded.

One responds by admitting what was posited and by denying the conjunctive proposition. And when someone proposes, "you are a man", I deny it because it is inconsistent with what was posited together with the opposite of what was correctly denied because its contradictory follows. For it follows "every man is in Rome; and you are not a man or you are not in Rome; therefore, you are not a man". The inference is clear because the conclusion follows from what was posited plus either part of a disjunctive proposition. Therefore, it follows from what was posited and the entire disjunctive proposition. The inference is clear and the antecedent is likewise intuitively clear. Whereby [the ninth rule is valid].

Section 3 – Interchangeable Propositions

With regard to the interchangeability of propositions this sophism is proposed. I pose to you this proposition. " 'God is and man is a donkey' are interchangeable". When this is admitted because it is possible, I propose "God is". This is conceded because it is necessary *per se*. Next, I propose "man is a donkey". Either you concede it or you deny it. If you concede it, then to the contrary: Let the time of the obligation cease. And I point out to you that you conceded something impossible *per se* in the time of the obligation; therefore, you responded poorly. Hence, outside [130] the time of the obligation the truth of the matter *(rei veritas)* is always to be acknowledged, because in this way one can tell whether the respondent answers well or poorly in the time of the obligation. If, however, in the time of an obligation this proposition is denied, "man is a donkey", on the contrary: "God is" and "man is a donkey" are interchangeable. And this is to be conceded, "God is"; therefore, this is to be conceded, "man is a donkey". Yet you deny it; therefore, you respond poorly. Again when that case is admitted, I propose − "this is true, 'God is' ". This ought to be conceded because it is true and irrelevant. Then, this is true, "man is a donkey". This is to be conceded because it follows. For it follows: Those propositions are interchangeable; and the first is true. Therefore, the second is true. And then this is true, "man is a donkey", which adequately signifies man to be a donkey; therefore, "man is a donkey" is true; and consequently, "man is a donkey".

To the first one responds by admitting the case. And when someone proposes, "God is", I concede it and I deny the proposition, "man is a donkey". Then with respect to the argument I concede that "man is a donkey", is by me to be conceded. And to the counterargument I deny the inference. But it ought to be added that you are not obligated, which I deny. And if one argues, "man is a donkey", is to be conceded by you and "man is a donkey", is *per se* impossible; therefore, what is *per se* impossible is to be conceded by you, I deny the minor premise insofar as it is inconsistent with the major premise already conceded. In the same way, one may respond if in the first place this proposition is proposed, " 'man is a donkey', by you is to be denied". That would be conceded and consequently it would be said that this proposition, "God is", is to be denied by you. And it would be denied that it is necessary *per se* because it is inconsistent with what is conceded. For it follows: "God is", is denied by you; therefore, it is not necessary *per se*.

To the second, I concede that this is true, "man is a donkey" and I deny that the proposition signifies adequately man to be a donkey because it is inconsistent with the major premise already conceded. For it follows: that is true, ["man is a donkey"] therefore, it may not signify adequately man to be a donkey. Where, however, in the first place that proposition, " 'Man is a donkey' is false", is proposed, it would be conceded because it is true and irrelevant. Then, " 'God is' is false", is conceded because it follows. And it is denied as [131] inconsistent that it signifies adequately God to be. And if it should be asked how it signifies adequately, such a question is not to be determined here.[a]

It is to be noted that if it is posited: [Interchange,] "God is" and "man is a donkey", signifying adequately as before, one ought not to admit the case because when it is admitted, there follows an absurdity or a contradiction. This is proved: For admitting that, I propose, "this is true, 'God is' ". Either you concede it or you deny it. If you deny it, on the contrary, that proposition is not true, "God is", which adequately signifies God to be. Therefore, "God to be" is not true, which is impossible. If it is conceded, then I propose this proposition is true, "man is a donkey". One ought to concede it insofar as it follows. Then it is argued in this way. That is true, "man is a donkey," which adequately signifies man to be a donkey, therefore, it is true that man is a donkey. The consequent is impossible.

For a kind of response in this matter, I posit some rules.

Rule I.   Whenever two propositions are posited to be interchangeable thus signifying adequately of which one is necessary and the other one impossible the case is not admitted, because then from the necessary the impossible would follow.

E.g., God is; therefore man is a donkey. And I mean by the expression "thus signifying adequately", the customary significates.[b]

Rule II.   Whenever two propositions thus signifying adequately are posited to be interchangeable of which the one is possible and the other impossible the case is not admitted.

Hence, if these propositions are posited to be interchangeable thus signifying adequately, "you are a man" and "man is a donkey", it is not admitted because then from the possible the impossible would follow. It is proved. I pose the above case. When it is admitted, I draw the consequence, "you are a man; therefore, a man is a donkey". The inference is solid. The antecedent is possible, and the consequent is impossible. For it is possible [for you] to be a man, and this proposition "you are a man" adequately signifies so. Therefore, this proposition is possible; and it is the antecedent; therefore, the antecedent is possible. Similarly, for man [132] to be a donkey is impossible; and this proposition "a man is a donkey", signifies so adequately; therefore, this proposition is impossible. And it is the consequent; therefore, the consequent is impossible.

Rule III.   Whenever two propositions are posited to be interchangeable thus signifying adequately of which one is necessary and the other contingent, the case is not admitted.

Hence if these propositions are posited to be interchangeable "God is" and "Antichrist will be", thus signifying adequately [the case is not to be admitted], because then from the necessary the contingent would follow.

225

This is proved because, if not, let this case be admitted. And I draw this consequence, "God is; therefore, Antichrist will be". That inference is solid because it is argued from one interchangeable proposition to the other; yet the antecedent is necessary while the consequent is contingent. Therefore, the inference is not valid. But it is proved that the antecedent is necessary; for it is necessary for God to exist, and the antecedent thus signifies adequately; thus, the antecedent is necessary. Similarly, for Antichrist to be is contingent, and the consequent thus signifies adequately; hence, the consequent is contingent.

Rule IV.   Whenever two contingent propositions are posited to be interchangeable thus signifying adequately, of which the one is contradictorily inconsistent with the other, the case is not admitted.

For example, if these propositions thus signifying adequately are posited to be interchangeable, "you are" and "you are not", [the case is not to be admitted] because then from one of two opposites follows the other — of these each will be contingent. Indeed, it follows that two contradictories will be simultaneously true or simultaneously false, which is not possible. And note that I say "contradictorily" because if they are contrarily inconsistent the case ought to be admitted. And each of these ought to be said to be false. For instance, "you run; yet you move". For these propositions thus signifying adequately cannot be simultaneously true; but they [can be] simultaneously false. For I call those things inconsistent "contradictorily" which cannot be simultaneously true or simultaneously false thus signifying adequately. And I call those things inconsistent "contrarily" which can be simultaneously false but not simultaneously true.

Rule V.   Whenever two contingent propositions are posited to be interchanged, thus signifying adequately, of which neither is inconsistent with the other [133] the case is admitted.

To the first thing proposed one may respond as one does with respect to an irrelevant proposition. To the second [one may respond] as one does with respect to a relevant proposition which follows *(pertinens sequens)*. E.g., I pose to you this proposition, " 'you are a man' and 'you run', are interchanged thus signifying adequately". Let that be admitted. And if someone proposes "you are a man", let it be conceded insofar as it is true and irrelevant. And likewise that other proposition "you run". Similarly if someone proposes "this is true, 'you are a man' ", it is conceded insofar as it is true and not repugnant and consequently, [it is to be conceded] that the first is true, "you run", insofar as it follows. Again, if the order is varied so that in the first place is proposed, "you run", it is denied because it is false and irrelevant, and consequently this proposition is to be denied: "you are a man". And if someone says: This is false, "you run", it is conceded, and consequently [it is conceded] that this is false, "you are a man".

Rule VI. Whenever two propositions, either contingent or non-contingent, are posited to be interchanged, not making mention of the adequate significate, the case is admitted. And when they are proposed, with respect to conceding and denying, one may respond within [the time of the obligation] just as [one does] outside [the time of the obligation]. But if the first is conceded to be true or necessary; then the second is treated in the same way. If, however, the first is false or impossible the second is taken in the same way.

E.g., if this proposition is posited: "God is and man is a donkey", the response is in the beginning of this section.[a] But if I pose to you this, " 'you are a man' and 'you run' are interchanged", it is admitted. Once this is admitted, I propose "you are a man". That is conceded. Then "you run", is denied. But if someone says the first proposition is true, let it be conceded. Therefore, the second is true. I concede it. But then I deny that the second signifies adequately that you run insofar as that is inconsistent with a proposition conceded together with the opposite of what is correctly denied. For it follows: You do not run; yet this proposition, "you run", is true. Therefore it does not signify adequately that you run.

And if one argues in this way: That inference is solid: "you are a man; therefore, you run", and the antecedent is to be conceded by you; therefore, also the consequent, I concede. Then further: The consequent is to be conceded by you, yet you deny that very proposition; therefore, you respond poorly. This inference is not solid; but one ought to add in the antecedent "you are not obligated".

It is to be noted that however many times someone posits these inferences [134] in a case of interchangeability "God is; therefore, man is a donkey", "you are a man; therefore, you run", each of these is always denied because in the truth of the matter each of these is impossible. But to what is impossible one is to respond under the time of the obligation just as he would outside of the time of the obligation. However, it may be said that each of these is solid, just as this proposition is always denied, "man is a donkey", yet sometimes it is conceded [that] this exists; as in the proposition, " 'man is a donkey', is impossible". But it is not impossible for the entire proposition to be true. Similarly, any of these inferences is impossible; but for any one of them to be solid is not impossible.[a]

Section 4 — Similar and Dissimilar Propositions

Now we come to discuss similar and dissimilar propositions. Let this be the truth of the matter: You are in Paris. And I pose to you this proposition: " 'you are in Paris' and 'you are in Rome' are similar". And "similar propositions" means "similar in truth or in falsity". This having been admitted, I propose to you this proposition, "you are in Paris". This is conceded because it is true and irrelevant, as is clear to intuition. Then I propose "you are in Rome". If you deny it, and you already conceded the other proposition similar to it, you respond poorly. If you concede it, I propose to you this conjunctive proposition, "you are in Paris and you are in Rome". If you deny that and you already conceded both parts, you respond poorly. The inference holds according to the last rule in the first part of this Chapter.[b] If you concede it, let the time of the obligation cease. And I argue that, after a possible obligation has been made, you have conceded something which is impossible, i.e., "you are in Paris and you are in Rome". Therefore, you responded poorly.

One may respond by admitting what was posited. And when someone proposes, "you are in Paris", I concede it, and I deny "you are in Rome". And when someone replies, "you already conceded one of [these] similar propositions; and now you deny the other one; thus, you respond poorly", I deny the inference, just as it does not follow: "you already conceded one of these interchangeable propositions, and you deny the other; therefore, you respond poorly". But it does follow: "you already conceded one of these similar propositions to be true, and you deny the other to be true; therefore, you respond poorly". Therefore, if in the beginning, someone proposes "this is true:'You [135] are in Paris' ", let it be conceded; and consequently, that this is true: "You are in Rome." And at first, I had denied this proposition, "you are in Rome". Therefore I deny consequently that the proposition, "you are in Rome", signifies adequately that you are in Rome. For it follows: you are not in Rome; and that proposition "you are in Rome", is true; therefore, it does not signify adequately that you are in Rome.

To clarify this material, I posit some rules.

Rule I.   Whenever two propositions are posited to be similar, and no mention is made of the adequate significate, one may respond to them by conceding, denying or doubting under the time of the obligation just as he would outside of the time of the obligation.

For instance when someone posits these propositions to be similar, "God is" and "man is a donkey", "you sit" and "you run", always the first should be conceded and the second denied.

228

Rule II. Whenever two propositions are posited to be similar, and no mention is made of the adequate significate, with respect to the truth or falsity of the first proposition one may respond as he would outside of the time of the obligation and with regard to the truth or falsity of the second proposition he may respond in a consistent manner.

For example, I pose to you the proposition, " 'you are a man' and 'Antichrist is', are similar propositions". If this proposition is proposed first, "this is true, 'you are a man' ", let it be conceded. And consequently [let it be conceded], that this is true, "Antichrist is". If, however, one proposes first, "this is false, 'Antichrist is'", let it be conceded. And consequently [let it be conceded], that this is false, "you are a man".

Rule III. Whenever two propositions are posited to be similar thus signifying adequately, of which the one is contradictorily inconsistent with the other, the case is not to be admitted.

For instance, if someone posits propositions such as these to be similar: "God is" and "man is a donkey", thus signifying adequately, [or] "a king sits" and "no king sits", [the cases are not to be admitted]. This is proved because if not [i.e., if it is not so], therefore let the case be admitted. I ask whether that proposition is true or false, "God is". And if the respondent says that this proposition is false, [then] the same also signifies adequately that God exists; therefore, that God exists is false. If the respondent says that this proposition is true, then this other proposition is true, "man is a donkey". And this proposition signifies man to be a donkey *(hominem esse asinum)*; thus, that man is a donkey is true. This conclusion is absurd *(inconveniens)*. And in this way one can argue about contradictories, by proving that two contradictory propositions are simultaneously true or false.

Rule IV. Whenever two propositions are posited to be similar thus signifying adequately [136] of which one or each follows from the contradictory of the other, those propositions are similar in truth; and wherever and whenever they are proposed they are to be conceded.

Thus, positing that such propositions signifying adequately are similar, [these follow]: "it is proved to you; yet you do not know it is proved to you". "You do not run; yet you are moved." This is proved: for admitting the case, I ask whether these propositions are [similarly] true or [similarly] false. If they are true, I have my point. If they are false, the opposite of the second proposition is true; namely, "you know it is proved to you". Then, in this way: "you know it is proved to you; therefore, it is proved to you". That inference is solid, and the antecedent is true; therefore, it is not false — the opposite of which you already conceded. And the same may be said with regard to the other pair of propositions.

Rule V.   Whenever two propositions thus signifying adequately are
           posited to be similar and one follows from the opposite of the
           other, they are similar in falsity; and whenever one is proposed
           it is to be denied.

Thus when it is posited that these propositions thus signifying adequately
are similar, "to you it is not proved; and you know it is proved to you";
"you are white; yet you are not colored", the case admitted. I propose
"those propositions are false". If you concede that, I have my point. If
someone says that they are true, I argue in this way: "you are white; therefore, you are not colored". That inference is solid; the antecedent is true
according to you; therefore, the consequent is also true. And thus two
contradictories are simultaneously true, which the imagination does not
admit.

Rule VI.   Whenever two propositions thus signifying adequately are
           posited to be similar, of which each is irrelevant *(impertinens)*
           to the other, they can be similar in truth or in falsity, and they
           may be conceded or denied.

For example, I pose that those propositions thus signifying adequately
are similar: "you are a man" and "you run". If first one proposes "you
are a man", let it be conceded and said that it is true. And consequently,
let that proposition "you run", be conceded and said to be true. If, however, in the first place one proposed "you run", that proposition is denied
and one concedes that it is false. And consequently, in the same way one
may respond to that proposition, "you are a man". [Thus, the rule is
proved.] [137]

Propositions are called "dissimilar" when one is true and the other is
false.

In order to clarify this material, I set forth some rules.

Rule I.   Whenever two propositions are posited to be dissimilar with-
           out any mention of an adequate significate one may respond
           to either of them when proposed, by conceding or denying it
           within the time of the obligation just as he would outside of
           the time of the obligation.

For example, I pose that these propositions are dissimilar: "you are a man",
"you are white". With that posited, each of those propositions may be
conceded.

Rule II.   Whenever someone posits two propositions to be dissimilar
           without any mention of an adequate significate, with regard
           to the truth or falsity of the first one proposed one may re-
           spond under the time of the obligation just as he would out-
           side of the time of the obligation. And to any other proposition,
           he may respond in the opposite way.

For example, I pose that these propositions are dissimilar: "you are a man"
and "you are an animal". Once this is admitted, I propose: "this is true,

'you are a man' ". Let this be conceded. And consequently [let it be conceded] that this proposition is false, "you are an animal".

Rule III. Whenever two propositions thus signifying adequately are posited to be dissimilar of which each is interchangeable with the other, this case is not to be admitted.

E.g., "man is", "God is", or "man runs", and "a risible being runs". For if it is conceded that that proposition, "man is" is true, one ought to concede this to be false, "God is". And so from one of two interchangeable propositions to the other the argument does not follow.

Rule IV. Whenever two propositions thus signifying adequately are posited to be dissimilar of which one is necessary and the other impossible or contingent, then the necessary one is always to be conceded and the other one denied.

E.g., "God is", and "man is a donkey"; "God is", and "you are".

Rule V. If two contingent propositions thus adequately signifying are posited to be dissimilar of which the one implies the other and not vice versa, the antecedent wherever it is proposed always is to be denied, and the consequent is to be conceded.

E.g., "you run" and "you are moved". For if the antecedent were conceded one would have to concede the consequent, and consequently to say that each of those propositions is true, which is contrary to this case.

Rule VI. If two propositions thus signifying adequately are posited to
[138] be dissimilar of which each one is irrelevant *(impertinens)* to the other, one may respond to the first one proposed under the time of the obligation just as he would outside of the time of the obligation and to the other one in the opposite way.

For example, having posited that these propositions thus signifying adequately are dissimilar, "you run" and "you are in Paris", whichever of them is proposed first ought to be denied, and the other one conceded. And the same thing may be said even if both are true outside the time of the obligation. E.g., "man runs", and "you see". [Thus, the rule is valid.]

Section 5 — Depositions

Other rules for the opposite species [of obligation] which is called "deposition" [rejecting], are here presented.

Rule I. Everything rejected *(depositum)* and admitted under the proposed time of the obligation is always to be denied.

For example, if someone rejects this proposition, "some man is in Rome", which is admitted, then when it is proposed, always it is to be denied. From this rule it follows that never is one to admit what is necessary *per se* in a deposition; but one is to admit whatever is impossible or contingent. For to deny what is impossible or contingent is not absurd *(inconveniens)*. But it would be absurd to deny what is necessary *per se*.

Rule II.   Everything that implies what is rejected, either *per se* or together with one or more conceded opposites of what has been correctly denied always is to be denied.

E.g., with this proposition rejected and admitted "man runs", if one should propose that proposition, "man runs", it ought to be denied because it implies what is rejected. For it follows: "this man runs; therefore, man runs". Again, if one should reject "some man does not run", and that is admitted and then it is proposed, "you do not run", it may be conceded because it is true and irrelevant. But if it is proposed secondly, "you are a man", it is to be denied because together with a conceded proposition it implies what was rejected. For it follows: "you do not run, and you are some man; therefore, some man does not run".

Rule III.   Everything inconsistent with what is rejected and every proposition following from that inconsistent proposition [either] *per se* or together with one or more conceded opposites of what has been correctly denied is to be conceded.

E.g., I reject to you this proposition, "some [139] animal does not run". Having rejected this proposition and admitted it, I propose its contradictory, i.e., "every animal runs". This proposition is to be conceded and this proposition also is to be conceded: "every animal is moved", because it follows from the contradictory of what was rejected. Next, if someone proposes, "you are an animal", it may be conceded because it is true and irrelevant. And further, that proposition "you run", may be conceded because it follows from the contradictory of what was rejected together with what was conceded. For it follows: "every animal runs; you are an animal; therefore, you run".

Rule IV.   Everything inconsistent with the contradictory of something rejected [either] *per se* or together with one or more conceded opposites of what has been correctly denied is to be denied.

Thus in the previous case, if someone proposed either this proposition, "some animal is not moved", or this proposition, "you do not run", the first is denied because it is *per se* the contradictory of what was rejected. The second proposition is inconsistent with the same rejected proposition together with a conceded proposition.

Rule V.   With regard to every proposition following from the rejected and with regard to every irrelevant proposition one is to respond according to its quality.

E.g., I reject this proposition, "you are white". This having been admitted, I propose, "you are colored". Let this be conceded because it is true and follows from what was rejected. For it is not absurd to deny the antecedent and to concede the consequent. Again, if someone proposes this proposition, "you are hot", it is to be conceded because it is true and irrelevant both to what is rejected and to the contradictory of the rejected. Hence properly speaking something "irrelevant" in this kind of an obligation is that which neither follows nor implies what is rejected; nor is it inconsistent with it; nor does it follow from the opposite of what is rejected; nor is it inconsistent with it [either] *per se* or together with another proposition or propositions, as was said. Therefore, if someone rejects, "Socrates runs", and this is admitted, and this proposition is proposed, "Plato runs", one may respond under the time of the obligation just as he would outside of the time of the obligation because it is an irrelevant proposition since it does not belong *(se habere)* to any of the mentioned modes.

Some sophisms are to be posited so that the rules of deposition may be made clearer.

First, I reject to you, therefore, this proposition, [140] "you are a man or you are in Rome". When this is rejected and admitted, I propose "you are a man". If you deny it, you deny something true yet irrelevant; therefore, you respond poorly. If you concede it, and that proposition implies what was rejected; then what implies what was rejected is to be conceded. One may respond by admitting what was rejected. And if some-one proposes "you are a man", I deny it because it implies what was rejected insofar as it is an inference from part of a disjunctive proposition to the entire disjunctive proposition.

Second, I reject to you this proposition, "some propositions are not true". When this is admitted, I propose: "these are propositions: 'You run', 'You do not run' ". That is to be conceded because it is true and irrelevant. Then, I propose "two contradictories are simultaneously true". If it is denied, then to the contrary: All propositions are true. But these are pro-positions; therefore, these are true. And these are mutually contradictory. Therefore, two contradictories are simultaneously true.

One responds by denying that these are contradictories, because that implies what was rejected. For it follows that those propositions are con-tradictory; therefore, some propositions are not true.

Third, I reject to you this proposition, "Antichrist is not white or Anti-christ is colored". If you do not admit this proposition, then to the con-trary: This is a contingent disjunctive proposition because both of its parts are contingent and neither is inconsistent with the other; therefore, it is to be admitted. The inference is clear from the first rule. This having been admitted, I propose to you, "Antichrist is colored". If you concede it, you concede what implies the rejected; and thus, you respond poorly. For it follows, "Antichrist is colored; therefore, Antichrist is not white or Anti-christ is colored". The inference is clear according to the rule "from part of a disjunctive proposition to the entire disjunctive proposition is a solid inference". If, however, you deny the proposition you deny what follows from the contradictory of what was rejected; therefore, you respond poorly. The antecedent is proved. For it follows: "Antichrist is white and Antichrist is not colored; therefore, Antichrist is white". This inference is clear according to the rule "from an entire conjunctive proposition to either of its parts is a solid inference". Furthermore, "Antichrist is white; therefore, Antichrist is colored". The inference is clear for it follows the rule "from a lower-level term to its higher-level term without an impediment is a solid inference". Therefore, from the first to the last, "Antichrist is white [141] and Antichrist is not colored: therefore, Antichrist is colored".

One responds by not admitting what is rejected because it is a necessary disjunctive proposition whose contradictory is impossible; namely, "Antichrist is white and Antichrist is not colored". And then with respect to the argument, "each of its parts is contingent and neither is inconsistent with the other; therefore; that disjunctive proposition is contingent", I deny the inference. But one ought to add into the antecedent, "that no contradictories of those parts are mutually inconsistent". But this is false because these propositions are mutually inconsistent, "Antichrist is white and Antichrist is not colored", which are the contradictories of the parts of the [original] disjunctive proposition.

Fourth, I reject to you this proposition, "you are and everything rejected to you is to be denied by you". When this is admitted and denied, I propose, "everything rejected to you is to be denied by you". If it is conceded I propose to you that proposition, "you are". And it is clear that it is to be denied, from which [it follows that] a conjunctive proposition is to be denied and either part is to be conceded. Then, I propose, "nothing rejected to you is to be denied by you". If you concede it, you concede the opposite of the rule plus a conceded proposition: therefore, you respond poorly. The antecedent is proved, for it follows: "you are not; therefore, nothing rejected to you is to be denied by you". The inference is clear because the contradictory of the consequent is inconsistent with the antecedent insofar as it [i.e., the contradictory of the consequent] asserts you to be.

One may respond by denying that what was rejected to you is to be denied by you because it implies what was rejected. For it follows: "everything rejected to you is to be denied by you; therefore, you are and everything rejected to you is to be denied by you". The inference is solid for it goes from part of a conjunctive proposition to the entire conjunctive proposition where the antecedent implies the other part. And if it is said, "you deny the rule", it may be said that "this is not the rule", but rather this is the rule: Everything rejected to you *which is admitted* is to be denied. Or, on the other hand, it may be said that any rule is contingent because rules are made by convention. Therefore, any such rule is to be rejected *(deponenda)*, and it is to be admitted or denied in a deposition. When it is denied one says [142] that this is not the rule insofar as it is true but insofar as it is something [inconsistent.] For it follows: "not every thing rejected is to be denied [by you]; therefore, this is not a rule: 'Everything rejected is to be denied [by you]' ".

And here ends the Fifth Treatise "On Obligations".

Notes

[121]^a "Every true affirmative proposition about the past whose truth does not depend on the future is necessary." For the background of this thesis see Aristotle, 1, *De Interpretatione*, Chapters 7–9.

[122]^a This sentence implies that in the context of the *obligatio* a statement is to be adjudged true or false relative to the time at which it is admitted into the *obligatio*. See p. [126].

  ^b Paul uses the rules of *obligatio* in the activity of challenging those very rules. His purpose is, of course, pedagogical: to provide a concrete example of the method he has just presented.

[123]^a The distinction Paul is getting at here is this: By Rule I a respondent must admit any possible proposition taken singly; but it does not follow that he must admit every possible proposition taken together. For many propositions are possible which are nonetheless false.

[124]^a Apparently the statement "you are not obligated", was conjoined by some opponents to their initial *posita*. But since those *posita* are initial statements in an *obligatio* the addition of "you are not obligated", would render them systematically false. Hence, any propositions whatsoever would follow from them. But Paul rejects this additional premise as "false and irrelevant".

[126]^a In other words, a response is inconsistent if the respondent concedes and denies the same statement in the same *obligatio*. Only this warrants the evaluation, "you respond poorly". But to doubt and concede or to doubt and deny the same proposition are not sufficient grounds for calling the response "poor".

[131]^a This remark suggests that some questions are extraneous to the course of an *obligatio*. A respondent should simply state that they are "irrelevant" without trying to decide how they are to be answered.

  ^b This in an important remark; in the *Logica Parva* the concept of "the adequate significate" of a proposition and of a proposition's "signifying adequately" are central to the concept of truth and to the rules for resolving insolubles. See below p. [162].

[133]^a See above p. [129].

[134]^a This passage seems to be saying that under normal conditions "man is a donkey", is an impossible proposition. However, in the present context which deals with the rules for interchanging propositions it is conceivable that the same proposition could be interchanged with some possible proposition, e.g., "God is" or "you are"; and then "man is a donkey", would be possible and even true.

^b That is, Rule IX, see above p. [122].

Chapter VI
On Insolubles

Section 1 – Definitions, Divisions and Rules

An insoluble is a proposition assertively signifying itself to be false. For example, "this proposition is false", pointing to itself. Among insolubles, however, there is a difference with regard to their signifying themselves to be false. Some insolubles signify themselves to be false immediately, e.g., "this proposition is false", pointing to itself. Some signify themselves to be false mediately; for another proposition is required in order to infer that they are false. E.g., "every proposition is false; hence, this is not true, pointing to itself". For it does not follow: "Every proposition is false; therefore, this proposition is false", pointing to the universal proposition. But it follows with the intermediate statement, "this is a proposition".

Similarly, "this is not true; therefore, that is false", pointing to the first proposition, because from a negative proposition an affirmative proposition does not follow; however, it follows with an intermediate proposition like, "that is a proposition".

In order to clarify the definition I posit two divisions.

The first division is this: some insolubles arise from our own act; others from a property of the expression. Insolubles having their origin in our act are these: "Socrates says something false", "I do not say what is true", "this man understands what is false", "you do not understand what is true". Insolubles having their origin from a property of the expression are: "every proposition is false", "no proposition is true", "this is false", "this is not true".

The second division is this: some propositions are insoluble simply *(simpliciter)*; others are insoluble according to a condition *(secundum quid)*.

A proposition insoluble simply is that to which a case is annexed and when it is admitted, a contradiction follows. E.g., I pose that this proposition (A) "no proposition is true", signifies precisely as the terms indicate, [143] i.e., that no proposition is true; and let this be every proposition. Having posited this, I ask whether (A) is true or false. If it is true, then it signifies precisely as is the case; but (A) signifies precisely that no proposition is true; therefore, no proposition is true. Therefore, (A) is not true; and previously I said that it was true. Thus, there is a contradiction. If

237

someone says that (A) is false, therefore (A) signifies otherwise than is the case. But (A) signifies precisely that no proposition is true. Therefore, it is not the case that no proposition is true. Therefore, some proposition is true; and (A) is every proposition. Hence (A) is true; but previously I said that it was false. Thus, there is a contradiction.

A proposition insoluble according to a condition is one to which a case is annexed and once it is admitted, a contradiction does not follow. For example, I pose this proposition (A) "no proposition is true", and that this is every proposition; and further, that this proposition signifies as its terms indicate — not, however, precisely. With this posited, one says that (A) is false because it signifies itself to be false. And if someone argues in this way: "(A) is false; therefore, (A) signifies otherwise than it is; but (A) signifies that no proposition is true; therefore, it is not the case that no proposition is true, I deny the inference, because one ought to add in the antecedent an exclusive or exceptive expression *(dictio)*. I.e., "(A) signifies precisely that no proposition is true" or "(A) does not signify *save* that no proposition is true". This assertion is denied insofar as it is inconsistent, because if someone should posit it together with the original case, that case would not be admitted.

Having set forth these divisions, I give some rules.

Rule I.   Every singular insoluble without a demonstrative pronoun arising from our act, in order that it be an insoluble simply, requires three conditions. The first condition is that one such be every such. The second condition is that one says or understands such a proposition and no other. The third is that it signify precisely as the terms indicate.

E.g., (A) "Socrates says something false", is an insoluble simply in this way: by stipulating that one Socrates is every Socrates who says that proposition and no other: "Socrates says something false", which signifies precisely that 'Socrates says something false'. This is proved for [144] when it is admitted, let (A) be that insoluble; and I ask whether (A) is true or false. If one says that it is true, then it signifies precisely as is the case; but (A) signifies precisely that Socrates says something false; therefore, it is the case that Socrates says something false. But Socrates says (A); therefore, (A) is false, which is the opposite of what was conceded. For Socrates says nothing except (A). And if someone says that (A) is false, then it signifies otherwise than is the case. But (A) signifies precisely that Socrates says something false; therefore, it is not the case that Socrates says something false; and Socrates says (A). Therefore, (A) is not false. Thus there is a contradiction. The first stipulation is made because without it it would be possible that there could be two Socrateses of whom one would say (A) and the other would say that man is a donkey. And then (A) would be true. The second stipulation is made because otherwise it would be possible that the same Socrates would say (A) and this proposition, "man is a donkey". And then (A) would be true. But the third stipulation is made because without it it would be possible that (A) would signify only that man is a donkey, and then (A) would be false; or it would signify only that man is an animal, and then (A) would be true. And in neither of these ways of signifying would (A) be insoluble.

Rule II.   Every singular insoluble without a demonstrative pronoun arising from our act, in order to be an insoluble according to a condition requires the same conditions except for the exclusive expression.

E.g., when it is posited that one Socrates is every Socrates and that he says this proposition and no other (A) "Socrates says something false", and that (A) signifies as the terms indicate. When this is posited, (A) is conceded. And one says that it is false because [it signifies a conjunctive proposition] just as any insoluble does, i.e., "Socrates says something false and (A) is true". Therefore, (A) is said to be false not by reason of the first significate but by reason of the second significate. And if someone argues in this way: "(A) is false; therefore, it signifies otherwise than is the case", I concede the inference and I deny this proposition, "(A) signifies otherwise than is the case". Rather (A) signifies that Socrates says something false; therefore, it is not the case that Socrates says something false, because one ought to add in the antecedent an exclusive or exceptive expression.

Rule III.   Every non-singular insoluble or every singular insoluble with a demonstrative pronoun arising from our act, in order that it be an insoluble [145] simply, requires only two conditions.

E.g., in order that this proposition, "I say something false", be insoluble simply one need not state the first stipulation, i.e., "one I is every I", but only that I say that proposition and no other thus signifying precisely. And an insoluble according to a condition ought to be made in the same way; for the same conditions without the exclusive expression are required and suffice. An example of a non-singular insoluble is this: "something false was said". Here one need not posit the second stipulation, i.e., that someone says that proposition and no other; but it suffices to posit that this is every proposition, which signifies precisely as the terms indicate; and then it is an insoluble simply. It would be an insoluble under a condition, however, by removing the exclusive expression.

Rule IV.   Every insoluble arising from the property of an expression requires only two conditions or only one condition.

I mean to say that an insoluble arising from the property of an expression requires two stipulations alone and some [of them] only one stipulation. Example of the first kind: "some proposition is false". In order to make this an insoluble simply one ought to posit that that proposition is every proposition, and that it thus signifies precisely. And with the exclusive expression removed it would be an insoluble according to a condition. Example of the second kind: "this is false", pointing to itself, and positing only that it thus signifies precisely, is an insoluble simply; and it is an insoluble according to a condition by removing the exclusive expression. In the same way one may speak of this proposition, "This is not true", pointing to itself.

Rule V. Every insoluble which is not an insoluble without a case, when one sets aside some required condition is thoroughly doubtful.

E.g., positing all the conditions except the first, (A) "Socrates says something false", is doubted. And [it is doubted] too whether it is true or false. For it is consistent with the case posited that it be true, given that one Socrates would say that proposition, (A); and another Socrates would say "no God is". It would be consistent also that it be false, given that one Socrates says (A) and any other Socrates says that "God exists". And the same would apply [146] if the second or third stipulation were set aside; because it would be consistent for (A) to be true and for (A) to be false as was exemplified above. And note that I said, "every insoluble which is not an insoluble without a case", because some insolubles are without a case and others are with a case. Examples of the first kind: "every proposition is false", "no proposition is true", of which I say that each is false and insoluble with no case being posited. Examples of the second kind: "Socrates says something false", "you understand something false", – neither of these is to be called "insoluble" without a case. Therefore, with respect to insolubles lacking some necessary particulars, one can doubt whether it is true or false, because without a case it could be that the proposition is true; and with the same case it could be that the proposition is false, as is clear to intuition.

From the foregoing rules two conclusions follow:

First, never is a case to be admitted from which an insoluble simply takes its origin. E.g., if someone should pose that every proposition is false, and that it is every proposition and signifies precisely, the case is not to be admitted because a contradiction follows. This is proved for let (A) be an insoluble. I ask if (A) is true. If someone says it is, then it signifies precisely as is the case. But (A) signifies precisely that every proposition is false. Therefore, it is the case that every proposition is false. But (A) is a proposition. Therefore, (A) is false. If, on the other hand, it is conceded that it is false; then (A) signifies otherwise than is the case. But (A) signifies precisely that a proposition is false; therefore, it is not the case that every proposition is false [and some proposition exists]. Therefore, some proposition is true. But (A) is [every] proposition; therefore, (A) is true, which is a contradiction.

240

Second, every case from which an insoluble according to a condition originates is to be admitted; and one concedes a proposed insoluble by saying that it is false, e.g., by positing that this proposition, (A) "this is false", pointing to itself, signifies as the terms indicate. Then, the case is admitted and (A) is conceded; and one says that (A) is false. And if someone argues, "(A) is false; therefore, it signifies otherwise than the case is; but (A) does not signify except that it is false; therefore, it is not the case that (A) is false", I deny the minor premise. And if someone asks "what else does it signify?", one replies that it signifies (A) to be true; and by this reason (A) is false. [147] Hence it was stated that any insoluble according to a condition signifies conjunctively, i.e., as the terms indicate and that it is true.

Section 2 – Objections

Against what was said I will object and I will solve the problems so that the difficulties with insolubles may become better known to the mind.

First, I pose that one Socrates is every Socrates and he says this proposition and no other, (A) "Socrates says something false", which signifies as the terms indicate, not positing precisely, because the case is not admitted with that posited. I ask whether (A) is true or false. And someone responds that it is false because it signifies a false significate, namely, that Socrates says something false and that (A) is a true proposition, but the second part of its signification is false. But it is proved that (A) is true. "Everyone saying (A) says something false; Socrates says (A); therefore, Socrates says something false." That conclusion is valid because it is a syllogism in the third mood of the first figure; and the antecedent is true; therefore, the conclusion is true. The consequent is (A); therefore, (A) is true.

Second, one can argue in this way. "Something false is said by Socrates; therefore, Socrates says something false." The inference holds from a passive verb to its active; and the antecedent is true. Therefore, the consequent is true; and the consequent is (A); therefore, (A) is true. That the antecedent is true is proved; for this proposition is said by Socrates, pointing to (A); and this is false; therefore, something false is said by Socrates. The inference is clear from resolving statements to what is resolved.

Third, one can argue that the contradictory of (A) is false; therefore, (A) is true. The inference holds; and the antecedent is proved. For this is false, "Socrates does not say something false"; and this is the contradictory of (A). Therefore, the contradictory of (A) is false. The inference holds together with the minor, and I prove the major. For Socrates says something false; and [this proposition], "Socrates does not say something false", signifies precisely that Socrates does not say something false; therefore, this proposition is false. The inference holds because it is similar to this deduction: "you run; and this [proposition], 'you do not run' signifies precisely that you do not run; therefore, the [proposition] is false".

To the first, one may respond when (A) is proposed, "I concede". And it is said that (A) is false; and then to the argument I concede the inference and the consequent; yet I deny that the conclusion is (A). Rather it is one similar to (A). And if someone says that the conclusion is (A) or interchangeable with (A), I say then that the inference is not solid. Nor is it a syllogism in the third mood of the first figure, for the conclusion of a syllogism in the third mood of the first figure ought to signify only in a categorical way. But that conclusion signifies hypothetically because it is [148] an insoluble proposition.

To the second, when someone says, "what is false is said by Socrates: therefore, Socrates says something false", I concede the inference and the consequent by saying that it is true. But the conclusion is not (A) nor is it interchangeable with (A). If however this is posed [in] the case, I concede the inference again; and I say that it is solid and then to the argument "from a passive verb to its active form there is a solid argument", one says that this is true. But that verb is not its active form. For the passive signifies only categorically and the active hypothetically. And if someone asks what is its active form, I say, "Socrates says something false", pronounced by you or by me, which is not interchangeable with (A) but only with propositions similar to (A).[a]

To the third one says that the contradictory of (A) is true; but it is not this proposition, "Socrates does not say something false". Rather it is this proposition, "not: Socrates says something false", which is true because it signifies disjunctively that Socrates does not say something false or [that (A)] is not true, the second part of which significate is true; and consequently its total disjoint significate [is true]. Whereby also the proposition stated is true whose significate is this. And if someone says that in singular [propositions] it does not matter (non refert) whether one puts the negation before or after [the proposition] one replies that with regard to insolubles it matters very much, as well as for any propositions signifying hypothetically. The same verdict is to be upheld in treating insoluble singular propositions having their origin in the property of an expression. E.g., "this is false, 'this is not true'", by saying that the contradictory of the first is not the statement, "this is not false", but the statement: "not: this is false". For the first insoluble signifies that this is false and this is true, pointing to the same insoluble proposition. Therefore, its contradictory signifies disjunctively that this is not false or this is not true. Similarly, the contradictory of the second insoluble is not the proposition, "this is true", but rather the proposition, "not: this is not true", so that the negation is always placed before, just as the contradictory of this "only you are not a man", is not "only you are a man", but rather, "not: only you are not a man".

Section 3 — Particular and Indefinite Insolubles

Having spoken of singular insolubles, now I will treat particular or indefinite insolubles.

I pose, therefore, that this be every particular proposition. [149] (A) "Some particular proposition is false". And let it signify as the terms indicate, not positing precisely. For the case would not be admitted with this posited. It is false, as is clear from what was said.

But against this view one can argue in this way: "every particular proposition is false; therefore, some particular proposition is false". That inference is solid — "from a universal proposition to its subalternate [there is a solid inference]"; and the antecedent is true; therefore, the consequent is true as well. But the consequent is (A); therefore, (A) is true. That the antecedent is true is proved; for a particular proposition is false since there is no particular proposition unless it is false; therefore, every particular proposition is false. The inference holds from exponents to an expounded proposition, and the antecedent is true; therefore, the consequent is true as well.

Second, one can argue in this way: "a particular proposition is false; therefore, some particular proposition is false". The inference holds from an indefinite proposition to its particular; and the antecedent is true; therefore, the consequent is true also. And the consequent is (A); therefore, (A) is true. That the antecedent is true is clear, because its contradictory is false, namely, "no particular proposition is false", because it is already conceded that this particular proposition (A) is false.

Third, one argues is this way: "this is false, pointing to (A); and this is some particular proposition; therefore, some particular proposition is false". The inference holds from resolving sentences to the resolved one and the antecedent is true; therefore, the consequent is true as well and the consequent is (A).

To the first argument one may reply by conceding this inference: "every particular proposition is false; therefore, some particular proposition is false", because before the case is posed I would have conceded that; however, I say that the inference is not solid. Nor does it argue from a universal proposition to [its subalternate or to] its particular, because a universal signifies only categorically and this particular signifies hypothetically, namely that some particular proposition is false; because (A) is true. And if someone should say, "what is its particular?", one replies that it does not have any particular since it was posited that that proposition was every particular proposition. Nevertheless, this same proposition (A) would be its particular, given that it were not an insoluble proposition.

To the second argument I reply similarly by conceding the inference and by denying it to be solid. And then to the argument I say [150] that this is not a particular of that indefinite proposition, because the particular is an insoluble proposition signifying hypothetically; but the indefinite proposition is not of this kind. The same proposition would be its particular, however, if neither of those were insoluble propositions.

To the third argument the inference is conceded and that it is solid I deny. Nor is it argued from resolving sentences to the resolved one for a particular or indefinite insoluble is not resoluble because it signifies hypothetically. But it is to be proved in this way: "its principal significate is true; therefore it is true"; and it is clear that the antecedent is false. And if someone argues in this way, "this particular proposition is false; therefore, some particular proposition is false", the inference holds from a lower-level term to its corresponding higher-level one affirmatively and without any sign impeding.

One says that an inference is not valid from a lower-level sentence to its higher-level sentence unless the inferior proposition and the superior proposition uniformly signify, namely, categorically, which is not the case in what was proposed. Whence if this proposition, "man is an animal", would signify principally that man is an animal and that man is a donkey, then none of these consequences would follow: "this is animal, and this is man; therefore, man is animal"; "this man is an animal; therefore, man is an animal". And this is the case because the consequent would signify conjunctively and no part of the antecedent would signify in this way. And if some of these rules should be brought forth, one responds as was said.

One says also as in another chapter that the contradictory of this statement, "some particular proposition is false", is not the statement, "no particular proposition is false", but rather, "not: some particular proposition is false".[a] And if someone says that these are equivalent because of the preposed negation, one replies that that rule is true only with regard to a categorical proposition, signifying categorically only; but this is not the case in what was proposed. The same point holds for these statements, "some particular proposition is not true", "some particular proposition signifies otherwise than is the case", and also for indefinite statements like, "an indefinite proposition is false", "an indefinite proposition is not true".

Section 4 – Universal Insolubles

Now we turn to universal insoluble propositions.

I pose [151] that this, "every universal proposition is false", is every universal proposition, which signifies as its terms indicate. Let this be (A). It is not stated that it signifies "precisely" because [with "precisely" posited] the case would not be admitted. With this posited one says that "(A) is false because it falsifies itself".

Against this position one argues, "some universal proposition is false; and there is no universal proposition unless it is false; therefore, every universal proposition is false". The inference holds because there is a valid inference from exponents to what they expound; and the antecedent is true; therefore, the consequent is true also.

Second, one argues, "only something false is a universal proposition; therefore, every universal proposition is false". The inference holds from an exclusive proposition to its universal with transposed terms. And the antecedent is true; therefore, the consequent is true. And the consequent is (A). That the antecedent is true is proved: "something false is a universal proposition; and nothing non-false is a universal proposition; therefore, only something false is a universal proposition". The inference holds from exponents to what they expound; and the antecedent is true; therefore, the consequent is true.

Third, one argues, "this is false, pointing to (A). And this is every universal proposition; therefore, every universal proposition is false". This inference is solid and the antecedent is true; therefore, the consequent is true also. That the inference is solid is clear by a similar one: "this runs; and this is every man; therefore, every man runs". It is confirmed by destroying the first case and by positing that these are all universal propositions: "every universal proposition is false" and "every man is a donkey", signifying thus. With this posited, one argues in this way: "this universal proposition is false, pointing to the first one. And this universal proposition is false, pointing to the second one. And these are all universal propositions. Therefore, every universal proposition is false". The inference holds from singulars sufficiently enumerated to their universal; and the antecedent is true; therefore, the consequent is true.

To these arguments one may reply; and firstly to the first one I concede the insoluble, but I deny that it is true. And then to the argument I concede the inference, but I deny that it is solid. And with regard to the argument, where it is argued "from exponents to what they expound", I deny it because (A) is not an exponible proposition unless [152] it should signify categorically only. Hence if this proposition, "every man is an animal", should signify principally that every man is an animal and that you

245

are a donkey, then it is clear that this inference would not be solid: "man is animal; and nothing is a man unless it is an animal; therefore, every man is animal", because the antecedent is true and the consequent is false. And then if the rule[a] should be appealed to, one ought to say that the consequent is not exponible for the reason stated; but it may be proved or disproved through its conjoint significate, just as any insoluble proposition.

To the second, I concede the inference; yet I deny that the inference is solid. Nor does it argue from an exclusive proposition to its universal since the exclusive proposition signifies categorically and the universal proposition hypothetically. And if someone asks "which is its singular proposition?", one replies that it has none. Hence if this proposition, "every man is animal" would signify hypothetically what is true or what is false, and this proposition, "only an animal is man", in the customary way, I would say then that this universal proposition would not be the universal of this exclusive proposition or vice versa. So it is to be said in the case at hand.

To the third argument, I say similarly that the inference is not solid. And if someone says that it follows a similar argument, I say that there is not a likeness because the consequent of the one argument signifies categorically only and the consequent of the other signifies hypothetically. Hence if "every man runs" signified that every man runs and that God does not exist, this inference then would not be solid: "this runs and this is every man; therefore, every man runs", for the reason stated, i.e., because the consequent would signify hypothetically.

In order to confirm this point, with the case admitted as previously, I say that the inference is not solid. Regarding the argument "from singulars sufficiently enumerated to their universal", I say that it is not argued with the due middle which should be, "these are all universal propositions, and (A) is true", which certainly is denied. For this inference is not solid: "this man runs, and that man runs and these are all men; therefore, every man runs", given that the consequent would signify hypothetically, as previously. But one ought to add the other part of the significate, namely, "no God exists", by which addition the inference is solid. But the antecedent is false. And if someone asks about the contradictory of (A), one says that it is this: "not every universal proposition is false", signifying disjunctively in the opposite way [153] from (A). In the same way one is to speak of these universal propositions: "Every universal proposition signifies otherwise than is the case", "no universal signifies as the case is", "no universal proposition is true", "no universal proposition is negative".

Section 5 – Exclusive Insolubles

An exclusive insoluble contains similar difficulties.

I pose that Socrates and you are all speakers; and Socrates says "God exists", and you [say] "only Socrates says something true", and let that be (A), and nothing else [is said]; let it signify as the terms indicate. With this posited, I ask whether (A) is true or false. If it is true, then it signifies precisely as is the case; but (A) signifies precisely that only Socrates says something true; [therefore, it is the case that only Socrates says something true]; therefore, you do not say something true. But you say (A); therefore, (A) is not true. If one says that (A) is false, then it signifies otherwise than is the case; but (A) signifies precisely that only Socrates says something true; therefore, it is not the case that only Socrates says something true; but you and Socrates are everyone speaking; therefore, you say something true; and you do not say anything other than (A); therefore, (A) is true. And thus there is a contradiction.

One may respond by not admitting the case because from it originates an insoluble simply. If, however, one does not posit "precisely" I admit the case and I say (A) is false. And then to the argument, "(A) signifies other than is the case", I concede the point; but (A) signifies precisely that only Socrates says something true; therefore, [you say something true; and you say (A); therefore, [(A)] is true.] I deny the minor premise because it is inconsistent with the case. And if someone says "then what else does it signify?", I say that (A) signifies that only Socrates says something true and that (A) is true. Not by reason of its first significate is (A) false, however, because it is true that only Socrates says something false. But by reason of its second significate [(A) is false] because one concedes that (A) is false.

Against this response one argues. "Everyone saying something true is Socrates; therefore, only Socrates says something true." This inference is solid, from a universal to its exclusive with transposed terms. And the antecedent is true; therefore the consequent is true. And the consequent is (A); therefore, (A) is true. That the antecedent is true, is proved: "for [someone] saying something true is Socrates; and nothing is saying something true save Socrates; therefore, everyone saying something true is Socrates". [The inference is clear because there is a solid inference from exponents to what they expound.]

Second, one can argue, "no one except Socrates says something true; therefore, only Socrates says something true". This inference is solid; and the antecedent is true; therefore, the consequent is true. [154] That the antecedent is true is clear through its exponents.

247

Third, one can argue: "Socrates says something true; and no non-Socrates says something true; therefore, only Socrates says something true". This inference is solid because it proceeds "from exponents to what they expound"; and the antecedent is true; therefore, the consequent is true as well. But the consequent is (A); therefore, (A) is true.

To all of these arguments one can respond at the same time that never is one of these implied consequents (A) or interchangeable with (A) but rather similar to (A). But if one posits with the whole case that it be (A) or interchangeable with (A), then one responds by conceding all of the inferences made but by denying that they are solid.

To the first argument, therefore, where someone says that it is argued from a universal to its exclusive [with transposed terms], I deny it, because the universal proposition signifies categorically and the exclusive proposition signifies hypothetically since it is an insoluble. And if someone asks about its exclusive, one may say that it is one similar to the one uttered by Socrates, which is not an insoluble; namely, "only Socrates says something true".

And to the other argument, one says also that it is not solid. Nor is its conclusion the exclusive of the exceptive mentioned, but rather it is the exclusive which I just now mentioned.

To the third one says that it is not argued from exponents to what they expound because this exclusive proposition is not exponible since it signifies hypothetically. For if this proposition, "only man is capable of laughter", signified principally that only man is capable of laughter and that no God exists, then none of these inferences would be solid: "every being capable of laughter is a man; therefore, only man is capable of laughter". "Nothing except man is capable of laughter; therefore, only man is capable of laughter." Again, "man is capable of laughter; and no non-man is capable of laughter; therefore, only man is capable of laughter". In the same way one must speak with regard to these exclusive propositions: "only an exclusive proposition is false", "only an exclusive proposition is not true", — given that one of these is every exclusive proposition, which is correctly admitted because "precisely" is not posited. And in this way one responds as previously to the arguments proving some of these to be true.

Concerning exceptive propositions the same thing is to be said as in the previous case: "nothing except Socrates says something true", "no proposition except an exceptive proposition is false". "Every exceptive proposition except this one is true", pointing to itself.

Section 6 – Conjunctive Insolubles

Next, we examine hypothetical insolubles. And first with respect to conjunctive insolubles, I set forth some rules. [155]

Rule I. With respect to a conjunctive insoluble one of whose parts is necessary *per se*, if in the case all of the conditions along with the sign of exclusion are added to it, it is an insoluble simply; and the case is not to be admitted.

For example, I pose that conjunctive proposition, (A) "God exists and no conjunctive proposition is true", be every conjunctive proposition, signifying precisely as the terms indicate. With this posited and admitted, I ask whether (A) is true. If someone says (A) is true, then the second part is true; but the second part signifies precisely that no conjunctive proposition is true; therefore, no conjunctive proposition is true; therefore, (A) is not true. If someone says that (A) is false, then some part is false; but it is not the first part; therefore, it is the second part. Then the second part is false; therefore, it signifies otherwise than is the case; but it signifies precisely that no conjunctive proposition is true; therefore, it is not the case that no conjunctive proposition is true; and (A) is every conjunctive proposition; therefore, (A) is true.

Rule II. With regard to a conjunctive insoluble one of whose parts is possible or contingent, by adding to it all conditions with the sign of exclusion, it is an insoluble according to a condition; and the case is to be admitted.

For example, I pose that this conjunctive proposition, (A) "you are a man and no conjunctive proposition is true", be every conjunctive proposition, signifying precisely as the terms indicate. With this posited and admitted, I ask whether (A) is true. If one says that (A) is true, then the second part is true and it signifies precisely that no conjunctive proposition is true; therefore, it is the case that no conjunctive proposition is true; therefore, (A) is not true. If someone says that (A) is false, then some part is false; and it is not the first part; therefore, it is the second part. Then one argues in this way: the second part is false; therefore, it signifies otherwise than is the case; but it signifies precisely that no conjunctive proposition is true; therefore, it [is] not the case that no conjunctive proposition is true; and (A) is every conjunctive proposition; therefore, (A) is true. And in this way a contradiction follows in this case as in the previous one, and consequently [it seems] that the second rule is not true.

One responds by admitting what was posited; and one says that (A) is false. And then consequently one ought to say that the first part is false and the second part is true. And if one argues in this way: "you are a man, and the first part thus signifies precisely; [156] therefore, that part is true", one denies the first part of the antecedent because it is inconsistent with the case together with a conceded sentence. For it follows: "the first part is false and that part signifies precisely that you are a man; therefore, you are not a man". In the same way, one responds if one part were impossible; for instance, "man is a donkey, and this conjunctive proposition is false".

Rule III.   Every conjunctive insoluble is insoluble according to a condition by adding to it all of the conditions except the sign of exclusion; and the case is to be admitted.

For example, I pose that this is every conjunctive proposition: (A) "God exists and no conjunctive proposition is true", signifying as the terms indicate. With this posited one says that (A) is false not, to be sure, because of the first part but because of the second part. And if one argues in this way, "the second part is false; therefore, it signifies otherwise than is the case", I concede the point; but it signifies precisely that no conjunctive proposition is true; therefore, it is not the case that no conjunctive proposition is true. I deny the minor premise because the second part signifies conjunctively that no conjunctive proposition is true and that (A) is true. And, therefore, (A) signifies three significates conjointly, i.e., that God exists, and that no conjunctive proposition is true, and that (A) is true. And one does not say that (A) is false because of the first significate, or the second significate but because of the third significate. In the same way, one can treat that insoluble, "you are and this conjunctive proposition is not true", by posing the case just stated.

From the first rule this point follows: If someone posits this proposition, "God exists" or any other proposition to be every proposition, and to signify precisely that God exists. or anything else necessary *per se,* and this is false, pointing to the same propositions, this case is not to be admitted because a contradiction follows from it.

From the second rule this point follows: If someone posits this proposition, "God exists", or any other proposition, to be every proposition, and to signify precisely man to be a donkey, or you to be [a donkey], and that this is false, by pointing to the same propositions, the case is to be admitted and one says that the proposition, "God exists", is false.

From the third rule this point follows. If someone posits, "God exists", or any other proposition, to be every proposition and to signify as one pleases and that this proposition is false, not positing "precisely", the case is to be admitted. And one says as previously that the same proposition is false. [157]

Section 7 – Disjunctive Insolubles

We now have to speak consequently about the disjunctive insoluble. To make this clear, let this be the first rule.

Rule I.   A disjunctive insoluble one of whose parts is [impossible] *per se*, if in the case all of the conditions with the sign of exclusion are added to it, is insoluble simply.

For example, I pose that the disjunctive proposition (A) "no God exists or no disjunctive proposition is true", is every disjunctive proposition, signifying precisely as the terms indicate. With this posited and admitted, I ask whether (A) is true. If someone says that it is true, then some part is true; and it is not the first part; therefore, the second part is true. Then one argues in this way: the second part is true; therefore, it signifies precisely and principally as is the case; but the second part signifies precisely that no disjunctive proposition is true; therefore, it is the case that no disjunctive proposition is true; and consequently, (A) is not true. If one says that (A) is false, therefore, the second part is false. But the second part signifies precisely that no disjunctive proposition is false; therefore, some disjunctive proposition is true, and (A) is every disjunctive proposition. Therefore, (A) is true. Therefore, one says that (A) in this case is insoluble simply; and thus the case is not to be admitted because it implies a contradiction.

Rule II.   A proposition appearing to be a disjunctive insoluble one of whose parts is contingently false is an insoluble according to a condition, by adding to it in the case all conditions with the sign of exclusion.

For example, I pose to you this proposition (A), "you are not a man or no disjunctive proposition is true". Let this be every disjunctive proposition signifying precisely as the terms indicate. With this posited and admitted, I ask whether (A) is true. If someone says that it is true; therefore, one of its parts is true; but it is not the first part; therefore, the second part is true. Then one argues in this way: the second part is true; therefore, it signifies precisely as is the case; but that proposition signifies precisely that no disjunctive proposition is true; therefore, it is the case that no disjunctive proposition is true; therefore, (A) is not true. If someone says, that (A) is false, then the second part is false. But it signifies precisely that no disjunctive proposition is true; therefore, it is not the case that no disjunctive proposition is true; therefore, some disjunctive proposition is true [158] and (A) is every disjunctive proposition; then, (A) is true. And in this way as it appears a contradiction follows in this case as it did in the first case; and consequently, the rule is not true.

One responds by conceding the rule and by admitting the case. And one says that (A) is true; and then when one says the first part is not true; therefore, the second is true, I say that the first part is true because for that part to be true follows from the case; and the second part is false. And from this claim no absurdity follows. Nevertheless, a disjunctive proposition of this kind is not an insoluble except apparently as was stated in the rule because every insoluble is false and (A) is true; therefore, (A) is not insoluble.

Rule III.   Every disjunctive insoluble is insoluble according to a condition by adding to it in the case all conditions except the sign of exclusion.

For example, when it is posited that this disjunctive proposition, (A) "a man is a donkey or this disjunctive proposition is false", is every disjunctive proposition, signifying as the terms indicate, the case is admitted. With this admission I say that (A) is false and the second part signifies otherwise than is the case; but I deny that the second part signifies only that this disjunctive proposition is false – indeed it also signifies otherwise, namely, that (A) is true. One could treat this statement in the same way if it should be posed that "you are not a man or this disjunctive proposition is not true", were every disjunctive proposition, and that it signified as the terms indicate. It is to be noted that no disjunctive is insoluble, either of whose parts is true; nor would it be insoluble given those conditions frequently named. Thus, "God exists or every disjunctive proposition is false", "you are a man or this disjunctive proposition is false". For by positing any named case, that would be admitted. And any of those disjunctive propositions would be conceded because of the truth of the first part.

Against this response one can argue in this way: "every (A) is false; but every (A) is this disjunctive proposition, [a man is a donkey or this disjunctive proposition is false]. Therefore, that disjunctive proposition is false". The inference holds because it is a syllogism in the first mood of the third figure, and the antecedent is true; therefore, the consequent is true as well. But the consequent is the second part of that disjunctive; therefore, the second part is true; and consequently, (A) is true.

Second one argues in this way: "the opposite of (A) is false, therefore, (A) is true". The antecedent [159] is proved: For this is false: "no man is a donkey and this disjunctive proposition is not false; and this is the opposite of (A); therefore, (A) is false". The inference holds together with the minor premise; and I prove the major premise: For this proposition is a conjunctive proposition whose second part is false because it has already been conceded that (A) is false.

To the first argument one can respond by conceding the inference and by denying that the inference is solid. And when someone says that it is a syllogism in the first mood of the third figure, I deny it because the conclusion signifies hypothetically in a way which does not happen with the conclusion of any valid syllogism.

To the second, one says that the opposite of (A) is not ["no man is a donkey and this disjunctive proposition is not false"] but rather, "nothing which is man is a donkey and not: this disjunctive proposition is false", whose second part signifies in two ways just as its contradictory does.[a]

These arguments could be applied to the chapter on conjunctive insolubles; but it is not useful to repeat them so often.[b]

From the first rule it follows that if someone should pose "a man is a donkey", or any other proposition, to be every proposition and to signify precisely that a man is a donkey or that no proposition is true, the case is not to be admitted because a contradiction would follow.

From the second rule it follows that if someone should pose, "'A man is a donkey' to be every proposition and to signify precisely that you are not or that no proposition is true", the case should be admitted and one should say that the proposition is true, "a man is a donkey".[c]

From the third rule it follows that if someone should pose, "man is man" to be every proposition and to signify man to be a donkey or that no proposition is true, — not positing "precisely" the case ought to be admitted; and consequently, one ought to say that this proposition is false, "man is man".[d]

Section 8 — Non-Apparent Insolubles

Lastly, we treat insolubles which do not appear to be insolubles. For example, "Socrates will not have a dime", "Plato will not cross the bridge".

I pose that everyone saying something true will have a dime, and only such a person, and that you say this proposition and no other (A) "I will not have a dime" — signifying precisely as the terms indicate. With this posited, I ask whether you will have a dime or not. If someone says that you will have a dime; and everyone who will have a dime [160] says something true; then you say something true; and you do not say anything except (A); therefore, (A) is true. And then [we argue] thus: (A) is true and signifies precisely that you will not have a dime; therefore, you will not have a dime, which is the contradictory of what was previously conceded. If, however, someone says that you will not have a dime; therefore, you do not say something true, and you do not say anything except (A); therefore, (A) is not true, then if (A) is not true, and (A) signifies precisely that you will not have a dime; therefore, it will not be the case that you will not have a dime. Therefore, you will have a dime. And thus a contradiction follows.

Similarly, one can ask in the beginning whether (A) is true or false, just as we asked in connection with the other insolubles.

Therefore, the case is not admitted because out of that case arises an insoluble simply.

If however, in the case the exclusive expression is not posited, I admit the case, and I say that you will not have a dime, that you do not say something true and that (A) is not true. But then to the argument: "(A) is not true but (A) signifies precisely that you will not have a dime; therefore, it is not the case that you will not have a dime", I deny the minor premise because (A) signifies that you will not have a dime and that (A) is true. And not in virtue of its first significate is (A) false, but in virtue of its second significate.[a] Nevertheless, if there were an inference not stipulating "precisely" in the minor premise, I would deny the inference.

In the same way one may respond to the case concerning the bridge when someone posits that everyone saying something true will cross the bridge and only such a person, and Socrates who is every Socrates says that proposition and no other, "Socrates will not cross the bridge", signifying precisely as the terms indicate. This case is not admitted. If, however, the exclusive expression were removed, it may be admitted; and one says consequently that Socrates will not cross the bridge, and that (A) is false.

Against this response one argues in this way: "no one saying something false will cross the bridge; but Socrates says something false; therefore, Socrates will not cross the bridge". The inference is solid because it is a syllogism in the fourth mood of the first figure; and the antecedent is true; therefore, the consequent is true also. But the consequent is (A); therefore, (A) is true.

Second, one can argue [161] in this way: the contradictory of (A) is false; therefore, (A) is true. The antecedent is proved. For this proposition is false, "Socrates will cross the bridge; and this proposition is its contradictory; therefore, [(A) is false]". The first part of the antecedent is proved, for Socrates says something false; therefore, he will not cross the bridge; and this proposition "Socrates will cross the bridge", signifies precisely that Socrates will cross the bridge; therefore, this proposition is false.

To the first argument, one responds by conceding the inference and by denying that the inference is solid. Nor is it a syllogism in the fourth mood of the first figure because the consequent signifies hypothetically and conjunctively; and this is so under the supposition that the conclusion is (A) or interchangeable with (A).

To the second argument, one may respond that what is stated is not the contradictory of (A) but rather this, "not: Socrates will not cross the bridge", signifying disjunctively in a way opposite to (A) just as is often recited [in these lessons].[a]

Now I argue against the whole foundation of insolubles by proving that not every insoluble according to a condition signifies conjunctively in the way stated because then any insoluble would be impossible simply.

This conclusion is false because an insoluble is to be conceded in a case, as is plain; and no proposition impossible simply is to be conceded within the time of an obligation; therefore, [not every insoluble according to a condition signifies conjunctively in the way stated]. And that this would follow is proved: for any such insoluble [according to a condition] signifies conjunctively, something impossible simply; and this precisely and principally; therefore, any insoluble according to a condition is impossible simply. The inference holds; and the antecedent is proven by taking this insoluble, "this statement is false", pointing to itself. For it signifies that [it] is false and [it] is true. But that [it] be false and that [it] be true is impossible simply; therefore, [this insoluble according to a condition signifies conjunctively something impossible simply].

This argument is very difficult. But briefly, it may never be solved by conceding an insoluble just as one concedes other statements. I did not concede this one and then say that any insoluble is a proposition impossible simply; for in that way the argument would not go forward. Indeed, because I conceded the insoluble proposed and I denied that it was true, I could not say in responding to that insoluble that it is impossible simply but only possible. And then [162] with regard to the argument, "its principal significate is impossible; therefore, an insoluble is impossible", the argument is not solid. With regard to this it is to be noted that an insoluble has two significates — one "adequate" and the other "principal". An adequate significate is a categorical significate like the expressed insoluble. Whence the adequate significate of the proposition, "Socrates says something false", is this "[for] Socrates to say something false", or that, "Socrates says something false". The principal significate, however, is the hypothetical significate as "[for] Socrates to say something false and [for] this proposition to be true". *(Sortem dicere falsum et istam propositionem esse veram.)* I say, therefore, that owing to something outside of it the possibility of an insoluble is brought to mind; and owing to something outside of it, its falsity [is established]. For the possibility of an insoluble arises owing to the possibility of its adequate significate. The falsity of an insoluble occurs due to the falsity of its principal significate. This proposition, therefore, is possible: "Every proposition is false" because it is possible [for] every proposition to be false. But that proposition is false because its principal significate is false, namely, [for] every proposition to be false *and* [for] that proposition to be true. However, beyond the matter of insolubles it is due to the same thing that the possibility, the truth or the falsity of a proposition arises; because it is due to the adequate significate.

It is to be noted that whenever I have spoken either here or in the other treatises I did not speak according to a proper intention; but in part also according to the intention of other instructors so that young beginners may be introduced [to logic] more easily.[a]

Notes

[148][a] For the definition and rules of "similar" propositions see above pp. [134]–[137].

[150][a] See above Chapter I, p. [12].

[152][a] The Rule: "There is a solid inference from exponents to what they expound." See above, Chapter III, p. [76] ff.

[159][a] According to Paul's rules for solving insolubles a self reflexive proposition like (A) which asserts its own falsity has in fact two significates. It has an adequate significate "(A) is false", and a principal significate " '(A) is false' and '(A) is true' ".

[b] See above pp. [155]–[157].

[c] In effect such a *positio* would make "a man is a donkey", interchangeable with "you are", or "no proposition is true", and then the rules for interchangeable propositions would apply. See above pp. [130]–[135].

[d] Here, again, the effect of such a *positum* would be to make "man is man" interchangeable with "man is a donkey" or "no proposition is true". And the rules for interchangeable propositions would apply.

[160][a] The first significate is "the adequate significate" or "the customary significate". The second significate is "the principal significate".

[161][a] As Paul insists throughout the *Logica Parva* the correct form of a negation has the negative term placed before the entire expression. See above p. [12].

[162][a] Is this a disclaimer of the views which Paul elaborates in the *Logica Parva?* It seems to be rather an explanation that counter-arguments are chosen not because Paul endorses them but because of their pedagogical and instructional value.

Chapter VII
Objections to Chapter I

Section 1 – Objections to Section 5

In order that the knowledge of this small logic book may be commited to memory, I present certain objections against its rules and definitions, and the solution of these will bring out new clarity.

First, against the definition of a proposition i.e., "a proposition is an indicative expression *(oratio indicativa)* signifying what is true or false", one can argue in this way. [163] This expression, "Antichrist were white", *("Antichristus esset albus")* is a proposition; yet it is not indicative; therefore, the definition of a proposition is not sufficient. The inference is solid with regard to the minor premise; and I prove the major premise. For every antecedent of a conditional is a proposition; but "Antichrist were white", is an antecedent of a conditional; therefore, it is a proposition. The conclusion is valid because this is a syllogism in the third mood of the first figure. And the major is also clear because a conditional proposition is that in which many categorical propositions are joined together by means of a sign of a condition. I prove the minor premise; for the antecedent of this conditional proposition, "if Antichrist were white, Antichrist would be colored", is that expression, "Antichrist were white".

One may respond by conceding the definition of a proposition; but I deny that this expression, "Antichrist were white", is a proposition. And then with regard to the argument I deny this major premise, "every antecedent of a conditional is a proposition". And when this is proved through a definition of a conditional, viz. "a conditional proposition is that in which many categoricals are joined together by means of a sign of a condition", I say that this definition is false taken in virtue of expression *(de virtute sermonis).*[a] For it means that a conditional is that in which either many categorical [propositions] are joined together or many expressions are related through a categorical mode *(se habentes per modum categoricae).* However, in the conditional proposition in question not many categorical [propositions] but rather many expressions are related through a categorical mode. Whence, this expression, "Antichrist were white", is not a categorical proposition, but an expression related through a categorical mode. For it has its principal parts through the mode *(per modum)* of subject, of predicate and of copula.

Section 2 – Objections to Section 6

Second, [one argues] against the rule of a universal proposition, viz., "a universal proposition is that in which a common term determined by a universal sign occurs as subject". For this proposition, "not any man runs", *(non quilibet homo currit)* is not a universal proposition. Yet in it a common term determined by a universal sign occurs as subject; therefore, the rule is false. The inference is solid; and the first part of the antecedent is proved. For this [proposition] "not any man runs", is equivalent to *(aequivalet)* this proposition in the square: "some man does not run", because the negation of something proposed makes it equivalent to its contradictory. But that proposition, "some man does not run", [164] is not a universal proposition; therefore, that proposition "not any man runs", is not a universal proposition either. The second part of the antecedent is proved. For every adjective is a determination of its substantive; but "any" *(quilibet)* is the adjective of the term "man". Therefore, it is a determination of that term; and consequently, "man" is determined by a universal sign, which was to be proved.

One may respond that the argument comes to a conclusion verbally. But it does not go against the sense of the rule which is this: A universal proposition is that in which a common term determined mobily by a distributive universal sign occurs as subject. But in the proposition in question the subject is not determined through a universal distributive sign; but the adjective alone; and thus the argument does not succeed.

Third, one can argue against the rule of a particular proposition, viz., "a particular proposition is that in which a common term determined by a particular sign occurs as subject". For this proposition, "not some man runs", *(non aliquis homo currit)* is not a particular proposition. Yet in it a common term determined by a particular sign occurs as subject. Therefore, the rule is false. The inference is solid with respect to the major because it is equivalent to this proposition, "any man runs", *(quilibet homo currit)* which is not a particular proposition. The minor is proved for every adjective of a substantive is the determination of that substantive. But "some" is an adjective of the term "man"; therefore, it is a determination of that term. Thus, "man" is determined by a particular sign, which was to be proved.

One may say in response that this argument does not go against the sense of the rule which is: A particular proposition is that in which a common term determined by a particular sign alone occurs as subject. But in the proposition in question the common term is determined by a sign which is an adjective and is also a distributive negation; and consequently, it is not determined by a particular sign alone.

Fourth, one can argue against the rule for an indefinite proposition, viz., "an indefinite proposition is that in which a common term without a sign occurs as subject". I posit that this universal proposition, "every man runs", comes before (A) "man runs". And I argue: (A) is an indefinite proposition; [165] yet in (A) a common term is mediated by a sign; therefore, the rule is false. The inference is solid with respect to the major premise; and the minor premise I prove: for the subject of the universal proposition and of (A) is the same; and the subject of the universal proposition is mediated by a sign; therefore, the subject of (A) is mediated by a sign, which was to be proved.

One says in response that this argument does not go against the sense of the rule: namely, that an indefinite proposition is that in which a common term without a sign occurs as the subject. Now something of that sort is relevant to what was proposed, i.e., the subject of (A) is subjected by means of a sign — not however, by means of some sign existing in that proposition, since the universal sign is not part of that which precedes (A); but rather it is a part of the preceding universal proposition.

Fifth, one can argue against the rule for a singular proposition, namely, a singular proposition is that in which a discrete term or a common term with a demonstrative pronoun occurs as subject. The proposition, "all of these run", *(omnes isti currunt)* is not a singular proposition; yet in it a discrete term occurs as subject; therefore, [the rule is false]. The inference is solid with respect to the major because it would be erroneous to add a universal sign, and the minor premise is clear. For every demonstrative pronoun is a discrete term; but the subject of the third proposition stated is a demonstrative pronoun; therefore, it is a discrete term.

One may respond that any of these propositions, "all of these run", "either of these is moved", is a universal proposition. Yet I deny that a discrete term occurs as subject in them. And then with regard to the argument, "every demonstative pronoun is a discrete term", this is true of a demonstrative pronoun which is singular in number but not of one plural in number: since I call a term "discrete" when it cannot apply at the same time to any more than one thing, e.g., "this" (masculine, feminine, neuter) and "this" (masculine, feminine, neuter) *(iste, ista istud; hic, haec, hoc)*. I call a term "common" when it can at the same time apply to many, e.g., "man", "animal", and demonstrative pronouns plural in number, e.g., "these" and "of these" *(isti, istorum)* and the like.

Sixth, one can argue against the rules for affirmative and negative propositions; namely, "an affirmative proposition is that in which the principal verb is affirmed, and a negative proposition is that in which the principal [166] verb is denied". For preceding that negative universal proposition, "no man runs", there is an affirmative proposition ["man runs"]; yet in that [affirmative] proposition the principal verb is denied; therefore, the rule is false. The inference is solid with regard to the major premise because "man runs", and anything similar to that proposition is affirmative. And I prove the monor premise: for the same point applies both to what is said of a universal negative proposition and of what precedes it. But the principal verb of a universal negative is denied, therefore, the verb of the preceding principal proposition is denied.

One says in response that the argument goes verbally against the rule; but it does not destroy the sense of the rule. For a negative proposition is that in which the principal verb is denied through some existing negation of that proposition. In this way the principal verb of that preceding part is negated; not, however, through some negation existing in this proposition "man runs", but in that proposition, "no man runs".

Section 3 — Objections to Sections 8, 9, 10

In the matter of equipollent propositions or of propositions existing in the figure, some rules were presented.

The first rule was this one, "two contraries cannot be simultaneously true".

Against this rule one argue. These propositions are simultaneously true: "any man is animal, and any man is not animal" *(quilibet homo animal est et quilibet homo animal non est)*. And these are two contraries; therefore, two contraries are simultaneously true. The inference is solid, and the first part of the antecedent is clear. For this is true, "any man is animal", as is clear through its exponents. And that the other proposition is true is clear: for this man is not animal and that man is not animal and thus of singulars and these are all masculine things; therefore, "any man is not animal". The inference is solid from singulars sufficiently enumerated to their universal; and each singular of the antecedent is of this kind, "this man is not a donkey; and every donkey is an animal; therefore, this man is not an animal". The inference is solid from lower-level terms to their corresponding higher-level ones with a negation placed in front and with the due mean. The second part of the antecedent is solid: a universal affirmative and a universal negative of like subject and predicate taken precisely for the same thing or things are contraries on the figure. But those two universal propositions in question are of this kind; therefore, they are contraries. [167] The inference is solid with regard to the minor; and the major is the very rule posited.

One may respond briefly that any of these propositions in question is true, but they are not contraries. And then with regard to the rule, I say that one ought to add into the rule that a common term not distributed in one may be distributed in the other; but in what was proposed in both cases "animal" stands merely confused *(confusa tantum)*. For that reason it remains that these are contraries "any man is animal", and "any man is not animal", of which the second is false. Similarly, these are contraries: "any man is not animal" and "any man is every animal" *(quilibet homo animal non est et quilibet homo omne animal est)*, of which the second is false. In a similar way one must treat the oblique cases, i.e., that they are not contraries. "Of any man a donkey runs and of any man a donkey does not run", are not contraries in virtue of the common rule: When an oblique case precedes a direct [nominative] case the oblique case is the subject and the direct [nominative] case goes with the predicate *(se tenet a parte praedicati)*, as for example in what was proposed.[a] But when the direct [nominative] case precedes the oblique case, which is a determination of the direct [nominative] case, either of those is put into the subject, e.g., "every donkey of a man runs", *(omnis asinus hominis currit)* the first universal is this contrary: "of any man no donkey runs", *(cuiuslibet hominis nullus asinus currit)* and the second universal is this proposition, "of any man every donkey runs" *(cuiuslibet hominis omnis asinus currit)*.

The second rule [for equipollent propositions] was this one: "two contradictories cannot be simultaneously true; nor can they be simultaneously false". Against this rule one may argue in this way. These propositions are simultaneously true, "any man is animal" and "some man is not animal", and these are two contradictories; therefore, two contradictories are simultaneously true. The inference is solid with respect to the minor premise because a universal affirmative and a particular negative with a similar subject, predicate and copula taken precisely for the same thing or things are contradictories in the figure; but the above propositions are of this kind; therefore, [two contradictories are simultaneously true]. The major premise is proved; for that this is true, "any man is an animal", is clear through its exponents. The second proposition is proved, "you are not an animal; and you are some man; therefore, some man is not an animal" *(tu animal non es et tu es aliquis homo; ergo aliquis homo animal non est)*. The inference is solid from a lower-level term to its higher-level term with a negation placed after it and with the due mean. The first part of the antecedent is proved: "you are not a goat, and every goat is an animal; therefore, you are not an animal". The inference is clear through the same rule. [168] One says that any of these is true; but they are not contradictories. And then with regard to the argument, I say that beyond what was said it is understood that a term not distributed in one may be distributed in the other; but it is not this way in what was proposed because "animal" in the universal proposition stands in a merely confused way

261

(confusa tantum), and in the particular proposition it stands determinately *(determinate)*. For that reason the contradictory of this proposition, "any man is an animal", *(quilibet homo animal est)* is said to be: "some man is no animal" *(aliquis homo nullum animal est)*. And the contradictory of this proposition, "some man is not animal" *(aliquis homo animal non est)*, is "any man is every animal" *(quilibet homo omne animal est)*. In the same way one says that these propositions are not contradictories: "of any man a donkey runs", and "of some man a donkey does not run" *(cuiuslibet hominis asinus currit et alicuius hominis asinus non currit)*. But the first contradicts this proposition, "Of some man no donkey runs" *(alicuius hominis nullus asinus currit)*, and the second [contradicts] this proposition, "of any man every donkey runs" *(cuiuslibet hominis omnis asinus currit)*.

The third rule was this one: "two sub-contraries cannot be simultaneously false; but they may be simultaneously true".

Against this rule one can argue in this way. These propositions are simultaneously false; "some man is every animal", and "some man is no animal" *(aliquis homo omne animal est et aliquis homo nullum animal est)*. And these are subcontraries; therefore, two subcontraries are simultaneously false. That those propositions are simultaneously false is clear because of any man pointed out it is false to say that of the same thing "every animal is", or of the same thing "no animal is". But that these are subcontraries is patent because a particular affirmative and a particular negative of similar subject, predicate and copula taken precisely for the same thing or things are subcontraries in the figure. But the above propositions are of this kind; therefore, they are subcontraries.

One may respond that these propositions are simultaneously false, but they are not, in turn, subcontraries; and then with regard to the criticism of the rule one says that beyond what the rule asserts it is understood that a common term distributed in one may not be distributed in the other, as is not the case in what was proposed. For "animal" stands in both propositions distributively. For that reason these are subcontraries, "some man is every animal", and "some man is not animal" *(aliquis homo omne animal est et aliquis homo animal non est)*. And these likewise: "some man is no animal", and "some man is animal" *(aliquis homo nullum animal est et aliquis homo animal est)*. For this reason always what is predicated stands [difformly] [*predicatum difformiter supponat*]; that is, if it is distributed in one, it is determinate in the other and conversely. This is not the case, however, with respect to the subject because always it ought to stand determinately. The same point applies to this proposition, [169] "of some man every donkey runs and of some man no donkey runs" *(alicuius hominis omnis asinus currit et alicuius hominis nullus asinus currit)*. For in the first proposition "donkey" continuously is distributed; and in the second proposition it is never distributed. For that reason neither the first nor the second is a subcontrary. But these are subcontraries: "of some man every donkey runs and of some man a donkey does not run" *(alicuius hominis omnis asinus currit et alicuius hominis asinus non currit)*. Further, "of some man a donkey runs and of some man no donkey runs" *(alicuius hominis asinus currit et alicuius hominis nullus asinus currit)*, are subcontraries.

Concerning equipollent propositions the first rule was this one. "[A sentence with] a negation placed in front is equipollent with the contradictory of the sentence."

Against this rule one can argue in this way. This proposition, "not by some man running you are a donkey" *(non aliquo homine currente tu es asinus)*, is not equipollent with "by no man running you are a donkey" *(nullo homine currente tu es asinus)*; therefore, the rule is false. The inference is solid, and the antecedent is proved. For the first proposition is true, and the second is false; therefore, neither of those is equipollent with the other. The inference is solid, and the antecedent is proved. First, that this proposition is true, "not by some man running you are a donkey" *(non aliquo homine currente, tu es asinus)*, is clear because its contradictory is false; namely, "by some man running you are a donkey" *(aliquo homine currente, tu es asinus)*. This is proved because this proposition has three causes of truth: namely, "some man runs", "you are a donkey", and "while a man runs you are a donkey"; and "if some man runs, you are a donkey". But any of these propositions is false, as is evident; therefore, this proposition, "by some man running you are a donkey", [is false]. Second, it is proved that this proposition is false: "by no man running, you are a donkey" *(nullo homine currente, tu es asinus)*. For any of its causes of truth is false; namely, "no man runs", "you are a donkey", "while no man runs, you are a donkey" and "if no man runs, you are a donkey". For that reason one may respond by denying the first inference in which it is concluded that the rule is false; but one ought to argue in this way: "not by some man running you are a donkey", is not equipollent with "by no man running you are a donkey". And these propositions contradict one another; namely, "by some man running, you are a donkey", and "not by a man running you are a donkey". Therefore, the rule is false. And then I deny the minor premise because they are two affirmative propositions proved through their causes of truth; and neither one of them is of some quantity.

Similarly, it does not follow [170] that these propositions are not equivalent: "not any man is animal", and "some man is not animal" *(non quilibet homo animal est et aliquis homo animal non est)*. Therefore, the rule is false because the first is false, and the second is true. But one ought to add into the antecedent that these propositions contradict one another: "any man is animal", and "some man is not animal" *(quilibet home animal est et aliquis homo animal non est)*. This is denied as was clear in the other chapter.[a]

The second rule was this one. [A sentence with] a negation placed after it is equipollent with the contrary of the proposition.

Against this rule one may argue. This inference is not solid: "any man every animal is not; therefore, no man is an animal" *(quilibet homo omne animal non est; ergo nullus homo animal est)*. But this is argued through the rule; therefore, the rule is false. The inference is solid with respect to the minor because it is argued from a negation posited afterwards; and I prove the major premise. The antecedent is true; and the consequent is false; therefore, the inference is not solid. That the antecedent is true was proved above.[b] But that the consequent is false I prove because its contradictory is true: "some man is an animal" *(aliquis homo animal est)*.

One responds by denying that this is argued according to the rule. And then with regard to the proof where [one says] it is argued from a post-posited negation, therefore, it is argued by the rule, the argument is not solid. But one ought to add into the antecedent that those are contraries, "any man is every animal" and "no man is animal" *(quilibet homo omne animal est et nullus homo animal est)*. This claim is false because the predicates of both are distributed. One says, therefore, that these are contraries; "any man is animal", and "no man is animal" *(quilibet homo animal est et nullus homo animal est)*. However, the postposited negation of the predicate does not make the first with that negation equipollent with the second. But there should be a negation placed after the subject and before the predicate by saying, "any man no animal is; therefore, no man is an animal" *(quilibet homo nullum animal est; ergo, nullus homo animal est)*. Further, if the negation were posited after the sign and not after the subject, it would not be argued according to the rule. For example, "no non-man is grammatical; therefore, any man is grammatical" *(nullus non homo est grammaticus; ergo, quilibet homo est grammaticus)*. The conclusion is false, as is clear; and the antecedent is true because its contradictory is false; namely, "some non-man is grammatical" *(aliquis non homo est grammaticus)*. Therefore, the negation of a negative term ought to be placed after the subject; as in this proposition "no man is not grammatical; therefore, any man is grammatical" *(nullus homo non est grammaticus; ergo, quilibet homo est grammaticus)*. Since the inference is solid and the antecedent is false, the consequent is false as well.

The third rule was this one. [A sentence with] a negation placed before it and a negation placed after it is equipollent with the subalternate of the proposition.

Against this rule one can argue. That inference does not follow: "not any chimera is not man; therefore, some chimera is man" *(non quaelibet chimera est non homo; ergo, aliqua chimera est homo)*. Yet this is argued according to the rule; therefore, the rule is false. The inference [171] holds with respect to the minor premise because it argues from a negation placed before and after. And the major premise is proved: For the antecedent is true; and the consequent false; therefore, the inference is not solid. That the consequent is false is evident. But that the antecedent is true is proved because its contradictory is false, namely, "any chimera is not man" *(quaelibet chimera est non homo)*, from which it follows that "any chimera is" *(quaelibet chimera est)*. [From a three-termed statement to a two-termed statement there is a solid inference. *(A tertio adjacente ad secundum adjacens [valet consequentia])*[a] The consequent is false; therefore, the antecedent is false as well. One says that this inference does not follow: "not any chimera is not man; therefore, some chimera is man" *(non quaelibet chimera est non homo; ergo, aliqua chimera est homo)*, according to which the argument is proved. Nor is it argued by the rule. And if someone says that the criticism is argued from a negation placed before and after; therefore, it argues according to the rule, I deny the inference. For the rule does not assert that howsoever a negation is placed before and after it makes [the sentence] equipollent with its subalternate. But it ought to be stated that it is placed before the entire proposition and it is placed immediately after the subject so that it may precede the principal verb. And it does not occur in this way in what was proposed because the second negation is put after the copula and for that reason it well follows: "not any chimera is not man; therefore, some chimera is man" *(non quilibet chimera non est homo; ergo, aliqua chimera est homo)*. The inference is solid; but the antecedent is false because its contradictory is true, namely, "any chimera is not man" *(quaelibet chimera non est homo)*. For no chimera is man *(nulla chimera est homo)*.[Thus, the rule is true.]

Section 4 — Objections to Section 11

The Chapter on Conversion contains three definitions.

The first definition was this one. "Simple conversion is the transposition of a subject into a predicate and conversely — the quality and quantity of the proposition remaining the same."

Against this definition one can argue in this way. Some proposition is converted simply; yet its quantity is changed; therefore, the definition is false. This inference holds; and the antecedent is clear. This proposition, "Socrates is animal", is converted simply into this proposition, "some animal is Socrates" *(aliquod animal est Sortes)*. This conversion is not *per accidens*, since no proposition is universal. Nor is it *per* contraposition because of the absence of an infinite term. Therefore, it is a simple conversion. Yet the quantity is changed because the converse is singular and the convertend is particular. The same difficulty occurs in this conversion, "man is animal", into "some animal [172] is man". The first proposition is indefinite; and the second one is particular. Therefore, the quantity is changed; yet it is a simple conversion because it is neither *per accidens* nor *per* contraposition.

For that reason I respond that the criticism proceeds verbally against the definition but not against the correct understanding of the rule. It may be said, therefore, that any of these conversions is simple. And if someone says that there the quantity is changed, one may reply that this is true according to the common way of taking "quantity". But it is not true according to the interpretation [of "quantity"] in the rule which specifies quantity with regard to supposition. Thus the definition may be glossed: simple conversion is the transposition of a subject into a predicate and conversely – the quantity remaining the same in supposition so that if in some converse a term should stand *(supponeret)* distributively, determinately or discretely in the convertend it stands *(supponit)* in the same way. And if someone says according to Aristotle's teaching in Book I of the *Prior Analytics*, that in the above examples "quantity" is taken in the sense of an indefinite universal or a singular, I respond that in the examples cited quantity is not taken in those senses but rather in the way indicated by the specifications added to the examples.[a]

The second definition was this one. "Conversion *per accidens* is the transposition of a subject into a predicate with the quality remaining the same but with a reduction in quantity."

Against this rule one can argue. This proposition is a conversion *per accidens*: "every man is capable of laughter; therefore, everyone capable of laughter is man". Yet the quantity is not changed. Therefore, the definition is insufficient. The inference holds with regard to the minor premise, for any of its [terms] is universal. The major premise is proved, for this [operation] is a conversion because it is [the transposition of a subject into a predicate] and conversely; yet it is not a simple conversion because a universal affirmative is not converted simply. Nor is it a conversion *per* contraposition because of the absence of infinite terms. Thus, it is a conversion *per accidens*.

One may respond that the conversion under examination is *per accidens*. And if someone says that the quantity is not changed, I deny the assertion taking quantity in the sense of supposition. Whence in the converse "man" stands *(supponit)* distributively and "capable of laughter" stands *(supponit)* in a merely confused way *(confusa tantum)*, and in the convertend "capable of laughter" stands *(supponit)* distributively and "man" stands *(supponit)* in a merely confused way *(confusa tantum)*. Thus let the definition be glossed in this way: Conversion *per accidens* is a transposition [173] of extremes [subject and predicate] remaining the same quality but of changed quantity, i.e., in supposition.

From this reply it follows first that this is a conversion *per accidens*: "man is capable of laughter; therefore, everyone capable of laughter is man". For this conversion is neither simple nor *per* contraposition; thus, it is *per accidens*. Second, it follows that this verse,

> *Feci simpliciter convertitur.*
> *Eva per accidens.*
> *Asto per contrapositionem.*
> *Sic fit conversio tota.*

does not express the truth but only affords some examples. Since not only a universal proposition can be converted *per accidens* but an indefinite and a particular proposition as well [can be converted *per accidens*]. Third, it follows that just as in a conversion *per accidens* the converse is false and the convertend true, in the same way the converse is true and the convertend false. This can be proved in the following way: I make two conversions *per accidens*. First, "every animal is man; therefore, man is animal". Second, "man is animal; therefore, every animal is man". It is clear that in the first the converse is false, and the convertend is true. In the second the converse is true, and the convertend is false.

The third definition was this one. Conversion *per* contraposition is the transposition of a subject into a predicate with the quantity and quality [of the proposition] remaining the same but with the change of a finite term into infinite terms.[a]

Against this definition one can argue in this way. The definition implies a contradiction; therefore, the definition is impossible. The inference holds; and the antecedent is proved. For if in a converse the subject and the predicate are finite terms, and in the convertend the subject and predicate are infinite terms, it follows that there is no conversion. The inference holds because a finite term cannot be an infinite term and conversely. E.g., "every man is animal", has for a subject "man" and for a predicate "animal". But the proposition, "every non-animal is non-man", has neither for a subject nor for a predicate some of those [finite] terms nor does it have any like them. Therefore, there is no conversion of the second proposition with the first.

One may respond by denying that the stated definition implies a contradiction. And then to the criticism the inference is denied because the definition does not say that the subject becomes the predicate or conversely; but rather that there may be a transposition of terms or of extremes so that the subject may be transposed into the predicate [position] without its becoming the predicate; and the predicate may be transposed into the subject [position] without its becoming the subject. Whence *ad hoc* for the subject to be transposed [174] into the predicate it suffices that it become the predicate or part of the predicate, in the way stated. And the rule states just what has been proposed.

From what is stated it follows that there is no conversion universally of a formal consequent apart from simple conversion. This is proved because there is no conversion *per accidens*, for when the convertend is true the converse is false and conversely, as was pointed out.[a] Nor is there conversion *per* contraposition because when the convertend is true the converse is false and conversely. This is proved in the following way: that proposition is true, "a chimera is not animal", and its convertend is false. I.e., "some non-animal is not non-chimera", because its contradictory is true: namely, "every non-animal is non-chimera". This is clear through the exponents of the proposition. Similarly, this proposition is false, "every chimera is animal", yet its convertend is true: namely, "every non-animal is non-chimera", as is clear through its exponents. Here are its exponents: "some non-animal is non-chimera; and nothing is non-animal unless it is non-chimera; therefore, every non-animal is non-chimera".

Section 5 – Objections to Section 12

In the matter of hypothetical propositions some rules are set forth. The first rule. "For the truth of an affirmative conditional proposition it is required that the contradictory of the consequent be repugnant to the antecedent." From this rule another rule follows: "For the falsity of [an affirmative conditional proposition] it is required and it suffices that the contradictory of the consequent stand with *(stet cum)* the antecedent."

Against these rules one can argue in this way. There is a true affirmative conditional proposition the contradictory of whose consequent stands with the antecedent; therefore, the rule is false. The inference holds, and the antecedent is proved. Of any affirmative conditional in which the antecedent is true and the consequent is false the contradictory of the consequent stands with the antecedent. But there is some true affirmative conditional whose antecedent is true and whose consequent is false; therefore, there is some true affirmative conditional the contradictory of whose consequent stands with the antecedent. The inference holds because it is a syllogism in the third mood of the first figure. The major premise is proved: for if the antecedent of that conditional is true and the consequent is false, then the contradictory of the consequent is true and the antecedent similarly is true. But all true [propositions] stand simultaneously: therefore, of any such conditional the contradictory of the consequent will stand with the antecedent. I prove the minor premise, for this conditional [proposition] is affirmative and true: [175] "unless you are animal you are not man". It is clear that the antecedent is true – namely, "you are animal", and the consequent is false, "you are not man".

One may respond that the rules given concerning the truth and the falsity of a conditional apply only to a conditional formed by *(denominata a)* "if" *(si)* and not to a conditional formed by "unless" *(nisi)*. For that reason it is proved that there is some true conditional [proposition] the contradictory of whose consequent stands with the antecedent; namely, a conditional proposition formed by "unless"; but there is no mention in the same place of a conditional proposition of the kind formed by "if".

Section 6 – Objections to Section 13

The second rule: "For the truth of an affirmative conjunctive proposition it is required that both principal parts be true." From this rule it follows that for the falsity of [an affirmative conjunctive proposition] it suffices that one of its parts be false.

Against these rules one can argue in this way. There is a true affirmative conjunctive proposition one of whose principal parts is false: therefore, the rule is false. The inference holds, and the antecedent is proved: This proposition is a true affirmative conjunction: "some animal is; and if you are that, you are a donkey". The second principal part of this proposition is false; therefore, the rule is false. The inference holds; and the principal part of the antecedent is proved: "this animal is, and if you are that, you are a donkey", – pointing to Brunellus; and this is some animal. "Therefore, some animal is; and if you are that, you are a donkey." The inference is clear because there does not seem to be another way of proving that conjunctive proposition. The second part of the antecedent also is proved: For this proposition, "if you are that, you are a donkey", does not seem to signify assertively anything other than "if you are animal, you are donkey". But this significate is false: "if you are animal, you are donkey" *(si tu es animal, tu sis asinus)*. Therefore, the second principal part is false.

One says that this conjunctive proposition is true, and the second part is true as well as the first part. But I deny that it signifies in the way stated, namely, that "if you are animal, you are donkey". Because then a relative term would stand [in the consequent] in a merely confused way and in the antecedent in a determinate way. But the opposite of this was said in the chapter on relatives.[a] It was said also that it is permissable to replace a relative term by an antecedent term where the same supposition *(suppositio)* is maintained. But "animal" in the first part stands determinately, [176] and posited in place of the relative term it stands in a merely confused way. For that reason the significate of the second part is grasped ineptly where the opponent states that it signifies the very same thing: "if you are animal, you are donkey". Therefore, a relative ought to be interchanged with its antecedent [term] standing determinately, by saying in the second part of the significate that, "some animal if you are, you are a donkey" *(aliquod animal si tu es, tu es asinus)*. And this is true because if you are this — pointing to a donkey — you are a donkey. And this is some animal; therefore, if you are some animal, you are a donkey. The inference is solid resolubly.

The third rule: "For the possibility of a conjunctive proposition it is required that either part be possible and no other part incompossible." From this one may infer that for the impossibility [of a conjunctive proposition] it is required and it suffices that one part be impossible or incompossible with another.

Against these rules one can argue. There is an impossible affirmative conjunctive proposition any of whose parts is possible and none of whose parts is repugnant to the other. Therefore, the rules concerning these propositions are false. The inference holds; and the antecedent is proved. For this conjunctive proposition is impossible: "every man runs, and you are man; yet you do not run", for from the first two statements follows the contradictory of the third statement in the third mood of the first figure, as is clear to intuition. Yet any of its parts is possible, as is clear. And it is proved that any of its parts is compossible with any other part. For these two propositions are compossible, "every man runs, and you are man". And these are compossible, "you are man, and you do not run". And these as well [are compossible]: "you do not run, and every man runs". Therefore, any of these propositions is compossible with any of the others. For that reason one says that the two rules given do not apply except to two-part conjunctives. But this is not the case in what was proposed where the conjunctive proposition is composed of three parts. If, therefore, one is seeking a general rule of the possibility of a conjunctive it is this: For the possibility of a conjunctive it is required that any of its parts is possible, and that no part be incompossible with any other part or with any other proposition. However, this is not the case in what was proposed because in that case any part is compossible with any other part; but it is not compossible [177] with any other proposition. For this proposition, "every man runs", is not compossible with this proposition, "you are man and you do not run". Similarly, this proposition, "you do not run", is not compossible with this proposition, "you are man, and every man runs", because from those two singular propositions follows the contradictory of a universal proposition. For it follows: "you do not run, and you are a man; therefore, not: every man runs".

The fourth rule: "For the necessity of a conjunctive proposition it is required that any of its parts be necessary." From this one can infer that for the contingency of a conjunctive proposition it suffices that one of its parts be contingent, and no part be incompossible with another part.

Against the second [part of the] rule, the argument already made applies.[a] But against the first part of the rule one argues in this way: Some conjunctive [proposition] is necessary one of whose parts is contingent; therefore, the rule is false. The inference holds; and the antecedent is proved. I quote this conjunctive proposition, "not: no God is and you are a man". This proposition is necessary because its opposite is impossible. I.e., "no God is and you are a man", because no truer contradictory of a proposition is given than that in which a negation is placed before the entire proposition. That one of the parts of this proposition is contingent, however, is clear, viz., "you are a man", which is the second part of the proposition.

One responds that this rule, just as any other rule given, is understood with respect to an affirmative conjunction and not [with respect] to a negative conjunction, as was stated in Chapter I.[b]

Section 7 – Objections to Section 14

The fifth rule: "For the truth of a disjunctive affirmative proposition it suffices that one part be true." From this one infers that for the falsity [of a disjunctive affirmative proposition] it is required that both parts be false.

Against these rules one can argue in this way. There is a false disjunctive; yet one of its parts is true; therefore, both rules are false. The inference is solid, and the antecedent is proved. This is a false disjunctive proposition. [178] "All men are donkeys, or men and donkeys are donkeys."[a] And one of its parts is true; therefore, both rules are false. The antecedent is proved and I posit that this is a disjunctive proposition because in it many categorical propositions are joined through a sign of disjunction. That, however, the same proposition is false is clear because any principal part of it is false; therefore, the same proposition is false. The inference holds, and the antecedent is proved for this is false, "all men are donkeys", and similarly, "men and donkeys are donkeys", and these are its principal parts, as is clear, That, however, one of its principal parts is true is argued. For any of these is true, "all men are donkeys or men", which is one part. And this is another part, "donkeys are donkeys". Therefore, one of its parts is true.

One may respond when someone proposes, "all men are donkeys or men and donkeys are donkeys", [by asking] whether the opponent wants to take the proposition as a conjunction or as a disjunction. If [he wants to take it] conjunctively, the proposition is true because both of its principal parts are true. And then to the criticism one says that it does not apply to what was proposed. If on the other hand [the opponent] wants to take it as a disjunctive proposition, the same proposition is denied because both of its principal parts are false, as was proved. And if someone says "one of its parts is true", I concede it. For according to what is understood in the rule by "principal part" it is conceded that some disjunctive proposition is false, yet one of its parts is true. But this does not militate against the rule because "principal part" is not assumed in this sense in the foregoing argument.

The sixth rule: "For the possibility of a disjunctive proposition it suffices that one part be possible; and for the impossibility of [a disjunctive proposition] it is required that any of its parts be impossible."

Against both rules one argues in this way: Some affirmative disjunctive proposition is impossible, and any of its principal parts is possible. Therefore, both rules are false. The inference holds; and the antecedent is proved. For this is impossible "contingently you are or you are not", granted *(supposito)* that the adverb determines the entire proposition, yet any of its principal parts is possible; therefore, [an affirmative disjunctive is impossible, yet any of its parts is possible.] The inference holds, and the first part of the antecedent is proved because its opposite is necessary, i.e., "necessarily you are or you are not". The second part also is clear because any of these propositions is possible, "you are" and "you are not". For that reason one responds that the rule is understood with regard to affirmative disjunctive propositions to be proved hypothetically and not categorically.[b] And this is not the case in what was proposed. From this it follows that any of these propositions, "contingently you are or you are not", "necessarily a king sits or no king sits", are to be proved exponibly [179] just as these propositions, "contingently you are", "necessarily God is".

The seventh rule: "For the necessity of an affirmative [disjunctive] proposition it suffices that one part be necessary or that all [the propositions] mutually contradict." From this it follows that for the contingency of the affirmative disjunctive proposition it is required that any part be contingent and no part be repugnant to another part.

Against these rules one argues: some disjunctive proposition is necessary any of whose parts is contingent; and no part is repugnant to another; therefore, both rules are false. The inference holds; and the antecedent is proved. For this disjunctive proposition is necessary, "Antichrist is not white or Antichrist is colored", and any of its parts is contingent, and no part is repugnant to another part. Therefore, [some disjunctive proposition is necessary any of whose parts is contingent; and no part is repugnant to another part.] The antecedent is clear with respect to any part; and first, it is clear that this proposition is necessary because its opposite is impossible, namely, "Antichrist is white and Antichrist is not colored". Second, it is clear; namely, that any of its parts is contingent because indifferently either can be true or false, as is clear. Third it is clear; namely, that none of these parts is repugnant to another because it is possible that Antichrist be black. And with this posited these propositions would be simultaneously true, "Antichrist is not white", and "Antichrist is colored". Therefore, they are not mutually repugnant.

One may respond that the rule of a contingent disjunctive was set forth in a brief form. But one ought to add "that the contradictories of parts are not repugnant".

Now with regard to what was proposed, the proposed disjunctive proposition is necessary and any of its parts is contingent, and no part is repugnant to another part. But the opposites of those parts are mutually repugnant, namely "Antichrist is white", "Antichrist is not colored", wherefore, there is nothing contrary to the rule.

It is to be noted that against any of these rules contained in the material on hypotheticals one can argue from the sign of a negative hypothetical or from a non-principal part. Where such objections are made, it may be said that [the rules] do not hold for negative hypotheticals.[a]

Section 8 – Objections to Section 15

The matter of predicables contains definitions of which the first is this one. "Genus is a univocal term [180] predicable *in quid* of many things different in species, e.g., 'animal'."

Against this definition one argues in this way. "Animated body" is a genus; yet it is not a univocal term. Thus the definition is insufficient. The inference holds with regard to the major premise, and I prove the minor premise. For every univocal term is a simple term; but "animated body" is not a simple term; therefore, it is not a univocal term.

One says [in response] that "animated body" is not a genus. Nor is "rational animal" [a genus] because any genus ought to be a simple term. And if someone cites Porphyry saying that he counts these terms as genera, one may reply that he did not say [that these terms were genera] but that he posited them by way of example, or because he lacked a simple term. Therefore, in place of this term "animated body" one ought to put one of these simple terms, "living" or "lived" mediating between "animal" and "body". Whence "every animal is living", but not conversely – declaring that a living thing composed of matter and form is a "rational animal". Therefore, it is erroneous to posit this as a genus because it is a definition of man. But Porphyry said that because he was following the opinion of Plato who said that the heaven was a rational animal. But this opinion we deny for the present.

The second definition. "A most general genus is that which, if it is a genus, is not able to be a species." From this one infers another rule: a subalternate genus is that which, if it is a genus, is able to be a species.

Against these definitions one argues in this way: "Substance is a most general genus; yet it can be a species. Therefore, the definitions are insufficient". The inference holds with respect to the major premise; and the minor premise I prove. For "substance" can be converted with this term "man"; therefore, it can be a species. The inference holds; and the antecedent similarly [is true] through a new imposition.[a]

One may respond that the argument proceeds verbally, but it does not militate against the sense of the definitions. This is the case for two reasons: first, a most general genus is that which, if it is a genus, is not able to be a species – *thus signifying adequately*. And a subalternate genus [181] is that which, if it is a genus, can be a species thus signifying adequately. Second, with regard to what was proposed, "substance can be a species", but not , however, by signifying adequately, viz., substance.

The third definition. "Species is a univocal term which is not the highest term predicable *in quid* of many things." *(Species est terminus univocus non supremus praedicabilis in quid de pluribus.)*

Against this definition one can argue in this way. "Substance" is a univocal term which is not the highest term predicable *in quid* of many things. Yet it is not a species; therefore, the definition is sufficient. The inference holds with respect to the minor premise; and the major premise is proved: For that "substance" may be predicated *in quid* of many things is clear. And that it is not the highest term is proved: For some term is above it; therefore, it is not the highest term. The inference holds. The antecedent is proved from this term "being" *(ens)* which is above the term "substance" because every substance is a being but not conversely.

One may respond that, in a way, "substance" is a most general genus.

For that reason it is a highest term; and if someone says that "being" is above it, I deny the point because superiority and inferiority are not found except in a category, and "being" is not in a category. Therefore, it is neither above nor below [some other term]. And when someone says, "every substance is a being but not conversely; therefore, 'being' is a higher-level term", the inference does not follow. But this does follow: "every substance is man or non-man and not conversely; therefore, 'man' or 'non-man' is a higher-level term". For no composite term is above or below a categorical term.

The fourth definition. "A most special species is a term which, if it is a species, is not able to be a genus." From this one can infer that a sub-alternate species is a term which, if it is a species, can be a genus.

Against both definitions one can argue in this way: This term "man" is a most special species; yet it can be a genus; therefore, neither definition is sufficient. The inference holds with regard to the major premise; the minor premise I prove. For ["man"] can be converted with that term "animal".

One replies that the criticism does not conflict with the sense of the rule which is this: a most special species is a term which, if it is a species, cannot be a genus — thus signifying adequately, e.g., "man". And a sub-alternate genus is a term which, if it is a species, can be a genus, thus signifying adequately, [182] e.g., "animal". But in what was proposed if "man" were converted with "animal", it would not adequately signify man.

The fifth definition. "Difference is a univocal term predicable *in quale essentiale*."

Against this definition one can argue. "Rational" is a difference; yet it is not a univocal term; therefore, the definition is [insufficient]. The inference holds with respect to the major premise and the minor premise I prove: for "rational" signifies man or angel under different concepts *(diversis rationibus)*; therefore, it is not a univocal term. The inference holds, and the antecedent is proved for it signifies man under the aspect of *(sub ratione qua)* sensitive and, further, angel under the aspect of intellective only. Therefore, ["rational" signifies man or angel under different concepts].

One responds that "rational" which divides animal — when one says animal is divided into rational and irrational — does not signify [anything] unless man because it does not signify [anything] unless [it signifies] rational animal. But no angel is a rational animal; therefore, it does not signify an angel. And for that reason one of the points assumed [in the criticism] was false.

The sixth definition. "A property is a univocal term predicable of many things in the sense of 'how' accidentally and convertibly *(in eo quod quale*

275

accidentale convertibiliter)." E.g., "risible" is predicated of Socrates and Plato accidentally and convertibly.

Against this definition one argues in this way: "Risible" is a property; yet is it not predicable of many things convertibly. Therefore, the definition is insufficient. The inference holds with respect to the major premise; the minor premise is proved. For "risible" is predicated of Socrates and Plato; yet [it is not predicated] convertibly because Socrates and "risible" are not interchanged. Whence it does not follow: "a risible thing runs; therefore, Socrates runs". Therefore, ["risible" is not predicated convertibly].

It must be said that "convertibly" in the definition does not apply [directly] to "many things" but to that by reason of which it is predicated of such things. For example, the subject, which is this term "man" is converted with this term "risible". For that reason this inference does not follow: " 'Risible' is predicated of Socrates and of Plato; yet it is not converted with those terms; therefore, it is not converted". For it argues from a lower-level term to its corresponding higher-level term with a negation placed before it.

The seventh definition. "An accident is a univocal term predicable of many things in the sense of 'how' accidentally and non-convertibly *(in quale accidentale non convertibiliter)*."

Against this definition one can argue in this way: This term "this whiteness" *(haec albedo)* is an accident because [183] it is an accidental term; yet it is not predicable of many things because it is a discrete term. Therefore, the definition is insufficient.

This criticism is solved through the definition by pointing out that "accident" may be taken broadly for all accidental terms common or discrete; and it is not taken in this way in what was proposed. In another way "accident" [may be taken] for a common accidental term; and this is the way it is assumed for the present. But according to this assumption it is clear that this term "this whiteness" *(haec albedo)* is not an accidental term nor is it a term qualifying [for predication] of many things accidentally.[a]

The eighth definition. "A direct predication is that in which a higher-level term is predicated of its lower-level term." An indirect predication is just the reverse of this rule.

Against these definitions one argues in this way: From them it follows that there is a predication which is neither direct nor indirect. For example: "man is man", "animal is animal", because neither a higher-level [term] nor a lower-level [term] is predicated.

For that reason one may respond to this criticism by conceding the original thesis.

The last definition. "An essential predication is that in which a higher-level term is predicated of its lower-level terms or of the differences of some of these [lower-level terms] or conversely."

Against this definition one can argue in this way: "man is not an animal", is not an essential predication; yet a higher-level term is predicated of its lower-level term. Therefore, the definition is insufficient. The inference holds with respect to the minor; and the major premise I prove because this predication is impossible.

One responds that some essential predication is impossible. Similarly, some contingent predication is an essential predication. For example, "you are a man", and "Antichrist is an animial". Further, some necessary predication is an accidental predication: e.g., "man is risible", or "animal is counted or colored" *(quantum aut coloratum)*.

Section 9 — Objections to Section 17

Some objections are to be made equally in the matter of syllogisms, so that what was not expressed may be brought more fully to light.[b]

First, one argues by proving the insufficiency of the [three] figures. There are four figures; therefore, three figures are too few. The inference holds. The antecedent is proved: for this is the optimum syllogism: "Every man is animal; every animal is substance; therefore, every man is substance". Therefore, there is a syllogism of some figure but it is not the first figure because what is the subject in the first proposition [184] is not the predicate in the second proposition. Nor is it in the second figure because the same term is not a predicate in both the premises. Nor is it in the third figure because the same term is not a subject in both the premises. Therefore, there ought to be a fourth figure in which the predicate in the first premise is the subject in the second premise.

One responds that there are not more than three figures. Nor does the syllogism proposed constitute a fourth figure because it is in the first figure and in the first mood. Nor was it said that it is not in the first figure because there is not in the first figure any syllogism other than that in which the subject of the first proposition is the predicate of the second. But one says that if the subject of the first premise is the predicate of the second premise, the first figure results. One may say, therefore, that the syllogism in question is in the first figure; for the subject of one premise is the predicate of the other premise.

Second, one argues for the insufficiency of the moods of the first figure. "No animal is a stone; any man is an animal; therefore, some man is not a stone." This is a syllogism in the first figure; yet it is not in one of the

277

nine moods, as is clear to intuition. Or one might say that it is in Baralipton. But this is not correct because Baralipton reaches a conclusion indirectly, and the syllogism in question reaches its conclusion directly. Therefore, [it is not Baralipton]. Or again, one says that the syllogism is in Celarent — not immediately but mediately — because the first premise leads to this conclusion in Celarent: "no man is a stone". And from this it follows formally, "some man is not a stone", in the figure of existence in *(de inesse)*. Similarly, one must say with regard to the second syllogism that it is in the first mood of the first figure not immediately but mediately by reaching this conclusion in the figure of existence in *(de inesse)* from a proper conclusion. For that reason this syllogism is immediate in the first mood of the first figure: "every animal is a substance; any man is animal; therefore, any man is substance". This follows because there does not occur *ad hoc* some intermediate which is in the first mood of the first figure. But another [kind of] syllogism is mediate because that conclusion does not follow unless mediately under this interpretation; namely, "any man is a substance", insofar as [one reasons] from a universal [term] to its subalternate. And if from this [185] one concludes that [the syllogism is in] Barbara or Celarent, it reaches its conclusion indirectly or indefinitely or particularly thereby conceding that it is not immediately [concluded] but mediately [concluded].

Third, one can argue to the insufficiency of the moods of the second figure. "No stone is an animal; any man is an animal; therefore, some man is not a stone." Or on this way: "any man is an animal; no stone is an animal; therefore, no man is a stone". Both of these syllogisms are in the second figure; yet they are not in some of the four moods [of that figure] as is clear by examining individual cases. For the first of these two syllogisms made from two universal propositions reaches its conclusion indirectly in a way which is not reducible to one of those four moods.

One may respond as previously that the first is mediate in Cesare because from its proper and immediate conclusion the conclusion drawn follows formally. The second syllogism is indeed in Camestres and is mediate as well because from its proper and immediate conclusion the conclusion of that syllogism follows by simple conversion.

Fourth, one can argue to the insufficiency of the moods of the third figure. "Every man is a substance; every man is an animal; therefore, a certain substance is an animal." Or "any man is risible; some man is one man; therefore, some risible [being] is one man". These are the best syllogisms in the third figure; and they are not in one of the moods of the third figure because all of the moods of the third figure reach their conclusions directly, and the syllogisms offered reach their conclusions indirectly; therefore, [the moods of the third figure are insufficient.]

278

For that reason one says as previously that the first syllogism is in Darapti and the second syllogism is in Datisi — not immediately but mediately — by simple conversion immediately of the conclusion. And thus it is not absurd that the moods of the third figure reach their conclusions indirectly not immediately, but rather only mediately.

One argues commonly against the moods of the figures by proving that the syllogisms made in them are not equally tenable.

And first, against the first mood of the first figure, this syllogism does not follow: "every man or donkey is a donkey; every risible thing is a man or a donkey; therefore, every risible thing is a donkey". And this syllogism occurs in the first mood of the first figure; therefore, this mood is insufficient. The inference holds with regard to the major premise because all of the requirements of the first mood of the first figure are sufficiently satisfied. However, that this syllogism would not follow is proved: the consequent is false and the antecedent is [186] true. For the minor premise is true, as is clear from its exponents. And the major premise I prove inductively: "this man or donkey and that man or donkey is a donkey and thus of singulars; and these are all men; therefore, every man or donkey is a donkey". The inference is clear from singulars sufficiently enumerated to their universal.

One may respond by asking of the subject of the distribution of that universal, "every man or donkey is a donkey", what is distributed? Is the total disjunct [distributed]? Or the first part of the disjunct only? If the total disjunct, I deny the major premise and with regard to the inductive proof, I say that any singular in which man is pointed out is false. For that reason this proposition is false: "this is man or donkey is a donkey" — pointing to a man. Because it signifies that this which is man is a donkey; and this proposition is false. If, on the other hand, the first part of the disjunct alone is distributed, I deny the inference because more is predicated in the minor premise than was distributed in the major premise. For it ought not to be that the entire subject of the major proposition be predicated in the minor; but it suffices that the distributed subject [of the major be predicated in the minor]. So that according to this reply a universal proposition which is a major premise has as a subject of distribution the first part of the disjunct, and it has as a subject of the proposition the entire disjunct. The first subject and not the second is predicated in the minor. Nor is the rule of the first figure thought to apply to a proposition of this kind.

Against the second mood one argues in this way. This syllogism does not follow: "no conclusion is true; but every conclusion made in Celarent is a conclusion, therefore, no conclusion made in Celarent is true". Yet this syllogism is in Celarent; therefore, [the second mood of the first figure is invalid]. The minor premise is clear because all the requirements [of Celarent are satisfied]. The major premise is proved by positing that the syllogism made is every syllogism. With that posited the antecedent of that syllogism is true with respect to any part; and the consequent is false because it falsifies itself. For that reason I said in the chapter on insolubles that the syllogism stated is not in the second mood of the first figure because its conclusion is an insoluble proposition signifying hypothetically in a way which does not occur in its premises.[a]

Against the third mood of the first figure one argues in this way: This syllogism does not follow: "of any man a donkey runs: Brunellus is a donkey of a man, [187] therefore, Brunellus runs". Yet this is argued according to the third mood; therefore, this mood is insufficient. The inference holds with regard to the minor premise; the major premise I prove. I posit that any man has two donkeys of which one runs, and the other does not run; and further, of the number not running Brunellus is one. With this posited, the antecedent is true, as is clear. The consequent goes against the case. For that reason one says that the criticism does not follow because more is predicated in the minor premise than was distributed in the major premise. For precisely "man" was distributed in the major premise and stated in the minor premise was this entire term, "donkey of a man".

But, again, one may say that the criticism stands. One may argue: "of any man a donkey runs; Brunellus is of a man; therefore, Brunellus runs".

One replies that this is not a syllogism in the third mood of the first figure because into oblique cases one ought to predicate the subject of the major premise and into the nominative case one ought to predicate the subject of the minor premise, by saying, "Brunellus is a man". And this is denied because on that account it follows: "of any man a donkey runs: Socrates is a man; therefore, of Socrates a donkey runs". It is to be noted concerning the first mode that if some of the premises were not quantified, one would not argue in this way. E.g., "necessarily every man is an animal; Socrates is a man; therefore, necessarily Socrates is an animal". And again, "every man is an animal; but only a risible thing is a man; therefore, only a risible thing is an animal". But in both of these inferences the antecedent is true, and the consequent is false. The paralogisms are not, therefore, syllogisms in Darii because in the first the major premise is not of some quantity, and in the second the minor [premise is not of some quantity] because it is an exclusive proposition of the first order.[a]

Against the fourth mood of the first figure one argues in this way: this syllogism does not follow: "every animal, if it is capable of braying *(rudibile)* is not a man; but you are an animal if you are capable of braying; therefore, you are not a man". Now this is argued according to the fourth mood of the first figure; therefore, [this mood is insufficient]. The inference holds; the antecedent is proved. For the consequent is false as is clear, and both of the premises are true, i.e., the first as well as the second, as is plain through their exponents. For some animal, if it is capable of braying, is not man; and nothing is animal unless, if it is capable of braying, it is not man. It is clear also from all of its singulars of which any is true.

One responds as in the first case that if the entire conditional is distributed, the major premise is denied; [188] and then to the criticism I say that it is not expounded well. First, because there is a universal negative which is not expounded. Second, because one ought not to assert the second exponent; rather one ought to say, "nothing is an animal, if it is capable of braying, unless this is not a man". But this proposition is false because there is some animal, if it is capable of braying, which is a man. For this is a man − pointing to a man; and this is an animal if it is capable of braying; therefore, [something is an animal which, if it is capable of braying, is a man]. Further, many singular propositions are false: "This animal, if it is capable of braying, is not a man" − pointing to a man − because this ought to be resolved in this way: "this is not a man, and this is an animal if it is capable of braying", of which the first proposition is false. If, however, someone says in the beginning that the first part only of what is conditioned is distributed, then it is clear that the inference does not follow because more is predicated in the minor premise than was distributed in the major premise. For that reason one ought to argue in this way: "every animal, if it is capable of braying, is not a man; but you are an animal; therefore, if you are capable of braying, you are not a man". The inference is conceded, and the conclusion is conceded as well. It is to be noted, however, in the foregoing and in other moods that the middle term ought always to stand precisely for the same thing or for the same things. For that reason this syllogism does not follow: "no man is a woman; Bertha is a man; therefore, Bertha is not a woman", because the minor ought to be this kind of statement: "Bertha is some man *(aliquis homo)*", which is denied. Against other moods of the first figure I do not argue because from what has been said objections can be elicited sufficiently against the other moods.

Against the first mood of the second figure one can argue in this way: This inference does not follow: "every God is not a substance; every first cause is a substance; therefore, every first cause is not God", for the antecedent is true, the conclusion is false, and this syllogism is in the first mood of the second figure.

One responds that that syllogism is not in the first mood of the second figure because such [a syllogism] ought to be made from a negative proposition in the customary way of speaking and not from an uncustomary way of speaking as occurs in what was proposed. Because all of these negatives exemplify an uncustomary way of speaking, since a negation precedes the predicate.[a] But this would follow: "every God is no substance; every first cause is a substance; therefore, every first cause is not God". But the major premise is false just as the conclusion is false. This criticism can be made against all of the other moods of this figure by transposition of the premises and by a change [in their] quality. [189]

Against the first mood of the third figure one can argue: This syllogism does not follow: "of any man a donkey runs; of any man a donkey rests; therefore, a resting donkey is a running donkey", because in the above case the antecedent is true, and the conclusion is false. Yet it is in the first mood of the third figure.

One says that this is not in Darapti because just as the premises are made from a nominative and an oblique [case] the conclusion ought to be made in the same way. For that reason this proposition ought to be the conclusion: "therefore, a resting donkey is of someone of whom there is a running donkey". Whence "donkey" is not part of what is subjected in the premise but part of what is predicated; and that is how it ought to be stated in the conclusion.

Against the second mood of the third figure one can argue: This syllogism does not follow: "every man or donkey is not a man; every man or donkey is capable of laughter; therefore, something capable of laughter is not a man". For the antecedent is true, as is clear from its exponents or from [its] singulars; and the conclusion is false.

One responds that if in any of the premises the total disjunct is distributed any of these is false, and it has many false singular propositions, as was shown previously.[a] For concerning the first universal proposition any of its singular propositions is false in which a man is pointed to. And concerning the second, any singular is false in which a donkey is pointed to, as is clear from its resolvents. If, however, the total disjunct is not distributed but only the first part, one does not argue according to the second mood of the third figure because in such a mood the total subject of the proposition ought to be distributed which is not the case in what was proposed.

Against other moods of this [third] figure I do not argue in a special way. First, because the two earlier objections can be advanced against all the other moods; and second, because a writing of great length would cause tedium in the mind of a student.

This is the end of the "Objections to Chapter I" edited by brother Paul of Venice.

Notes

[163]ᵃ   On the background of the qualification "in virtue of expression" *(de virtute sermonis)* see Boehner, 6, pp. 248—253.

[167]ᵃ   On the distinction between the direct and oblique cases see above n. [80]ᵃ.

[170]ᵃ   See above pp. [167]—[168].
    ᵇ   See p. [167].

[171]ᵃ   On this rule see above, n. [61]ᵃ.

[172]ᵃ   Aristotle, 2, Chapter I.

[173]ᵃ   "man" is a finite term; "non-man" is an infinite term.

[174]ᵃ   This was discussed above pp. [13]—[14].

[175]ᵃ   See above pp. [51]—[58].

[177]ᵃ   That is the argument made in defense of Rule Three, see
       pp. [176]—[177].
    ᵇ   See Chapter I on the negation of hypothetical propositions, pp. [15]—[18].

[178]ᵃ   The proposition unpunctuated in the Latin is ambiguous. As Paul's response shows, the task of the dialectician is to determine whether the original proposition is a conjunction or a disjunction. On this puzzle see Boehner, 3, p. 97 ff.
    ᵇ   To prove a proposition "categorically" means to exhibit the elementary categorical propositions which make it decidably true or false. To prove a proposition "hypothetically" means to exhibit the concatenation of elementary propositions which make it decidably true or false.

[179]ᵃ   "One can argue beyond the sign of a negative hypothetical or from a non-principal part." This statement means that objections based on these other factors can be raised against the rules of hypothetical propositions; but Paul rejects such objections as irrelevant to the rules for hypothetical propositions.

[180]ᵃ   That is by defining "substance" as "man" in the present context.

[183]ᵃ   The point here is that the criticism presupposes the definition in question; hence, it amounts to a confirmation of that definition rather than a disconfirmation of it.
    ᵇ   For discussions of the theory of syllogistic see Ashworth, 2; Prior 2, pp. 103—125.

[186]ᵃ   The proposition, "this conclusion is not true", is an insoluble proposition which has its origin in the property of an expression. It signifies hypothetically in the sense that its principal significate is: "this conclusion is not true and this conclusion is true". See above Chapter VI, p. [162].

[187]ᵃ   See above Chapter IV for definitions of the kinds of exclusive propositions recognized in the *Logica Parva*, p. [100] and n. [100]ᵃ.

[188]ᵃ   See the Chapter I treatment of negation, p. [12] ff.

[189]ᵃ   See above p. [186].

Chapter VIII
Objections to Chapter III

Section 1 – Objections to Section 1

Having understood the objections against the small logic book here follows last as was stated in the beginning: namely, the material to strengthen the rules of inferences.

I argue, therefore, against the prime and principal rule which is this: A solid inference is that in which the contra- [190] dictory of the consequent is repugnant to the antecedent. From this rule another may be inferred; an unsolid inference is that in which the contradictory of the consequent stands with *(stat cum)* the antecedent.

[Against these rules one can argue.] Some inference is solid; yet the contradictory of the consequent stands with the antecedent; therefore, both rules are false. The inference is solid; the antecedent is proved. This inference is solid: "you believe precisely that some man is deceived; therefore, some man is deceived"; yet the contradictory of the consequent stands with antecedent. Therefore, [both rules are false]. The first part of the antecedent is proved because this follows: "you believe precisely that some man is deceived; therefore, you believe precisely what is true or you believe precisely what is false. If you believe precisely what is true, and you believe precisely that some man is deceived; then some man is deceived. If you believe precisely what is false; then you are deceived, and you are some man; therefore, some man is deceived". The second part of the antecedent is proved. I pose the antecedent in the case with this condition: let none other than you be deceived. With this posited, you believe precisely that some man is deceived; and no man is deceived; therefore, the contradictory of the consequent stands with the antecedent. The case posits the first part of the antecedent; and the second part I prove. For no one other than you is deceived according to this case; nor are you deceived; therefore, no man is deceived. The minor premise I prove because if it is not granted, the opposite follows; and one argues in this way: "you believe precisely as the case is; therefore, you are not deceived". The inference is solid and the antecedent is proved; for you believe precisely that some man is deceived according to the case. And yet it is the case that some man is deceived because you are deceived according to the response. Therefore, you believe precisely as the case is.

One may respond that this inference is solid: and that the opposite of the consequent does not stand with the antecedent — indeed it is repugnant to the antecedent. And with the case admitted, I concede, "you believe precisely that some man is deceived". And I deny this proposition, "no man is deceived", because I concede that you are deceived as a consequence *(tamquam sequens)*. For it follows: "some man is deceived and none other than you is deceived and you are; therefore, you are deceived". Furthermore, with regard to the criticism I deny this proposition, "you believe precisely as the case is". And in order to prove this claim I deny the inference: "you believe precisely that some man is deceived; and for that reason it is the case that some man is deceived; therefore, you believe precisely as the case is". Just as it does not follow: "you believe precisely that some man runs; and for that reason it is the case [191] that some man runs. Therefore, you believe precisely as the case is". Again, let it be posited that Socrates runs and Plato does not run; and you believe precisely that Plato runs *(Platonem currere)*. With this posited, the antecedent is true; and the consequent is false; but it follows: "you believe precisely that some man runs; and for that reason it is the case that that one whom you precisely believe to run, runs. Therefore, you believe precisely as the case is". But the minor premise is false in this case. For that reason it follows in what was proposed, "you believe precisely that some man is deceived; and for that reason it is the case that that one whom you believe precisely to be deceived is deceived; therefore, you believe precisely as the case is". The inference is solid; but the minor premise is false because in this case you believe that someone other than you is deceived *(tu credis aliam a te decipi)*.

It is to be noted that under the second rule two other rules are set down: namely, from an impossible proposition any proposition follows; a necessary proposition follows from any proposition.[a]

Against these rules one can argue in this way. It does not follow, "some man is a donkey; therefore, no man is a donkey". And this is argued according to both rules; therefore, both rules are false. The inference holds with regard to the minor premise; and the major premise I prove. First, because from one of two opposites the remaining one does not follow. Second, because the contradictory of the consequent stands with the antecedent insofar as it is interchanged with that very proposition. For that reason one may respond that this inference is solid in matter, and it is not absurd from one of two opposites to infer the other one — given that the proposition in question is impossible. I deny, however, that the opposite of the consequent stands with the antecedent. And I deny the opposite inference: "the consequent is interchanged with the antecedent; therefore, it stands with that same proposition". Whence I say that any proposition in the world follows from that proposition, "you are a donkey"; and any proposition is repugnant to that same proposition. Indeed it is repugnant to its very self because it implies *(infert)* the opposite of its very self.

Section 2 – Objections to Section 2

The first rule of a formal inference is this (1.1): "If in some inference the contradictory of the antecedent follows from the contradictory of the consequent, that inference is solid." From this rule one may infer another (*1.1.1): "if in some inference the contradictory of the consequent is not supportive *(non est illativum)* of the contradictory of the antecedent, that inference is not solid".

Against both rules one argues in this way. There is a solid inference; yet the contradictory of the antecedent does not follow from the contradictory of the consequent. Therefore, these rules are false. The antecedent is proved: this inference is solid, "you believe precisely that every man is deceived; [192] therefore, you are deceived". And from the contradictory of the consequent the contradictory of the antecedent does not follow. Therefore, [the rule is false]. The first part of the antecedent is proved. For this proposition follows: "you believe precisely that every man is deceived; therefore, you believe what is true or what is false. If you believe what is false, then you are deceived. If [you believe] what is true and you believe precisely that every man is deceived, then since it is the case that every man is deceived, and you are a man; therefore, you are deceived". This inference is solid, and the second part of the principal antecedent is proved because it does not follow: "you are not deceived; therefore, you do not believe precisely that every man is deceived". This claim is proved; for I posit that you believe precisely that every man is deceived, and that this be the case and that every man [who is] not you be deceived. With this posited, the consequent is false according to the case. And that the antecedent is true is proved, for if it is not granted the opposite proposition follows. And one argues in this way: "you believe precisely that every man is deceived, and it is the case that every man is deceived because every man [who is] not you is deceived according to the case. Yet you are deceived according to the response; therefore, you believe precisely as the case is; therefore, you are not deceived" – which was to be proved.

One is to respond by not admitting the case because it is not possible that you believe precisely that every man is deceived. For in that way it follows that you are deceived, as was shown. Either, therefore, you are deceived in believing every man to be deceived or otherwise in not believing every man to be deceived. Because every man is deceived is true according to the case [you are deceived] in believing otherwise, and from this it follows that a man is a donkey or some other false proposition. And consequently, you do not believe precisely that every man is deceived, which is the opposite of one claim in the case. From the same argument it follows that it is not possible that you believe precisely yourself to be deceived. This claim is proved; for if you believe precisely yourself to be deceived, then you are deceived either in believing yourself to be deceived or [you are deceived in believing] something else. It is not the first alternative, because [that] you yourself are deceived is true; therefore, [you are deceived in believing] something else false; and consequently, you do not believe precisely yourself to be deceived.

The third rule (1.2; 1.2.1; *1.2.2) was this one: "If in some solid inference the antecedent is true, the consequent is true; then, if the antecedent is true and the consequent is false, this inference does not follow *(non valet)*."

Against this rule one argues in this way: It is possible that [193] some inference is solid in which the antecedent is true and the consequent is false; therefore, the rule is false. The inference holds; and the antecedent is proved. I posit that this inference "you are a man; therefore, you are not a man", is interchanged with a solid inference having an antecedent and a consequent signifying as previously. The case is possible, because an inference is distinguished from an antecedent and a consequent taken simultaneously because one adds on to these the sign of an inference. Having admitted the case, this inference is solid: "you are a man; therefore, you are not a man", because it is interchanged with a solid inference. But the antecedent is true, and the consequent is false because it signifies in every way as previously was stated in the case. Therefore, [it is possible that some inference is solid in which the antecedent is true and the consequent is false].

For this reason one replies that the criticism proceeds verbally against the rules. However, it is not contrary to the sense of these rules if the first statement is understood in this way: If in some solid inference signifying precisely according to the composition of its parts the antecedent is true, the consequent similarly is true.

The rule, however, is understood in this way: if in some inference signifying precisely according to the composition of its parts the antecedent is true and the consequent is false, the inference does not follow. But while in the above case, the proposed inference is solid it does not, however, signify according to the composition of its parts. For it posits [that] the very same proposition is interchanged with a solid inference with the antecedent and consequent signifying, as previously, in every way. So that, therefore, in order to argue against the rule one ought to take this antecedent, "it is possible that some inference is solid, signifying precisely according to the composition of its parts and that the antecedent is true and the consequent is false". And this [claim] is denied, for it is impossible. This [is the correct] way of understanding, "signification of parts", with regard to a rule of inference even if it is not stated explicitly. However, any rule of inference against which that criticism or a similar criticism can be advanced verbally implies this interpretation [of "signification of parts"], unless the stated gloss is [not] applied to those rules.

The fourth rule (1.3; *1.3.1): "If in some solid inference the antecedent is necessary and the consequent is also necessary, it is inferred that if an antecedent is necessary and a consequent is contingent, the inference does not follow."

Against these rules one argues in this way. There is a solid inference in which the antecedent is necessary and the consequent is contingent; therefore, the rules are false. The inference holds and the antecedent is proved. For this inference is solid: "God is; therefore, this proposition is true, 'God is' ". But the antecedent is necessary and the consequent is contingent; therefore, [there is a solid inference in which the antecedent is necessary and the consequent is contingent]. [194] That the antecedent is necessary is patent. That the consequent is contingent is proved. For this proposition, "God is", can be false and the same proposition is true; therefore, it is contingent for that proposition to be true. This inference is known with regard to the minor premise; the major premise is proved insofar as it is interchangeable with a false proposition. For this reason the principal inference is proved to be solid; for if it is not, the opposite of the consequent would stand with the antecedent. This point is argued in this way: "this proposition is not true, 'God is'; yet the same proposition signifies adequately that God is *(Deum esse)*; therefore, that God is *(Deum esse)* is not true; and consequently, God is not" – which is the opposite of the other [antecedent] part of the original proposition.

One may respond that this inference does not follow: "God is; therefore, this proposition is true, 'God is', unless this minor premise is added to the argument, 'God is' signifies adequately God to be *(Deum esse)*", which is contingent; and I concede that the opposite of the consequent stands with the antecedent. Then when someone posits [this proposition] with the admitted antecedent I concede this proposition, " 'God is' and this proposition is not true: 'God is' ". And then with regard to the argument, "this proposition is not true, 'God is' and the same proposition signifies adequately that God is *(Deum esse)*; therefore, that God is is not true", I deny the minor premise because it is repugnant to the two conceded [propositions]. For it follows: "God is and this proposition is not true, 'God is'; therefore, the same proposition does not signify adequately that God is

(Deum esse)". Whence in this criticism there is an obligation and it does not appear; for when one states that the opposite of the consequent stands with the antecedent, this is a position *(positio)* implicitly [i.e., something posited in an obligation] as if I should say, "I posit to you this proposition, 'God is', and the same proposition is not true, 'God is' ". This proposition is to be admitted and to be responded to as previously.[a]

The fifth rule (1.4; *1.4.1): "If in some solid inference the antecedent is possible the consequent is similarly possible; then, in some inference when the antecedent is possible and the consequent is impossible, the inference does not follow."

Against these rules one argues in this way. This inference is not solid: "every proposition is affirmative; therefore, no proposition is negative". The antecedent is possible, yet the consequent is impossible; therefore, the rule is false. The inference holds and the first part of the antecedent is clear [because of the rule: everything repugnant to the consequent is repugnant to the antecedent]. Thus, the inference is solid. And the antecedent is clear; for these propositions are repugnant: "every proposition is affirmative, and some proposition is negative". That the antecedent is possible is clear because it is possible that this proposition "you are", is every proposition. But now it is proved that the consequent is impossible. [195] For the same [proposition] cannot be true signifying as it does. For if it can be true, this is either through itself existing or not existing. It is not through itself not existing because, if so, this proposition "no proposition is negative", would not be. And thus the same proposition would be neither true nor false. Nor is it through itself existing because, while this proposition is, some negative proposition is. And consequently, this proposition is always false, "no negative proposition exists" *(nullam negativam esse)*. [Wherefore, the above criticism of the rule is false.][a]

It is to be said, moreover, that this inference is solid: "every proposition is affirmative; therefore, no proposition is negative". And the consequent is possible just as the antecedent is possible. And then concerning the criticism, "the consequent cannot be true signifying as it does; therefore, the same proposition is impossible", I deny the inference. For many propositions are possible which are not able to be true such as: "every proposition is false"; "no proposition is true" – thus signifying adequately – "this is false", "this is not true", the propositions pointing to themselves, as was determined in the discussion of insolubles.[b] Also, beyond the discussion of insolubles these expressions have a place: "this is not true, 'God is', in the mind of Socrates". Or "this is not", – pointing to the very subject of the proposition. Any of these propositions is possible, yet none of them signifying in the way they do is able to be true.

The sixth rule (1.5; 1.5.1; 1.5.2): "Whatever follows from the consequent follows from the antecedent." From this rule one may infer two additional rules: (1) Whatever implies the antecedent implies the consequent. (2) In a chain of propositions when all of the intermediate inferences are solid and formal and unvaried, the inference is solid and formal.

Against these rules one argues in this way. There is a solid inference, and something follows from the consequent of the same argument which does not follow from the antecedent. Therefore, all three of the rules are false. The inference holds and the antecedent is clear. This inference is solid: "Four is; therefore, two is; and something follows from the consequent which does not follow from the antecedent; therefore, [there is a solid inference, and something follows from the consequent of the same argument which does not follow from the antecedent]". The inference holds with respect to the major premise because the contradictory of the consequent is repugnant formally to the antecedent. I prove the minor premise; for it follows "two is; therefore, its half is precisely one", yet it does not follow in a chain of propositions, "four is; therefore, its half is precisely one". For half of four is not one but two. [196] In a similar way, it is argued: "a four-footed thing is; therefore, a twofooted thing is; a two-footed thing is; therefore, its half is precisely a one-footed thing". Yet it does not follow: "a four-footed [thing] is; therefore, its half is precisely a one-footed thing" because half of a four-footed thing is not a one-footed thing but rather a two-footed thing.

One says that these rules hold beyond the matter of relatives; and this is due to a change in the ultimate significate of the consequent because of a relative which varies the significate according to the variation of the antecedent.[a] For that reason this proposition "of that one-half is one", signifies one thing conjoined with this proposition, "two is", and it signifies another thing [conjoined with this proposition], "four is". For with the first it signifies that half of two is one, which is true; and with the second it signifies that half of four is one, which is false. The first rule is understood, therefore, in this way: Whatever follows from the consequent follows from the antecedent *the first signification remaining*. And because the last consequent, in virtue of a relative term, cannot retain the first signification, for that reason it is no wonder that it does not follow from the first antecedent. In its place, therefore, one puts this proposition signifying the same thing interchangeably by arguing in this way: "four is; therefore, two is; two is; therefore, its half is one". Therefore, from the first to the last, "four is; therefore, half of two is one". And in the same way one ought to infer the following: "a four-footed thing is; therefore, half of a two-footed thing is a one-footed thing". This is conceded.

The seventh rule (1.6; 1.6.1): "If in some solid inference something stands with the antecedent that same thing stands with the consequent." From this it follows that whatever is repugnant to the consequent is repugnant to the antecedent.

Against these rules one argues in this way. This inference is solid. "Wood was destroyed; therefore, it is impossible for that to be".[b] Yet this proposition, "an animal is", stands with the antecedent; and the same thing does not stand with the consequent. Thus, the rules are false. The inference is solid, and the antecedent is proved. That the inference is solid is clear because what was once destroyed is not able to be anymore. That, however, this proposition, "an animal is", stands with the antecedent is clear, for these stand at the same time: "Wood was destroyed", [197] "an animal is" because both of them are true. But now it is proved that that proposition, "an animal is" does not stand with the consequent because this conjunctive proposition is impossible, "an animal is; and it is impossible for that to be".

One may respond that this inference is solid: "Wood was destroyed; therefore, it is impossible for that to be". And just as this proposition, "an animal is", stands with the antecedent it stands also with the consequent. And when someone says that this conjunctive proposition is impossible, "an animal is; and it is impossible for that to be", it is true; therefore, this proposition, "an animal is", does not stand with the consequent, I deny the inference. For the second part of this conjunctive proposition is not the consequent of the first inference, nor is it interchangeable with [the consequent of the first inference]. Because the relative term would have one or another significate according to a change of the antecedent.[a] And if someone asks how this proposition, "an animal is", stands with the consequent, one answers that one ought not to conjoin that proposition in the form of a conjunction; but it suffices that any of these propositions is true. Whence these stand simultaneously: "you are a man", "you are white", yet from these propositions there is no conjunctive proposition. And if the opponent desires just one conjunctive proposition let it be this, "an animal is, and wood was destroyed and it is impossible for that to be", "that" referring always to "wood". This conjunctive proposition is true; therefore, the first part stands with the last part.

The eighth rule (1.7; 1.7.1; *1.7.2): "If some inference is solid and is known by you to be solid, and the antecedent is to be conceded by you, then its consequent also is to be conceded by you." From this one may infer that if the antecedent is to be conceded and the consequent is to be denied, the inference does not follow.

Against these rules one argues in this way. I posit that in this inference, "a man runs; therefore, a risible being runs", the antecedent is posited to you and admitted by you. The consequent, however, is rejected to you *(depositum)* and admitted by you.[b] With this posited, one argues in this way: This inference is solid and is known by you to be solid: "a man runs; therefore, a risible being runs", because you know that it is argued from one interchangeable proposition to the other. And the antecedent is to be conceded by you because it was posited to you and admitted by you. Yet the consequent is to be denied; because it was rejected to you *(depositum)* and admitted by you. Thus the rules are false.

For that reason one replies by admitting the case. And I concede that in this inference the antecedent is to be conceded and the consequent is to be denied according to the argument made. But I deny that this inference is solid and known by me to be solid. For from the two propositions conceded [198] the opposite of that proposition follows. For it follows: if the antecedent is to be conceded by you and the consequent is to be denied, this inference is not known by you to be solid.

The last [ninth] rule (1.8): "If there is some solid inference known by you to be solid; and the antecedent is known by you, its consequent also is known by you." From this [rule] it follows that if an antecedent is known by you and a consequent is not known, the inference is not known to be solid.

Against these rules one argues in this way. This inference is known by you to be solid. "This is unknown by you; therefore, this is unknown by you", – pointing to the consequent with both demonstratives. This antecedent is known by you and the consequent is not [known by you]. Therefore, the rule is false. The inference holds. The first part of the antecedent is proved; for you know that where it is argued from one proposition interchangeable with another, and that the opposite of the consequent is repugnant to the antecedent; therefore, you know that inference to be solid. The second part of the antecedent is proved. For the consequent is unknown by you and the antecedent you know to signify adequately that the very consequent is unknown by you. Therefore, the antecedent is known by you and the consequent is unknown. The inference is clear; for either the consequent is known by you or it is unknown [by you]. If it is unknown, I have made my point. If it is known and the same consequent signifies adequately that this is unknown by you – pointing to the same consequent – then that consequent is not known by you.

One responds that this inference does not follow: "this is unknown by you; therefore, this is unknown by you". Nor is it argued from one proposition interchangeable with another. Nor is the opposite of the consequent repugnant to the antecedent because the antecedent is not an insoluble. But the consequent is an insoluble signifying hypothetically in the way of a conjunction "that this is unknown by you and that this is known by you". But the contradictory of this proposition is not the proposition, "this is not known by you". Or that other proposition, "this is known by you". But rather, "it is not the case that this is known by you", *(non hoc est scitum a te)* signifying disjunctively "that this is known by you or that this is not known by you", which is true by reason of the second part.[a]

In the same way one may reply to the reason or to the inference stated. And he may reply to this proposition, "this is false; therefore, this is false" — pointing always to the consequent — by conceding such inferences. And I say that these propositions do not follow because the consequent is a false insoluble; and the antecedent is a true proposition which is not insoluble. [Thus, the rules are true.]

Section 3 — Objections to Section 3

Of the categorical rules the first is this (2.1): "From a lower-level term to [199] its corresponding higher-level term, affirmatively and without a distribution and without a sign of confusion impeding there is a solid inference."

Against this rule one argues in this way. This inference is not solid: "you are appearing as a donkey; therefore, you are a donkey of some kind". Yet this is argued through the rule; therefore, the rule is false. The inference holds with respect to the minor premise because "appearing" is a term on a lower-level than "of some kind". The major premise is clear because the antecedent is possible; and the consequent is impossible. For it is possible that you appear as a donkey; but it is not possible that you are a donkey of some kind: since it is not possible that you are a donkey.

One may respond that this is not argued according to the sense of the rule which is this. "From a lower-level term to its higher-level term by reason of the entire extreme without an impediment preceding there is a solid argument." However, the above case is not argued by reason of the entire extreme but by reason of a part only because "appearing as a donkey" is not a term on a lower level than "donkey of some kind" but rather [it is on a lower level than] "of some kind", as well as "appearing". For just as it follows, "you are appearing; therefore, you are of some kind", it follows: "you are appearing as a donkey; therefore, you are of some kind". Yet similar inferences in other areas do not follow: "you are the father of Socrates; therefore, you are something of Socrates' " *(tu es pater sortis; igitur, tu es aliquid sortis)*. "You are the lord of Plato; therefore, you are something of Plato's." *(Tu es dominus platonis; igitur, tu es aliquid platonis.)*

The second rule (2.2): "From a lower-level term to its corresponding higher-level term in a distributive way an argument does not follow."

Against this rule one argues in this way. This inference is solid; "no number two is; therefore, no number is". And this is argued according to the rule; therefore, the rule is false. The inference holds with respect to the major premise. Because the opposite of the consequent is repugnant to the antecedent. Namely, "no number two is; and some number is; there is not some number unless it is two or including two". In the same way one can argue "no true proposition is known; therefore, no proposition is known". The inference is most solid because the opposite of the consequent is repugnant to the antecedent; yet it is argued distributively from a lower-level term to its higher-level term. For "true proposition" is a term on a level lower than "proposition"; since every true proposition is a proposition but not conversely. Just as every two is a number but not conversely. For that reason one says that the rule does not [200] say that an inference never follows from a lower-level term to its higher-level term distributively. But rather that many times it does not follow formally; and never are the inferences stated above formal according to form *(formales de forma)*.[a] Yet they are formal because in any of these the opposite of the consequent is repugnant formally to the antecedent. But they are not solid according to form *(bonae de forma)* because [propositions] similar in form do not follow. For it does not follow: "no number three is; therefore, no number is". Nor does this follow: "no true proposition is seen or is understood; therefore, no proposition is seen or is understood". If, then, these inferences are solid, this is only owing to the matter. For the first is solid thanks to the matter because it is impossible for number to be and there not to be number two. The second holds similarly because of the matter or the terms because nothing is known unless it is true; nor is it possible that some false proposition be known.

The third rule (2.3): " From a lower-level term to its corresponding higher-level term with a negation placed after it and with the due mean there is a solid argument."

Against [this rule] one argues in this way. This inference does not follow: "knowing a proposition is not something", − pointing to this proposition, "a man is a donkey". And this proposition is some proposition; therefore, knowing some proposition is not something; however, it is argued according to the rule. Thus the rule is false. The inference holds with respect to the minor premise; and the major premise I prove, for the antecedent is true and the consequent is false. Therefore, this inference does not follow. That the antecedent is true is clear with regard to the second part and with regard to the first part as well because its contradictory is false, namely, "every knowing some proposition is some thing".

One may respond that this inference does not follow. Nor is it argued with the due mean because the subject of the first proposition ought to be the subject of the second proposition, arguing in this way: "knowing this is not something and knowing this proposition is; therefore, [knowing some proposition is not something]". And then I concede the inference; but the minor premise is denied. It is to be noted concerning this rule that if one should argue from a lower-level term to its higher-level term distributively with the negation placed after the term he would not argue according to the rule as is clear in this example. "Every man does not run; every man is an animal; therefore, every [201] animal does not run." For one understands the rule in this way: From a lower-level term to its higher-level term not distributed with a negation placed after it there is a solid inference.

The fourth rule (*2.4): "From a higher-level term to its corresponding lower-level term affirmatively and without a distribution an argument does not follow."

Against this rule the arguments made against the second rule set forth above apply, by arguing from the opposite of the consequent to the opposite of the antecedent.[a] E.g., "some number is; therefore, number two is". "Some proposition is known; therefore, a true proposition is known." But one argues especially in this way: This inference is solid: "you are an animal; therefore, you are a man". But this is argued from a higher-level term to its lower-level term without a distribution; therefore, the rule is false. The inference holds, and the antecedent is proved because this follows: "you are an animal; therefore, you are", by the rule "from a three-term statement to a two-term statement is a solid inference". Then, moreover, "you are; therefore, you are you". The inference is clear because the opposite of the consequent is formally repugnant to the antecedent. And, still more, "you are you; therefore, you are a man". The inference holds through the first rule, "from a lower-level term to its higher-level term, affirmatively and without an impediment; therefore, it follows from first to last: "you are an animal; therefore, you are a man".

On this account one replies as previously that any of these inferences is solid and formal; however, [they] do not argue against the rule implicitly asserting that no inference of this kind is solid in virtue of form *(bona de forma)*. For arguments similar in form do not follow: "Some number is; therefore, three is." "Some proposition is understood; therefore, a true proposition is understood." Nor does this follow: "This is an animal — pointing to a donkey; therefore, this is a man."

The fifth rule (*2.5): "From a higher-level term to its corresponding lower-level term distributively and affirmatively an inference does not follow unless with the due mean."

Against this rule one can argue. This inference is solid: "every animal runs; therefore, every man runs". Yet it is argued from a higher-level term to its lower-level term distributively and affirmatively without a due mean;

therefore, the rule is false. This inference holds with respect to the minor premise; the major premise I prove. The contradictory of the consequent is repugnant to the antecedent; therefore, the inference is solid. The antecedent is proved, for these propositions are repugnant: "every animal runs", "a man does not run". Because from these propositions the impossible follows, namely, "man is not an animal" in the fourth mood of the second figure.

One must reply [202] that this inference is solid *(bona)*; however, it is not formal *(formalis)* or of a form *(de forma)*. It is not formal because the opposite of the consequent is imaginable with the antecedent without a contradiction. Nor also is it of a form because some inference similar to it in form does not follow: e.g., "every animal runs; therefore, any man runs". But this is solid materially *(bona materialiter)* or thanks to the matter because it is impossible for man not to be [animal]; for it holds through this necessary mean, "every man is an animal". Similarly, this follows because of the matter: "every animal is; therefore, every man is", because the consequent is necessary. Also, it follows: "every man is a donkey; therefore, you are not a donkey", because the antecedent is impossible simply. For that reason there is no rule against which an argument does not proceed owing to the matter either because the antecedent is impossible or because the consequent is necessary or because of some other necessary and inevitable mean, as was pointed out in earlier inferences.[a]

The sixth rule (2.6): "From a higher-level term to its corresponding lower-level term with a negation placed before the term distributing the higher-level term there is a solid argument."

Against this rule one argues in this way. This inference does not follow: "non-contingently man is an animal; therefore, non-contingently you are an animal". Yet it is argued according to the rule; therefore, the rule is false. The inference holds and the first part of the antecedent is proved because the antecedent is true. The consequent is false, as is clear by assigning its contradictory; for this proposition is false: "Contingently, man is an animal". And this is true, "contingently, you are an animal". And the second part of the antecedent is proved for it is argued from a higher-level term to its lower-level term. And that it is distributed by a negation is manifest because with the negation removed "man" would not stand distributively; therefore, through its addition ["man"] stands distributively. The inference is clear through this rule. Whatever mobilizes the immobilized immobilizes the mobilized. *(Quicquid mobilitat immobilitatum immobilitat mobilitatum.)*

One may respond that a term stands mobily distributive when only one distributive sign precedes it, e.g., "every man is". It stands immobily distributive when two signs precede it. Of these two signs, one has the force of distributing; the other [has the force] of confounding in a merely confused way and immobily. For this reason I say that the above argument does not go against the sense of the rule which is this: From a higher-level term to its corresponding lower-level term with a negation placed before the term in a mobily distributive way there is a solid inference. [203] But in what was proposed above the higher-level term is not distributed mobily because of the impediment of this term, "contingently". Thus, it is not legitimate to descend as the argument clearly shows. For the same reason it does not follow: "you do not begin to be colored; therefore, you do not begin to be white". Because from an opposite, the opposite does not follow, as was pointed out in the chapter "On Begins" *(incipit).*[a] Yet it is argued in a distributive and negative way. If, then, someone asks what impedes it? I reply that the verb "begins" *(incipit)* impedes the inference because it immobilizes the very term which the preceding negation distributes.

Section 4 — Objections to Section 4

Against the rules of the fourth section [of Chapter III] we argued sufficiently in discussing the matter of insolubles.[b] More specially, however, I argue against the rules in the fourth section [of Chapter III].

The first was this (3.1): "From a universal proposition to its indefinite, particular or subalternate there is a solid inference."

Against this rule one argues in this way. This inference does not follow: "every being begins to be; therefore, some being begins to be". *(Incipit omne ens esse igitur incipit aliquod ens esse.)* However, it is argued according to the rule; therefore, the rule is false. This inference holds; and the first part of the antecedent is proved. For the antecedent is true; and the consequent is false. Therefore, the original inference does not follow. That the antecedent is true is proved: for "every being is and immediately before an instant which is present every being was not because a *present* instant never *was*. Therefore, every being begins to be". The inference is clear from exponents to what is exposited. That, however, the consequent is false is clear because now [in the present instant] something is and immediately before an instant which is present something was [and immediately after an instant which is present something will be]; therefore, it is false that *now* something begins to be or some being [begins] to be, which is the same thing. But the second part of the principal antecedent is argued. For this proposition is universal: "every being begins to be", because in that proposition a common term is the subject determined in a distributive way by a universal sign; and this proposition is its particular, "some being begins to be", because in that proposition a common term is the subject determined by a particular sign. Therefore, this is argued according to the rule.

One must reply briefly that this is not argued according to the rule. For neither the antecedent nor the consequent is of some quantity. And then with regard to the proof: "in this proposition, 'every being begins to be', a common term is the subject determined in a distributive way by a universal sign; thus, it is universal", I deny the inference. And if someone should appeal to the rule, I say that the rule is understood in the sense of "mobile distribution" [204] and not "immobile" [distribution] but in the case in question "being" is distributed immobily. For that reason the rule is glossed in this way: A universal proposition is that in which the subject is a common term distributed mobily by a universal sign and determined with respect to something existing [under this very term]. I claim this also with regard to what occurs before this proposition, "every man is an animal", in which the subject is a common term determined in a mobily distributive way by a universal sign. That sign [every] is not part of what goes before the term; it is part of the universal term itself. Concerning the particular [proposition], however, the criticism does not apply because to the rule one adds: "determined *alone* by a particular sign". But in the above case beyond the determined sign "being" there is this verb "begins"; and because of that, the subject stands in a merely confused way. For that reason there is this rule: "A particular proposition is that in which the subject is a common term determined alone by a particular sign [and determined] with respect to something existing [under this very term]"; this qualification applies to the above mentioned particular proposition.

The second rule was this one (*3.2): "From a particular or indefinite proposition to its universal proposition an inference does not follow."

Against this rule one argues in this way. This inference is solid: "an animal is a man: therefore, every animal is a man"; and consequently, any other [proposition] follows from an indefinite proposition to its universal. This inference holds; the antecedent is proved. This proposition, "an animal is a man", signifies every animal to be man; but every proposition signifies whatever follows from it; therefore, the inference is solid. This inference holds with regard to the minor premise because it is the rule. The major premise I prove: the subject of this proposition, "an animal is a man", signifies every animal and the predicate [signifies] man and the copula [signifies] to be; and the entire proposition signifies according to the composition of its terms; therefore, this proposition signifies every animal to be man. This inference is clear because in this way one investigates the significate of a proposition.

One may respond by denying the second inference. And with regard to the proof I concede that this proposition, "an animal is a man", signifies every animal to be a man [and that every proposition signifies whatever follows from it]. And with regard to the criticism, I deny this inference, "this proposition, 'an animal is a man', signifies every animal to be man. And every proposition signifies whatever follows from it; therefore, this inference is solid". Because then every proposition would signify whatever follows from it; it would not, however, signify any *proposition* which follows from it.[a] Indeed, this follows: "An animal is a man", signifies adequately [205] every animal to be man; therefore, this inference was solid. But the antecedent is denied because no proposition about the world signifies adequately every animal to be a man, unless it is a proposition such as, "every animal is a man".

The third rule (3.3): "From an affirmative universal proposition to all of its singulars, taken as much collectively as divisively accompanied by the due mean there is a solid argument, and conversely collectively."

Against this rule one argues in this way. This inference does not hold: "necessarily every man is an animal; and these are all men; therefore, necessarily this man is an animal and necessarily that man is an animal and thus of singulars". However, this is argued according to the rule; therefore, the rule is false. The inference holds with regard to the minor premise; and the major premise is clear through the exponents of this term "necessarily".[a] In the same way one argues that an argument does not hold from a universal proposition to its singular with a due mean, by arguing in this way: "necessarily every man is; but you are a man; therefore, necessarily you are". For the antecedent is true, and the consequent is false. From the same base also one argues that an inference does not hold from singulars sufficiently enumerated with a due mean to their universal proposition because this does not follow: "contingently this man is and contingently that man is, and thus of singulars and these are all men; therefore, contingently every man is". This is clear through the exponents of this term "contingently"[b]. And the antecedent is true while the consequent is false. And consequently, the inference does not follow.

For that reason briefly I respond and I say that in no way is this argued according to the rule because none of these propositions is of some quantity; namely, "necessarily every man is an animal", "contingently, every man is an animal", "necessarily this man is an animal", "contingently this man is an animal". The first two propositions are not universal because in them the subjects are distributed immobily. The other two are not singular propositions because their subjects are not common terms determined alone by a demonstrative pronoun; on the contrary, they are determined by another provable term, namely a modal term. In this sense —

one understands the definition of a singular proposition: A singular proposition is that in which the subject is a discrete term or a common term with a demonstrative pronoun – preceded by ([no] provable sign.[c] From this definition it follows that if a pronoun [206] plural in number is a discrete term this proposition is not singular: "all of these run", because the subject of this proposition is a common term preceded by a provable sign.

The fourth rule (3.4): "From a universal negative proposition to any of its singulars there is a solid argument."

Against this rule one argues in this way. This inference does not follow: "no chimera which runs is moved; therefore, this chimera which runs is not moved". Yet this is argued according to the rule; therefore, the rule is false. This inference holds with respect to the minor premise; and the major premise I prove. For the antecedent is true as is clear and the consequent is false; therefore, the inference does not follow. That the consequent is false is proved: for this proposition follows: "a chimera which runs is not moved; therefore, this chimera runs and that one is not moved". The inference holds because the relative term is resolved into "and" and "that" (masculine, feminine and neuter).[a] But the consequent is false because it is an affirmative conjunctive proposition whose first part is false; therefore, the antecedent is false, which was to be proved.

One may respond by conceding the stated inference. And when someone says that the antecedent is true and the consequent is false, I deny that the consequent is false because its contradictory is false, namely, "this chimera which runs is moved". And then for the proof of its falsity, I deny this inference, "this chimera which runs is not moved; therefore, this chimera runs and this [thing] is not moved". And then with regard to the rule of the relative terms, "which" (masculine, feminine and neuter), [which says that] they are resolved into a conjunction and a demonstrative pronoun, this rule is true in an affirmative proposition but not in a negative proposition. For that reason this follows: "this chimera which runs is moved; therefore, this chimera runs and the same is moved", because "which" in an affirmative proposition is resolved into a conjunction and a demonstrative pronoun. For that reason in a negative proposition, the contradictory ought to be resolved into a disjunction and a demonstrative pronoun – saying in this way, "this chimera runs or the same is not moved", because whatever signifies one of two contradictories conjunctively signifies the remaining one disjunctively.

It is to be noted concerning this rule that if the subject of a singular proposition stands for *(supponit pro)* some thing for which the subject of the universal does not stand *(non supponit pro)* in the arguing, then one does not argue from a universal proposition to its singular according to the rule; for this [referent] is not the singular of *that* universal proposition.

E.g., "no man (masculine) runs; therefore, this man (feminine) does not run", "no man (feminine) is some man; therefore, this man (masculine) is not some man".[b] The first singular is not the singular of this; "no man (masculine) does not run", but of that, [207] "no man (feminine) runs". The second singular is not the singular of this; "no man (masculine) is some man", but of that, "no man (feminine) is some man".

The fifth rule was this one (3.5): From a particular proposition to its corresponding indefinite affirmative as well as negative and conversely there is a solid inference."

Against this rule one argues in this way. This inference does not follow: "animal is a genus; therefore, something animal is a genus". However, it is argued according to the rule; therefore, the rule is false. The inference holds; the antecedent is proved, for the antecedent is true as is clear, and the consequent is false. Therefore, the inference does not follow. That the consequent is false is proved because its contradictory is true, namely, "no animal is a genus". For "neither this animal is a genus, nor that animal is a genus and thus of singulars; therefore, no animal is a genus". The second part is proved, namely that this is argued according to the rule. For "animal" stands in both cases [materially. This is proved for if in some of these ["animal"] should stand personally], this would be because of the limitation of this sing, "something" *(aliquod)*. But this sign "something" in those other propositions does not limit [the terms it modifies] to personal supposition; therefore, it does not limit [the terms it modifies] in this case either. This inference holds with regard to the major premise; the minor premise I prove. For in any of these, "some man is a species", "some man is a name", "man" stands *(supponit)* materially. Therefore, ["animal" stands materially] in this proposition, "some animal is a genus". The inference is clear; for just as "animal" is neuter in kind so "man" taken materially [is neuter in kind].[a]

One may respond that this is not argued according to the rule because in this proposition, "some animal is a genus", "animal" stands *(supponit)* personally because of the limitation of the particular sign. And if someone says in this proposition, "some man is a species", ["some"] does not limit ["man"] to personal supposition; therefore, it does not do so in the other proposition either, the argument does not follow. For "man" taken personally is not neuter in kind and "some" *(aliquod)* is neuter in kind. And for that reason added to ["man"] it cannot limit ["man"] to personal supposition; just as if someone added some sign of the same (i.e., neuter) kind. E.g., "some man is a species" *(aliquis homo est species)*. "Some man is not a name" *(aliqua homo non est nomen)*. But "animal" taken personally is neuter in kind; and for that reason a sign neuter in kind added to it limits it to personal supposition, by saying "some animal is a genus" *(aliquod animal est genus)*, or "no animal is a noun" *(nullum animal est no-*

men). If, therefore, someone asks, what is the indefinite proposition of this particular, "some animal is a genus" *(aliquod animal est genus)?*, one replies that it is this proposition, "living animal is a genus" *(animal vivens est genus).* And of this indefinite proposition, "animal [208] is a genus" *(animal est genus),* this is the particular proposition, "some 'animal' is a genus" *(aliquod ly animal est genus).* [a]

It is to be noted that it ought to be the case that terms stand *(supponat)* precisely for the same thing. Thus of that proposition, "a man runs", this is not the particular, "some man runs", but rather, "something which is man runs". And of this proposition, "some man runs" *(aliquis homo currit),* this is the indefinite proposition, "a masculine man runs". And the same thing applies in a corresponding way to negative propositions.

The sixth rule (3.6): "From a particular or indefinite proposition to all of its singulars taken disjunctively and with a due mean there is a solid argument."

Against this rule one argues in this way. This inference does not follow: "necessarily man is; and these are all men; therefore, necessarily this man is or necessarily that man is and thus of singulars". However, this is argued according to the rule; therefore, the rule is false. The inference holds with respect to the major premise because the antecedent is true and the consequent is false as is clear through its exponents. The minor premise is proved for this proposition, "necessarily man is", is a proposition and it is not a hypothetical proposition. Therefore, it is a categorical proposition and consequently of a quantity. If it is not universal, particular or singular, then it is an indefinite [proposition] whose singulars do not seem to be other than what was said.

For this reason one says that this is not argued according to the rule; for this proposition is not indefinite, "necessarily a man is an animal", since the subject is a common term mediated by a sign. Then with regard to the argument, "this proposition is categorical; therefore, it is of a quantity", I deny the inference. And if someone should advance this argument *ad hoc* proving that this inference is solid, I respond that I similarly asserted the opposite. [b] Wherefore, [the rule is true].

Section 5 – Objections to Section 5

In the fifth section of Chapter III certain rules were set down.

The first rule (4.1): "From an exclusive proposition to the corresponding universal with the terms transposed and conversely there is a solid inference."

Against this rule one argues in this way. This inference does not follow: "only a donkey is a man's; therefore, of any man there is a donkey". And this is argued according to the rule; therefore, the rule is false. The inference holds with regard to the minor premise; and the major premise is proved, by stating that there is no possession of a man except a donkey; however, there is some man who does not have a donkey in his possession. With this posited the consequent is false, as is clear; and the antecedent is true because a donkey is of a man, and nothing not-a-donkey is of a man; therefore, the major is proved. Secondly, one argues against the second part of the rule in this way. This inference [209] does not follow: "of any man there is a donkey; therefore, only a donkey is a man's". However, this is argued according to the rule; therefore, the rule is false. The inference holds with respect to the minor premise; and the major premise I prove by stating that whichever man has a donkey also has a horse. With this posited the antecedent is true according to the case and the consequent is false. For "something not-a-donkey is a man's; therefore, not only a donkey is a man's". This inference holds from one cause of truth to a proposition having that [truth].[a]

To the first criticism, one replies that it is not argued according to the rule because [the consequent] is not the universal of this exclusive but rather this is the universal, "every being of a man is a donkey". And the reason is that in this proposition, "only a donkey is a man's", ["man"] is not distributed for all men but only for men having something. To the second criticism, one says similarly that [the consequent] is not the exclusive of the universal; but rather this proposition: "only someone having a donkey is a man", because this proposition, "of every man there is a donkey", is equivalent to this, "of every man there is something having a donkey". Moreover, because some people have few words and are dense, in order to free themselves, say that these rules do not hold in the oblique cases.[b] For that reason, I argue first in the nominative case against the first rule. This inference does not follow: "only being necessarily is substance; therefore, every substance necessarily is being". Yet this is argued according to the first rule; thus, the first rule is false. The inference holds with regard to the minor premise and the major premise is proved, for the antecedent is true, and the consequent is false, as is clear through its exponents; therefore, the inference does not follow. Secondly, one argues against the second rule. This inference does not follow: "all of the Lord's apostles are twelve; therefore, only twelve are apostles of the Lord", – taking "all" collectively. Therefore, the rule is false. This inference holds, and the antecedent is proved. For the antecedent is true, as is supposed; and the consequent is false because its second exponent is false, namely, "no non-twelve are apostles of the Lord". Because Peter and Paul are apostles of the Lord; and Peter and Paul are some ones non-twelve; therefore, some ones non-twelve are apostles of the Lord.

To the first, one replies that [the above-mentioned consequent] is not the universal of that exclusive proposition; but rather this proposition, "every being necessarily substance is being"; because just as in an exclusive proposition "necessarily" does not determine this term "being" but only "substance" so also in a universal proposition that same thing applies. To the second criticism one replies that "all" is taken collectively: but an exclusive proposition is not expounded through [210] infinitated negation but rather through a sign of plurality. E.g. "twelve are the Lord's apostles, and no more than twelve are apostles of the Lord".[a] And this proposition is true; and the exclusive proposition similarly [is true]. When, however, "all" is taken divisively, and then to the same term corresponds an exclusive expression exponible through an infinitated negation, as much the universal as the exclusive proposition would be impossible because a contradiction [would be among] its exponents.

The second rule (4.2): "From a negative exceptive proposition to its corresponding affirmative exclusive proposition there is a solid inference."[b]

Against this rule one argues in this way. This inference does not follow: "no man except Socrates runs; therefore, only Socrates runs". And this is argued by the rule; therefore, the rule is false. This inference holds with respect to the minor premise because it does not seem to be other than an exceptive proposition. The major premise is proved because in a possible case posited, the antecedent is true, and the consequent is false. This is proved; for I posit that Socrates runs and no other masculine [being runs]; however, many women [run]. With this posited, the antecedent is true through its exponents, and the consequent is false because some non-Socrates runs; therefore, it is not the case that only Socrates runs.

One may respond that this exclusive proposition does not correspond to that exceptive proposition; but rather this proposition, "only Socrates is some man running", according to what was stated concerning the proofs of terms in the section on exceptive propositions where this rule was declared.[c]

The third rule was this one (4.3): "From a lower-level term to its corresponding higher-level term on the part of the subject with an exclusive expression added there is a solid inference."

Against this rule one argues in this way. This inference is not solid; "only substance is not accident; therefore, only something is not accident". However, this is argued according to the rule; therefore, the rule is false. This inference holds with regard to the second part of the antecedent and the first part of the antecedent is proved; for the antecedent is true and the consequent is false; therefore, the inference does not follow. That the antecedent is true is proved because substance is not accident; yet any non-substance is accident; therefore, only substance is not accident. That the consequent is false is clear because the second exponent is impossible, namely, "anything not something *(non aliqua)* is accident", because the first exponent of this is impossible: namely, "something not something is accident", as is very clear through its resolvents. For that reason one replies that the criticism is not argued by the rule. Nor is it argued from a lower-level term to its higher-level term because originally it was declared that a transcendent term is neither [211] higher than nor lower than something else.[a] For that reason it is not in a category unless improperly by taking "higher" in the sense of "prior" or "more common" − in a way not assumed in the rule under attack. In another way, however, one may reply, and more nicely, that the rule is understood affirmatively and not negatively. Whence this does not follow; "only body is not indivisible; therefore, only substance is not indivisible". The antecedent, however, is true because body is not indivisible and any non-body is indivisible. But the consequent is false because according to its exponent [it is] false; namely, "any non-substance is indivisible", for whiteness on the wall is non-substance; yet it is not indivisible. For it is extended to the limit of the wall.

The fourth rule was this one (*4.4): "From a lower-level term to its corresponding higher-level term on the part of the predicate with an exclusive expression added on the part of the subject there is not a solid inference; but conversely and with a due mean [there is a solid inference]."

Against this rule one argues. Universally this follows: "Something only man runs; therefore, something only man is moved." "Something only Socrates is man; therefore, something only Socrates is animal", for the opposite of the consequent does not stand with the antecedent. This is argued according to the rule; therefore, the rule is false. This inference holds with regard to the minor premise because an exclusive expression is added into this proposition. And it is added neither to the copula nor to the predicate; therefore, it is added to the subject. Secondly, I argue that conversely and with a due mean there is not a solid argument. For this does not follow: "only man is risible; Antichrist is risible; therefore, only man is Antichrist". Yet this is argued according to the rule; therefore, the rule is false. This inference holds with regard to the minor premise; and the major premise I prove. For the antecedent is true; and the consequent is false; therefore, the inference does not follow. That, however, the consequent is false is manifest; but the antecedent is proved. For "every risible [being] is a man; therefore, only man is risible". This inference holds from a universal proposition to its corresponding exclusive proposition and thus the first part is true. The second part is proved:

for Antichrist can laugh; therefore, Antichrist is risible. This inference is clear according to the rule, "from one proposition interchangeable with another there is a solid inference".

To the first reason I say that an exclusive expression is not added to the subject alone but also to the predicate because from [this expression] and another term there is one subject. But it is added to the subject in saying, "only man runs", because "man" is the subject and it is not part of the subject. This inference, therefore, is denied: "an exclusive expression is posited in that proposition, and it is added neither to the [212] copula nor to the predicate; thus, it is added to the subject". It suffices, however, that it is added to a part of the subject or the predicate.

To the second reason one says that "risible" is taken in two senses, namely, ampliatively and non-ampliatively.[a] In the first way it is not interchanged with "man"; but in the second way [it is interchanged with "man"]. Therefore, taking "risible" in the first way as much in the minor premise as in the major premise, the inference is denied. For in the antecedent "man" as much as "Antichrist" is ampliated; though it is not so in the consequent. For that reason it well follows: "therefore, only man is able to be Antichrist". If, however, "risible" is taken in the second way, I concede the major premise to which corresponds a universal expression; and I deny the minor premise. And then to the criticism, "Antichrist is able to laugh; therefore, Antichrist is risible", this argument does not follow. Nor is it argued from one proposition interchangeable with another because it was said that "risible" is not taken ampliatively.

I do not argue against the other three rules (*4.5; 4.6; *4.7) because they also are inferred from the previous ones.

Section 6 – Objections to Section 6

Concerning pertinent and non-pertinent terms the first rule (5.1) was this: "From the affirmation of one disparate term to the negation of another disparate term there is a solid argument."

Against this rule one argues in this way. This inference does not follow: "Brunellus is a donkey; therefore, Brunellus is not risible". Yet this is argued according to the rule; thus, the rule is false. The inference holds with regard to the minor premise because "donkey" and "risible" are disparate terms just as "man" and "donkey" are [disparate terms]. The major premise is clear; for the antecedent is true. And it is clear as well that the consequent is false. This is proved, and I make this inference; "Brunellus is human *(hominis)*; therefore, Brunellus is risible". The inference holds from one term interchangeable with another. And the ante-

306

cedent is true, as I take it; therefore, the consequent is true also. But this consequent is the contradictory of the first consequent; therefore, the first consequent is false, which was to be proved.

One replies by doubting this inference, "Brunellus is a donkey; therefore, Brunellus is not risible *(risibilis)*", because one doubts how the term "risible" is taken — whether in the nominative or in the genitive case. If it is taken in the first way, the inference is conceded and also the consequent. Then with respect to the proof I deny the inference, "Brunellus is human *(hominis)*; therefore, Brunellus is risible", because "man" and "risible" are converted *(ly homo et ly risible convertantur)* or "human" and "risible" are converted *(hominis et risibilis)* in the oblique case. This is not so in the objection in question; for they are taken difformly: namely, one is taken in the nominative and the other in an oblique case. If, however, "risible" is taken [213] in the genitive case, I deny that inference, "Brunellus is a donkey; therefore, Brunellus is not risible", because it is not argued according to the rule. For "donkey" and "risible" *(asinus et risibile)* are disparate terms; but donkey and risible *(asinus et risibilis)* in the oblique case are not [disparate terms]. For that reason I concede these two propositions to stand at the same time: "any donkey is risible", "no donkey is risible", — taking "risible" in the first proposition in the genitive case and in the second in the nominative case. Nor are they contraries or opposites of each other.

The second rule was this one (5.2): "Whenever there is a pair of propositions whose subjects and predicates are interchangeable, the propositions remaining the same in denomination, there is a solid inference from one to the other."[a]

Against this rule one argues in this way: this inference does not follow, "any man is one man; therefore, every man is one man". Yet it is argued according to the rule; therefore, the rule is false. The inference holds with respect to the minor premise because the predicates and the subjects are converted remaining the same in denomination. The first part of the antecedent is proved; for that the antecedent is true is clear through its exponents. And the consequent is false because something is a man which is not one man.

One may respond that the subjects are not converted; although they are similar. For this does not follow: " 'man' and 'man' are converted; therefore, the subjects are converted". Because "man" and "man" are converted just as "man" and "man" are not converted, for that reason the subjects of these propositions are not converted: "man runs", and "man is a species", the fact that they are similar notwithstanding. Because "man" in the first stands personally; and "man" in the second stands materially. So that in what was proposed the subjects of these propositions are not converted: "any man is one man", *(quilibet homo est unus homo)*, "every man is one man" *(omnis homo est unus homo)*, because they are similar and stand *(supponant)* personally; they do not stand, however, precisely for the same thing, but in the first for the masculine sex alone and in the second for either sex. But "man" and "man" are converted when they stand *(supponunt)* in the same way and precisely for the same thing, e.g. "every man is rational", "every man is risible". One must take "man" and "risible" in the same way whenever they are converted or whenever they are not converted.

The third rule was this one (5.3): "From one interchangeable proposition to another there is a solid inference."

Against this rule one argues. This inference does not follow: "Socrates you know to be a man; therefore, Socrates you know [214] to be risible". Yet it is argued according to the rule; therefore, the rule is false. The inference holds with regard to the minor premise because "man" and "risible" are interchanged. The major premise is proved for in the possible case posited the antecedent is true, and the consequent is false; therefore, the inference does not follow. I prove the antecedent. I posit that you know Socrates to be a man. You do not know, however, what is the proper passion of a man; but you believe that risible is the proper passion of a donkey. With this posited the antecedent is true; and the consequent is false because you believe firmly Socrates not to be risible just as you believe the same one [Socrates] not to be a donkey. Therefore, Socrates you do not know to be risible.

For that reason one says that from one convertible proposition to another, by reason of its total extreme, there is a solid argument. By reason, however, of a part [of its extreme] the inference fails, just as it does in what was proposed. Because "man" and "risible" are not the predicates but rather these: "knowing to be man" and "knowing to be risible" which in turn are not interchanged. The example is clear in the case of another [kind of] term; for the contradictory of a contradictory and that contradictory are in turn interchanged because if a contradictory is true or false then the contradictory of a contradictory is of this kind. Yet this does not follow: "the contradictory of A is true; therefore, the contradictory of the contradictory of A is true", − posited that every A is this proposition, "a man is a donkey". For the antecedent is true, and the consequent is false. If, however, the contradictory of the contradictory of A is true, every A is the contradictory of the contradictory of A; therefore, A is true, which is false. The defect, therefore, stands in this: because it is not argued by reason of the total extreme but by reason of a part [of the extreme]. For "the contradictory" and "the contradictory of the contradictory" are interchanged; but "the contradictory of A" and "the contradictory of the contradictory of A" [are not interchanged].

The fourth rule was this one (5.4): "From one of two correlatives to the other in two-termed propositions there is a solid argument."

Against this one can argue. This inference does not follow: "a father is; therefore, a son is". Yet it is argued according to the rule; thus, the rule is false. The inference holds with respect to the minor premise; and the major premise I prove. For in a possible case posited the antecedent is true; and the consequent is false. Therefore, the inference does not follow. The antecedent is proved: For given that [215] every father has a daughter and does not have a son; then, the antecedent is true and the consequent is false.

It is to be said, [in reply] that this criticism is not argued according to the rule because "father" and "son" are not correlatives. Nor are "mother" and "daughter" correlatives. For one may be a father and not have a son just as one may be a mother and not have a daughter. But these disjunctives are correlatives: "father or mother", "son or daughter", because it follows: "a father or a mother is; therefore, a son or a daughter is", and conversely.

The fifth rule (5.5): "From a privative term to an infinite term there is a solid inference [but not conversely]."

Against this rule one argues. This inference does not follow: "A was infinite; therefore A was not finite". Yet this is argued according to the rule; therefore, the rule is false. The inference holds with respect to the minor premise; and I prove the major premise. I posit that A was the whole infinite past time terminated at the first instant of the past hour. With this posited, A was infinite because of the earlier part [of the statement] and A was finite because of the later part [of the statement]. Therefore, it is false that it was not-finite because from this consequent it follows that it was not finite.

In the same way one argues, "a line is indivisible; therefore, a line is not divisible". This does not follow because the antecedent is true, as is clear, because it has neither width nor depth. Yet the consequent is false because a line is divisible according to its length.

One must reply that "infinite" and "indivisible" are not privative terms because they are not called "defective", as is clear. For they meet in God. Thus, it is no wonder if none of those inferences follows because none argues according to the rule. But one argues according to the rule in this way: "you are unjust; therefore, you are not just". "Socrates is blind; therefore, Socrates is not seeing", because "blind" and "unjust" are privative terms — calling it a defect in those in whom they are found.

The sixth rule (5.6): "From an affirmative with a privative or infinite predicate to a negative there is a solid inference [but not conversely]."

Against this rule one argues in this way. This inference does not follow: "you were not-white; therefore, you were not white". Yet it is argued according to the rule; therefore, the rule is false. The inference holds with respect to the minor premise and the major premise [216] I prove. For in a possible case posited the antecedent is true, and the consequent is false. [Therefore, the inference does not follow.] The antecedent is proved, and I posit that yesterday you were white and today black. With this posited, the antecedent is true because whenever you were black you were not white. And the consequent is false because its contradictory was posited in the case.

One may respond that one does not solidly infer *(non bene infertur)* a negative proposition from a finite predicate. One ought to argue in this way: "you were not-white; therefore, *at some time* you were not white". "You will be not-running; therefore, *at some time* you will not be running."

It is to be noted, however, that in the case of an oblique term, the rule does not hold. For that reason this does not follow: "a donkey is not-Socrates'; therefore, a donkey is not Socrates' " — posited that every donkey belongs as much to Socrates as it does to Plato. Then the antecedent is true, and the consequent is false. Similarly, this does not follow: "Socrates is not-donkey; therefore, Socrates is not a donkey".

The seventh rule was this one (5.7): "From a negative proposition with a finite predicate to an affirmative proposition with an infinite predicate, with the due mean, there is a solid inference [and conversely]."

Against this rule one argues in this way: This inference does not follow: "*A* whose contradictory is false is not-true, and *A* is; therefore, *A* whose contradictory is false is true". Yet this is argued according to the rule; therefore, the rule is false. The inference holds with regard to the minor premise and the major premise I prove, given that *A* is this proposition, "man is a donkey". The antecedent is true, and the consequent is false; therefore, the inference does not follow. That the antecedent is true is proved. The second part is true, as is clear. The first part is true also because its contradictory is false, namely, "*A* whose contradictory is false is true". That, however, the consequent is false is argued in this way. I make to you this inference, "*A* whose contradictory is false is not-true; therefore, *A* whose contradictory is false is false". The inference holds because "false" and "not-true" are interchanged. The consequent is impossible; therefore, the antecedent is impossible as well.

One may respond by conceding the rule and the inference made against it. And I deny that the consequent is false. And then with respect to the criticism "*A* whose contradictory is false is not-true; therefore, *A* whose contradictory is false is false", I deny the inference. And when one says "not-true" and "false" are interchanged, I concede the point. [But when he says that this inference is solid, I deny the criticism because it is not argued from [217] one proposition interchangeable with another by reason of the entire extreme but only by reason of part [of the extreme]. For "not-true" and "false" are interchanged; however, "not-true whose contradictory is false" and "false whose contradictory is false", are not interchanged.

It is to be noted concerning "the due mean" that this does not follow: "of Socrates there is not a donkey; and Socrates is; therefore, of Socrates there is a non-donkey". Because the antecedent is true, and the consequent is false — given that Socrates has nothing. Nor is this argued according to the rule because the due mean is not the one cited but rather this: "Socrates is someone". And it does not follow: "a donkey is not Socrates'; and a donkey is; therefore, a donkey is not-Socrates' ", — given that no donkey is owned by anyone. Then the antecedent is true, and the consequent is false. It is not, however, argued according to the rule because the due mean is not the one cited but rather, "a donkey is of someone" which is [repugnant to the case].

Section 7 — Objections to Section 7

In the seventh Section [of Chapter III] the first rule was this one (6.1): "From all of the exponents of a proposition — taken simultaneously — to the exponible proposition there is a solid inference."

Against this rule one argues in this way. This inference does not follow: "some sort of man runs; and there is not some sort of man unless the sort that runs; therefore, any sort of man runs". Yet this is argued according to the rule; therefore, the rule is false. The inference holds, and the first part of the antecedent is proved. I posit that there are not in the world any men save white ones of which some run and some sit. With this posited, the consequent is false, as is clear; yet the antecedent is true, because some sort of man runs; and there is not any sort of man other than such a sort itself as: it runs. In the same way one argues into another term: "some size of man runs; and there is not any size of man unless that size runs; therefore, any size of man runs". For posited that any man is three feet tall; and that some run and some sit, then the antecedent is true and the consequent is false. For a relative of accident is not required to stand for that for which its antecedent [stands] *(non necessitatur supponere pro illo pro quo suus antecedens)*.

For that reason one says that none of these inferences follows: because none is argued according to the rule since a nominative *(recte)* is not assigned in any of them in the second exponent. For of this universal proposition, "any sort of man runs" *(qualislibet homo currit)*, the second exponent is this proposition, "nothing is some sort of man unless that runs" *(nihil est aliqualis homo quin illud currat)*. Of this proposition, "any size of man runs" *(quantuslibet homo currit)*, the second exponent is this proposition, "there is not [218] any size of man unless that runs" *(nulla est aliquantus homo quin illud currat)*.

The second rule was this one (6.2): "From every exponible proposition to each of its exponents there is a solid inference [but not conversely except in virtue of matter]."

Against this rule one argues in this way. This inference does not follow: "you begin to be white; therefore, you are white; and immediately before an instant which is present you were not white". Yet it is argued according to the rule; therefore, the rule is false. The inference holds with respect to the minor premise because 'begins' is expounded in one way through the positing of the present and the removal of the past; therefore, the consequent is one of its exponents. The major premise I prove because in a possible case posited the antecedent is true and the consequent is false; therefore, the inference does not follow. The antecedent I prove; and I posit that you are not white; but immediately after the instant which is present you will be white. With this posited, it follows that you begin to be white, insofar as it is from its exponents. Yet you are not white according to the case, which is opposed to the first part of the consequent.

One may respond that this inference does not follow: "you begin to be white; therefore, you are white, and immediately before an instant which is present you were not white". Nor is this argued from an exponible proposition to some of its exponents. Secondly, one says that these verbs "begins" and "ceases" are not expounded properly: rather they have conjunctive causes of truth one of whose parts is an affirmative of the present [time] and the other a negative of past [time]. One says, moreover, that there is a conjunctive cause of truth one of whose parts is a negative [proposition] of the present and the second of whose parts is an affirmative [proposition] of the future. These are called causes of truth and from any of those conjunctive propositions to a proposition of inception *(propositionem inceptionis)* there is a solid argument; conversely, however, [the argument] does not follow — just as was asserted in the same part [Chapter III, Section 7] of this treatise.[a] In the same way one must speak concerning "ceases". And if at any time I said that these verbs ought to be expounded I was not using "exposition" in the proper sense: rather I meant it according to the common understanding, i.e. that intended in any proof of terms.[b] For that reason in this case one argues very strictly; this inference does not follow: "only not every man is an animal; therefore, not every man is an animal". Yet this is argued according to the rule; therefore the rule is false. The first part of the antecedent is proved. For the antecedent is true, and the consequent is false. Therefore, this inference does not follow. That the consequent is false is manifest. And the antecedent is proved in this way: "every animal is not every man; therefore, only not every man is an animal". This inference holds [219] from a universal affirmative proposition to its corresponding exclusive proposition. The antecedent is true, as is clear; therefore, the consequent is true also. And the second part of the antecedent is proved; for the first exponent of an exclusive proposition is of its first part *(eius praejacens)*. But "not every man is an animal" is the first part of that exclusive proposition because it is that which remains minus the exclusive expression; therefore, it is its exponent — which was to be proved.

One may respond by conceding the inference and by denying the antecedent. And with regard to the criticism I deny the inference because this proposition is not the corresponding exclusive of that universal proposition; but rather this, "only a being not every man is an animal", which is true *(tantum ens non omnis homo est animal, que est vera)*. And if someone asks what is the universal proposition of that exclusive, "only a being not every man is an animal", one answers that it does not have a universal proposition because it is a negative exclusive proposition.

The third rule was this one (6.3): "From any contradictory of an exponent the contradictory of the expounded proposition follows [but not conversely]."

Against this rule one argues in this way. This inference does not follow: "you are an animal; therefore, you do not differ from an animal". And this is argued according to the rule; therefore, the rule is false. This inference holds with respect to the minor premise, and the major premise I prove. The antecedent is true, as is clear; and the consequent is false — since its contradictory is true, namely, "you differ from an animal". This is proved in this way: "you differ from an animal which is a donkey; therefore, you differ from an animal and that is a donkey". The inference holds through the resolution of a relative term into a conjunctive and a demonstrative pronoun. And the antecedent is true, as is clear through its exponents; therefore, the consequent is clear also: "you differ from an animal; and that is a donkey; therefore, you differ from an animal". The inference holds from a conjunctive proposition to either of its parts, and the antecedent is true, as was proved; therefore, the consequent is true, which was to be proved.

One may respond briefly by conceding the first inference and by denying the proposition, "you differ from an animal". Then with regard to the proof, "you differ from an animal, which is a donkey; therefore, you differ from an animal, and that is a donkey", the inference is denied. Nor is a relative term governed by a confused term always resoluble in this way: for these do not follow: "you are every man who is in house A; therefore, you are every man, and that is in house A". Again, "every man who runs is moved; therefore, every man is moved and that runs", and thus of countless others. However, a relative term existing in a proposition without a sign would have to be resolved in this way: for it follows: "Socrates who runs is moved; therefore, Socrates is moved and this [220] runs". "Antichrist will be a man who is; therefore, Antichrist will be a man and that is."

The fourth rule was this one (6.4): "From resoluble propositions to a resolvent there is a solid inference [but not conversely]."

Against this rule one argues in this way: This inference does not follow: "this is not a man — pointing to a donkey; yet this is an animal if it is risible; therefore an animal, if it is risible, is not a man". However, this is argued according to the rule; therefore, the rule is false. This inference holds with regard to the minor premise; and the major premise I prove. For the antecedent is true, as is clear; and that the consequent is false is proved because its contradictory is true, namely, "every animal, if it is risible, is a man", as is clear through its exponents, i.e. "some animal, if it is risible, is a man; and there is no animal unless it, if it is risible, is a man".

One says that the inference is solid, and the consequent is true just as the antecedent is true; and when one says that its contradictory is true, namely, "every animal, if it is risible, is a man", I say that the second exponent is not sufficiently analyzed *(assignata)*. For this is the second exponent, "nothing is an animal, if it is risible, unless it is a man", which is false because its contradictory is true, namely, "something is an animal which, if it is risible, is not a man". This is proved: "this is not a man — pointing to a donkey — yet this is something animal, if it is risible and this is some thing; therefore, something is an animal which, if it is risible, is not a man".

The fifth rule was this one (6.5): "From officiating propositions to their officiates there is a solid inference [but not conversely]."

Against this rule one argues in this way. This inference does not follow: "this proposition is necessary 'an animal is a man', which adequately signifies animal to be man: therefore, for an animal to be a man is necessary". However, this is argued according to the rule; therefore, the rule is false. This inference holds with regard to the second part of the antecedent; the first part I prove because the antecedent is true, and the consequent is false. That the antecedent is true is clear. That the consequent is false is proved. "For an animal to be a man is impossible; therefore, it is false that for an animal to be a man is necessary." This inference is solid; and the antecedent is proved. "For this to be man is impossible — pointing to a donkey; yet this is an animal: therefore, for an animal to be a man is impossible." The inference holds from a lower-level term to its corresponding higher-level term in an affirmative proposition without an impediment.

One may respond by conceding the first inference as well as its antecedent and the consequent and by denying that "for an animal to be a man is impossible". And with regard to the proof, I deny the inference and then with regard to that rule, I respond in two ways: first, that it is not argued by reason of the entire extreme; second, that one understands the rule in a way which argues [221] with an impediment, for "impossible" immobilizes this term "animal". Moreover, the rules of inference say that from a lower-level term to its immobilized higher-level term, an inference is not solid. If, however, one desires to strengthen that argument by saying that it is argued from resolvents to a resoluble [proposition], I deny this claim because this proposition "for an animal to be a man is impossible", is not a resoluble proposition. But it is provable officiably as was clear in the section on the proofs of terms.[a]

The sixth rule was this one (6.6): "From a description to the described there is a solid inference and conversely."

Against this rule one argues in this way. This inference does not follow: "you understand man; therefore, you understand something under the aspect of man" *(sub ratione qua homo)*. This inference holds with respect to the minor premise; and the major premise is proved. I posit that you have no concept *(intellectionem)* except the simple concept *(intellectionem)* of man. With this posited, you understand man; yet you do not understand something under the aspect of man. For every concept *(ratio)* of man is a definition; but you do not understand something under a definition because you have no definition in your mind, as I set down in the above case. Therefore, you do not understand something under the aspect of man.[b]

One must say that the first inference is solid; its antecedent and consequent are conceded in this case. And when one argues, "every concept *(ratio)* of man is a definition of that very thing", I deny the point. For the concept "of man" *(ratio hominis)* is a denomination of man himself; just as from humanity *(ab humanitatae)* man *(homo)* is named. For that reason humanity is said to be the concept *(ratio)* of that very thing; and this is the concept *(ratio)* beneath which you understand this thing — pointing to a man.

The seventh rule was this one (*6.7): "From a proposition in the composite sense to one in the divided sense and conversely there is not a solid inference."

Against this rule one argues in this way. This inference is solid: "you are able to run; therefore, it is possible for you to run", and conversely. "It is possible for Antichrist to be; therefore, Antichrist is able to be", and conversely.

One replies that in the case of simple and discrete terms, without the impediment of some sign, there is a solid inference; but with the limitation of a sign the inference does not follow. E.g., "for every animal to be is necessary; therefore, every animal necessarily is to be". "Your soul necessarily is; therefore, necessarily, your soul is." [222] "White is able to be black; therefore, it is possible for white to be black."

Against this reply one argues that the last inference follows; for this follows: "white is able to be black; therefore, white is something-able *(potens)* to be black". The inference is clear by resolving this verb "is able" into "I am", "you are", "it is", and its participles and then beyond, "white is something-able *(potens)* to be black; therefore, a white is a black being". The inference is clear from one proposition interchangeable with another because "something-able to be" *(potens esse)* and "a being" *(ens)* are interchanged; because every thing which can be is a being; therefore, everything-able to be is a being *(nam omne quod potest esse est ens; igitur omne potens esse est ens)*. This inference is clear, and the antecedent is similarly clear through its exponents. Moreover, "a white is a black being; and furthermore, white is black; therefore, it is possible for white to be black". The inference is clear because any proposition of the present implies a proposition of the possible in the composite sense. Therefore, from the first to the last: "white is able to be black; therefore, it is possible for white to be black".

One replies briefly that this inference does not follow: "white is something-able to be black *(potens esse nigrum)*; therefore, a white is a black being *(ens nigrum)*". And with regard to the proof where he argues from one proposition interchangeable with another, I deny the point. And when he says "something-able to be" *(potens esse)* and "a being" *(ens)* are interchanged, I concede the point. And also, "something-able to be" taken nominally is interchanged with "a being"; but taken participially it is not interchanged with that [term]. Because this does not follow: "Antichrist is something-able to be; therefore, Antichrist is a being". Yet in what was proposed "something-able to be" is taken participially, and for that reason the criticism is ineffective.

The eighth rule was this one (6.8): "From one cause of truth to a proposition having that cause of truth there is a solid inference [but not conversely]."

Against this rule one argues in this way. This inference does not follow: "proposition *A* is true; and immediately before an instant which is present it was not true; therefore, proposition *A* begins to be true". However, this

316

is argued according to the rule; therefore, the rule is false. This inference holds; and the antecedent is proved. I posit that proposition A in the first proportional part of the past hour terminating at this present instant was true, in the second part false and in the third part [223] true, and so forth in alternating succession through all proportional parts of the past hour. For that reason in every odd-numbered part it was true; and in every even-numbered part it was false, and thus now in the present instant it is true. And in this way continuously with this posited it will be the case that the antecedent is true, and the consequent is false. Therefore, the inference does not follow. That the antecedent is true is clear because now A is true through what is posited; and immediately before this [instant which is present] it was false; and whenever it was false it was not true; therefore, immediately before this [instant which is present] it was not true. However, that immediately before an instant which is present A was false I prove. For immediately before an instant which is present there was some even-numbered part; but whenever there was some even-numbered part A was false; therefore, immediately before an instant which is present A was false. That, however, the principal consequent is false is argued because now A is true, and immediately before an instant which is present A was true; because immediately before an instant which is present there was some odd-numbered part; therefore, [proposition] A does not begin to be true.

One says briefly that A does not begin to be true. Then with regard to the criticism, I deny the inference made first. Nor is it argued according to the rule for that is not a cause of truth; but rather this, "A is true, and immediately before an instant which is present A was not true". And this is false because it is contradictory. Whence it is conceded that immediately before an instant which is present [A was true and immediately before an instant which is present] A was not true. [The latter part, viz., "immediately before an instant which is present A was not true",] is not conceded with the former part, viz., "immediately before an instant which is present A was true", because these are contradictories.

The ninth rule was this one (6.9): "From an active proposition to its passive proposition and conversely there is a solid inference."

Against this rule one argues in this way. This inference does not follow: "I promise you a dime; therefore, a dime is promised to you be me".[a] However, it is argued according to the rule; therefore, the rule is false. The inference holds with regard to the minor premise; the major premise I prove: For in the possible case posited the antecedent is true; and the consequent is false; therefore, the inference does not follow. The antecedent is proved: and I posit that to you a dime is promised in a general way *(in confuso)*; however, promising no single dime to you. With this posited, the antecedent is true; and the consequent is false according to the case; [therefore, the rule is false]. Similarly, this does not follow: "Any man sees some man; therefore, some man is seen by any man; for it is posited that any man sees precisely himself". The antecedent is true, [224] and the consequent is false.

One may respond that none of these inferences is solid. Nor are they argued according to the rule because terms ought always to stand *(suppone-re)* in the same way. But in the active-voiced proposition "dime" and "man" stand *(suppon [unt])* in a merely confused way, and in the passive-voiced proposition [they stand] in a determinate way. For that reason one ought not to analyze the passives of these propositions in this way: "I promise you a dime", corresponds to "by me to you is promised some dime", and "any man sees some man", corresponds to this passive proposition, "some man is seen by any man".[a]

The tenth rule was this one (6.10): "From a three-termed proposition to a two-termed affirmative proposition without a distracting term there is a solid inference."

Against this rule one argues. This inference does not follow: "only man is risible; therefore, only man is". However, it is argued according to the rule because it is an affirmative proposition, and it is without a distracting term; therefore, the rule is false. This inference holds with regard to the minor premise, on the supposition that "risible" is not an ampliative term. The first part of the antecedent is manifest; since the antecedent is true; and the consequent is false, as is known to anyone.

For that reason one may respond also that the rule does not hold in the case of a first order exclusive; and the reason is that it is argued implicitly from a lower-level term to its corresponding higher-level term distributively. For when someone says, "only man is", "is" includes the participle "being" standing in a confused way and distributively because of the exclusive expression.

Against this gloss one also argues; for this does not follow: "chimera is a term; therefore, a chimera is". Yet it is argued affirmatively, and it is without a distracting term and without an exclusive expression.

One replies that this is not a two-termed proposition; but rather this: " 'chimera' is", for terms ought to stand in the same way.[b]

Section 8 – Objections to Section 8

The eighth and last section of Chapter III sets forth some rules of hypotheticals.

The first was this one (7.1): "From an affirmative conjunction to either of its principal parts there is a solid inference [but not conversely unless owing to the matter]."

Against this rule one argues. This inference does not follow: "as far as Socrates sees, to that extent Plato sees; therefore, only Plato sees" *(aliquantum videt Sortes et tantum Plato videt; igitur, tantum Plato videt)*. And this is argued according to the rule; therefore, the rule is false. This inference holds with respect to the minor premise; and the major premise is proved. In a possible case posited the antecedent is true, and the consequent is false; therefore, the inference does not follow. The antecedent is proved and I posit [225] that Socrates as much as Plato sees [a distance of] one foot. With this posited, the antecedent is true. For Socrates sees [one] foot and Plato sees [one] foot; therefore, as far as Socrates sees, to that extent Plato sees. But that the conclusion ["only Plato sees"] is false is clear since its second exponent is false, namely, "nothing non-Plato sees". Indeed, it is contrary to the case for Socrates sees, and Socrates is something non-Plato; therefore, something non-Plato sees, which is the opposite of the second part.

One must state that this expression "to that extent", "only" *(tantum)* can be taken exclusively and relatively. If it is taken exclusively in both the antecedent and the consequent, the inference is very solid. But one denies the second part of the above conjunction, and with regard to the proof the inference is denied. If, however, in both the antecedent and the consequent, "only" *(tantum)* is taken relatively, I concede the inference and the conclusion. And with regard to its disproof, I say that it does not have to be expounded; but rather it signifies interchangeably that as far as Socrates sees, to that extent Plato sees, which is true. Where, however, an opponent wants "only" *(tantum)* to be taken in an antecedent relatively and in a consequent exclusively, it is clear then that he does not argue according to the rule.

From that rule there is a corollary: "From an entire conjunct to either part there is a solid inference."[a]

Against this rule one argues. This inference does not follow: "Socrates and Plato are two; therefore, Socrates is two". For the antecedent is true and the consequent is false. Nor does this follow: "Socrates and Plato by themselves *(de per se)* carry stone A; therefore, Socrates by himself carries stone A". For it is given that A would be carried by both at the same time, and it can be carried by no one by himself. Then the antecedent would be true, and the consequent [would be] false. Similarly, it does not follow: "you differ from a man and from a donkey; therefore, you differ from a man". For the antecedent is true, and the consequent is false as is clear through its exponents. Therefore, none of these inferences is solid; yet they are argued according to the rule, as is known; thus, the rule is false.

One may respond that a conjoined conjunction taken conjunctively can be interpreted in two ways: i.e. collectively or divisively. "Collectively" means either extreme exists in *(in est)* both joined at the same time, and it is not divided; or it is determined by a confusive sign. It is taken in the first way as much in the first as in the second example; and it is taken in the second way in the third example. Taking the expression "collectively" therefore, it is not a solid inference to go from a total [226] conjunct to either part. An expression is taken "divisively", however, when it is not limited by a confusive sign, and any of its conjuncts exists in *(in est)* the other one; for example, "Socrates and Plato are men", "Socrates and Plato run or see". Taking the expression in this way one has a rule in truth.[a]

The second rule was this one (7.2): "From the principal part of an affirmative disjunction to the same [total] disjunctive proposition there is a solid inference [but not conversely]."

Against this rule one argues. This inference does not follow: "Contingently you are; therefore, contingently you are, or you are not." Yet it is argued according to the rule; therefore, the rule is false. This inference holds with regard to the minor premise; and the major premise I prove. For the antecedent is true, as is clear; and the consequent is false. It is proved that the consequent is false because "you are or you are not, and it cannot be otherwise than you are or you are not. Therefore, necessarily you are or you are not", which is the opposite of the consequent. The antecedent is true; therefore, the consequent is true.

For that reason one replies that if "contingently" determines in the consequent the entire disjunctive expression, then it is not argued according to the rule. For taken in this way there is no first or second part in a categorical sense. If, however, "contingently" determines the first part only, I concede the inference and the consequent; and I deny the proposition, "necessarily you are or you are not", by analyzing "necessarily" in the same way, [i.e., with respect to one part]. Where, however, ["necessarily"] determines [both disjuncts] a second time, I concede the proposition; but then the disjuncts are not opposites, for they determine in different ways.

From this rule one infers another corollary: "From a disjunct part to an entire disjunct there is a solid inference."

Against this rule one argues in this way. This inference does not follow: "you differ from a donkey; therefore, you differ from a man or a donkey", because the antecedent is true, and the consequent is false, as is clear through its exponents. Also, it does not follow: "a donkey is a donkey; therefore, this man or donkey is a donkey".

320

One replies as previously that a disjunctive expression taken disjunctively is interpreted in two senses: namely, collectively and divisively.[b] It is taken collectively when it is determined by a confusive sign or a discrete [sign] or a relative [sign]. Example of the first: "you differ from [you or from me]". Example of the second: "this man or donkey is a donkey". − letting "this" operate over the entire disjunct. Example of the third: [227] "Socrates who is a man or a donkey is capable of braying". An expression is taken divisively, however, when it is taken in none of these ways: e.g. "a man or a donkey runs", "you are a man or a donkey".

It may be said, therefore, that from a disjunct part to a total disjunct taken divisively there is a solid inference, and this is the sense of the rule. But from a disjunct part to a total disjunct taken collectively an argument does not follow, just as [we saw] in the opposite case which was argued against the intention of the rule.

The third rule was this one (7.3): "From an affirmative disjunctive proposition with the destruction of one of its parts to the other part there is a solid inference."

Against this rule one argues in this way. This inference does not follow: "you are a donkey or you are not a donkey; but you are not a donkey; therefore, you are a donkey". For the antecedent is true, and the consequent is false, as is clear; yet it is argued according to the rule. Therefore, the rule is false.

One may respond that it is not argued according to the rule because in the second part of the antecedent the contradictory of the first part of the disjunctive proposition occurs. Or one takes the second part of the disjunctive expression, if the opposite of the first part is assumed. It is clear that this [objection] is not argued according to the rule because the other part is not implied: namely, "you are not a donkey". And with that implication, the inference and the conclusion is conceded. If, however, one says that for the second part of the antecedent there is another disjunctive expression implying a different [proposition] one responds that it is not argued according to the rule. For its contradictory ought to be taken in this way: "you are a donkey or you are not a donkey; but you are a donkey; therefore, you are a donkey". The inference is solid; however, the minor premise is denied.

The fourth rule was this one (7.4): "From a negative conjunctive proposition to an affirmative disjunctive proposition made from the contradictory parts of the affirmative conjunctive proposition and conversely there is a solid inference."

From this rule a fifth rule (7.5) follows: "From a negative disjunctive proposition to an affirmative conjunctive proposition made from the con-

321

tradictory parts of the affirmative disjunctive proposition there is a solid inference, and conversely."

Against these rules one can argue. From no negative proposition follows an affirmative proposition; therefore, each of these rules is false. And because one may respond that this rule does not hold in the case of hypothetical propositions but in the case of categorical propositions of which an affirmative posits "existence in" and a negative nothing, I argue more especially. The opposite of an affirmative disjunctive proposition assigned through a preposed negation of the whole is not interchanged with its opposite [228] assigned through a conjunctive proposition made from the parts of the opposite disjunctive; therefore, both rules are false. This inference holds. The antecedent I prove; and I quote this disjunctive proposition, "necessarily, you are or you sit". It is clear that this proposition is false; therefore, this proposition is true: "not necessarily you are or you sit", and yet this proposition is false, "necessarily you are not and you do not sit". One argues, therefore, that just as the former negative disjunctive proposition is true, the latter conjunctive proposition is false. Moreover, any of those affirmative disjunctive propositions proffered earlier are opposed; therefore, they are not interchanged. The inference is clear because what is true is not interchanged with what is false.

For that reason briefly one may respond that if an affirmative disjunctive proposition has two opposites of this kind these propositions are mutually interchanged; but it does not always have for an opposite a conjunctive proposition made from the parts of the opposite disjunctive, as the argument makes clear. And this is the case when the disjunctive proposition is a categorical proposition provable, as in those proposed above, by reason of this term, "necessarily".[a] Infallibly and regularly, however, it may be held that an affirmative disjunctive proposition as much as [an affirmative] conjunctive proposition is given a contradictory through a negation placed in front of the entire proposition. The same thing applies to an affirmative conjunctive proposition; for this is false, "necessarily you are a man, and you are white", as is clear. And similarly, any of these is false: "necessarily you are a man, or you are not white". "Contingently you are not a man, or you are not white". For any of these yields this disjunctive proposition: "you are not [a man], or you are not white", which is false since each of its parts is false.

The sixth rule was this one (7.6): "From an affirmative conditional proposition with its antecedent to the consequent of this same proposition there is a solid inference."

Against this rule one argues in this way. This inference does not follow: "necessarily you are an animal, if you are a man; but you are a man; therefore, necessarily you are an animal". However, this is argued by the rule;

322

therefore, the rule is false. This inference holds with respect to the minor premise; the major premise I prove. For the consequent is false, as is clear; and the antecedent is true. This is proved with respect to the first part because with regard to the second part it does not apply. "For you are an animal, if you are a man; and it is not able to be otherwise than you are an animal, if you are a man; therefore, necessarily you are an animal if you are a man."

It is to be said [in reply] that "necessarily" is able to determine in two ways: either precisely the consequent of the stated conditional proposition or the entire conditional proposition. In the first way, I concede the inference, and I deny the first [229] part of the antecedent, namely, "necessarily you are an animal, if you are a man", because it is equivalent to this, "if you are a man, necessarily you are an animal", which is false. With regard to the proof I deny the inference because that conditional proposition is not in this case a provable categorical proposition. If, however, "necessarily" determines the entire conditional proposition, I deny the inference. Nor is it argued according to the rule because it implies this proposition, "necessarily you are an animal", which is not its consequent. But this proposition alone is its consequent, "you are an animal", because in the way it is taken the *modus* is not part of the consequent; nor is it [part of] the antecedent, and it is not [the sign of] a condition; rather ["necessarily" operates] over the entire conditional proposition.

For that reason one ought to argue in this way: "necessarily you are animal if you are a man; but you are a man; therefore, you are an animal". Whence a conditional proposition without the modifier "necessarily" is interchanged with itself having this mode. For that reason this follows: "if you are a man, you are an animal; therefore, necessarily if you are a man, you are an animal and conversely".

The seventh and last rule was this one (7.7): "From an affirmative conditional proposition with the contradiction of the consequent there follows the contradiction of the antecedent."

Against this rule one argues as previously, "necessarily if Antichrist is white, Antichrist is colored; but Antichrist is not colored; therefore, necessarily the same one is not white". It is very clear that the antecedent is true, and that the consequent is false. However, one argues more specially in this way: This inference does not follow: "if you are a man, necessarily you are an animal; but not necessarily you are an animal; therefore, you are not a man". However, this is argued according to the rule; therefore, the rule is false. The inference holds with respect to the minor premise. The major premise I prove, for the antecedent is true, and the consequent is false; therefore, the inference does not follow. That the consequent is false is clear, and it is proved that the antecedent is true. For the proposition is true, "not necessarily you are an animal", because its opposite is false. But the other part [of the proposition] is proved: "if you are a man, necessarily you are an animal", for you are an animal if you are a man necessarily. "Thus, if you are a man, necessarily you are an animal."[a] This inference holds from one proposition interchangeable with another; since it is the same thing to say, "an animal runs, if a man runs", and "if a man runs, an animal runs".

For that reason one may respond to the first argument just as to the criticism of the other rule; that it is not argued according to the rule, [230] for this proposition alone ought to be concluded: "Antichrist is not white", since "necessarily" is not part either of the antecedent or the consequent. And with regard to the other argument one doubts whether this inference is solid, "if you are a man necessarily you are an animal; but not necessarily you are an animal; therefore you are not a man". One doubts whether "necessarily" is part of the antecedent or part of the consequent.[a] If, however, "necessarily" is part of the antecedent, I deny the inference. Nor is it argued according to the rule because the opposite of the consequent is not assumed. Rather it ought to be argued in this way: "you are not an animal; therefore, you are not a man necessarily", and in this way the inference is conceded, but the minor premise is denied. If, however, "necessarily" is part of the consequent, I concede the inference, yet I deny the conditional proposition because then it would be equivalent to this conditional proposition: "if you are a man, you are an animal necessarily". And then with respect to the argument, "you are an animal if you are a man necessarily; therefore, if you are a man, necessarily you are an animal". I deny this inference. Nor is it argued from one proposition interchangeable with another. Nor is this exemplified in what was proposed because in the antecedent "necessarily" is part of the antecedent of [one] conditional, and in the consequent it is part of the consequent of another conditional; therefore, [the rule is true].

With good reason many other things could have been added to the foregoing statements within what was proposed. About those things from the outset I decided to remain silent — so that an abundance of words or writings would not generate tedium in the mind of the student — just as I promised in setting forth my first introduction.[b]

The End
Thanks be to God
The year of the Lord
July 14, 1472

Notes

[191]^a These are the paradoxes of strict implication. See above Chapter III, n. [65]^b.

[194]^a See Chapter V on Obligations, p. [118] ff.

[195]^a For Buridan's treatment of this sophism see Scott, pp. 184–185.
^b See above Chapter VI, p. [142] ff.

[196]^a See the discussion of relative terms, pp. [51]–[58].
^b The point of this example is this. "Wood was destroyed", is in the past perfect tense, and once something is destroyed it is impossible for it to be at any later time.

[197]^a The relative term mentioned here is "that" in the sentence, "An animal is, and it is impossible for that to be".
^b See the treatment of deposition in Chapter V, p. [138] ff.

[198]^a The opposite of the consequent "this is unknown by you and this is known by you", is: "it is not the case that this is unknown by you and this is known by you", which is equivalent to: "it is not the case that this is unknown by you or it is not the case that this is known by you". Cancelling for double negations, this amounts to the tautology: "this is known by you or this is not known by you". Far from being repugnant to the antecedent, this conclusion is consistent with the antecedent.

[200]^a See Chapter III, pp. [66]–[67].

[201]^a See p. [199].

[202]^a See earlier discussions of the paradoxes of strict implication, p. [65] ff. and n. [191]^a.

[203]^a See Chapter IV, pp. [110]–[111].
^b See Chapter VI, pp. [149]–[153].

[204]^a To say that "an animal is a man" does not signify adequately "every animal to be a man", is to say that the original proposition is false. To say that "an animal is a man" signifies "assertively" "every animal to be a man", is simply to acknowledge that the opponent has asserted that proposition.

[205]^a See Chapter IV, p. [84].
^b See Chapter IV, p. [84].
^c A "provable sign" is one which calls for an analysis of truth-conditions according to one of the methods elaborated in Chapter IV.

[206]^a See Chapter IV, p. [80].
^b This argument turns on the fact that *"homo"* in Latin may signify either masculine, feminine or neuter things.

[207]^a For a discussion of the gender of terms taken in material supposition see Perreiah, 3, p. 59.

[208]^a Note that "animal" in this proposition is taken in material supposition.
^b Paul says here that the inference, "this proposition is categorical therefore, it is of a quantity", is a non sequitur. For the antecedent proposition may be of no quantity. Moreover, because the critic's claim is *ad hoc* it may be met by a counter claim equally *ad hoc*.

[209]^a A "cause of truth" is simply a truth-condition or a condition which renders a proposition decidably true or false.

    ^b There is no hint of whom Paul is referring to here.

[210]^a See Chapter IV, pp. [101]–[104].

    ^b The term "affirmative" does not occur in the original statement of this rule. See p. [74].

    ^c See Chapter IV, pp. [103]–[106].

[211]^a On "transcendent terms" see Adams and Del Punta in Adams, 3, p. 293.

[212]^a See Chapter II on Ampliation, pp. [58]–[61].

[213]^a "to interchange", "to convert" — these words are synonymous in the present context; they mean "to replace" or "to substitute for".

[218]^a See Chapter III, Rule 6.8 is the one in question, p. [77].

    ^b This remark indicates that the word "exposition" has in Latin the same double meaning it has in English: namely, the technical sense elaborated in Chapter IV and the common notion of "explication".

[221]^a See Chapter IV, p. [86] ff.

    ^b The point here is the difference between understanding a man simply and understanding something as *(sub ratione qua)* a man. For you may have the former understanding without the latter. This point is argued in the following paragraph.

[223]^a See Chapter IV, p. [89]. Also, Scott, p. 137 ff.

[224]^a See above Chapter II, n. [53]^a.

    ^b The point of this criticism is that the first argument is fallacious. It proceeds from an antecedent with a term in material supposition to a consequent with the same term in personal supposition.

[225]^a See p. [78].

[226]^a Note that the distinction between the "collective" and "divisive" senses of a conjunct term is crucial to the principle of simplification.

    ^b Here the distinction between a "collective" and a "divisive" sense is applied to disjunct terms.

[228]^a See above p. [226].

[229]^a Note that the original statements are unpunctuated; hence the propositions in question are ambiguous and require analysis in order to establish their correct meanings and logical forms.

[230]^a Here, again, the original statements are unpunctuated and thus call for analysis to determine their correct meanings.

    ^b See Chapter I, p. [1].

Appendix
Concordance
Logica Parva – Logica Magna

In recent years interest in the *Logica Magna* attributed to Paul of Venice has grown. Partly to further that interest and partly to enhance the usefulness of the present volume, we offer the following guide which cross-references topics in the *Logica Parva* to those in the *Logica Magna*. It is hoped that this index will facilitate the research of those who may wish to compare methods and doctrines in the two works.

The *Logica Magna* exists in one manuscript (Vat. lat. 2132) and two fragments. For present purposes all references are to the edition published by Octavianus Scotus (Venice, 1499) Hain 12.505.

Section 1 – Form

The 1499 edition of the *Logica Magna* includes a Table of Contents (f 200) which divides the work into two parts and, in turn, subdivides each part into tracts. According to this *tabula* Part I has 23 tracts; Part II has 15 tracts.

Tractatus Primae Partis

Primus tractatus de terminis
Secundus de suppositionibus terminorum
Tertius de terminis confundentibus
Quartus de dictionibus exclusivis

Quintus de regulis exclusivarum
Sextus de dictionibus exceptivis
Septimus de regulis exceptivarum

Tractatus Secundae Partis

Primus de propositione
Secundus de propositione cathegorica
Tertius de propositione in genere
Quartus de quantitate propositionum
Quintus de figuris propositionum
Sextus de aequipollentiis
Septimus de natura situatorum in figura

Corresponding to this table, the contents of the 1499 edition of the *Logica Magna* are divided, subdivided, numbered and titled. An examination of the *actual contents* of the *Logica Magna* reveals a number of errors and inaccuracies in this table of contents. Here I note only a few. Part I Tracts 12 and 13 (ff. 39-56ra) are listed in the *tabula* as separate items; they are, however, one continuous unit. Tract 19 is identified in the *tabula* as *De propositione exponibili* whereas the text itself speaks about *De terminis officiabilibus* of which describable, exponible, and officiable propositions are subordinate topics. Tract 20 is identified in the *tabula* as *De propositione officiabili* whereas this is the third topic of tract 19. Tract 22 *De scire et dubitare* and tract 23 *De necessitate et contingentia futurorum* are listed as discrete items; yet the introduction to the former tract makes clear that the latter is continuous with it. Hence, their presentation as separate tracts is misleading. In part II tracts 2 *De propositione cathegorica* and tract 3

328

De propositione in genere cover subtopics of the main topic of tract 1 *De propositione.* Thus the tracts numbered 2 and 3 should be treated as mere subdivisions of tract 1. In addition to these points of detail the table of contents and the corresponding chapter numbers and titles in the 1499 edition are misleading in a fundamental way. As a serial list of items the *tabula* reduces all of the topics of the numbered chapters to the same level of generality. But the subject matters of those chapters are plainly not on the same level of generality. For example, in Part I each of the chapters listed 4 through 20 pertains not to a multiplicity of isolated topics but to a coherent group of items under a single topic which in the *Logica Parva* is called the Proof of Terms *(probatio terminorum)*. Moreover, none of those special problems is on a par with the general topics of Tract 1 *De terminis* or Tract 2 *De suppositionibus* as the table of contents and the corresponding organization of the text in the 1499 edition makes them appear. In Part II each of the tracts from 1 through 9 deals with a specific topic under the general topic of tract 1 *De propositione,* which in the body of the text is subdivided quite clearly into two groups of discussions, one on Categorical propositions (Tracts 2 through 8) and another on Hypothetical Propositions (Tract 9). These two groups of discussions correspond, of course, to the two species of proposition recognized in the *Logica Magna*; but this point of doctrinal order is not reflected in the 1499 *tabula.* Thus, because it is both inaccurate and misleading the Table of Contents and the corresponding Chapter titles and divisions published in the 1499 edition of the *Logica Magna* should be replaced.

The sole surviving manuscript of the *Logica Magna* (Vat. Lat. 2132) has no Table of Contents, no corresponding numbered divisions and no titles of chapters. There is only one main marked division between the "First Part" and the "Second part" and blank spaces between various possible subdivisions of the text. Hence as the manuscript stands its materials could be grouped in a variety of ways. Here I propose a grouping of the text which reflects its contents. Section 2 will develop these in greater detail. Because the manuscript itself is divided into two parts I retain that division here.

The proposed table of contents for the *Logica Magna* includes subdivisions with chapter numbers and titles which represent the actual doctrinal content of the text. Moreover, the suggested ordering of those materials parallels more closely the patterns of organization which had become standard in logical treatises of the 15th century. Contrasted with the 38 chapter list of the 1499 edition, the proposed 12 chapter table for the *Logica Magna* has a number of practical advantages. For one, it invites comparison at a glance of doctrines in the *Logica Magna* with doctrines in other texts from the 14th and 15th centuries. Second, it greatly facilitates examination of parallels with other texts by Paul of Venice, especially the *Logica Parva, Quadratura,*

330

Lectura posteriorum analyticorum and *Expositio praedicabilium et prae-dicamentorum.*

Chapter 1 of the *Logica Magna* omits many topics treated in Chapter 1 of the *Logica Parva* which includes the main ideas in the *summulae* tradition; yet both still cover the same ground. Note also that Chapters 1 and 7 and Chapter 3 and 8 are combined for the purposes of comparison with the *Logica Magna.* This is done for the following reason. In the *Logica Parva* definitions, divisions and rules are propounded in the earlier chapters and then in the later chapters are established by a method of objections and resolutions. In the *Logica Magna* all of these operations — theory, objections and replies — are carried out in one place when a topic is first introduced. Despite the fact that a "tract on consequences" is referred to explicitly in one chapter of the *Logica Magna* (178 rb) no single chapter by that name exists in that work. Rules of consequences, one of the topics of such a chapter, are formulated in connection with discussions of the various kinds of propositions, for that reason, I compare the *Logica Magna* II, 6 with Chapters 3 and 8 of the *Logica Parva* where such rules are elaborated. Chapter 4 of the *Logica Parva* deals with the proof of terms, i.e., the elucidation of the truth or falsity of propositions in function of the kinds of terms they contain. Chapters 3 and 4 in the proposed analysis of the *Logica Magna* manuscript (Vat. lat. 2132) thus compare neatly to Chapter 4 of the *Logica Parva.* Finally, Chapter 5 *De obligationibus* and Chapter 6 *De insolubilibus* in both texts may also be readily compared.

Section 2 – Content

In this section I explore several doctrines discussed both in the *Logica Magna* and in the *Logica Parva.* Although there are a few points on which the two works agree, there are many more on which they disagree. I will note the former by and by; but the latter will be the main focus of attention in this section. My procedure is twofold: First, I review chapter by chapter particular difficulties expressed or implied by other scholars. Some of these issues have been noted by scholars for well over 500 years; but no one to my knowledge has successfully answered them. Second, I offer some general observations about the development and presentation of doctrines in the *Logica Magna* and the *Logica Parva.*

The *Logica Magna* defines a term as that *"in quem resolvitur proposi-tio ut praedicatum et de quo praedicatur"* (f. lr). The *Logica Parva* defines a term as a *"signum orationis constitutivum ut pars propinqua eiusdem"* (p. [1]). Whatever can be made of the differences between these definitions, there are clear differences between the *Logica Magna* and the *Logica Parva* conceptions of the divisions of terms.

Logica Magna (ff. 1r-16r)	Logica Parva (pp. [1]-[4])
Part 1	Chapter 1
Chapter 1-Terms	Section 1-Terms
1. Categorematic/syncategorematic	1. Significative/nonsignificative
2. Natural/conventional	2. Natural/Conventional
3. Common/Singular	3. Categorematic/Syncategorematic
4. Mediate/Immediate	4. 1st/2nd intention
	5. 1st/2nd imposition
	6. Complex/noncomplex

The contrasts between these divisions of terms in the two works are remarkable for several reasons. First, the *Logica Parva* addresses the problem
of non-significative terms which the *Logica Magna* ignores. Second, the
Logica Parva recognizes a distinction between 1st and 2nd intention and 1st
and 2nd imposition which the *Logica Magna* Chapter 1 omits. This is doubly
surprising because the *Logica Magna* Chapter 2 invokes and employs this
very distinction. Third, where the *Logica Parva* incorporates the distinction
between common and singular terms into its rules of supposition (Chapter
2), into its rules of consequences (Chapter 3), into its rules of proof (Chapter 4) and into its typology of insolubilia (Chapter 6), the *Logica Magna*
deals with this as an independent topic. Finally, the *Logica Magna* Chapter 1
ignores the important linguistic phenomenon captured in the distinction
between complex and noncomplex terms. Again, this is notable because the
Logica Magna chapter 2 introduces this very distinction (f 17v).

It is not, of course, the mere existence of diverse sets of principles for the
analysis of terms which is remarkable. The fact that the author of the *Logica
Magna* and the author of the *Logica Parva* use these principles to arrive at
opposite conclusions is, however, worthy of note. For example, Mengus
Bianchellus shows that the author of the *Logica Magna* holds that a verb
cannot be a categorematic term *(Quaest.* f 66r). It cannot be because a
categorematic term must have a proper significate and not unite the extremes of a proposition. But every verb *qua* verb unites the extremes of a
proposition. Therefore, no verb can be a categorematic term. The author
of the *Logica Parva*, however, holds that a categorematic term is that which
has a proper significate as much *per se* as *cum alio* and it does not have the
function of determining (*officium determinandi*). A syncategorematic term
is that which *per se* signifies nothing (p. [2]). It follows from this definition
that a verb is a categorematic term. Whether these two positions can be
reconciled was not settled by Bianchellus, nor has it been settled for the
past five centuries.

The *Logica Magna* defines supposition as the *"significatio termini extremaliter se habentis et non extremaliter unitivi pro aliquo vel aliquibus in
propositione"* (f 16 r). The *Logica Parva* defines supposition as the *"acceptio*

termini in propositione pro aliquo vel pro aliquibus" (p. [30]). It is noteworthy that the *De universalibus* for which we have eight manuscripts employs the *Logica Parva* definition of *suppositio* as *acceptio* and shows no trace of the *Logica Magna* definition or vocabulary. Beyond basic definitions the organization of the topic in the two works differs greatly:

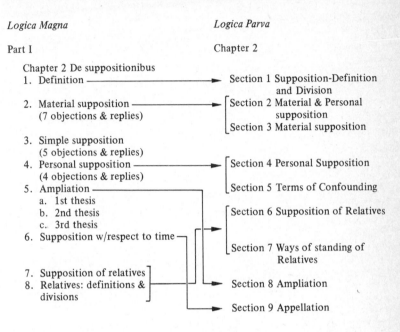

Logica Magna	*Logica Parva*
Part I	Chapter 2

Chapter 2 De suppositionibus
1. Definition ⟶ Section 1 Supposition-Definition and Division
2. Material supposition ⟶ Section 2 Material & Personal supposition
   (7 objections & replies) Section 3 Material supposition
3. Simple supposition (5 objections & replies)
4. Personal supposition ⟶ Section 4 Personal Supposition
   (4 objections & replies) Section 5 Terms of Confounding
5. Ampliation
   a. 1st thesis
   b. 2nd thesis
   c. 3rd thesis Section 6 Supposition of Relatives
6. Supposition w/respect to time
   Section 7 Ways of standing of Relatives
7. Supposition of relatives
8. Relatives: definitions & divisions ⟶ Section 8 Ampliation
   ⟶ Section 9 Appellation

These two approaches to supposition theory may be contrasted in several ways. First, the *Logica Magna* divides supposition into three species: Material, Simple and Personal. The *Logica Parva* division is twofold — Material and Personal — omitting any mention of Simple supposition. Second, the *Logica Magna* treats terms of confounding *(termini confundendi)* outside the chapter on suppositions. The *Logica Parva* treats such terms as a part of supposition theory. Third, the *Logica Magna* deals with the supposition of terms with respect to past and future time without any mention of the word 'appellation" *(appellatio)*. The *Logica Parva* has a section on Appellation (pp. [61]-[64]). The treatments of each of the topics which do have counterparts in both works are highly diverse. Here are a few illustrations.

The *Logica Magna* subdivides personal supposition into discrete and common and these in turn into several more subdivisions; it recognizes no subdivisions for either material or simple supposition. The *Logica Parva* subdivides Personal supposition in the same way and it also recognizes a parallel subdivision of Material supposition.

Paulus Venetus, *Logica Magna.*

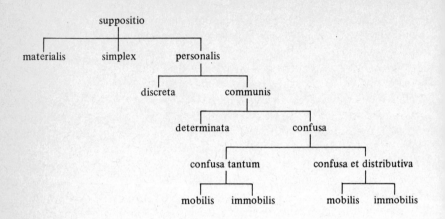

Paulus Venetus, *Logica Parva.*

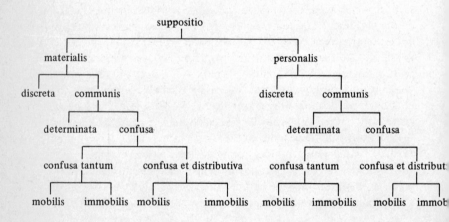

The implications of these two schemata are quite different: on the *Logica Magna* account one may quantify over individuals (personal supposition) but not over concepts or natures (simple supposition) or terms (material supposition). On the *Logica Parva* account one could quantify over both individuals (personal supposition) and *in the same ways* over terms (material supposition).

With regard to the theory of ampliation the *Logica Magna* defends three theses which are thought to regulate the supposition of common or discrete terms with respect to a verb of present time (1st thesis), the supposition of a term in subject position with respect to an ampliative verb (2nd thesis), the supposition of a term following an ampliative verb (3rd thesis) (ff. 22r-25r). The *Logica Parva* takes an entirely different approach to ampliation and offers six rules which have no discernible connection with those of the *Logica Magna* (pp. [58]-[61]). Moreover, only one example *(Antichristus est futurus)* out of almost two dozen used to illustrate the rules occurs in both works; yet not even this is employed in the same way in each work. A similar observation could be made about the treatment of relative terms in the two works. Although the typologies of relative terms are practically the same in the *Logica Magna* and the *Logica Parva* (the *Logica Parva* has an additional division under relatives of accident), the rules for relative terms and the examples used to illustrate them are quite different in the two works (LM ff. 26v-31r; LP pp. [51]-[58]). If we take into consideration the fact that the rules of supposition have a practical purpose, i.e. to help a dialectician keep track of the way or ways in which a term was accepted in the course of an argument, it is difficult to see what advantage there would be in a single author's holding two approaches to the theory of supposition as dissimilar as those in the *Logica Magna* and the *Logica Parva*.

With regard to the theory of deduction and inference we must examine both the theory of syllogism and the theory of consequences in both works. In this guide I do not attempt to compare the two accounts of syllogistic. I note only one clear contrast: the *Logica Magna* makes a fundamental distinction between "regular" and "irregular" syllogisms (ff. 172-177). This should not be confused with the distinction between "perfect and imperfect" syllogisms. The notion of an "irregular" syllogism is not so much as mentioned in the *Logica Parva*. Nor have I been able to find any reference to it in any of Paul of Venice's genuine works. With regard to the theory of consequences there are some close parallels between the *Logica Magna* and the *Logica Parva*. Despite the fact that reference to a tract on consequences is made in the text (f. 178rb) of the *Logica Magna* no single chapter is devoted to an *ex professo* treatment of *consequentia*. Instead a number of separate chapters otherwise devoted to discussions of the varieties of categorical and hypothetical propositions expound rules of consequences. In this guide I do not elaborate contrasts between the rules themselves which are markedly different in form between the two works. Rather I comment on the principal disagreement between the two works about the nature of a *consequentia.*

The *Logica Magna* treats the class of *consequentia* as coextensive with the class of conditional propositions. Professor Bottin who has studied the question carefully follows the Kneales in criticizing the author of the *Logica Magna* for clouding the distinction between consequences and conditionals. He refers to the "oscillations" *(oscillazioni)* and "constant ambiguity" *(costante ambiguità)* on this point in the *Logica Magna.* In the end he recognizes that the *Logica Magna* identifies the one with the other saying that consequences differ from conditionals "only graphically" *(solo graficamente)* (Bottin, 1, p. 336). By identifying consequences including syllogisms with hypothetical, i.e. conditional propositions, the *Logica Magna* reduces the concept of a *sequence* of propositions to the concept of a proposition. In so doing it obliterates important differences between inference and judgment. Finally, it obviates the distinction between the theory of argumentation and the theory of propositions. The *Logica Parva* follows Strode's definition of a *consequentia* as *"illatio consequentis ex antecedente"* (p. [64]). It remains faithful to Strode's insistence that the passage from the one to the other involves an intellectual act. It thus preserves in practice the distinction between one kind of intellectual act (judgment) and another kind of intellectual act (argument). The *Logica Parva* in this way maintains separate accounts for propositions and for argumentation.

The *Logica Magna* and the *Logica Parva* both recognize three types of *bona consequentia*: (1) *Bona formalis* (2) *Bona de forma* (3) *Bona materialis.* (LM. ff. 124-127; LP pp. [64]-[80]). Moreover, the definitions of (2) and (3) are similar in both works. Where the *Logica Parva* adds a fourth type, viz. *bona de materia*, the *Logica Magna* distinguishes three levels of formality for consequences: (a) formally *(formaliter)*, (b) more than formally *(plus quam formaliter)* or (c) most formally *(formalissime)* (f. 169va). Because the necessity of a formally valid consequence is defined by the impossibility of the denial of its consequent with the affirmation of its antecedent there must be three grades of impossibility corresponding to the three grades of formality elaborated here. These are distinguished according to the ways in which the impossible conditional implies a contradiction: (a') if a contradiction follows naturally only *(naturaliter solum)*, the consequence is formal (e.g., *homo est asinus*). (b') If a contradiction follows naturally as much as supernaturally *(tam naturaliter quam supernaturaliter)* the consequence is more than formal (e.g., *homo est non risibilis*). (c') If a contradiction follows supernaturally, i.e. it contradicts anything either intelligible or known *(contradictio apud quodlibet intelligibile vel intellec-*

tum) the consequence is most formal (e.g., *tu est aliud a te*). As a standard of impossibility (c′) appears to have a connection with the priciple of divine omnipotence. The *Logica Parva* maintains only one grade of formal validity. Needless to say, the diverse treatments of formally valid consequences in the *Logica Magna* and the *Logica Parva* have important ramifications not only for inference theory but for modal logic and the paradoxes of implication as well. Whether the two accounts are, in the last analysis, reconcilable has never been established.

Controversies over the analysis of *consequentia* go much deeper than the theory of consequences. They stem in part from two very different conceptions of the proposition which are contained in the two works. The *Logica Magna* defines a proposition as an *"enuntiatio congrua et perfecta veri aut falsi significativa"* (f. 101ra). The *Logica Parva* defines a proposition as an *"oratio indicativa verum vel falsum significans"* (pp. [4]-[5]). Over 500 years ago Mengus Bianchellus sought to reconcile these definitions by noting that *enunciatio* is one species of *oratio.*(Exp. 8v) Professor Gabriel Nuchelmans has recently proposed a similar view: "[The author of the *Logica Magna*] uses the word *enunciatio* in a rather wide sense, practically as a synonym of *oratio*, and defends the view that not only the indicative *enunciatio* but also imperative, deprecative, optative, and subjunctive *enuntiationes* are rightly called *propositiones*". Professor Nuchelmans calls it "a remarkable feature of the definition that it does not contain the element of *oratio indicativa*" (Nuchelmans, p. 266). It is unfortunate that Professor Nuchelmans' careful studies of the *propositio* in medieval logic omit the *Logica Parva* doctrine on propositions. Neither of his books on the subject even cites the *Logica Parva*, which is nonetheless on several points quite relevant to Professor Nuchelmans' claims: (1) a *propositio* is an *oratio indicativa*, (2) imperatives, optatives, subjunctives etc. are not *propositiones* and (3) such locutions are not "rightly called" *propositiones*. A contrast between two works on a point of theory could hardly be clearer than that between the *Logica Magna* and the *Logica Parva* on the analysis of propositions. The *Logica Magna* explicitly rejects not only the definition of a proposition fundamental to the *Logica Parva*. It goes on to accept *the very example* of a subjunctive, *"antrichristus esset albus"*, which is explicitly rejected in the *Logica Parva* (LM f. 101rb; LP p. [163]).

With regard to the theory of truth both texts say that the "primary and adequate significate" determines the truth or falsity of a proposition. The *Logica Magna*, however, defines the adequate significate as that of which the proposition actually or virtually is signi*ficative* (ff. 167rb-167vb). The *Logica Parva* distinguishes between the principal and the adequate significate and then defines the adequate significate as that which the proposition customarily (i.e. actually) signi*fies* (p. [131]). Additional conflict between these two conceptions arises in the case of insoluble propositions. As Adams and Del Punta have observed, the *Logica Magna* stipulates that an insoluble proposition may have an adequate significate which is true but that the proposition may be false, e.g., "This proposition (pointing to itself) is false" (Adams, 3, pp. xiii-xiv). The *Logica Parva* states unequivocally, "A true categorical proposition is one whose primary and adequate significate is true. ... A false categorical proposition is one whose primary and adequate significate is false" (p. [6]). The *Logica Parva* makes no exception for insolubles. Thus, with regard to truth theory there are at least two major discrepancies between the *Logica Magna* and the *Logica Parva*.

Turning now to the theory of proof *(probatio terminorum* or *probatio propositionum)* there are significant differences between the two works. There is, first of all, an astonishing contrast in the organization of standard topics:

Logica Magna	*Logica Parva*
Part I, Chapter 3	Chapter 4
[De probatione terminorum]	De probatione terminorum
a. De terminis confundentibus	1. De Prop. resolubili
b. De dictionibus exclusivis	2. De Prop. exponibili
c. De regulis exclusivarum	3. De Prop. officiabili
d. De dictionibus exceptivis	4. De Prop. descriptibili
e. De regulis exceptivarum	5. De li necessiter et li contingenter
f. De reduplicativis	6. De gradu positivo
g. De dictione li sicut	7. De gradu comparativo
h. De comparativis	8. De gradu superlativo
i. De superlativis	9. De li differt
j. De maximo et minimo	10. Expressiones exclusivae
k. De li toto	11. Expressiones exceptivae
i. Syncategorematice	12. Expressiones reduplicativae
ii. Categorematice	13. De li immediate
l. De li semper et eternum	14. De li incipit et li desinit
m. De isto termino li immediate	
n. De li incipit et li desinit	15. De li toto
o. De terminis officiabilibus	16. De li semper
i. Descriptibilibus	17. De li ab eterno
ii. Exponibilibus	18. De li infinite
iii. Officiabilibus	

Beyound the format of these two chapters, the treatment of specific topics in the *Logica Magna* diverges considerably from the treatment of their counterparts in the *Logica Parva*. Three sections have no counterparts in Chapter 4 of the *Logica Parva*. a. *"De terminis confundentibus"* is treated as a part of supposition theory in Chapter 2 of the *Logica Parva*. j. *"De maximo et minimo"* is not discussed in the *Logica Parva*. Resoluble propositions investigated in Chapter 4 of the *Logica Parva* are not treated in Chapter 3 of the *Logica Magna*. In making comparisons I pay close attention to two aspects which dominate the discourse in each text: (a) doctrinal claims, including rules and (b) examples including paradoxical theses.

Logica Magna	*Logica Parva* and comment

1. Exclusives (ff 34r-35v)
  a. Five orders of exclusives depending upon how the exclusive sign operates
  b. No theses
	1. Exclusives (pp. [100]-[103])
	  a. Three orders of exclusives none reducible to the five in LM.
	  b. Four paradoxical theses

2. Exceptives (ff 38r-39r)
  a. Two orders of exceptives
 	
  b. No paradoxical theses
	2. Exceptives (pp. [103]-[106])
	  a. Two orders of exceptives not reducible to those in LM.
	  b. Four paradoxical theses.

3. Reduplicatives (ff 41r-42r)
  a. Analysis of truth-conditions and suppositions.
  b. No theses.
	3. Reduplicatives (pp. [106]-[107]
	  a. Does not parallel LM account.
	
	  b. Four paradoxical theses.

4. *"Sicut"* – Positives (ff 42r-43v)
  a. Analysis of truth-conditions
  b. Four theses.
	4. Positives (pp. [94]-[96])
	  a. Does not parallel LM account.
	  b. Four theses; none the same as LM.

5. Comparatives (ff 43v-47v)
  a. Analysis of truth-conditions
  b. Four theses.
	5. Comparatives (pp. [96]-[98])
	  a. Does not parallel LM account.
	  b. Four theses; none like LM.

6. Superlatives (ff 47v-49r)
  a. Analysis of truth-conditions
  b. Various theses
	6. Superlatives (pp. [98]-[99])
	  a. Does not parallel LM account.
	  b. Four theses; none like LM.

7. Maximum and Minimum (ff 49r-56r)
  a. Four part analysis with rules, objections and replies
	7. Maximum and Minimum
	  a. No treatment in *Logica Parva*. Treatment in *Summa Naturalium* is entirely different from LM.

8. "Whole" (ff 56r-57v)
  a. Analysis of truth-conditions
 	
  b. No formal theses
	8. "Whole" (pp. [112]-[113])
	  a. Different treatment; similar examples.
	  b. Four theses.

9. "Always", "eternal" (ff 57v-58v)
 	
  a. Analysis of truth-conditions
  b. Three theses plus note
	9. "Always", "Eternal" (pp. [113]-[115])
	  a. Different treatment from LM.
	  b. Four theses; none like LM.

10. "Infinite" (ff 58v-61r)
  a. Analysis of categorematic and syncategorematic senses and truth-conditions.
  b. Numerous theses
	10. "Infinite" (pp. [115]-[118])
	  a. Does not parallel LM account.
	
	  b. Six theses; none like LM.

11. "Immediate" (ff 61r-63r)
  a. Analysis of nominal and adverbial senses and truth-conditions.
  b. Theses
	11. "Immediate" (pp. [107]-[110])
	  a. Analysis of nominal and adverbial senses; but accounts do not parallel.
	  b. Four theses; none like LM.

Logica Magna	Logica Parva and comment
12. *"incipit"*, *"desinit"* (ff 63r-70v)	12. *"Incipit"*, *"desinit"* (pp. [110]-[112])
a. Three methods of analysis; the 2nd of these is like the main one in LP, author rejects the 2nd method.	a. Method of analysis like 2nd in LM which is rejected by the author of the LM.
b. LM proposes alternative analysis by reference to a cause of truth.	b. The alternative analysis by means of a cause of truth is not in LP.
13. Describable propositions (ff 70v-71r)	13. Describable propositions (pp. [89]-[92])
a. Analysis of truth-conditions	a. No parallel in LM.
b. No formal theses	b. Four theses; none like LM.
14. Exponible propositions (ff. 71r-73r)	14. Exponible propositions (pp. [92]-[94])
a. Analysis of truth-conditions	a. Treatment does not parallel LM account.
b. Eight theses	b. Four theses; none like LM.
15. Officiable propositions (ff 73r-76r)	15. Officiable propositions (pp. [86]-[89])
a. Analysis of truth-conditions	a. Treatment does not parallel LM account.
b. Six theses	b. Four theses; none like LM.

In sum, a careful investigation of each of these items of proof theory shows that there is practically no correspondence between the two works with respect to doctrine, rules, examples and the characteristic paradoxical theses which were associated with this theory in medieval logic. Because proof theory brings together a unique blend of term-theory, proposition-theory, supposition-theory and inference-theory in order to establish the truth-conditions of propositions, it shows in a concrete and practical way the method unique to each logician. With this in mind, the wide disparities between the *Logica Magna* and the *Logica Parva* approaches to truth-theory call for explanation.

The *Logica Parva* defines an *obligatio* as an *"oratio composita ex signis obligationis et obligato"* (p. [118]). The *Logica Magna* repeats this definition verbatim (f 177 va). It elaborates what the author of the definition means by it and then declares: *"Descriptio in se est falsa; quia obligatio non est oratio sed relatio. ... Declaratio vero istius descriptionis continet tria falsa."* After reciting the three ways in which the [*Logica Parva*] description is false, the author of the *Logica Magna* insists on his point, *"obligatio est relatio, ut dictum est"*. The *Logica Parva* nowhere defines an *obligatio* as a *relatio*. The *Logica Magna* distinguishes three species of obligation: *"Ultima suppositio est ista et principalis. In hac materia tres sunt species obligationum et non plures coincidentes in respondendo videlicet suppositio, positio et depositio"* (f. 178v). The *Logica Parva* distinguishes only two species of obligation, viz. *positio and depositio:* and it makes no connection between *obligationes* and *suppositiones* in any sense of that term. (p. [118])

Despite these divergencies in theory, the rules of obligations in the two works are comparable.

Rules of obligations

Logica Magna (ff. 179r-180r)	*Logica Parva* (pp. [118]-[122])
Rule I	Rule I
Rule II	Rule II
Rules III & V	Rule III
Rules IV & VI	Rule IV
Rule VII	Rule V
Rule VIII	Rule VI
Rule IX	Rule VII
Rule X	Rule VII Corollary
Rule XI	Rule VIII
Rule XII	Rule IX

It is apparent that the *Logica Parva* has a smaller number of rules and it normally gives a simplified expression to the rules themselves. A major point of difference in the formulation of the rules is that the rules in the *Logica Magna* systematically include the phrase, *"scitum esse tale infra tempus obligationis"* whereas this phrase is omitted in the *Logica Parva* account. Because the phrase involves reference to an intentional act on the part of the respondent in the *obligatio* it could complicate seriously issues of possibility or impossibility (and the problem of admission or non-admission) as well as issues of truth or falsity (and the problem of concession, or denial) of any statement tendered in an *obligatio.* Whether these two approaches to obligations can be reconciled is an open question.

Turning to the objections and replies to each rule in both works we find, nonetheless, some close parallels.

Logica Magna (ff. 181-189)	Comment relative to *Logica Parva* (pp. [122]-[129]).
Rule I	Seven arguments with responses in LM. The first counter argument and reply is the same including the very examples used.
Rule II	Four arguments with responses; none is like the ones in LP.
Rules III & V	Seven arguments with replies against Rule 3 in LM; the third counter argument is almost verbatim in LP including examples. Four arguments with replies against Rule 5 in LM; none is like counter arguments against Rule 3 in LP.

341

Rules IV & VI	Eight arguments with replies against rule 4 in LM; First and second are the same as those against Rule 4 in LP. Three arguments with replies against rule 6 in LM; None is like the those against Rule 4 in LP.
Rule VII	Three arguments with replies against Rule 7 in LM; The first of these is practically identical to those against rule 5 in LP. Similarity is very close: both have the same *extra* examples.
Rule VIII	Four arguments with replies against Rule 8 in LM; None is like those against Rule 6 in LP.
Rule IX	Five arguments with replies against Rule 9 in LM; The first of these is practically verbatim in LP.
Rule X	There are no arguments against Rule 7 corollary in LP.
Rule XI	One argument with replies against Rule 11 in LM; These are practically the same in LP.
Rule XII	Four arguments and replies against Rule 12 in LM; The first and second of these are almost verbatim in LP.

Throughout the remaining sections of the chapter on obligations the relationship between the two works is at times quite close at other times very remote. For example, the *Logica Magna* has no rules for interchangeable propositions *(propositiones convertibili);* the *Logica Parva* has six rules for such propositions. Rules for similar propositions compare in this way:

Logica Magna (ff. 190v-191r)	*Logica Parva* (pp. [134]-[136])
Rule I	Rule I Similar to LM; different examples.
Rule II	Rule II Similar to LM; one of two examples the same.
Rule III	Rule III Similar to but briefer than LM; one of two examples the same.
Rule IV	Rule IV Verbatim with same examples.
Rule V	Rule V Verbatim with two examples the same.
Rule VI	Rule VI Similar to LM; examples similar.

Rules for dissimilar propositions display the following parallels:

Logica Magna (f. 191r)	*Logica Parva* (pp. [137]-[138])
Rule I	Rule I Similar rules; examples the same.
Rule II	Rule II Rules are the same; examples are different.
Rule III	Rule III Simpler than LM; examples are similar.
Rule IV	Rule IV Simpler than LM; examples are the same.
Rule V	Rule V Verbatim; examples are the same.
Rule VI	Rule VI Similar rules; examples are different.

Concerning rules of deposition, the *Logica Magna* has 12 rules; the *Logica Parva* has 6 rules (LM 191v; LP pp. [138]-[139]). The list of brief theses which follows the rules in the former work is not in the latter work.

Finally there is a group of sophisms in each work. The *Logica Magna* presents 8 sophisms; the *Logica Parva* gives 4 (LM 191vb-192rb; LP pp. [139]-[142]). Two of the sophisms in the *Logica Parva*, viz. the second and fourth are like two of the sophisms in the *Logica Magna*, viz. the third and sixth. The remaining ones are different.

The treatment of obligations in the two works thus reveals a close kinship. Apart from the initial definition and typology of obligations which are markedly different in the two works, the rules of obligation including the examples used to illustrate them are strikingly close. Because the *Logica Parva* expressions are normally simpler and briefer and because of a reduction in the number of rules in several groups, the *Logica Parva* account would appear to derive either from the *Logica Magna* treatment or more likely from a source which both works have in common.

I cannot within the limits of this paper go very far into the long and complicated topic of insolubles in the *Logica Magna* and the *Logica Parva*. The former work lays down eight dichotomies plus seven corollaries. It then defines an insoluble as, a *"propositio habens supra se reflexionem suae falsitatis aut se non esse veram totaliter vel participaliter illativa"* (f. 194vb). In fact solution is the central topic as this chapter concludes with a long section reviewing 15 proposed solutions to the paradox of the liar. The *Logica Parva* approaches *insolubilia* within the context of the *obligationes*. Following the definition of an insoluble as a *"propositio se esse falsam assertive significans"*, which does not occur in the *Logica Magna*, its treatment of insolubles divides into three areas: (1) Identification, (2) Admission or non-admission and (3) Solution (p. [142]). Moreover, the rules for insolubles in the *Logica Parva* are quite clearly continuous with the rules of obligations. They are in fact rules which govern *either* the admission or nonadmission of a statement initially posed in an obligation *or* the solution of an insoluble impossible *secundum quid* once an initial statement has been admitted. With regard to solving insolubles we have already noted one important difference between the *Logica Magna* and the *Logica Parva*. Professor Spade has demonstrated the close reliance of the *Logica Magna* solution to the Liar paradox on other authors. For example, he says, "Some of these (i.e. solutions) are taken verbatim from Bradwardine. ... The eighth and ninth opinions (192vab) are the second and third in Heytesbury's *Regulae*", although as Professor Spade observes, the replies of the author of the *Logica Magna* are interspersed among them (Spade, 3, pp. 82-84). Overall it is noteworthy that the *Logica Magna* approach to the solution of insolubles is a version of Roger Swyneshed and it rejects outright Heytesbury's approach. The *Logica Parva* solution is essentially based on Heytesbury and does not show even the faintest trace of Swyneshed.

343

References

Adams, M.M.	1973	"Did Ockham Know of Material and Strict Implication: A Reconsideration", *Franciscan Studies* 33, 5–37. [1]
	1976	"What Does Ockham Mean by 'Supposition'?", *Notre Dame Journal of Formal Logic* XVII, 3. [2]
Adams, M.M. (tr.) and F. del Punta (ed.)	1976	*Logica magna of Paul of Venice, Fasc 6.2: De veritate et falsitate propositionis et De significato propositionis* (Classical and Medieval Logic texts), Oxford: Oxford University Press. [3]
Alessio, F. (ed.)	1971	*Lamberto d'Auxerre: Logica (Summa Lamberti)* (Pubblicazioni della facoltá di lettere e filosofia dell'Universitá di Milano, Vol. 59), Firenze: La Nuova Italia Editrice.
Angelelli, I.	1970	"The Techniques of Disputation in the History of Logic", *The Journal of Philosophy* 67, 800–815.
Aristotle	1963	*Categories* and *De Interpretatione*, transl. with notes by J.L. Ackrill, Oxford: The Clarendon Press. [1]
	1968	*Analytica Priora* in: *The Works of Aristotle* transl. into English by A.J. Jenkinson, Oxford: Oxford University Press. [2]
	1968	*Analytica Posteriora* in: *The Works of Aristotle* transl. into English by G.R.G. Mure, Oxford: Oxford University Press. [3]
	1968	*Topica* and *De Sophistics Elenchis* in: *The Works of Aristotle* transl. into English by W.A. Pickard-Cambridge, Oxford: Oxford University Press. [4]

Ashworth, E.J.

1969   "The Doctrine of Supposition in the Sixteenth and Seventeenth Centuries", *Archiv für Geschichte der Philosophie* 51, 260–285. [1]

1970   "Some Notes on Syllogistic in the Sixteenth and Seventeenth Centuries", *Notre Dame Journal of Formal Logic* XI, 1, 17–33. [2]

1972   "The Treatment of Semantic Paradoxes from 1400 to 1700", *Notre Dame Journal of Formal Logic* XIII, 1, 34–52. [3]

1973   "The Theory of Consequence in the Late Fifteenth and Early Sixteenth Centuries", *Notre Dame Journal of Formal Logic* XIV, 3, 289–315. [4]

1973   "The Doctrine of Exponibilia in the Fifteenth and Sixteenth Centuries", *Vivarium*, Vol. XI, 2, 137–167. [5]

1974   *Language and Logic in the Post-Medieval Period* (Synthese Historical Library, Vol. 12), Dordrecht: D. Reidel. [6]

1976   "Will Socrates Cross the Bridge? A Problem in Medieval Logic", *Franciscan Studies,* Vol. 36, XIV, 75–83. [7]

1978   *The Tradition of Medieval Logic and Speculative Grammar from Anselm to the End of the Seventeenth Century: A Bibliography from 1836 Onwards* (Subsidia Mediaevalia), Toronto: Pontifical Institute of Mediaeval Studies. [8]

1978   "A Note on Paul of Venice and the Oxford *Logica* of 1483", *Medioevo* IV, 93–99. [9]

Barth, E.M.

1974   *The Logic of the Articles in Traditional Philosophy*, Dordrecht-Holland/Boston-U.S.A.: D. Reidel.

Bedell, G.

1979   "Teaching the Material Conditional", *Teaching Philosophy* 2, 225–236.

Bird, Otto:

1961 "Topic and Consequence in Ockham's Logic", *Notre Dame Journal of Formal Logic* 2, 65–78. [1]

1962 "The Tradition of the Logical Topics: Aristotle to Ockham", *Journal of the History of Ideas* 23, 307–323. [2]

Bocheński, I.M.

1956 *Formale Logik* (Orbis Academicus, Bd. III, 2), Freiburg: Verlag Karl Alber, transl. in Bocheński (1961). [1]

1961 *A History of Formal Logic*, Notre Dame, Ind: University of Notre Dame Press, Translation of Bocheński (1956). [2]

1962 "Formalization of a Scholastic Solution of the Paradox of the 'Liar' ", *Logico-Philosophical Studies* edited by Albert Menne, Dordrecht: D. Reidel, 64–66. [3]

Boehner, P.

1951 "Does Ockham Know of Material Implication?", *Franciscan Studies* 11, 203–230, Reprinted in Boehner (1958, pp. 319–351). [1]

1951– *William Ockham: Summa Logicae, Pars*
1954 *Prima et Pars secunda et tertiae prima*, Vols. 1–2 (Franciscan Institute Publications Text Series, Vol. 2), St. Bonaventure, N.Y.: The Franciscan Institute. *Pars Prima* translated in Loux (1974). [2]

1952 *Medieval Logic: An Outline of Its Development from 1250 to circa 1400*, Manchester: Manchester University Press. [3]

1955 *Walter Burleigh: De puritate artis logicae tractatus longior, with a Revised Edition of the Tractatus Brevior* (Franciscan Institute Publications Text Series, Vol. 9), St. Bonaventure, N.Y.: The Franciscan Institute. [4]

1957 *Ockham: Philosophical Writings*, London: Thomas Nelson and Sons. [5]

| | 1958 | *Collected Articles on Ockham* (Franciscan Institute Publications Philosophy series, Vol. 12), St. Bonaventure, N.Y.: The Franciscan Institute. [6] |

1958   "A Medieval Theory of Supposition", *Franciscan Studies* 18, 240–289. [7]

Boh, Ivan   1963   "Burleigh: On Conditional Hypothetical Propositions", in *Franciscan Studies* 23, I, The Franciscan Institute, New York. [1]

1963   "Walter Burleigh's Hypothetical Syllogistic", *Notre Dame Journal of Formal Logic* 4, 241–269. [2]

1965   "Paul of Pergula on Supposition and Consequences", *Franciscan Studies* 25, 30–89. Translation of part of Brown (1961). [3]

1966   "Propositional Connectives, Supposition and Consequences in Paul of Pergula", *Notre Dame Journal of Formal Logic* VII, 1. [4]

forthcoming, "A Late Mediaeval Assessment of the Scope of Logic: An Analysis of *Parvulus Logicae*", (a copy was kindly made available to me). [5]

Bottin, F.   1976   "Proposizioni Condizionali, 'Consequentiae' e Paradossi Dell' Implicazione in Paolo Veneto", *Medioevo, Rivista di Storia della Filosofia Medioevale* II, 289–330. [1]

1976   *Le antinomie semantiche nella logica medievale* (Pubblicazioni dell' istituto di storia della filosofia e del centro per ricerche di filosofia medievale, nuova serie, Vol. 25), Padova: Editrice Antenore. [2]

Brown, M.A. (ed.)   1961   *Paul of Pergula: Logica and Tractatus de sensu composito et diviso* (Franciscan Institute Text Series, Vol. 13), St. Bonaventure, N.Y.: The Franciscan Institute. [1]

Brown, M.A.   1966   "The Role of the *Tractatus de obliga-*
                                     tionibus in Mediaeval Logic", *Francis-*
                                     can Studies 26, 26–35. [2]

Brown, S.F.   1972   "Walter Burleigh's Treatise *De suppo-*
                                     sitionibus and its Influence on William
                                     of Ockham", *Franciscan Studies* 32,
                                     15–64.

Burge, T.   1978   "Buridan and Epistemic Paradox", *Phi-*
                                     losophical Studies, 34, 21–35.

Bursill-Hall, G.L.   1963–   "Mediaeval Grammatical Theories", *Ca-*
                           1964   *nadian Journal of Linguistics* 9, 40–
                                     54. [1]

                           1971   *Speculative Grammars of the Middle*
                                     Ages, The Doctrine of the Partes Oratio-
                                     nis of the Modistae, The Hague/Paris:
                                     Mouton. [2]

Chomsky, N.   1966   *Cartesian Linguistics*, New York: Harper
                                     and Row.

Christensen, N.E.   1967   "The Alleged Distinction Between Use
                                     and Mention", *The Philosophical Re-*
                                     view, 358–367.

Cittadini, A.   1474   *Logica Minor,* Cod. Urb. lat. 1381.

Clagett, Marshall   1961   *The Science of Mechanics in the Middle*
                                     Ages, Madison: The University of Wis-
                                     consin Press.

Colligan, O.F.M., O.A.   1953   *St. John Damascene: Dialectica* (The
                                     Franciscan Institute Publications Text
                                     Series Vol. 6), St. Bonaventure, N.Y.:
                                     The Franciscan Institute.

Davidson, D. and   1971   *The Semantics of Natural Language*,
Harman, G. (eds.)   Dordrecht: D. Reidel. [1]

                           1975   *The Logic of Grammar*, California:
                                     Dickenson Publishing Company, Inc.
                                     [2]

De Medicis, M.   1502   Annotations on the *Logica Parva*, A
                                     copy is in the Franciscan Institute Li-
                                     brary, St. Bonaventure, New York.

De Rijk, L.M. 1962– *Logica Modernorum: A Contribution to*
         1967   *the History of Early Terminist Logic*,
                Vols. 1–2 bound in 3 (Wijsgerige Tek-
                sten en Studies), Assen: Van Gorcum.
                [1]

         1964   "On the Chronology of Boethius'
                Works on Logic", *Vivarium* 2, 1–49
                and 125–162. [2]

         1966   "Some Notes on the Mediaeval Tract
                De insolubilibus with the Edition of a
                Tract Dating from the End of the
                Twelfth Century", *Vivarium* 4, 83–
                115. [3]

         1970   *Petrus Abaelardus: Dialectica, First*
                Complete Edition of the Parisian Manu-
                script, 2nd ed. (Wijsgerige Teksten
                en Studies), Assen: Van Gorcum. [4]

         1971   "The Development of *Suppositio Natu-*
                ralis in Mediaeval Logic", *Vivarium* IX,
                2, 71–107. [5]

         1972   *Peter of Spain, Tractatus, Called after-*
                wards Summulae Logicales (Wijsgerige
                Teksten en Studies), Assen: Van Gor-
                cum. [6]

         1973   "The Development of *Suppositio Natu-*
                ralis in Mediaeval *Logic",* *Vivarium* XI,
                1, 43–79. [7]

         1975   "*'Logica Cantabrigiensis'.* A Fifteenth
                Century Cambridge Manual of Logic",
                Revue Internationale de la Philosophie
                29, 297–315. [8]

         1977   "*Logica Oxoniensis",* Medioevo, Rivista
                di Storia della Filosofia Medioevale* III,
                121–164. [9]

         1974– "Some Thirteenth Century Tracts on
         1976   the Game of Obligation", *Vivarium* 12,
                94–123; 13, 22–54; and 14, 26–49.
                [10]

Dumitriu, A. 1979   *History of Logic*, Four Volumes, Tun-
                bridge, Kent: Abacus Press.

Dürr, K.   1937   "Aussagenlogik im Mittelalter", *Erkenntnis* 7.

Ebbesen, Sten   1979   "The Dead Man is Alive", *Synthese* 40, 43–70.

Erasmus, D.   1971   *Praise of Folly*, translated by Betty Radice, Great Britain: Penguin Books,

Erickson, K. (ed.)   1974   *Aristotle: the Classical Heritage of Rhetoric*, Metuchen, New Jersey: Scarecrow Press.

Evans, J.D.G.   1977   *Aristotle's Concept of Dialectic*, Cambridge: Cambridge University Press.

Faventinus, Mengus Bianchellus   *Commentarius super Logicam Pauli Veneti*, Tarvisii, 1476.
(Domenico Bianchelli)

Frege, Gottlob   1960   *Begriffsschrift* (Chapter I) translated by Peter Geach and Max Black in: *The Philosophical Writings of Gottlob Frege*, Oxford: Basil Blackwell.

Gál, G. and S.F. Brown   1974   *Venerabilis Inceptoris Guillelmi de Ockham Summa logicae* (Opera philosophica, Volume 1), St. Bonaventure, N.Y.: The Franciscan Institute.
(eds.)

Garin, E.   1960   "La cultura fiorentina nella seconda metá del '300 e i 'Barbari brittani' ", *La Rassegna della Letteratura Italiana* 64, 181–195.

Geach, P. and   1961   *Three Philosophers,* Oxford: Basil Blackwell. [1]
Anscombe, G.E.M.

Geach, P.   1968   *Reference and Generality* (emended edition), Ithaca, New York: Cornell University Press. [2]

                      1972   *Logic Matters*, Berkeley, CA: University of California Press. [3]

Gilbert, N.   1974   "The Early Italian Humanists and Disputation", in: *Renaissance Studies in Honor of Hans Baron* edited by Anthony Molho and John A. Tedeschi, Biblioteca Storica Sansoni Nuova Serie XLIX, Firenze: G.C. Sansoni. [1]

	1976	"Richard De Bury and the 'Quires of Yesterday's Sophisms' ", in: *Philosophy and Humanism*, edited by E. Mahoney, Leiden: E.J. Brill, 229–257. [2]
Grabmann, M. (ed.)	1937	*Die Introductiones in Logicam des Wilhelm von Shyreswood* (+ nach 1267) (Sitzungsberichte der Bayerischen Akademie der Wissenschaften, Phil.-Hist. Abt., Jg. 1937, Heft 10), München: Verlag der Bayerischen Akademie der Wissenschaften.
Green, R.		forthcoming, *The Logical Treatise 'De obligationibus': An Introduction with Critical Texts of William of Sherwood and Walter Burley*, St. Bonaventure, New York: The Franciscan Institute.
Hamblin, C.L.	1970	*Fallacies*, London: Methuen and Company.
Henry, D.P.	1963	"The Early History of *Suppositio*", *Franciscan Studies* 23, 205–212. [1]
	1964	*The De Grammatico of St. Anselm: The Theory of Paronymy* (Publications in Mediaeval Studies, Vol. 18), Notre Dame, Indiana: University of Notre Dame Press, Contains text, translation and study. [2]
Heytesbury, W.	1494	*Tractatus Gulielmi Hentisberi de sensu composito et diviso, Regulae ejusdem cum sophismatibus, Declaratio gaetani supra easdem....*Bonetus Locatellus for Octavianus Scotus, Venice.
Howell, Wilbur Samuel	1956	*Logic and Rhetoric in England, 1500–1700*, Princeton, New Jersey: Princeton University Press.
Hubien, H. (ed.)	1976	*Johannis Buridani Tractatus de Consequentiis*, Louvain: Publications Universitaires.
Hunt, R.W.	1964	"Oxford Grammar Masters in the Middle Ages", *Oxford Studies* Presented to Daniel Callus, Oxford Historical Society, New Series 16.

Jackson, B.D.   1975   Augustine *De Dialectica*, Dordrecht,
                                Holland: D. Reidel.

James, T.E.   1974   "Peter Alboini of Mantua: Philosopher-
                                Humanist", *Journal of the History of
                                Philosophy* 12, 161–170.

Jardine, L.   1977   "Lorenzo Valla and the Intellectual Ori-
                                gins of Humanist Dialectic", *Journal
                                of the History of Philosophy* 15.

Keenan, E.L. (ed.)   1975   *Formal Semantics of Natural Language*,
                                Cambridge: Cambridge University Press.

Kneale, W., and   1962   *The Development of Logic*, Oxford:
M. Kneale   The Clarendon Press.

Kretzmann, N. (tr.)   1966   *William of Sherwood's Introduction to
                                Logic*, Minneapolis: University of Minne-
                                sota Press. [1]

                       1968   *William of Sherwood's Treatise on
                                Syncategorematic Words*, Minneapolis:
                                University of Minnesota Press. [2]

Kretzmann, N.   1970   *"Medieval Logicians on the Meaning
                                of the Propositio", Journal of Philo-
                                sophy* 67, 767–787. [3]

                       1976   *"Incipit/Desinit"* in: P.K. Machamer
                                and R.G. Turnbull (eds.) *Motion and
                                Time, Space and Matter: Interrelations
                                in the History of Philosophy and Scien-
                                ce*, Columbus: Ohio State University
                                Press, 101–136. [4]

                       1977   "Socrates is Whiter than Plato Begins
                                to be White", *Nôus* 11, 3–15. [5]

Kristeller, P.O.   1961   *Renaissance Thought*, New York, N.Y.:
                                Harper and Row. [1]

                       1963   *Iter Italicum*, 2 Volumes, London:
                                Warburg Institute. [2]

Lohr, C.   1973   "A Note on Manuscripts of Paulus Ve-
                                netus, *Logica"*, *Bulletin de Philosophie
                                Medievale* 15, 145–146. [1]

353

	1972	"Medieval Latin Aristotle Commentaries: Paulus Nicolettus Venetus", *Traditio* 28, 314–320. [2]
Loux, M.J. (tr.)	1974	*Ockham's Theory of Terms: Part I of the Summa Logicae*, Notre Dame, Ind.: University of Notre Dame Press. Translation of Boehner (1951–1954, *pars prima*). [1]
Łukasiewicz, J.	1967	"On the History of the Logic of Propositions", (*Polish Logic* 1920–1939) edited by Storrs McCall, Oxford: The Clarendon Press, 66–87.
Maierú, A.	1972	*Terminologia logica della tarda scolastica* (Lessico intellettuale Europeo, Vol. 8), Roma: Edizioni dell'Ateneo.
Manzolus, B.	1523	*Dubia super logicam Pauli Veneti juxta viam realium philosophorum praesertim S. Thomae extricata et resoluta*, Venice. A copy is in the Houghton Library, Harvard University, Cambridge, Massachusetts.
Mates, B.	1965	"Pseudo-Scotus on the Soundness of *Consequentiae*", in: *Contributions to: Logic and Methodology*, In Honour of Joseph M. Bocheński, edited by Anna-Teresa Tymieniecka, Amsterdam, North-Holland Publishing Company, 132–141.
Matthews, G.B.	1964	"Ockham's Supposition Theory and Modern Logic", *The Philosophical Review* 73, 91–99. [1]
Matthews, G.B.	1973	"*Suppositio* and Quantification in Ockham", *Noûs* 7, 13–24. [2]
McKeon, R.	1942	"Rhetoric in the Middle Ages", *Speculum*, Volume XVII, No. 1, 1–32.
Mohan, G.E.	1952	"Incipits of Logical Writings of the XIIIth–XVth Centuries", *Franciscan Studies* 12, 349–489. [1]
		forthcoming, "Incipits of Philosophical Writings in Latin of the XIIIth–XVth Centuries" (Franciscan Institute Text

Series), St. Bonaventure, New York: The Franciscan Institute. See the announcement in *Franciscan Studies* 35, (1975), p. 279. [2]

Moody, E.A. 1935 *The Logic of William of Ockham*, New York: Sheed and Ward. [1]

1953 *Truth and Consequence in Mediaeval Logic* (Studies in Logic and the Foundations of Mathematics), Amsterdam: North-Holland Publishing Company. [2]

1965 "Buridan and a Dilemma of Nominalism", *Harry Austryn Wolfson Jubilee Volume on the Occasion of His Seventy-Fifth Birthday, English Section, Volume II*, Jerusalem, American Academy for Jewish Research, 577–596. [3]

1966 "The Medieval Contribution to Logic", *Studium Generale* 19, 443–452. [4]

1967 "Medieval Logic", in: P. Edwards (ed.), *The Encyclopedia of Philosophy*, New York: Macmillan Company and the Free Press, Vol. 4, 528–534. [5]

More, Sir Thomas 1961 *Selected Letters* edited by Elizabeth Frances Rogers, New Haven: Yale University Press.

Mullally, J.P. (ed. and transl.) 1945 *The Summulae Logicales of Peter of Spain* (Publications in Mediaeval Studies, Vol. 8), Notre Dame, Ind: University of Notre Dame Press. [1]

Mullally, J.P. (transl.) 1964 *Peter of Spain: Tractatus Syncategorematum and Selected Anonymous Treatises* (Mediaeval Philosophical Texts in Translation, Vol. 13), Milwaukee, Wisc.: Marquette University Press. [2]

Muñoz Delgado, V. 1973 "Juan Hidalgo (1516) comentarista del 'Compendio de lógica' de Pablo de Venecia", *La Ciudad De Dios, Rivista Augustiniana* 186, 20–36.

Murdoch, J.E.   1969   *"Mathesis in Philosophiam Scholasti-cam Introducta:* the Rise and Develop-ment of the Application of Mathema-tics in Fourteenth Century Philosophy and Theology", in: *Arts Liberaux et Philosophie au Moyen Age*, Actes du Quatrième Congres International de Philosophie Mediévale, Paris: Librairie Philosophique J. Vrin, 215–254. [1]

1974   "Philosophy and the Enterprise of Science in the Later Middle Ages", in: Y. Elkana (ed.), *The Interaction be-tween Science and Philosophy,* Atlantic Highlands, N.J.: Humanities Press, 51–113. [2]

1975   "From Social into Intellectual Factors: An Aspect of the Unitary Character of Late Medieval Learning", in: J.E. Mur-doch and E.D. Sylla (eds.) *The Cultural Context of Medieval Learning,* Dord-recht: D. Reidel Publishing Company, 271–348. [3]

1979   "Propositional Analysis in Fourteenth-Century Natural Philosophy: A Case Study", *Synthese* 40, 117–146. [4]

Murphy, J.J.   1974   *Rhetoric in the Middle Ages,* Berkeley: University of California Press.

Nardi, B.   1958   *Saggi sull' Aristotelismo Padovano*, Fi-renze: G.C. Sansoni.

Nuchelmans, G.   1973   *Theories of the Proposition: Ancient and Medieval Conceptions of the Bearers of Truth and Falsity* (North-Holland Linguistic Series, Vol. 8), Amsterdam: North-Holland Publishing Company.

Oberman, Heiko A.   1975   "Reformation and Revolution: Coper-nicus' Discovery in an Era of Change", in J.E. Murdoch and E.D. Sylla (eds.) *The Cultural Context of Medieval Learning,* Dordrecht: D. Reidel Publish-ing Company, 397–435.

O'Donnell, J.R. (ed.)   1941   "The *Syncategoremata* of William of Sherwood", *Mediaeval Studies* 3, 46–93.

Ong, S.J., Walter J.   1974   *Ramus, Method and the Decay of Dialogue*, New York, N.Y.: Octagon Books.

Owen, G.E.L. (ed.)   1968   *Proceedings of the Third Symposium Aristotelicum*, Oxford: The Clarendon Press.

Owens, J.   1951   *The Doctrine of Being in the Aristotelian Metaphysics*, Toronto: Pontifical Institute of Mediaeval Studies.

Pamphilus of Bologna   1565   *Logica...addidimus annotationes ad marginem, tabulas...daque omnia in emendavimus*, Venice. A copy is in the Houghton Library, Harvard University, Cambridge, Massachusetts.

Paul of Venice   *Logica Parva* (Venice, 1472) reprinted Hildesheim/New York: Georg Olms Verlag, 1970 [1]

Logica Parva, Venice, 1492. A copy is in the Henry E. Huntington Library, San Marino, California. [2]

Logica Parva, Venice, 1565. A copy is in the Folger Shakespeare Library, Washington, D.C. [3]

Logica Magna, Venice, 1499, *Manuscripta*, List 9, St. Louis University Library, St. Louis, Mo. [4]

Quadratura, Venice, 1493. A copy is in the Lily Library, Indiana University, Bloomington. [5]

Sophismata Aurea, Venice, Bonetus Locatellus, 1493. [6]

Perini, P.D.A.   1938 &   *Bibliographia Augustiniana* IV, Florence, 39–47.
1963

| Perreiah, A.R. | 1967 | "A Biographical Introduction to Paul of Venice", *Augustiniana* XVII, 450–461. [1] |

1971 "Approaches to Supposition-Theory", *The New Scholasticism*, XLV, No. 3, 381–408. [2]

Perreiah, A.R. (ed. & transl.)

1971 *Paul of Venice, Logica magna (Tractatus de suppositionibus)*, (Franciscan Institute Text Series, Vol. 15), St. Bonaventure, N.Y.: The Franciscan Institute. [3]

Perreiah, A.R.

1972 "Buridan and the Definite Description", *Journal of the History of Philosophy* X, no. 2, 153–160. [4]

1982 *"Obligationes* in Paul of Venice's *Logica Parva"*, *Analecta Augustiniana.* XLV, 89–116. [5]

1978 *"Insolubilia* in Paul of Venice's *Logica Parva"*, *Medioevo, Rivista di Storia della Filosofia Medioevale*, IV, 145–171. [6]

1982 "Humanistic Critiques of Scholastic Dialectic", *The Sixteenth Century Journal*, XIII, No. 3, 3–22. [7]

forthcoming, "Supposition Theory: A New Approach", *Franciscan Studies.* [8]

1984 "Logic Examinations in Padua *circa* 1400", *History of Education.* [9]

Pinborg, J.

1967 *Die Entwicklung der Sprachtheorie im Mittelalter, Beiträge zur Geschichte der Philosophie und Theologie des Mittelalters*, Band LXII, Heft 2, Münster, Westfalen: Aschendorffsche Verlagsbuchhandlung und Kopenhagen: Verlag Arne Frost-Hansen, [1]

1972 *Logik und Semantik im Mittelalter: Ein Überblick* (Grammatica Speculativa) Stuttgart-Bad Canstatt: Frommann-Holzboog. [2]

358

| | 1979 | "The English Contribution to Logic before Ockham", *Synthese* 40, 19–52. [3] |

Prantl, C.   1855–1867   *Geschichte der Logik im Abendlande*, Vols. 1–4, S. Leipzig: Hirzel.

Prior, A.N.   1961   "On a Family of Paradoxes", *Notre Dame Journal of Formal Logic*, Vol. II, No. 1, 16–32. [1]

   1962   *Formal Logic*, Second Edition, Oxford: The Clarendon Press.

Randall, Jr. J.H.   1940   "The Development of Scientific Method in the School of Padua", *Journal of the History of Ideas* 1, 177–206.

Reichenbach, H.   1947   *Elements of Symbolic Logic*, New York: The Free Press.

Reina, M.E. (ed.)   1957   "Giovanni Buridano 'Tractatus de suppositionibus' ", *Rivista critica di storia della filosofia* 12, 175–208 & 323–352.

Riccius de Arentino, J.   1502   Commentary on the *Logica Parva*, A copy is in the Franciscan Institute Library, St. Bonaventure, New York.

Risse, W.   1965   *Bibliographia Logica*, Band I: 1472–1800, Hildesheim/New York: Georg Olms.

Rist, J.M. (ed.)   1978   *The Stoics*, Berkeley: University of California Press.

Robinson, R.   1966   *Plato's Earlier Dialectic*, 2nd Edition, Oxford: The Clarendon Press.

Roth, F.   1958–1966   *The English Augustine Friars* in *Cassiciacum* VI published with *Augustiniana*, Volumes VIII–XVI.

Roure, M.L.   1970   "Le Problématique des propositions insolubles au XIIIe Siècle et au début du XIVe, Suivie de l'edition des traités de W. Shyreswood, W. Burleigh et Th. Bradwardine", *Archives d'histoire doctrinale et littéraire du moyen âge* 37, 205–326.

359

Ruello, F.	1980	*Paulus Venetus: Super Primum Sententiarum Johannis de Ripa Lecturae Abbreviatio*, Florence: Leo S. Olschki.
Ryle, G.	1939	"Plato's *Parmenides*", *Mind* 48, 129–151.
	1959	"Philosophical Arguments", in *Logical Positivism* edited by A.J. Ayer, Illinois: The Free Press, 327–346.
Salisbury, John of	1971	The *Metalogicon* translated with an Introduction and Notes by Daniel D. McGarry, Massachusetts: Peter Smith.
Seigel, J.E.	1968	*Rhetoric and Philosophy in Renaissance Humanism,* New Jersey: Princeton University Press.
Schenk, Gunter	1973	*Zur Geschichte der logischen Form* 2 Volumes, Berlin: VEB Deutscher Verlag der Wissenschaften.
Scott, T.K. (tr.)	1966	*John Buridan: Sophisms on Meaning and Truth* (Century Philosophy Sourcebooks), New York, N.Y.: Appleton-Century-Crofts, Translation of Scott (forthcoming). [1]
Scott, T.K. (ed.)		forthcoming, *Johannes Buridanus: Sophismata* (Grammatica Speculativa), Stuttgart-Bad Cannstatt: Frommann-Holzboog. [2]
Spade, P.V.	1971	"An Anonymous Tract on *Insolubilia* from Ms. Vat. Lat. 674", *Vivarium* IX, No. 1. [1]
	1973	"The Origins of the Mediaeval *Insolubilia*-Literature", *Franciscan Studies* 33, 292–309. [2]
	1975	*The Mediaeval Liar: A Catalogue of the Insolubilia-Literature* (Subsidia Mediaevalia, Vol. 5), Toronto: Pontifical Institute of Mediaeval Studies. [3]
	1977	"Roger Swyneshed's *Obligationes*: Edition and Comments", *Archives d' histoire doctrinale et littéraire du moyen âge* 44, 243–285. [4]

1978 "Richard Lavenham's *Obligationes*: Edition and Comments", *Rivista critica di storia della filosofia*: [6]

1979 "Recent Research in Medieval Logic", *Synthese* 40, 3–18. [5]

1980 "Robert Fland's *Obligationes*: An Edition", *Mediaeval Studies*, XLII, 41–61. [7]

Stegmüller, F.   1947   *Repertorium commentariorum in sententias Petri Lombardi*, 2 Volumes, Würzburg: Herbipoli, Volume I, Item 485.

Steele, Robert   1940   *Roger Bacon, Summa Grammatica and Summulae Dialectices*, fascicle XV *Opera Hactenus Inedita*, Oxford: The Clarendon Press.

Stump, Eleonore   1978   Boethius' *De Topicis differentiis*, translated with notes and essays on the text, Ithaca, N.Y.: Cornell University Press.

Swinarski, J.J.   1970   "A New Presentation of Ockham's Theory of Supposition with an Evaluation of Some Contemporary Criticisms", *Franciscan Studies* 30, 181–217.

Tarski, A.   1956   "The Concept of Truth in Formalized Languages", in: *Logic, Semantics, Metamathematics* translated by J.H. Woodger, Oxford, 152–197.

Thorndike, L.   1975   *University Records and Life in the Middle Ages*, New York, N.Y.: W.W. Norton and Company.

Trentman, J.A.   1967   "Vincent Ferrer and His Fourteenth-Century Predecessors on a Problem of Intentionality", *Arts Liberaux et Philosophie au Moyen Age*, Montreal-Paris: J. Vrin. [1]

1968 "Extraordinary Language and Medieval Logic", *Dialogue* 286–291. [2]

<table>
<tr><td></td><td>1973</td><td>"Speculative Grammar and Transformational Grammar: A Comparison of Philosophical Presuppositions", History of Linguistic Thought and Contemporary Linguistics edited by H. Parret, Berlin/New York: 279–301. [3]</td></tr>
<tr><td></td><td>1977</td><td>Vincent Ferrer: Tractatus de suppositionibus, a critical edition with an introduction, in Grammatica Speculativa, Theory of Language and Logic in the Middle Ages, Volume 2, Stuttgart-Bad Cannstatt: Frommann-Holzboog. [4]</td></tr>
<tr><td>Vasoli, C.</td><td>1968</td><td>La Dialettica e la retorica dell' umanesimo: 'Invenzione' e 'Metodo' nella cultura del XV e XVI secolo, Milano: Feltrinelli.</td></tr>
<tr><td>Veatch, H.B. and Ogden, J.B.</td><td>1956</td><td>"Putting the Square Back into Opposition", The New Scholasticism XXX, 4, 409–440.</td></tr>
<tr><td>Vives, J.L.</td><td>1979</td><td>Against the Pseudodialecticians (Contra Pseudodialecticos) translated by Rita Guerlac, Boston: D. Reidel.</td></tr>
<tr><td>Wallace, W.A.</td><td>1972</td><td>Causality and Scientific Explanation in Medieval and Early Classical Science, Ann Arbor: The University of Michigan Press, 117–155.</td></tr>
<tr><td>Weisheipl, O.P., James A.</td><td>1964</td><td>"Curriculum of the Faculty of Arts at Oxford in the Early Fourteenth Century", Mediaeval Studies XXVI, Toronto: Pontifical Institute of Mediaeval Studies. [1]</td></tr>
<tr><td></td><td>1966</td><td>"Developments in the Arts Curriculum at Oxford in the Early Fourteenth Century", Mediaeval Studies XXVIII, Toronto: Pontifical Institute of Mediaeval Studies. [2]</td></tr>
<tr><td>Wilson, Curtis</td><td>1966</td><td>William Heytesbury, Medieval Logic and the Rise of Mathematical Physics, Madison: University of Wisconsin Press.</td></tr>
<tr><td>Wooden, W.W.</td><td>1977</td><td>"Anti-Scholastic Satire in Sir Thomas More's Utopia", The Sixteenth Century Journal VIII, Supplement, 29–45.</td></tr>
</table>

Index of Names and Subjects

This index should be used with the Table of Contents and the cross-references in the notes. Some entries list only the most important occurrences.

Boethius, 117 n. 2.
Boh, I., 14 n. 14, 15 n. 21, 46 n. 2,
   68 nn. 11,5; 81 n. 1, 82 nn. 4,5.
Bottin, F.,68 n.1,108 nn.1,17,326.
Brown, M., 14 n. 14, 68 n. 1, 82 n.
   14, 97 nn. 2,3.
Brown, S., 14 n. 10, 46 n. 2.
Burge, T., 108 n. 1.
Bursill-Hall, G., 15 n. 23.

Cajetan of Thiene, 10.
case, 122, 124, 147.
 − direct / oblique (*rectus /obli-
   quus*), 212 n. [80] a, 261, 280,
   282, 307.
 − nominative, 146, 154, 307, 311.
 − genitive, 43, 307.
 − dative, 192.
 − accusative, 186.
 − ablative, 177, 192.
 − and insolubles, 237.
 − and proof, 181, 184, 186.
categorematic. See term, types of.
categorical. See proposition, types
   of.
category, 21, 136−139.
Chomsky, N., 15 n. 26.
Christensen, N., 47 n. 18.
Cittadini, A., 12.
Clagett, M., 14 nn. 5, 13.
complex / incomplex (*complexus /
   incomplexus*) see term, types of.
composite sense (*sensus compositus*),
   26, 127, 155, 182, 191, 315−
   316. See proposition, assertoric / modal; sense.
concept. See term.
   and definition, 315−316.
conceptual representation. See
   supposition.
concession. See obligation.
conclusion. See syllogism.
conditional. See inference, rules
   for; proposition, hypothetical.
confusion (*confusio*), confounding.
   See supposition, types of.
conjunction. See inference, rules
   for; proposition, types of hypothetical.
consequence (*consequentia*), 49−

68, 68 nn. 1,2,4, 6, 8, 10;
   compare *Logica Magna*, 335−
   338. See inference.
consequent (*consequens*). See inference, parts of.
contingency / necessity. See proposition, modes of.
contradictory, 127−128. See figures of the propositions.
contrary, 127−128. See figures of
   the propositions.
convention T, 27, 32 n. 25.
conventional, "by convention"
   (*ad placitum*). See signification,
   natural/conventional.
conversion, 129−130, 265−268.
copula, 22, 257.
correlative term. See term, correlative.

Davidson, D., 11, 15 nn. 22, 25;
   30 n. 1, 32 n. 25, 46 n. 9, 98 n. 15.
deduction, 49−50. See inference,
   syllogism.
Del Punta, F., 14 n. 12, 31 n. 16,
   32 n. 24, 68 n. 4, 97 n. 9, 141 n.
   [6] a, 166 n. [61] a, 213 n.
   [100] a, 326 n. [211] a, 337.
De Medicis, M., 12.
De Morgan Law, 58.
denial. See obligation.
deposition (*depositio*). See obligation.
De Rijk, L., 14 nn. 8, 9; 15 n. 19,
   45 n. 2, 46 n. 6, 47 n. 19, 48 n.
   24, 97 nn. 1, 3; 98 n. 12, 117 n.
   2, 141 n. [1] b.
description, describable proposition.
   See proof, methods of.
de virtute sermonis, 113, 118 n. 11,
   283 n. [163] a.
dialectic, 109−118. See argumentation.
direct predication. See predication,
   direct / indirect.
disjunction. See inference, rules
   for; proposition, types of hypothetical.
disparate term. See inference, rules
   for; term, disparate.

disposition. See category.
distribution. See proof methods of exposition; supposition, types of.
diversity. See supposition, rules for relative terms.
divided sense (*sensus divisus*). See composite sense; proposition, assertoric / modal.
Dominici, Bondii, 15 n. 29.
due mean (*debito medio*), 47 n. 16, 69 n. 19, 171, 173, 246, 299, 311.
Dumitriu, A., 97 n. 3.
Dürr, K., 68 n. 1.

education, 9.
epichireme. See argumentation, dialectical.
equipollence (*equipollentia*), 127–129, 260–265.
equivocation. See ambiguity.
Erasmus, D., 10, 15 n. 18.
Erickson, K., 15 n. 17.
Evans, J., 117 n. 2.
exception, exceptives. See proof, methods of exposition; proposition, types of categorical.
– expressions of, 39, 200–202.
– inference rules for, 55, 64, 173–175.
– proof of, 72–73, 200–202.
– supposition of, 39, 152, 154.
exclusion, exclusives. See proof, methods of exposition; proposition, types of categorical.
– expressions of, 39, 197–200.
– inference rules for, 55, 64, 173–175.
– proof of, 72–73, 197–200.
– supposition of, 39, 150, 151.
existence, existential import. See due mean.
existence clause. See insoluble, solution of.
exposition. See proof, methods of.
– as clarification, 312.
expression (*dictio*), 121, 147, 198, 238. See statement, term.
extreme of a proposition. See proposition, categorical extremes of.

fallacy. See inference, syllogism, insoluble.
false. See insoluble, solution of; proof, truth-conditions; proposition, modes of.
– simply / according to a condition (*simpliciter / secundum quid*), 99–107, 237–256.
falsity / truth. See proposition, modes of; truth.
figures of the propositions, 27, 33 n. 26, 126–129.
finite / infinite term, 65. See term, interchangeable.
formal. See inference, types of; supposition, rules for substantive terms.
formal logic. See logic.
Frege, G., 46 n. 10.

Gál, G., 14 n. 10.
Geach, P., 46 nn. 5, 10; 47 n. 19, 166 n. [53] a.
gender, 128, 142 n. [11] a, 300–301, 304, 308, 325 nn. [206] b, [207] a.
genus. See predicable.
Gilbert, N., 14 n. 17, 82 n. 17.
Giles of Rome, 9.
grades of comparison, 192–195.
grammar, 11, 15 n. 23.
Green, R., 97 nn. 1,3.
Gregory of Rimini, 9.
Grice, P. 98 n. 15.

Hamblin, C., 15 nn. 21, 25; 30 n. 1, 32 n. 25, 46 n. 9, 98 n. 15.
Harvey of Nedellec, 9.
Henry, D., 45 n. 2, 46 nn. 5,9; 47.
hierarchy, 21, 43. See predicable; term, higher-level / lower-level.
Hieronymous de Mutina, 15 n. 29.
higher-level term. See term, higher-level / lower-level.
Howell, W., 14 n. 13, 15 n. 17.
Hubien, H. 68 n. 1.
Hunt, R., 15.
hypothetical. See inference, rules for hypotheticals; proposition, types of hypothetical.

obligation, 83–98, 108 n. 1, 214–
236. Compare *Logica Magna*,
340–343.
— admission / non admission, 84,
217.
— and conversational implicature,
98 n. 15.
— *antiqua / nova responsio*, 97,
98 n. 12.
— desposition, 83–84, 88–90,
231–235.
— examination argument, 84 ff.
— explicit / implicit, 289, 98 n. 13.
— interchangeable propositions,
90–91, 223–227, 236 n. [134]a.
— position, 83–87, 214–223.
— relevant / irrelevant proposition,
86, 214, 235 n. [124]a.
— sequent proposition, 216.
— similar / dissimilar propositions,
92–96, 228–231.
O'Donnell, J., 30 n. 7.
of form (*de forma*). See inference,
types of.
of matter (*de materia*). See inference, types of.
Ong, W., 14 n. 8, 47 n. 11, 82 n. 17.
oral vs. written medium, 10, 80–
81, 96–97.
Owen, G., 117 n. 2.
Owens, J., 118 n. 6.

Pamphilus of Bologna, 12.
paradox
— of strict implication, 52, 142 n.
[16]a, 167–168, 179 n. [65]b,
285–286, 325 n. [191]a.
— as mnemonic device, 45, 48 nn.
23, 24; 71, 80–81, 183–211,
233.
participle. See speech, part of.
particular. See proposition, categorical quantity of.
passion (*passio*). See category.
Paul of Pergola, 9, 77, 97 n. 2,
98 n. 12.
Paul of Venice,
— biography, 13 n. 1.
— works attributed to, 9, 13 n. 2,
15 n. 27, 31, 46, 82 n. 17, 98 n.

12, 329–330.
Perini, D., 13 n. 2, 14 n. 7.
Perreiah, A., 13 n. 1, 14 nn. 11, 12,
17; 31 n. 14, 46 nn. 2–6; 47 n.
11, 97 nn. 3, 4; 108 nn. 1, 17;
141 n. [6]a, 142 nn. [11]a,
[26]a; 165 nn. [36]a, [40]a;
212 n. [90]a.
pertinent term. See term, pertinent/
non-pertinent.
Peter Abelard, 68 n. 8, 117 n. 2.
Peter of Ailly, 9, 98 n. 12.
Peter of Mantua, 14 n. 12.
Peter of Spain, 9, 14 nn. 3, 9;
46 n. 8.
philosopheme. See argumentation,
demonstrative, didactic.
Pinborg, J., 14 n. 13, 15 n. 23, 81 n.
1, 82 n. 4.
place. See category.
Plato, 117 n. 2.
Porphyry, 31 n. 12.
position. See category.
position / deposition (*positio /
depositio*). See obligation,
position.
possibility / impossibility. See proposition, modes of.
pragmatics, 34.
preciseness clause. See insoluble,
solution of.
predicable, 20, 31 n. 12, 133–136,
273–277.
predicament. See category.
predicate, 26, 46–47, 47 n. 10.
See proposition, extremes of.
predication,
— direct / indirect, 136, 276.
— essential / accidental, 136,
276–277.
premise. See syllogism.
primary and adequate. See significate, adequate and primary.
principal significate. See significate, adequate and primary.
Prior, A., 31 n. 19, 33 nn. 26, 27;
283 n. [183] b.
privative term. See term, privative.
pronoun. See speech, part of.
proof (*probatio*), 70–82, 142 n.

speech, part of
— adjective, 258.
— adverb, 122, 154, 192, 213 n. [110] a, 272.
— article, definite, 47—48, 48 n. 19, 165 n. [30] b.
— noun, 122, 147.
— participle, 123—124, 162, 166 n. [61] b, 212 n. [82] a, 318.
— pronoun, 42—43, 166 n. [53] a.
— — demonstrative, 149, 238, 259, 292, 299.
— — personal, 156—161.
— — relative, 156—161, 186—188.
— verb, 79, 123, 155, 162, 177, 208, 259.
square of opposition. See figures of the propositions.
state. See category.
Steele, R., 14 n. 9, 45 n. 2.
Stegmüller, F., 14.
Strode, R., 9, 15 n. 30.
Stump, E., 31 n. 12, 68 n. 1, 117 n. 2, 118 n. 5.
St. Augustine, 117 n. 2.
St. Vincent Ferrer, 9, 14 n. 11.
subalternate, 127—128. See figures of the propositions.
subcontrary, 127—128. See figures of the propositions.
subject. See proposition, extremes of; term.
supposition (*suppositio*), 34—44, 45—46 nn. 1—9; 47 nn. 12, 14; 69 n. 16, 143—166, 165 nn [30] a, [36] a; 166 n. [40] a. Compare *Logica Magna*, 332—336.
— ascent / descent (*ascensus / decensus*), 37—38, 147. See proof.
— as conceptual representation, 35, 46—47, 47 nn. 10, 11.
— as quantification, 46 n. 5, 144.
— rules.
— — for substantive terms
— — — formal (*formalis*), 36—40.
— — — material and personal (*materialis et personalis*), 145—147.

— — — material (*materialis*), 40—42, 47 nn. 18, 19; 147—149, 301.
— — — personal (*personalis*), 149—156.
— — for relative terms, 42—45, 156—161.
— semiotic interpretations of, 34, 46 nn. 3—6.
— similarity of, 301—302, 307—308.
— types of, 37—40, 143—165. Compare *Logica Magna* 332.
— — discrete / common
— — determinate / confused
— — confused merely / confused and distributed
— — mobily / immobily, 36, 153, 296—298.
substance. See category.
substantive. See term.
substitution. See equipollence.
superior. See term, higher-level.
Swinarski, J., 46 n. 5.
syllogism, 28, 33 n. 27, 139—141, 142 nn. [26] b, c; 277—282. Compare *Logica Magna*, 330.
syncategorematic. See term, types of.
syntax, 34.

Tarski, A., 32 n. 25.
term, 17—22, 29, 121.
— abstract / concrete, 21, 31 n. 14, 138—139, 142 n. [26] a. See category.
— correlative, 55, 171, 309.
— disparate, 65.
— expression (*dictio*), 121.
— higher-level / lower-level (*superius / inferius*), 19—21, 38, 54—62, 177, 179 n. [70] a, 293—297, 305.
— immediate / mediate, 38, 70, 81 n. 2, 82 n. 12, 212 n. [90] a.
— interchangeable, 310—311. See conversion.
— pertinent / non-pertinent (*pertinens / impertinens*), 55, 65, 173—176, 306.

- privative, 65, 309.
- properties of
- − signification. See significate, signification.
- − supposition. See supposition.
- − verification. See proof.
- types of
- − significative / non-significative, 19, 30 n. 5, 121, 141 n. [1] b. Compare *Logica Magna*, 332.
- − categorematic / syncategorematic, 19, 30 n. 7, 121, 125, 136.
- − natural / conventional, 19, 122, 30 n. 6.
- − prime intention / second intention, 19, 30 n. 8, 122.
- − prime imposition / second imposition, 19, 30 n. 9, 122.
- − complex / incomplex, 19, 31 n. 10, 74, 122.

Thomas Bradwardine, 343.
Thorndike, L., 98 n. 14.
time. See category.
- and supposition. See ampliation.
transposition. See conversion.
Trentman, J., 14 n. 11, 15 n. 23, 30 n. 5, 46 n. 2, 47 n. 10.
true, 22, 32 n. 25, 267.
- affirmative about the past, 235 n. [121] a.
- propositions stand simultaneously, 269.
- simply / according to a condition. See insoluble, solution of.
truth-conditions. See proof, and truth-conditions; proposition, types of.
truth
- cause of, 312.
- of the matter (*rei veritas*), 224.

uniqueness clause. See insoluble, solution of.
universal. See term, types of.
univocal. See ambiguity, predicable.
utterance (*vox*), 147, 188, 190.

Valla, L., 10.
valid / invalid. See inference, solid/unsolid.
Vasoli, C. 14 n. 4.
Veatch, H., 33 n. 26.
verb. See speech, part of.
verification. See proof, true, truth-conditions.
- as test of supposition, 42, 143 − 144.
Vives, J., 10, 15 n. 20, 117 n. 2.

Wallace, W., 14 n. 5.
Walter Burleigh, 9, 14 n. 10, 46 n. 2, 68 n. 1.
Weisheipl, J., 97 n. 2, 108 n. 1.
William of Heytesbury, 9, 14 n. 13, 16 n. 30, 82 nn. 6, 12, 17; 97 n. 2, 108 n. 6, 343.
William of Ockham, 9, 46 n. 2, 68 n. 1.
William of Sherwood, 9, 14 n. 9.
Wilson, C., 14 n. 13, 82 nn. 6, 10, 13, 17.
Wooden, W., 15 n. 19.

Φ

3285

N/ ИЛЗHPB

Paulus i.